CAMBRIDGE SKILLS FOR FLUENCY
Series Editor: Adrian Doff

Speaking 2

Joanne Collie
Stephen Slater

CAMBRIDGE
UNIVERSITY PRESS

Published by the Press Syndicate of the University of Cambridge
The Pitt Building, Trumpington Street, Cambridge CB2 1RP
40 West 20th Street, New York, NY 10011–4211, USA
10 Stamford Road, Oakleigh, Melbourne 3166, Australia

© Cambridge University Press 1991

First published 1991
Reprinted 1994

Printed in Great Britain at the University Press, Cambridge

ISBN 0 521 36789 1 book
ISBN 0 521 36610 0 cassette

GO

Contents

Map of the book   iv
Acknowledgements   vi

1   Planning improvements   1
Money and its uses

2   Music, music, music   5
Music and musical instruments

3   We lost touch   8
Lost friends, abilities, things

4   It wasn't my fault, it was an accident   11
Accidents, prevention and insurance

5   And so to bed . . .   15
Bedrooms and sleep

6   Oh, I do like to be beside the seaside . . .   19
Holidays, good and bad

7   Your number is up   23
Numbers and their applications

8   How can I get from A to B?   28
Cars and transport

9   Hands   32
Different ways of using our hands

10   Burning the candle at both ends   35
Being prudent or rash

11   Crash bang whizz!   38
Sounds

12   Small but deadly   42
Small things that are annoying or dangerous

13   Letters, words and pictures   46
Exploring letters and words

14   Please speak after the tone   50
Messages

15   Fire power   54
Fire and firearms

16   Is bad language good for you?   58
Bad language and its effects

17   Chuckers and hoarders   61
Collections, antiques and disposables

18   Sugar and spice   65
Stereotypes of males and females

19   Zoo story   70
Animals and humans

20   Book ends   75
Books, including this one

Key   78
Tapescript   80
To the teacher   88

Map of the book

Unit	Themes/Vocabulary areas	Areas of communication	Learner activities
1	Money, taxes, borrowing/lending.	Comparing and justifying choices and ideas; making guesses; discussing consequences.	Guessing in groups; brainstorming for ideas; designing (coins); preparing a short speech; completing a table.
2	Music, songs, films, busking.	Responding to music; giving opinions; talking about imagined situations/memories; asking/answering questions.	Matching visuals to sounds; group/pair listening to songs/film music; discussion.
3	Friends, losing things, skills.	Describing (friends, memories); narrating; asking/answering questions; discussing skills/abilities.	Group/pair discussion; listening for particular expressions; listening to identify speaker's topic.
4	Accidents, emergencies, insurance.	Discussing accidents, insurance; giving a report; comparing (lists).	Completing a questionnaire; pair discussion; listening/note-taking; preparation of a report in groups.
5	Bedrooms, bed, sleep, sleeping tablets.	Describing (bedrooms); justifying (bedtimes); checking/retelling narratives; giving opinions; interviewing.	Pair interpretation of a visual; pair discussion; listening to narrative; making/extending lists; simulating an interview.
6	Holidays, house exchange, souvenirs.	Making reports; planning/discussing (holidays, souvenirs); guessing (identity).	Listening/note-taking; completing a grid; note-writing; group role play.
7	Numbers, rich and poor, optimists and pessimists, life.	Guessing; comparing choices; discussing (life, rich and poor); giving reasons.	Pair guessing game; group completion of a table/cartoon; making a prioritised list.
8	Cars, highway codes, traffic problems.	Discussing/justifying choices; making suggestions; describing problems; reporting findings.	Choosing a visual; answering a questionnaire; listening; matching lists in pairs; administering a questionnaire; preparing a report in groups.
9	Hands, activities using your hands.	Communicating without speaking; discussing skills past and present; assessing skills.	Matching pictures/words; listening to a song; pair/group discussion; vocabulary building.

Unit	Themes/Vocabulary areas	Areas of communication	Learner activities
10	Dangerous and cautious actions, levels of risk.	Comparing (risks); discussing meanings (of poem); sharing narratives; asking/answering questions; preparing a formal warning.	Ranking actions; story building in pairs; group preparation of a broadcast.
11	Sounds, noises, jobs and voices, noise levels.	Comparing (lists, choices); talking about likes/dislikes; talking about oneself.	Making lists; listening and note-taking; group and pair discussion; matching.
12	Annoying small things, food colouring.	Comparing (lists); describing personal experiences; giving reasons; complaining (formally).	Rating (troubles); vocabulary building; pair discussion; planning a phone call; phoning in pairs.
13	Words, alphabet, typefaces, business cards.	Making guesses; comparing choices; making/reporting decisions.	Guessing game; building a poem; vocabulary building; choosing designs (pair and group work).
14	Messages, answerphones, complaints about the locality.	Describing and discussing feelings; comparing problems; leaving messages; complaining; giving a short talk.	Listening and guessing; group discussion and planning (messages); listening, then simulating a radio show; pair planning of talk.
15	Fires, burning, guns.	Seeking information; narrating; sharing comparisons/reasons; discussing opinions; giving reasons; speculating.	Listing (reactions); listening for gist; recounting memories in groups; listening for detail; group discussion (guns).
16	Bad language, swearing.	Explaining (answers); persuading; giving reasons; asking questions; making suggestions; oral reporting.	Answering a questionnaire; pair/group discussion; constructing a questionnaire in pairs; preparing/presenting a report.
17	Collections, antiques, disposable household items.	Comparing (choices); giving explanations; describing; completing (narrative); discussing the future.	Pair discussion of a visual; interpreting a questionnaire in groups; pair role play; listening for prediction; group discussion; completing a questionnaire.
18	Male/female stereotypes, upbringing, masculinity and femininity.	Interpreting (poem); comparing reactions, decisions, reasons; discussing opinions; presenting advice.	Listening/note-taking; group discussion of choices; whole class discussion; completing and discussing a grid.
19	Pets, endangered species, whales and whale products, zoos for humans.	Justifying choices; seeking opinions; evaluating views; describing (categories of people).	Responding to visuals in groups; matching words/pictures; guessing (statistics); preparing a recording.
20	Books, writing books, types of book.	Speculating; describing (books); discussing (character); giving opinions.	Responding to visuals in pairs; pair discussion; whole class/individual letter writing.

Acknowledgements

We should like to acknowledge the valuable help and support given by Adrian Doff and by Kendall Clarke, Peter Donovan, Peter Ducker, Jeanne McCarten, Peter Taylor, Barbara Thomas and Lindsay White of Cambridge University Press.

The authors and publishers would like to thank the teachers at the institutions which piloted *Speaking 2* for us. Without their constructive suggestions, the improvements in the book would not have been made.

The authors and publishers are grateful to the following individuals and institutions for permission to reproduce copyright material: The Royal Australian Mint (p. 2); J. Allan Cash Photo Library (pp. 5, 7, 12, 19, 28 caravan, 35, 36, 40, 44, 54, 55, 59, 66, 70); St Matthews County Primary School, Cambridge (p. 8); Jean Mohr (p. 15); The Kobal Collection (pp. 23, 57, 74); the Posy Simmonds cartoon on p. 25 is reprinted by permission of the Peters, Fraser and Dunlop Group Ltd; the Ford Motor Company Ltd (Ford car on p. 28); Rolls Royce Motor Cars Ltd (Rolls Royce car on p. 28); Falcon Cycles (bicycle on p. 28); the Standards Association of Australia for permission to reproduce on p. 29 five signs from the *Road Traffic Code South Australia*; the poem on p. 31 is by Jenny Boult; the illustrations on p. 32 are reproduced from *British Sign Language* by Dorothy Miles with the permission of BBC Enterprises Ltd; 3rd (volunteer) Battalion The Royal Regiment of Wales (p. 71); Greenpeace Ltd (p. 73); Harper Collins for the cover of *Twopence to Cross the Mersey* on p. 75; Penguin Books Ltd for the cover of *Coming up for Air* on p. 75; Mills and Boon for the cover of *Enter Dr Jones* on p. 75; the cover of *Love and Friendship* on p. 75 is reproduced by kind permission of Sphere Books, illustration © Mark Harrison.

The photographs on pp. 16, 28 (motorbike), 38, 52, 64 and 68 were taken by Jeremy Pembrey and on pp. 1 and 22 by Nicholas Collie.

Drawings by Chris Evans, Leslie Marshall, Chris Pavely, Clyde Pearson and Chris Rothero. Artwork by Hardlines and Wenham Arts.

Book design by Peter Ducker MSTD.

1 | Planning improvements

Money and its uses

1 Tuning-in

Sit with four or five other students. Write down the names of each student in your group.

Guess how much cash each student has in his/her pocket or bag today. Write your guesses next to each name (including your own). Then add up the total. Discuss your ideas with others in the group. As a group take out all your cash and count the total. Were your guesses right?

2 For the greatest good

Now that you know the total amount of cash in your group, consider this
task:
How could all the cash in your group be used for the greatest good of the
greatest number of people? For example, with a small amount of money you
could make some soup and feed many poor people in your city or town.
Choose one person in your group to write down each idea the group has.
After an agreed time, stop, discuss each idea on the list and choose the best
one.
Compare your best idea with those of other groups in your class.

In your group, talk about these questions:
- How much money is each person in your group really prepared to give to
  make your idea a reality?
- Have you given away any money so far this year?
- To what kind of organisations have you given money?

3 Designs for coins

Here are some examples of coins from
Australia. With another student, talk about
what the designs represent. What do they
tell us about Australia?

You have been asked to design new coins for your country or for the country
where you are studying.
Together, talk about the designs that already exist and then discuss some
ideas for new ones. When you have chosen your designs, describe them in the
table below and give reasons for your choices.

Value of coin	Design on coin	Reasons
5c	Beautiful tree surrounded by the words: 'Save our Forests'.	It shows that our country wants to save its environment.

Sit with another group. Describe your designs and ask about theirs.

4 Head of the government for a day

Nobody likes paying taxes but politicians continue to collect them. If you were head of government for one day, would you use the time to introduce some new taxes?

Which of these new taxes would you choose and why?

Tax	Reasons
A tax on people with two cars. A tax on people with more than two children. A tax on people who eat meat. A tax on people who watch more than 20 hours of TV per week. A tax on parents whose children break the law. A tax on .... A tax on	

When you are ready, share your ideas with another student.

In class or at home, prepare a short political speech describing your new taxes and your reasons for introducing them. If you like, you can begin in this way:

> 'My fellow citizens: Now that I am your head of government, I have decided to introduce .... new taxes to help our country. First . . .'

If possible, record your speech on cassette. In small groups, play your speeches or give them live and talk about the consequences of these new taxes.

5 Neither a borrower nor a lender be . . .

Which of these items would you happily lend to the people listed in the table?
Complete the table, then talk about your choices with one or two other
students. What has your teacher put? Find out.

Tick (√) the appropriate boxes:

Item	classmate	teacher	best friend	brother	sister
my car	☐	☐	☐	☐	☐
my bicycle	☐	☐	☐	☐	☐
my camera	☐	☐	☐	☐	☐
$1,000	☐	☐	☐	☐	☐
my swimming costume	☐	☐	☐	☐	☐
some jewellery	☐	☐	☐	☐	☐
my toothbrush	☐	☐	☐	☐	☐
my house/flat	☐	☐	☐	☐	☐
a book	☐	☐	☐	☐	☐
Others (list below)					
....	☐	☐	☐	☐	☐
....	☐	☐	☐	☐	☐
....	☐	☐	☐	☐	☐

Ask one or two other students these questions:
— How many of the things in the list have you in fact borrowed in the past
  year?
— Who lent them to you? Did you return them all?
— Do you agree with the English proverb: *Neither a borrower nor a lender be*?

2 | Music, music, music
Music and musical instruments

1 Tuning-in

A   B   C   D   E

Look at the photos of the instruments. Listen to the cassette. With another student, match each sound with the right instrument.
Were there any instruments you were not familiar with? Which ones did you like best? What other instruments do you like to listen to? Talk about your preferences with your partner.

2 Film music

 Listen to these musical extracts. With one or two other students, decide the most suitable kind of film for each extract.

Extract 1 ....

Extract 2 ....

Extract 3 ....

Extract 4 ....

When you have chosen the types of film that best suit the music, listen to the extracts again and for one of the films decide:
— a location for the film
— two key characters
— a brief description of each character
— an opening scene for the film

POSSIBLE KINDS OF FILMS:
a science fiction film
a horror film a war film
a thriller a cowboy film
a spy film a love story
a comedy
a historical drama

3 'New voices' talent show

 Get into groups of three or four students. Each group is a jury at a talent show for new singers. Choose a talent show host — either the teacher or one of the class. The juries listen to a new singer or group on the cassette, and each member of the jury notes down answers to these questions:
— What did you like about the song?
— Is it going to be a big hit record?
— Has the singer or group got a bright future?
— What advice will help them in their musical career?

After hearing a song, each person in the jury says what they thought of it and the jury gives the song a score from 1 to 10.

The host then plays the songs again. This time, after each song, the juries give their comments in turn. The host keeps the scores and announces the winner. You could bring in some songs of your own to play as well as the ones on the cassette.

4 Musical memories

Most people have strong memories of particular songs or pieces of music. When you hear a certain song, it often reminds you of a person, a holiday, music lessons or a particular dance or party you went to.

Write down the names of one or two songs or pieces of music that always remind you of something or someone from the past.

My musical memories:

1 .... reminds me of ....

2 .... reminds me of ....

When you are ready, exchange lists with another student and ask each other questions about your musical memories.

5 Busking for fun

Buskers are part of the street life of many cities of the world. Have you stopped and listened to them anywhere?
In some cities, busking is against the law but this does not stop it. With another student, talk about your views on this.

In a group of four students, imagine that you are going to form a band of buskers. Decide:
- if you will play instruments, sing, or both
- what types of music you could play in the street
- where in your town or city would be the best places to stand and perform
- a name for your group

Share your thoughts with other groups. Any group that is willing can perhaps perform at the end of one of your lessons. If you collect any money, you can use it for a class party.

3 | We lost touch

Lost friends, abilities, things

1 Tuning-in

Most people have old school photos or address books that remind them of friends from the past.
Think for a minute or two about a friend you remember well but haven't seen for a long time. Tell another student about your friend.
— When did you last see him/her?
— What was he/she doing then?
— What was she/he like?
— Where is she/he now? (Guess if you don't know.)
— Would you like to get in touch again? (Why? or Why not?)

2 I wonder where it went?

On a piece of paper write down the name of an interesting thing which you used to have but do not have any more. It could be: a car, a large amount of money, a rare clock, a doll . . . anything. Try to think of something unusual. Put your pieces of paper in a hat or bag. Your teacher will take them out one by one and read them. Guess who wrote each (except your own!).

With a partner, tell the story of how you lost or why you no longer have that particular thing. Ask your teacher to tell you his/her story.

3 Memories

Listen to the cassette. The speakers are trying to remember a pop group from the sixties. Which of these expressions does the woman use?

> Don't tell me, it's on the tip of my tongue.
> I can't think of their name.
> What was their name?
> What were they called again?
> Their name escapes me.
> I remember them vividly.
> I'm sure it was something like that.
> I can't remember it that well but I'm pretty sure that...
> I can see them clearly...
> It'll come back to me in a minute.

Compare your answers.

Now listen again for the name of the pop group they are trying to remember.

Do you sometimes have trouble remembering names or do you have a good memory for faces, names, facts? In groups, choose one or two of the following memories and describe them to each other.
— your earliest memory
— the clothes you had when you were eight or nine
— the name of your first primary school teacher
— your classmates in your first year at secondary school
— one of your first holidays
— a song or poem you learned as a child

4 Lost opportunities

Sometimes we lose opportunities because we
 — make a bad decision
 — move to a new place
 — have an accident
 — have a long illness
 — lose a job

Complete some of these sentences and then exchange sentences with other students. Ask other students about their sentences.

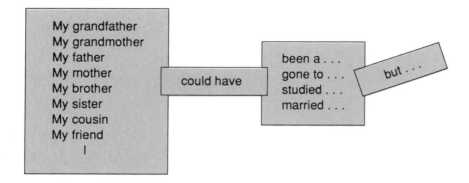

My grandfather
My grandmother
My father
My mother
My brother
My sister
My cousin
My friend
 I

could have

been a . . .
gone to . . .
studied . . .
married . . .

but . . .

5 One day I'm going to . . .

Think of something you used to be able to do quite well but can't do any longer. It could be . . .

knitting   playing the piano   dancing
playing a sport well   speaking another language

Talk about your lost skill with another student. Why did you lose the skill? Did you stop practising or lose interest?

Listen to these two people talking about their plans to regain lost skills. As you listen, write down the name of the skill which each person is talking about.

Are these skills that you have also lost? With one or two other students, discuss ways of regaining a lost skill.

4 | It wasn't my fault, it was an accident

Accidents, prevention and insurance

1 Tuning-in

Answer these questions about accidents and add some questions of your own.

		Yes	No
*	Have you ever had a road accident?	[ ]	[ ]
*	Have you ever had an accident with a knife?	[ ]	[ ]
*	Have you ever broken a bone in your body?	[ ]	[ ]
*	Have you ever dropped a valuable object and broken it?	[ ]	[ ]
*	Have you ever fallen down some stairs?	[ ]	[ ]
*	Have you ever left a tap running and flooded a room?	[ ]	[ ]
*	Have you ever broken a window?	[ ]	[ ]
*	....	[ ]	[ ]
*	....	[ ]	[ ]

Talk about your accidents with others. Are people who have a lot of accidents just unlucky?

2 Emergency procedure

You are driving alone along a quiet road. Suddenly in front of you, you see a car in a ditch at the side of the road. There is steam coming from the engine. The driver is lying near the overturned car. He is bleeding and seems to be unconscious.

With another student discuss, and then write down, the things that you would do in that kind of an emergency.

> First of all I would. . .
> Next, I. . .
> After that. . .
> Then. . .
> Following that. . .

Compare your list with that of another pair and explain the reasons for your decisions. Can the class agree on a final list that satisfies everyone?

3 Near misses

Everyone has a travel story involving a 'near miss' — in a plane, car, boat, motor cycle or even tractor.

[cassette icon] Listen to these near-miss stories and as you listen note down the type of transport involved and some of the details.

	Type of transport	Details
Person 1		
Person 2		
Person 3		

Check the details of the stories with one or two other students, then talk about your own near misses.
Ask your teacher about one of her/his near misses.

4 Safety first

Some accidents can be prevented, especially those in the home. If young children came to stay in your home, what things would you need to check or change in order to reduce the risk of accidents?

Ask another student to tell you what they would need to check or change in each of their rooms. Make notes of the answers in the spaces. You may wish to use some of the following expressions. Ask your teacher or use a dictionary if you need to.

leads or flexes of electrical appliances   loose sockets
slippery floors   loose rugs   sharp edges
sharp knives   dangerous medicines
cleaning fluids or powders in unlocked cupboards   pets
hot water taps   loose buttons on toys   open windows or stairs

	Checks	Changes
kitchen		
bathroom		
bedroom		
lounge/living room		

In groups, make a report from your notes. What are the high risk features of most homes?
Is your own home relatively safe for children or is it full of accidents just waiting to happen?

5 Just in case

Each year many people spend a lot of money trying to protect themselves against the effects of accidents. They take out insurance policies.

Which of these types of insurance have you or your family taken out recently?

travel   car   life   property
house contents   health   other. . .

Talk about your family's insurance policies with other students. Is insurance more expensive than it is worth? Is it better to save your money and trust your luck?

6 Special insurance

Certain people take out special kinds of insurance. Pianists insure their hands against injury; opera singers insure themselves against colds or sore throats. There is no limit to insurance if you are prepared to pay.

With one or two other students decide what these people could insure themselves against:

Teachers could insure themselves against ....

Buskers could insure themselves against ....

Private detectives could insure themselves against ....

Writers could insure themselves against ...... *writer's block.* ....

Accountants could insure themselves against ...... *double vision.* ....

Wine tasters could insure themselves against ...... *colds.* ....

.... could insure themselves against ....

.... could insure themselves against ....

Pin up your lists and see if you have all had similar ideas. Which insurance policies would be the most expensive? Compare your views.

5 | And so to bed . . .

Bedrooms and sleep

1 Tuning-in

With another student, look at the bedroom in the picture. Decide what kind of person lived there – a student? an artist? a burglar?

What things do you notice most in bedrooms:

> *The kind of bed:* colour of bedspread?
> *The other furniture:* chairs, sofa, chest of drawers?
> *Things on the bedside table:* lamps, books, photos, radio?
> *The furnishings:* rugs, curtains, things on the wall?
> *Anything else?* ....

Exchange ideas with your partner.

Choose one of the following people or one of your own. Decide what kind of bedroom your chosen person has.

> your country's leader
> one of your primary school teachers
> your dentist
> your bank manager

Sit with other students and take it in turns to describe the bedroom of your chosen person. Can they tell you what kind of person you had in mind?

2 Bedtime

When should children go to bed?
Fill in the table:

Age of child	Suggested bedtime	Your own bedtime at that age
5		
7		
9		
11		
13		

Compare your answers with another student's. Explain why you think your bedtimes are the right ones for children. Do you think that it is important for a child to have a fixed bedtime every night? Why?

3 My most unusual night's sleep

Work with a partner. Ask your partner to leave the classroom for a few minutes while you listen to the first person on the cassette talking about her most unusual night's sleep.

Check the details of the story with others who also listened. Then get your partner to come back, and tell him or her the story you heard. Now change roles. You step outside while your partner listens to the next story on the cassette.

Can you remember an unusual night's sleep? Describe your experience to one or two others in the class and ask them about their most unusual night.

4 If only I could get to sleep . . .

Do you sometimes (or often) have trouble falling asleep? Here are some possible cures for this problem which is called insomnia. How many can your class add to this list?

counting sheep   soft music
exercise before going to bed   a relaxing warm drink

What about sleeping tablets? Some people take them, others not. Pick out the sentence which is closest to your thoughts – or write your own.

1 They're good because they give you a deep sleep.
2 They're very bad because you get addicted to them.
3 They always have side effects.
4 They treat the symptoms, not the cause.
5 Doctors wouldn't prescribe them if they were not safe.
6 ....
7 ....

Find two or three other people in the class whose opinions are close to your own.

5 A television interview

In your group, prepare a television interview about sleeping tablets. Choose one person in the group to be the interviewer.

Instructions for the interviewer: Introduce the subject of the programme by saying a few words about sleeping tablets. Then ask members of the public to give their opinions.

Instructions for the rest of the group: You are members of the public – you are interviewed and give your opinions on sleeping tablets. Give your own views, or adopt one of these roles.

a doctor whose research shows that sleeping tablets cause loss of memory

the parent of a teenager with a broken arm, which is very painful at night

a person who has lost a job because of oversleeping and being late for work

a single parent with two young children and a full-time job, who needs plenty of sleep

make up your own role

Together, discuss and plan your interview. When you are ready, present it to the class.

6 Bedridden!

With another student, imagine that you are bedridden for a week. Make a
list of things which you would like to have, to help you get better – and to
give you something to do.
Compare your list with another group's.
What would you have on your list to help your teacher if she or he were
bedridden?

6 | Oh, I do like to be beside the seaside . . .

Holidays, good and bad

1 Tuning-in

🔲 Holidays are not always happy experiences. Listen to these people talking about their holidays. As you listen make notes about the places and what happened.

	Places	What happened?
Person 1		
Person 2		

Have you had similar experiences on holiday? With one or two other students, talk about something that happened to you, a friend, or relative. Here are some ideas to talk about:

souvenir shop   cancellation
double-booked seats or rooms
long delays   refund
rude staff   luggage
going through customs
food poisoning   sunburn

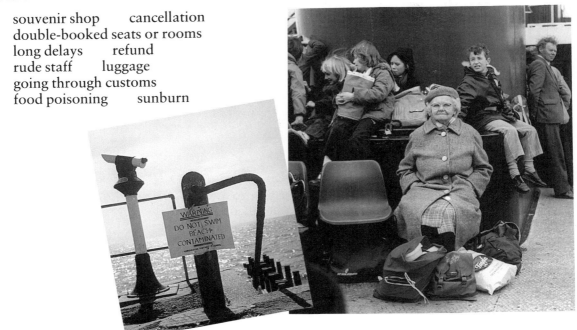

2 House exchange

Every year people 'swap' houses for a few weeks with people from different countries. But it is risky having strangers in your house or flat.

Look at this list of items that are in many homes. Before going on your house exchange, which items would you: leave? hide? remove? replace with cheaper items? Add some of your own to the list.

Household item	leave	hide	remove	replace
antiques	☐	☐	☐	☐
bed	☐	☐	☐	☐
rugs	☐	☐	☐	☐
video/stereo	☐	☐	☐	☐
home computer	☐	☐	☐	☐
piano	☐	☐	☐	☐
pottery	☐	☐	☐	☐
paintings	☐	☐	☐	☐
plants	☐	☐	☐	☐
best china	☐	☐	☐	☐
books	☐	☐	☐	☐
....	☐	☐	☐	☐
....	☐	☐	☐	☐

With other students, talk about your answers.

Do any of your homes have special features that you would have to leave notes about?

— where to turn the water off?
— dustbin days?
— where you hide a spare key?
— where the fuse box is?
— how to operate any of the electrical appliances?
— feeding any pets left behind?
— watering the plants?

Write one note each to leave on the table before you go away. Together, look at your group's notes. Are they easy to understand? Talk about ways of making your instructions very clear for the visiting family.

3 Holidays with a difference

You are starting a holiday company which specialises in unusual holidays. Each branch of your company will offer a different type of unusual holiday. In small groups, choose one of these company branches, and think up some good holiday ideas for it.

Adrenalin Holidays – holidays with a strong element of danger or risk and with high excitement.

Tranquil Holidays – holidays where peace and quiet are the key words.

Eccentric Holidays – holidays for people who don't want to take too many risks but who want something very unusual.

Ecological Holidays – activity holidays for people who are concerned about the future of our planet.

When you plan holidays make sure you talk about:

— where to go
— when to go (what season)
— what activities to organise
— where to stay

When you are ready, call a full company meeting of all the branches. One representative from each branch can report its group's ideas.

4 A surprise holiday

With another student organise a surprise holiday for one of the following:

— a well-known historical figure
— a well-known world leader
— your teacher
— a famous singer or film star
— two handicapped children
— your pet

Decide on: the destination, some of the activities you will arrange, accommodation, type of transport.
Remember: the holiday can be an unpleasant one if you choose an unpleasant world figure, past or present.

5 Where on earth did you get that . . .!?

Can you say from which country these souvenirs came? Talk about your guesses with another student.

With another student, talk about typical souvenirs that you associate with different countries. Write down a few countries and their souvenirs.

Then find another pair, take it in turns to read out the name of one of your souvenirs and see if the other pair can correctly identify the country.

Country	Typical souvenirs
Australia	boomerang
China	jade figurines
France	Eiffel tower paperweight
Malaysia	batik shirt

Many tourists just can't resist souvenir shops when they are on holiday. Often they buy things which they don't really like very much when they get home.

Do you have some interesting, exciting or embarrassing souvenirs from your travels? Bring in some examples (if you can) and talk about them with other students. Were they bargains? Where did you find them?

7 | Your number is up
Numbers and their applications

1 Tuning-in

 Listen to this extract from 'The Magic Flute'. The composer, Mozart, built into this music the 'magic' number 3: small parts of the music are repeated three times. With another student, see whether you can find examples of this in the music.

$\ggg\rightarrow$

Draw a circle on a piece of paper. Inside the circle write some numbers that are important to you.

The numbers can represent dates, lucky numbers, sizes, the number of teeth you have left, bank account number, your sister's age, house numbers – anything.

When you are ready, exchange circles with someone else. Try to guess what your partner's numbers represent.

2 Ideal numbers

Write numbers in these boxes to show your choices.

What is your ideal number of:

political parties in a country ☐	years in one job ☐
days for a holiday ☐	people in a city ☐
students in an English class ☐	TV channels in a country ☐
guests at a wedding ☐	hours of sleep per night ☐
hours in a plane ☐	guests at a dinner party ☐

When you are ready, compare your answers with others, and talk about differences in your choices.

3 Them and us

The cartoon on the next page uses the style of a child's book to show some differences between people who are rich and people who are poor. Some of the text beside some of the numbers is missing. With a partner, can you guess where these missing pieces of text should be?

nd hand clothes
nd cars
star restaurants
st class travel
rd World conditions

Talk about the cartoon. Are the differences between rich and poor similar in your country?

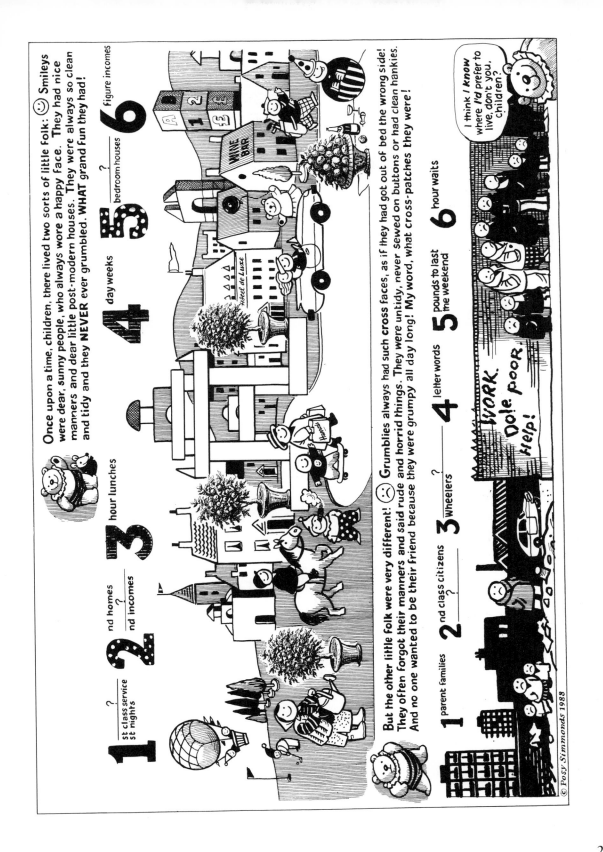

25

4 Half full and half empty

Are you an optimist 😊 or a pessimist 🙁 and why? Ask others in the class to give you their answers to these questions.

Work in small groups. Together, complete this cartoon and add any other items that you can think of.

How many optimists 😊 and pessimists 🙁 are there in your class? What about other people you know?

5 The most important things in life

In 1987 a survey was carried out in Europe amongst young people aged between 15 and 25. They were asked to list the five most important things in life. What is your answer to the same question?

The 5 most important things in life are:

1 ....

2 ....

3 ....

4 ....

5 ....

When you are ready, talk about your answers with other students and give reasons for them. Ask the teacher what is at the top of her or his list.

In the 1987 survey, what do you think young people in Europe considered the most important thing in life to be?

8 | How can I get from A to B?

Cars and transport

1 Tuning-in

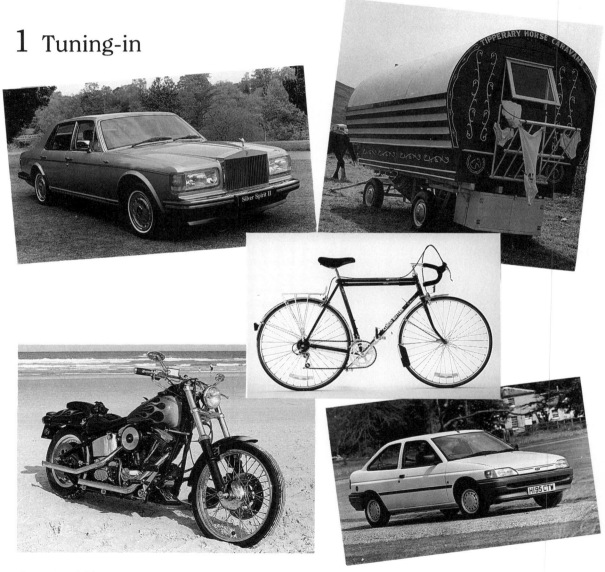

If you could have only one of these, which would you choose, and why? Find someone in the class who has made a different choice. Talk about the reasons for your choices.

2 The Highway Code

With two or three other students, consider these questions:

	Yes	No
Is there a Highway Code in your country?	☐	☐
Can car drivers use their horns in cities?	☐	☐
Do passengers have to wear seat belts?	☐	☐
Do drivers have to give way to ambulances?	☐	☐
Can drivers drink alcohol in moderation?	☐	☐
Can drivers use car phones?	☐	☐
Is there a speed limit on motorways?	☐	☐

Compare your answers.

Listen to two people from different countries answering these questions:
– How important is it to have a strict Highway Code?
– Are there any silly or useless rules in your country's Highway Code?
– Are there any new rules you would like to add?

Would your answers be similar to theirs or very different? Talk about the questions with one or two other students.

29

3 The Devil's Highway Code

With another student, match the two parts of the Devil's Highway Code:

Part I

- Don't stop for pedestrians . . .
- Use a portable television . . .
- Show your seat belt but . . .
- When you hear an ambulance behind you . . .
- Drink and drive . . .
- Don't signal . . .
- Don't drive under 160 k.p.h. . . .
- Carry a loudspeaker . . .

Part II

alcohol helps you relax.
other drivers like surprises.
to shout rude words at pedestrians.
the world is overpopulated anyway.
never fasten it.
it's bad for the engine.
to prevent boredom on long drives.
drive faster.

With another student, think of two more rules for the Devil's Highway Code. Write them down and tell the class about them.

In groups, consider these questions:
- How important is it to make young people think of road safety?
- Do you think the Devil's Highway Code is a good way of doing so?
- If so, how would you present it – advertising, a booklet . . . ?
- If not, what other ideas can your group suggest?

4 City traffic

Does your town have any traffic problems? Take the following questionnaire home, and ask someone who is not in your class the questions.

```
TRAFFIC PROBLEMS IN OUR TOWN - a questionnaire

What do you think our town's main traffic problems are?

Tick  (✓)  one or more:

Too many cars                [ ]
Streets too narrow           [ ]
Not enough traffic lights    [ ]
Not enough policemen/women   [ ]
Bad drivers                  [ ]
Not enough one-way streets   [ ]
Too many one-way streets     [ ]

Others:   . . . . . . . . . . . . . . . . . . . . . . . . . . . . .
          . . . . . . . . . . . . . . . . . . . . . . . . . . . . .
          . . . . . . . . . . . . . . . . . . . . . . . . . . . . .
```

Next class: In small groups, study the results of your questionnaires. Think about the two problems that were ticked most often. What possible solutions are there?
Try to think of as many solutions as possible for your town.

Prepare a report from your group to the class. One person will tell the class what problems you talked about and describe your solutions. Other members of the group can answer questions from your class.

5 Car problems

 Listen to this poem, called 'The car':

> i bought the car
> to travel to jobs
> to make money
>
> the car can't hack the pace*
>
> i'm taking buses
> to get to jobs
> to make the money
> to get the car back on the road
> to get to the jobs
> to make the money
> to keep the car on the road
> to get to the jobs
>
> when i've taken buses
> to the jobs
> to make the money
> to get the car back on the road
>
> i'm selling the car

> *the car has broken down

With another student, look at these one-line sentences about the situation in the poem. Discuss each one and then choose the one which is closest to your idea of the poem.

a) My car's broken down and it's too expensive to keep.
b) I only need a car to get to work, and I only work to pay for my car.
c) I'm caught in a situation I can't escape from.

Find another pair with a different choice and compare your reasons.

Have you ever owned a car when you didn't have enough money to keep it running?
Has anyone in your family had a car that gave them real problems? Describe the situation to one or two other students.
Are cars worth the expense and the trouble they cause?

9 | Hands

Different ways of using our hands

1 Tuning-in

Look at the pictures.
With another student, try to
match each picture with its
message.
The messages are:
— Are you deaf?
— Is that enough?
— It was you.

Now look at this picture. With another student discuss what it could mean.

2 What can I say with my hands?

Imagine that you can no longer speak. Could you use your hands to get a message across?

Your teacher will give you a message on a slip of paper. With a partner, decide what sign language you can use to make other students understand your message.

Try out your sign language with another pair. Can they understand what you are trying to say? Can they suggest ways of improving your sign language?

Now, with your partner, choose a topic of conversation: holiday plans, what you did last week-end . . . or an idea of your own. Try to have a conversation for as long as possible without using words. The two other students will watch, then they will retell your conversation using words – English words, of course!

3 What can I do with my hands?

Look at the words below. With another student, decide which of the words are actions that we can do with our hands.

Use a dictionary or ask your teacher if you need help with the meanings of the words.

Can you add any other words to the list of actions that we can do with our hands?

4 He's got the whole world in his hands

Listen to the song on the cassette. Is it a song you have sung? With another student, talk about what the expression 'in his hands' means. Can you give a definition? Who is the 'he' in the song?

5 How handy are you?

Which of these things can you do without help? Tick the appropriate ones.

change a light bulb	☐	develop your own photos	☐
connect wires to a plug	☐	give someone a nice haircut	☐
change oil in a car	☐	make bread	☐
sew a button on	☐	prune a fruit tree	☐
darn a hole in a sock	☐	tile a floor	☐
make a bookcase	☐	repair a bicycle puncture	☐
make a cushion	☐	type an essay	☐

In groups, show each other the skills you ticked. Talk about the way you learnt those skills. At school? From a parent? From a friend? From a 'How to . . .' book? From a radio or television programme?
Of the things you cannot do, which skills do you feel you need most?
Is there anyone in the group who could help you get started?

How important do you think it is to teach these kinds of skills at school?

10 | Burning the candle at both ends

Being prudent or rash

1 Tuning-in

Look at the following list of actions. Say whether you think they are careful, or rash. Give a number from 1 to 5. (1 = too careful; 2 = quite careful; 3 = just about right; 4 = quite rash; 5 = too rash.)

Keeping a single sock when the other is lost. ☐
Buying life insurance. ☐
Giving up your job to go on the holiday of your dreams. ☐
Travelling around the world by yourself. ☐
Giving up one home before you've found another. ☐
Buying something you really want even if you can't really afford it. ☐
Keeping receipts for everything you buy. ☐

Compare your numbers with another student's. Do you agree? If you disagree, try to explain why you put the number you did.

2 Near the edge

Have you — or someone you know — ever done anything that was quite dangerous or rash?
With another student, plan a story about a dangerous action. It can be: your own experience, a story that you have read about in a book, or a story you invent.

Use the following questions to help you:
— When did it happen? How old were you?
— Where were you?
— Did anyone try to stop you from doing it?
— What were the results?
— Are you glad you did it, or do you regret it?

When you are ready, one of you will tell the story to the class. They can ask questions about it and the partner who is not telling the story answers them. Can the class guess whether the story you have told really happened to you?

3 Does prudence pay?

Look at the beginnings of these news items:

Does prudence pay?

A MIDDLE-AGED couple in Vancouver found to their horror last week that the best plans can sometimes go wrong.

All their life, they had been very careful with their money. They didn't trust banks, and kept all their savings under the mattress.

Last week, they finally decided to buy their dream house. But when they ~~went~~...

From the frying pan into the fire!

FIREMAN Ted Jones decided last week that he needed a change of scene.

So he gave up his job, borrowed some money from a friend, and set off on the trans-Siberian express.

But he did...

Mad dash

POLICEMEN are searching the Melbourne area this morning for two young runaways.

The boys aged 12 and 13 disappeared after a sports master discovered them smoking behind the cricket pavilion.

They jumped on another teacher's motorbike, ~~and...~~

With another student, choose one of the stories and talk about what happened next. Then change partners. Imagine that you are the main character in your story, and tell your new partner what happened to you.

4 A radio warning

In one English-speaking town, children have started taking a short cut from school across the railway tracks to the shops. There have been no accidents yet, but this is a very dangerous thing to do.

With one or two other students, prepare a short warning for the local radio. Decide about these questions:
— Is it a good idea to have music or songs to help children remember your message?
— Should you mention possible punishment?
— Is it best to speak in a light, funny way or a strong, almost frightening tone?

When you are ready, 'broadcast' your warning to the class. If you can, record your warning on a cassette and then play it to the class.

11 | Crash bang whizz!

Sounds

1 Tuning-in

What sounds do you associate with your home environment? Make a list of as many as you can think of. Use these headings if you like:

Morning sounds	*Evening sounds*	*Sounds inside your home*	*Sounds outside*
....	....	....	....
....	....	....	....
....	....	....	....
....	....	....	....

Compare your list with another student's. Talk about the sounds which you like best in your list, and those which you like least.
If you became deaf, what sounds would you miss most? Compare what you think about this.

2 Pleasant sounds and annoying noises

With another student look at these sounds. For each one, think of as many situations as possible when that sound is nice or when it is annoying.

Sound	is pleasant when	is annoying when
A dog barking		
A baby crying		
A phone ringing		
A person laughing		
Traffic		
Music in a public place		
Others:		
....		

Compare your results with those of other groups.

3 Loud mouths?

Listen to three people talking about their jobs and why they like them. With another student, list the qualities of voice that each person mentions, then guess their occupation.

	Kind of voice needed for job	Occupation
Speaker 1		
Speaker 2		
Speaker 3		

Compare your answers with those of other groups.

Now, with your partner, match up the people on the left with a word that describes the kind of voice that helps each in their jobs.
If there are words you don't know, use a dictionary, or ask your teacher.

1 An auctioneer
2 A doctor
3 A street vendor
4 A politician
5 A lion tamer
6 A hotel receptionist

sweet loud hesitant persuasive powerful cheerful impersonal clear AUTHORITATIVE sincere soothing monotonous firm soft musical polite kind

⟫⟶

Sit with two or three other students. Compare your choices. Are any of these jobs you would really like to do? Say why or why not. What is your ideal job, and what sort of voice would you need to do that job well?

4 Silence is golden

Here is a traditional rhyme. With a partner, guess the missing words.

A wise old owl
Sat in an oak
The more he sat
The less he ....
The less he ....
The more he ....
Why can't we all be like that
Wise old bird?

Now listen to the cassette. Were your guesses right?
Do you agree with the rhyme? Are wise people usually quiet? Ask other people in the class what they think.

In these situations, are you: (a) mainly a silent listener, *or*
(b) mainly a chatterbox?
– at parties
– first thing in the morning
– last thing at night
– in your class
– on a bus, train, or plane
– at family gatherings

Talk about these situations with your partner.

5 Danger noise levels

Here is part of a newspaper article about noise level limits. Noise levels are measured in units called 'decibels'.

With two or three other students, read the article. Ask other groups or your teacher if you need help.

Danger noise levels set for Europe

EUROPEAN industry has approved noise level limits which could result in 50% of workers becoming partly deaf.

The noise level limit has been set at 90 decibels. Medical research in America and England shows that it is not only hearing that is affected at that noise level.

Noise levels

	decibels
Very quiet room	20
Quiet office	40
Office	60
Factory	100–120
Jet engine	130

The stress to the body is considerable and can cause heart problems.

In your groups, decide how many decibels you think these situations produce:

- roadworks
- sirens
- vacuum cleaner
- discos
- rush hour traffic
- your cafeteria

What are the noisiest situations that you are exposed to? Talk about them in your groups. What should the noise level limit be for your classroom?

12 | Small but deadly

Small things that are annoying or dangerous

1 Tuning-in

Here is a list of troubles that are small but very annoying. In the box after
each one, put a number from 1 to 5, to show whether you find them
annoying or not (1 = not at all annoying, 5 = very annoying).
Add any other small things that you find especially annoying.

gravel in your shoe
someone humming
a dripping tap
flies in the kitchen
milk boiling over
spiders in the bath
small chips on cups
scratches on furniture
a missing button

....

....

Compare your list with another student's. Are you both easily annoyed? . . .
or untroubled by small irritations?
In your class, which small thing got named most often?
What small troubles annoy your teacher most?

2 Small but deadly

Some small things are more than annoying: they are really painful or even deadly.
Here are four groups of small things that can produce pain, illness or even death. With another student, can you match each group with one of the headings in the box?

Virus or germ
Can bite or sting
Can cause allergies
Can contain poison

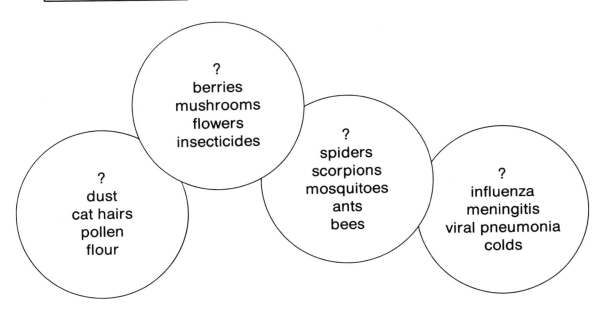

In a group, can you add anything to the lists? Use a dictionary if you wish.
Has anyone in your group or someone they know ever had a bad experience with any of these small things? Describe the experience to the group.

3 Food colouring tragedy

With a partner, read this newspaper article:

Food colouring tragedy

TORONTO: A father claimed yesterday that his nine-year-old son walked to his death in front of a car because he was over-excited as a result of eating sweets containing artificial colouring.

Police found on the boy half-eaten packets of sweets and a candy bar containing two different kinds of food colourings.

Mr Charles Johnson, 35, said: 'I am convinced he was killed because of the sweets and I want a total ban on artificial colourings.'

'We have gradually realised that within minutes of eating some kinds of sweets, Jimmie would lose his concentration, become very excited, and often could not put two words together.'

Jimmie Johnson, age 9, food colouring victim

'Fifteen minutes before the accident, I phoned home from work and I did not even recognise his voice. He was such a smashing kid but his personality would change completely when he ate the sweets.'

Mr Johnson added: 'The best thing that can come out of Jimmie's death is for these colourings to be banned.'

Here is what some people said when they read the article:

> I'm not convinced that food colouring was responsible for the boy's death.

> They should stop companies using artificial colourings in food.

> You shouldn't let a nine-year-old boy walk on the streets by himself.

> The parents knew that eating sweets had a strong effect on their son so why did they let him have them?

> We need stronger laws to make foods safe for everyone.

With a partner, choose the two opinions that you like best. Explain your reasons to others in the class.

4 Let's do something about it

Imagine that you want to take immediate action about the food colouring tragedy which you have read about in the paper. You decide to make a phone call to the managing director of the local company that makes sweets.

With your partner, make a list of things you want to say. These expressions might be useful:

I'd like to complain about. . .
I'm phoning about. . .
I'm really worried about. . .
I'm really concerned about. . .
I can't understand why you can't. . .
There must be other ways of. . .
Do you realise that. . .
Are you aware that. . .
Is there anything you can do to. . .
It must be possible to. . .

5 The phone call

One person in each pair: Make the first part of your 'phone call'.
The other person: You are the managing director of the company that makes sweets. Reply to the phone call and continue the conversation.

When you have completed your phone conversation, change partners and try the conversation again.

13 | Letters, words and pictures

Exploring letters and words

1 Tuning-in

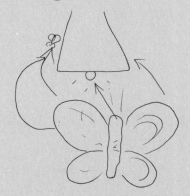

These drawings were used in a guessing game.
Can you guess what words they represent?
To play the game, you need an English
dictionary, pencil and paper.
Sit in pairs. Each person takes it in turn to
draw and guess.

> *Person A:*
> Let the dictionary fall open at any page but don't let the other person see.
> Look quickly at the words, then choose one. Draw a picture to represent
> your word. You cannot speak to your partner, but can try to help by
> nodding or by the expression on your face.

> *Person B:*
> You have two minutes to guess the word, from the moment your partner
> starts to draw the picture. You can keep guessing but your partner
> cannot speak during those two minutes.

When you have finished, compare your experiences: was it hard or easy to
guess or draw?

2 The Traveller's Alphabet

Here is a Traveller's Alphabet with some parts that are missing. With another student, talk about the gaps and choose suitable words to complete them.

A   is for the *A*NTS we found in the hotel bedroom.

B   is for the *B*................ which gave me backache.

C   is for the *C*OURIER who lost our ....

D   is for the *D*RIVER who couldn't see without his glasses.

E   is for the *E*................ on the plane that caught fire.

F   is for the *F*ISH that upset everyone's stomachs.

G   is for the *G*OATS that ate ....

H   is for the *H*................ where we recovered from sunstroke.

I   is for the *I*CE-CREAM that ....

J   is for the *J*EANS that ....

K   is for the *K*................ that didn't fit the motel lock.

L   is for the *L*IGHTHOUSE where we slept one stormy night.

M   is for the *M*................ where the monks made honey wine.

N   is for the *N*EON LIGHTS that ....

O   is for the *O*................ that were part of every meal.

P   is for the *P*................ that ....

Q   is for the *Q*UEUES that we found at every airport.

R   is for the *R*ADIO that ....

S   is for the *S*WIMMING POOL that ....

T   is for the *T*................ that were never on time.

U   is for the *U*MBRELLA ....

V   is for the *V*INES that ....

W   is for the *W*................ that nearly blew us off the rocks.

X   is for the *X*MAS LIGHTS that made the square so bright.

Y   is for the *Y*................ that took us round the islands.

Z   is for the *Z*OO that ....

Compare your alphabet with that of other pairs.

Do any of these letters remind you of your own travels? Choose one that does, and tell other students about that experience.

3 I love my armadillo

Here is a traditional alphabet game that English-speaking people sometimes play on long journeys. This is how to play it in small groups.

The first person chooses the first letter of the alphabet and says something like this:

I love my .... *armadillo* .... with an A.
Her name is .... *Alice* ....
She comes from .... *Argentina* ....
She eats ...*apples and avocados*...
I like her because she is .... *amusing* ....
But I hate her when she is .... *angry* ....

The second person chooses B, the third C, and so on. When a student can't think of a word, others in the group can help.

Is this game similar to ones you play or have played on long journeys?
In your groups, talk about ways of passing the time when travelling long distances. Which of these activities have you tried?

reading   crossword puzzles   writing letters
chess or draughts   backgammon   cards   Scrabble
guessing games (like 'I Spy')   chatting to strangers
Any others?

4 It's not my type

Look at these different types. With another student, choose the most suitable types for each of these:

— a birthday card for a grandparent
— a card of sympathy when someone has died
— a party invitation
— a dictionary
— a reading book for a six-year-old child
— the name of a town on a tee-shirt

Compare your choices. Do you like types that are:

— clear and simple?   — interesting to look at?
— unusual?   — decorative?

Goudy Old Style   Rockwell
Lazybones   Arnold Bocklin
Italian Old Style   CHROMIUM
Friz Quadrata   Avant Garde Gothic
Baskerville   Times New Roman
eurostile   Commercial Script
        Tintopetto
SCANNER   University Roman
Palatino Italic   Caxton Roman

5 Here's my card

With another student, imagine that you are both directors of a small language school. You need a business card. Together, decide:

— what the school's name will be
— whether to have a design as well as words
— what colour the card should be
— what colour the words or design should be
— where on the card to put the school name and design
— where to position the address, telephone number etc.
— what title to give yourself (e.g. director, head, principal, English language consultant)

Would you print the card in other languages besides English? Which ones? When you are ready with your ideas, tell the others in the class and your teacher what you have decided and why.

14 | Please speak after the tone

Messages

1 Tuning-in

Look at this list of jobs:

teacher

doctor's receptionist   electrician

TV announcer   plumber

hotel manager   film producer

secretary   tour operator

car mechanic

actor

Listen to the messages left on the answerphone.
With another student, try to guess each speaker's job.

Speaker 1 ....
Speaker 2 ....
Speaker 3 ....
Speaker 4 ....

Check your answers with other students.

In a small group talk about how you feel when you use a
telephone or an answerphone.
Do you feel comfortable in your own language? What do you
feel about leaving a message on an answerphone? Do you
hang up rather than speak to a machine?

What problems do you have when you use a telephone or answerphone in
English? Do you get nervous? Do you forget words that you know? Do you
have trouble understanding?
Compare your problems and talk about ways of making telephoning easier.

2 I'm sorry I can't take your call at the moment . . .

In small groups, think about the person and the situation your teacher gives you.
Imagine that person wants to record a message on his or her own answerphone for any possible callers.
Plan the message. Then, if you can, record it onto a cassette and give it to another group – or say it to the other group.
Ask them to guess the identity and situation of the person recording the message.

When you have played the other group's recorded message, imagine that you wish to leave a message after the tone. Plan your message together and then one of you will record it onto the cassette. Play both messages to the class.

3 Insultograms and praisograms

Nowadays you can send many different kinds of messages – sung messages, 'kissograms' (including a kiss from the messenger) 'cookiegrams' (a message on a biscuit) . . .
You have just started a company that specialises in delivering messages of praise or insult.
With one or two others, choose someone you know outside the classroom, or a famous person, past or present. Together, plan a message of praise or insult to that person.
When everyone is ready, deliver your praisogram or your insultogram to one of the other groups.
Can the other group guess what kind of person the message is intended for?

4 Community complaints

On a new local radio station, there is a programme called 'Community complaints'. It gives ordinary people the chance to complain about anything they don't like in their community.

 Listen to part of the programme and list some of the complaints and improvements that the people mention.

	Complaints	*Improvements suggested*
Speaker 1		
Speaker 2		

With one or two other students, talk about the complaints you listened to. Which does your group consider the most serious? Does your town have similar problems?

At home, think about problems in your own community. What would you complain about on the programme?

Next class: In your group, one person is the interviewer for the radio programme and asks the others for their views.

Did many of you complain about the same problems? As a class, talk about actions which the community could take to improve these unsatisfactory situations.

5 If there is anyone out there . . .

A space probe is about to be launched – on it will be a cassette containing many hundreds of short messages about life on our earth. You are invited to record one of the messages – about one minute.
With another student, plan a short informative talk about one of these topics, or choose one of your own.

1 What humans are like – their appearance.
2 History.
3 Food.
4 What humans enjoy doing.
5 What humans make/have made.
6 What humans believe in.
7 Problems on earth.
8 Hopes for our planet.
9 ....?
10 ....?

If you can, record your messages on a cassette. Otherwise, say your message to the class.

What was the most popular topic? Do you agree on which is the most important?
Did most people present optimistic or pessimistic messages about our planet?
Talk about your different approaches.

15 | Fire power
Fire and firearms

1 Tuning-in

Think about fire for a moment. Then complete the sentence below by listing as many words or expressions as you can. Use a dictionary or ask your teacher if you need help.

> When I think about fire, these things come into my mind. . .

When you are ready, sit in a small group and find out about one another's lists. Are most of your words positive or negative about fire? Can you say why?

2 Camp fires

Many people enjoy having parties around some kind of fire – a camp fire, bonfire, barbecue, or fireworks.

Listen to two people talking about their past experiences. What did they enjoy most?

Now listen to a third person telling a story about his son's birthday party. In small groups, take it in turns to retell the story, with each student saying only one sentence at a time.

In small groups, tell each other your own stories.
Do you ever have parties around a fire?
Have you any childhood memories involving fire?

3 Have gun, will shoot

Listen to some people talking about personal guns. How many details can you add to this table?

Reasons for allowing hand guns	Reasons for not allowing hand guns
dangerous society	If one person has one, more and more will buy them.

In a small group, compare your answers. What are your own ideas on these questions?
– Do you think having a personal gun is a good idea? Why/why not?
– What would cause you to buy a personal gun?
– Describe the circumstances that would make having a gun a necessary part of every home.

4 Designer guns

With two or three other students, read the following article. Help each other with difficulties. Here is a summary of the article to help you:

> In the United States, there is a big demand for guns. Now, a company wants to sell hand guns to women. Their advertising tries to make women think that guns are necessary to protect their families. But they also want women to think that guns are a part of fashion, like 'designer' clothes.

DESIGNER GUNS *The latest word in fashion*

NOWHERE is the demand for designer guns stronger than in the United States. In Washington, business is ready to fill the market of designer guns for women.

15.6 million women may buy a gun this year. Next month, a leading firm of manufacturers will launch a new line of revolvers for women, called Lady Smith Handguns. 'As more women have entered the job market, become heads of households and purchased their own homes, they've taken on a new set of responsibilities', says one advertisement with a photograph of a mother bending to kiss her young daughter good night.

The company is therefore trying to sell the Lady Smith gun for family protection but it also wants women to think of the gun as a fashionable, feminine, accessory.

In your group, choose two sentences from the article that you find either interesting or frightening. Discuss how you feel about them.
Find out what other groups think about the article. Did they find it:

strange?   boring?   interesting?   amusing?   saddening?
relevant to their lives?

5 Pyromania

Burning has always been one way of getting rid of unwanted things. In the pictures above from the film *Fahrenheit 451*, books are being burned.

With one or two other students, think about all the things that your community burns: autumn leaves? rubbish? used newspapers? dead bodies? other things?

Now imagine that you are a committee in your town. Your job is to destroy unwanted items. You can set fire to anything you dislike, anything that is useless, or harmful to society: buildings, vehicles, consumer goods. Together, make a list of the items that need to go.

Compare your list with that of another group. Did you all choose the same things?

16 | Is bad language good for you?

Bad language and its effects

1 Tuning-in

Ask another student the following questions and note the answers.

Do you swear or use a rude word in your own language when:	usually	sometimes	occasionally	never
You hit your thumb with a hammer?	☐	☐	☐	☐
You spill a drink on a good carpet?	☐	☐	☐	☐
A dog with dirty paws jumps up at you?	☐	☐	☐	☐
You just miss a train while on the way to an important meeting?	☐	☐	☐	☐
Another driver forces you to brake suddenly to avoid hitting his car?	☐	☐	☐	☐

Talk to each other about your answers. Are there other things which make you use rude language?

2 Can we learn some rude words, please?

Do you know any rude words in English? Are they a useful part of learning a language?

Choose either A or B. Find another student who made the same choice.
Together, think of one or two reasons for that choice.
Find a pair who chose the other statement. Can you make them change their minds?

A	B
When you learn a new language you should also learn the most popular rude words in that language.	It is not at all important to learn rude words in the language you are learning.
Reasons	*Reasons*
....	....
....	....
....	....

3 Any ideas?

Read about Sam's situation below.

Joan and David have a son Sam, aged eight. He is a lively and intelligent boy. The family is a caring one. They live in a good middle-income area. Sam uses swear words a great deal. He swears at the dog, his parents, his teacher and his school friends. Punishment for his behaviour has not made any difference. He is not a difficult child and there seems to be no stress in his life. His parents are getting worried and frustrated.

In a small group, talk about this situation. What do you feel about an eight-year-old child swearing? Can you think of positive suggestions that you could make to help the family deal with the problem?

4 Is bad language a good thing?

Which of these viewpoints is closest to your own? Choose one or make up your own in the space provided.

a) You should never use bad language under any circumstances as it is unnecessary and a sign of bad upbringing.
b) Although bad language is not usually acceptable, when emotions are running high, it is normal for people to use strong language.
c) Bad language doesn't do any harm; it is part of the richness of a language and adds colour to life.
d) There is no such thing as 'bad' language, only 'language'. Today's so-called bad language may become tomorrow's acceptable expression, so why worry?
e) (your own statement) ....

....

Sit with one or two students who chose a different statement from the one you chose. Try to understand each other's point of view.
Find out if most people in the class have a similar opinion of bad language.

5 Language interview

With another student make up a list of questions to find out what people think about bad language. You can use some of the sentences in this unit to help you with the questions.
When you are ready, decide on the best way to ask people if they are prepared to answer your questions.

Interview some English-speaking people if possible.* Make a note of the answers you get and record the interviews if you can.

When you have completed your interviews, prepare a short oral report with your partner and present it to another pair.
Try to speak for about the same length of time as your partner.
When the other pair give their report, ask questions if something is not clear to you.

* If you can't find any English-speaking people to interview, ask the questions in your own language but give your report in English.

17 | Chuckers and hoarders

Collections, antiques and disposables

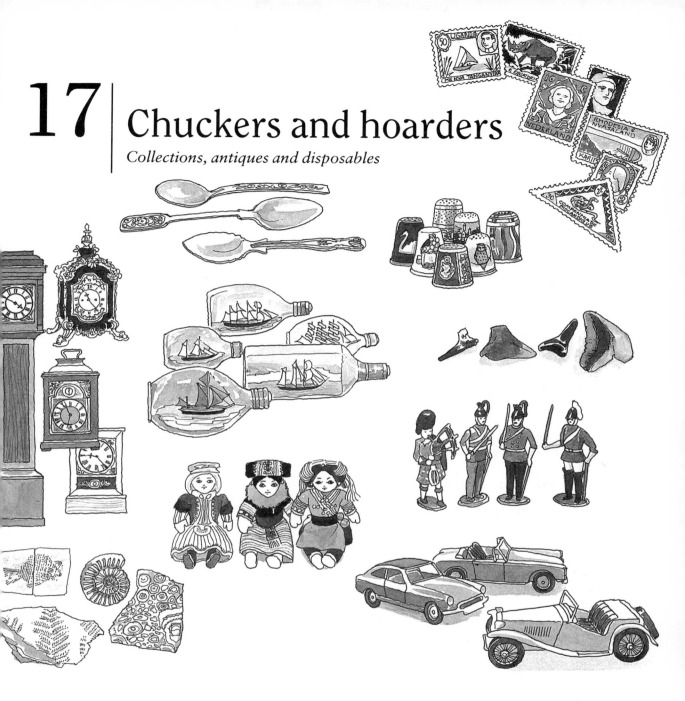

1 Tuning-in

Which of the things in the picture would you rather collect? Why? Compare
with another student. Have you ever collected anything? Talk to some other
students about any collections you have made. Ask them about their
collections.

2 Wilting flowers and socks with holes

Answer the following questions about yourself.

1. You have some cut flowers in a vase, but two have wilted. You:

   a) Throw them all out.
   b) Save the good ones.
   c) Dry the wilted flowers and put them in a bowl to make the room smell nice.

2. You have used a tin of drinking chocolate which has a lid. You:

   a) Throw the tin and lid out.
   b) Put it with other empty tins under the sink.
   c) Use the lid as: a saucer under plants or an ashtray; decorate the tin and use it to hold pencils.

3. A cupful of rice is left over after a meal. You:

   a) Throw it out.
   b) Store it in the fridge.
   c) Invent a new recipe that needs exactly one cupful of rice.

4. One of your socks has a big hole. You:

   a) Throw it out.
   b) Darn it.
   c) Use it as a cloth for cleaning.

5. You have a lot of postcards people have sent you. You:

   a) Throw them out.
   b) Leave them on the table for a while, then put them in a drawer.
   c) Create a colourful display to put on your kitchen wall.

6. At the end of the week, you have a pile of used newspapers. You:

   a) Throw them out.
   b) Put them in your garden shed.
   c) Take them to be recycled (or, if you live in a cold climate, press them into logs for the fire).

7. Your cheap ball-point pen runs out. You:

   a) Throw it out.
   b) Put it away until you buy a refill.
   c) Take out the old refill and give the empty pen to a child as a pea-shooter for rice grains.

Are the majority of your answers (a), (b), or (c)? Find one or two other people in the class who are the same. Your teacher will give you a 'profile' which tells you something about your personality.
Do you think it describes you accurately?

With your partners, think of a similar profile for the other two groups.
(For example, if you are Chuckers, write a profile for Hoarders and Creative Recyclers.)
When you are ready, find another group with a different profile from yours.
Tell them your profile, and compare it with the one the teacher gave them.
What differences are there?

3 Antiques

With another student, choose role card A or B. Prepare your role play, then team up with a pair that has chosen the other role.

A: You are an antique dealer selling one of the objects in the picture. Think of ways of persuading people to buy it: is it very old and valuable? Is it useful? Is it attractive? Is it something that can be stored easily? Think of a convincing date for it, and be prepared to talk also about the people who owned it.

B: You want to buy an antique as a present for an aunt. Ask the antique dealer what would be best. But make sure you find out all about the antique – where it came from, its date, who owned it before – remember there are a lot of fakes around!

4 If only I hadn't thrown it away!

Have you ever thrown away anything you had kept for a long time, and then regretted it later?

 Listen to two people telling stories about things they threw away. With another student, talk about what happened in each case. Has anything like this ever happened to you?

Now listen to the first part of the next story. What happened next? Work in small groups. Continue the story. Can you supply an ending? When you are ready, tell another group your ending and listen to theirs.

Finally, listen to the end of the story on the cassette.

5 Throw it away?

Nowadays, there are more and more disposable things – things that you use once or twice and then throw away.
With another student, choose the items that you consider disposable:

handkerchiefs   drinking glasses   nappies for babies
tablecloths   napkins   watches   pens   umbrellas   plates
gloves   books   toothbrushes   underwear   shower caps
slippers   hair bands   combs   sunglasses   briefcases   toys

With other pairs, talk about the items you haven't chosen.
Which ones will become disposable in the future?
Why are so many things disposable these days?

18 | Sugar and spice

Stereotypes of males and females

1 Tuning-in

▭ Listen to this very old nursery rhyme. Write down what little girls and boys are made of.

Little girls are made of:

sugar

....

....

Little boys are made of:

snips

....

....

....

Compare your two lists with another student.

What does the rhyme say about boys and girls? Which of these statements seem to be close to what you think the rhyme says? Choose three for boys, three for girls (you can add your own if you like):

boys are rough   boys are playful   boys are happy outdoors
        girls are sweet
boys like animals   girls can get angry suddenly   girls are pretty
        boys like active games   girls are happy indoors
girls are sometimes unpredictable   boys are stubborn
                                        girls smell nice
boys like to get dirty
        girls are like precious jewels

Have other students chosen the same statements? Find out why or why not.

2 Men and women

Which person interests you most? Why? In small groups, compare your reactions.

Andrea

Trevor and Don

Robert and Tanya

Marcia

In your groups, talk about these situations until you can decide on one person for each. If you cannot agree, be ready to explain why.

Situation 1: Each one of the people in the photos has invited your group to a party this Saturday.

Decision: We'll go to ....'s party.

Situation 2: Each of these people is also a qualified teacher and has applied to teach English to you.

Decision: We'll choose .... as our teacher.

Situation 3: Your group is looking after a friend's little girl, aged two. You have advertised for a baby-sitter. Each of these people applies for a job.

Decision: We'll hire ....

When you are ready, get together with another group and talk about your decisions.

3 Feminine and masculine

Listen to these people talking about masculinity and femininity.

With another student, jot down the qualities they mention under these headings:

What makes a man 'masculine'?

Speaker 1:

....

....

Speaker 2:

....

....

What makes a woman 'feminine'?

Speaker 1:

....

....

Speaker 2:

....

....

Which of these views is closest to your own? What qualities do you think are important?

Compare your ideas with those of other students in the class. Discuss reasons for differences.

Are your ideas about masculinity and femininity very different from those of your parents?

As a class, talk about those differences. Do you think there will be a lot of changes in the future?

4 What can I say to the children?

▭ Look at situation A. Listen to two parents discussing this situation.

> *Situation A:*
> A boy, aged 8, asks you to buy him a fashionable teenage girl doll for his birthday.

With another student, talk about the parents' decision. Do you agree with it? Why? Why not?

In a small group, discuss situation B. Imagine that you are the parents. Talk about what you would say to your daughter.

> *Situation B:*
> Your daughter, aged 16, wants to join a pop group who have long hair and small tattoos on each arm.

Make notes of your discussion. At home, prepare what you would say to your child.

Next class: In groups, take it in turns to present your advice. Listen to the others and comment. Is the advice presented in a balanced way?

5 Well brought-up . . .

In many countries the rules of behaviour for well brought-up men used to be different from those for well brought-up women. In some cases these rules still apply.

In your own country, are there rules of behaviour that apply to men or to women? With another student, write your ideas below:

A well brought-up man
never: ....
....
always: ....
....

A well brought-up woman
never: ....
....
always: ....
....

When you are ready, sit with another pair. Are your rules similar or different? What do you think about these rules of behaviour?
- Are they still necessary today?
- Should they be different for men and for women, or should they be the same for both?
- Which rule is the most important?

19 | Zoo story
Animals and humans

1 Tuning-in

Is it true that people become like the animals they keep? In that case, what
are the right animals for the following people:
- the Prime Minister or President of your country
- your English teacher
- your best friend
- your favourite actor or actress

Compare your choices – can you say why you chose those animals?

2 Mascots

Organisations often have animals as
mascots. Some army regiments, for
example, have goats. The goat in the
picture is the mascot of the 3rd Battalion of
the Royal Regiment of Wales.
With another student, choose an animal
mascot for at least three of the national
associations of these occupations:

racing drivers	lawyers	plumbers
magicians	builders	police officers
politicians	teachers	hairdressers
surgeons	dentists	

Find out what mascots other pairs have
chosen. Explain why you think each animal
is an appropriate mascot.

3 Can we save the whale?

buttons   candlewax   chessman   chicken feed
corsets   detergent   drum skin   fish bait   fishing rod
golf bag   lamp oil   lipstick   margarine   paint   pet food
medicines   printing ink   sausage skins   soap   tennis racket
wax crayons   whip

With another student, see if you can match each object with its name.
All of these objects are made from whales.
How many of them do you think are necessary? How many could be made in other ways?

To save the whale, is it enough to place limits on the numbers that we can catch, or should we stop hunting whales completely?
Find out if others in the class share your view.

4 Endangered species

There are now many animals or birds that are endangered species, that is their numbers are so small that they may disappear altogether.
Look at this table. With another student, try to guess the missing figures.

Endangered species

In the world, there are:

60	endangered species of cat (tigers, jaguars, ocelots, etc.)
....	endangered species of bear
4	endangered species of rhinoceros
....	endangered species of panda
....	endangered species of whale
1,000	endangered species of bird

In 1974, ... species were lost every year.
By 2000, ... species will be lost.

Compare your guesses with other groups.

 Listen to two people talking about the animals that they would most like to protect.

In small groups, talk about the views expressed by the speakers. Are there other animals which you would like to protect, so that your grandchildren can see them in a natural environment?

Discuss the best way to protect those animals: is it necessary to keep them in zoos? Or can they be protected in their own environments?

73

5 A human zoo

In groups of three, imagine that you are setting up the first human zoo.
To start with, you can only afford three cages or enclosures.
Decide what human 'species' you would like to show (for example –
politicians? teachers? dentists? football fans? wrestlers? poets? etc.)
What will each one of the enclosures be like? Think of an appropriate
environment for each 'species'.

At your zoo, visitors will be able to rent a personal cassette so that they can
listen to a description of the 'species' as they walk around.
Prepare the description for each one of your 'species'. If you have a cassette
recorder, make a recording.

When you are ready, hold a press conference to announce the opening of
your new zoo. Describe it to the members of the press (the class) and play
them your cassette (or describe each 'species' to them). Be ready to answer
questions about your zoo!

20 | Book ends

Books, including this one

1 Tuning-in

Look at the front covers of these paperback books. With another student try to imagine what each story might be about and talk about two possible characters in one of the books. Share your ideas with other students.

2 Special books

Think of some of the books, or magazine and newspaper articles, you have read in the last few years. They may be of any type. Write the names or a brief description of one or two that you remember well.

Describe one of your books or articles to some other students. Tell them why you remember it so clearly.
For example, was it about an important world event? Was it something that made you think differently about your life? Was it an exciting or unusual story?

3 They should write a book about . . .

Which person in your family or which one of your friends would make an interesting character in a novel or other kind of book?
When you have selected your family member or friend, discuss answers to these questions with another student:
— What would the book be about?
— What kind of book would it be: an adventure story, a crime story, a romantic novel?
— Where would the action take place?
— What would happen to your family member or friend in the book?

4 One day I'll write a book

Have you ever thought of writing a book? Imagine that you have decided to take six months off to write your first book.
Which of these types of book would you choose to write and why?

a novel   a book of poems   a biography   an autobiography
a travel book   a cookery book   a children's book
a book on a sport or hobby
a study of a social problem in your country
other (name it) ....

Talk about your ideas with another student.
Where in the world could you happily spend six months writing your book?
Choose a place that would help you to be creative.

5 About this book

In the first book in this series, we asked students to give us their reactions to the units they had tried.
Would you like to let us know what you think of this second book?

Write to Joanne Collie and Stephen Slater
c/o Cambridge University Press
The Edinburgh Building
Shaftesbury Road
Cambridge CB2 2RU
England

We would like you to tell us which activities you enjoyed doing.
Did the book help you to speak English more easily?
Did the group work help you get to know other members of the class better?

We look forward to hearing from you. Goodbye for now,
see you in Book 3! With all our good wishes,

Joanne Collie

Stephen Slater

Key

Unit 1 **1.3** $200 koala bear, $1 red kangaroo, 20¢ platypus, 5¢ echidna – they are all native animals that do not exist anywhere else, and they symbolise the importance of wildlife for Australians.

Unit 2 **2.1** The pieces of music on the cassette are, in this order: Alpine horn (picture C); Indian snake charmer (picture E); tuba (picture B); xylophone (picture A); African drums (picture D).

Unit 3 **3.5** Ballet, hockey.

Unit 5 **5.1** The room is in a women's prison.

Unit 6 **6.5** The souvenirs are from the following countries: *1* Lithuania; *2* Brazil; *3* Kenya *4* Nicaragua; *5* Mexico; *6* Canada; *7* Turkey; *8* Russia; *9* Greece. Also included are Kenyan elephants and Scottish stones.

Unit 7 **7.3** First class travel, second cars, five star restaurants, second hand clothes, third world conditions. **7.5** Good health.

Unit 8 **8.3**
Don't stop for pedestrians, the world is overpopulated anyway.
Use a portable television to prevent boredom on long drives.
Show your seat belt but never fasten it.
When you hear an ambulance behind you drive faster.
Drink and drive, alcohol helps you relax.
Don't signal, other drivers like surprises.
Don't drive under 160 k.p.h., it's bad for the engine.
Carry a loudspeaker to shout rude words at pedestrians.

Unit 9 **9.1** 1 It was you. 2 Are you deaf? 3 Is that enough? 4 Visit my house.

9.2 Examples of messages:

Please get up and open the door.
Can you lend me a pencil?
I'm cold. Please shut the window.
Bring me the book that is on the teacher's desk.
Can you tell me the time?
Can I use your phone, please?
Do you have a match?
Can you give me a lift back home after the class?
Where is the nearest post office, please?
I'd like a cup of coffee, please – black.
Have you got a room for the night, please?
Where is the parking lot?
May I introduce you to my wife/husband/mother/father?
There is a small red insect crawling up your back.
You've got two different socks on today, one red and one blue.
Can you lend me a pound/dollar/crown/zloti . . . etc.

9.3 Break, write, paint, wave, swim, stir, clap, phone, carry, signal, drive, strike, rub.

9.4 'In his hands' in this context means that the whole world is being cared for – 'he' is usually taken to refer to a divine being.

Unit 10 Burning the candle at both ends means 'to be excessively wasteful or extravagant' or 'to get up early and also stay up late'.

Unit 11 **11.3** Nurse, English teacher, actor.

Unit 12 **12.2** Left to right – can cause allergies, can contain poison, can bite or sting, virus or germ.

Unit 13 **13.1** Contact lens and moth.

Unit 14 **14.1** *1* a doctor's receptionist *2* a tour operator *3* a film producer *4* a plumber
14.2 Examples of people and situations: class gone on a picnic; a man whose company has gone bankrupt, being chased by debt collectors; a pop star who has gone on a world tour; a phone-in advisory service for desperate people, that is understaffed at the moment; an air-line that has a pilot strike; an artist who wants to be left alone.

Unit 17 **17.2** Profiles:

Majority (a) You are a born chucker.
Your motto is: When in doubt, throw it out.
Your main strengths are: you are lively and realistic.
Main danger: you may have nothing to eat tomorrow.
Your friends like you because you are never dull.

Majority (b) You are a born hoarder.
Your motto is: Waste not want not.
Your main strengths are: you are determined and totally dependable.
Main danger: over-timidity.
Your friends like you because they can always count on you.

Majority (c) You are a creative recycler.
Your motto is: Let's try it another way.
Your main strengths are: you are imaginative and open-minded.
Main danger: people may think you are slightly dotty (a bit mad).
Your friends like you because you are never completely predictable.

Unit 19 **19.2** The first goat mascot of the 3rd Battalion of the Royal Regiment of Wales was officially recorded in 1860 when Queen Victoria presented a billy goat from her Royal Herd at Windsor to the regiment and the tradition has continued. Today the goats come from the Royal Herd at Whipsnade Zoo. The goat in the photograph was called Dewi IV and died in 1990.

19.3 The objects are: *1* fishing rod; *2* corsets; *3* golf bag; *4* pet food; *5* drumskin; *6* lamp oil; *7* whip; *8* chicken feed; *9* detergent; *10* printing ink; *11* candlewax; *12* fish bait; *13* medicines; *14* soap; *15* paint; *16* tennis racket; *17* chessman; *18* wax crayons; *19* lipstick; *20* buttons; *21* margarine; *22* sausage skins.

19.4 10 species of bear, 2 species of panda, 23 species of whale. 1974: 1,000 species a year; 2000: 1 million.

Tapescript

Unit 2   Music, music, music

1   Tuning-in
(Different musical instruments.)

2   Film music
(Musical extracts from films.)

3   'New voices' talent show
(Pieces of music from talent show.)

Unit 3   We lost touch

3   Memories

A: What was the name of that group that had a
few hits at about the same time as the
Beatles? . . . (*oh . . . well*) . . . they were
from Liverpool as well . . .

B: Erm . . . well . . . there were so many
weren't there . . . erm . . . er . . . well there's
. . . there's the Swinging Blue Jeans (*no, no,
no*) . . . and there's Bi . . . Billy . . .

A: I can see them clearly . . . (*What . . .*) . . .
they wore suits.

B: Well they all wore suits.

A: No what was their name? . . . the Seekers or
something like that . . . (*yeah*) it was one
word . . . (*erm*) . . . I'm sure it was
something like that . . . (*the . . . no . . . like
the Seekers?*) . . . like the Seekers . . . one
word . . . (*erm . . . one word . . . er . . . erm
. . . Surf . . . Surfers?*) . . . no . . . no . . . no
. . . don't tell me . . . it's on the tip of my
tongue . . . the lead singer's name was
Pender. (*er . . .*) oh it'll come back to me in a
minute (*Bri . . . oh I . . . I know who you
mean*) . . . got it . . . Searchers (*ah!*) . . .
that's it . . . (*yes*) . . . the Searchers.

B: You see . . . I was thinking of erm . . . er . . .
Billy J. Kramer (*no . . . no*) . . . and the
Dakotas . . . (*fade*)

5   One day I'm going to . . .
Well, I got up to grade four, um, but then I got
tired of all the practice and oh, my feet! they
really started to hurt a lot. It gets harder as you
get older and heavier, and all that pointing
really hurts your feet. So, in the end, I just
found that I was too fat for it. But I've been
dieting, and it's worked, I'm kind of thin now,
and I'm thinking of starting up again. I know
it's going to be murder but if I start with regular
bar work and get supple and strengthen my leg
muscles, then after maybe six months or so I
should be up to the level I was at three years ago
. . . well, that's the plan anyway.

I used to play all the time, you know, I was,
really keen. But when I was about . . . uh . . .
sixteen or seventeen, I got more interested in
discos, girls, that sort of thing. Um . . . I'm
really keen to start again now, maybe it was the
Olympic Games that got me going I suppose,
inspired me. Um, you know there were really
some fantastic matches. I found my old stick
and I'm going training once a week. Uh, I know
I smoke a bit, but I'm not all that unfit and so
I'm sure that I can . . . uh . . . you know, it
won't take me too long to get back into . . . uh
. . . normal shape. So we had a practice match
last week and I was really aching after that in
the morning, but it hasn't put me off . . . uh . . .
and although I'm not used to all that bending
and running after the ball, I'm really looking
forward to the next match.

Unit 4   It wasn't my fault, it was an accident

3   Near misses
It had been a really beautiful sunny afternoon.
We were just coming home and I set foot across
the road, and suddenly, I was nearly at the
other side of the road, I heard this little voice

cry 'Mummy' and I turned round and looked back and there was this resounding bump, and I saw my three-year-old sailing through the air, and a great screech of brakes. Anyway, my heart stopped, I rushed across the road, picked him up, dashed with him to the doctor's . . . he had a huge bump on his head, and he was absolutely fine. So three-year-olds are obviously fairly indestructible.

When I first came to Europe, I was at university and I took a charter flight and we had the University of California at Los Angeles football team, or at least most of them, on the flight . . . and, I looked out the window, it was night, and there was this big fire on one of the engines. People started getting scared and the hostesses couldn't handle the people inside the plane, so they all went and locked themselves in the loo in the tail of the plane, where I hear it's the safest place if you're going to crash . . . and the football players decided to find something out and break down the door to the flight cabin. Eventually, the situation was sorted out and we went back and stayed for a day in Toronto. But it was an interesting introduction to aircraft.

I used to live in Darwin in the Northern Territory, top of Australia, and er . . . I remember an incident where we'd been scuba diving and I was coming back with three mates. We were going along quite fast, came round a corner and there were four cows, facing us, standing in the middle of the road, and completely blocking the road, and we were going maybe . . . erm . . . eighty miles an hour, and er I was driving, and all I could do was to throw the car off the road, . . . or hit them . . . and we went between two trees, and then slid sideways, around the cows and then back onto the road, kept going along . . . and it must have been a good three or four minutes of complete silence and then, all at once, everybody swore, at exactly the same second. Very exciting experience.

Unit 5   And so to bed . . .

3   My most unusual night's sleep
My most unusual night's sleep was some years ago when I went on holiday with my boyfriend. And we hadn't got a car in those days, and we borrowed his mother's car, and we hadn't booked anywhere, we were going to take pot luck, and we couldn't get in, all the hotels, all the bed and breakfasts were . . . were full . . . and it got to about ten, eleven o'clock on . . . on . . . on . . . one . . . on this first night, . . . and we thought well that's it we'll have to sleep in the car. So we drove around and we went up onto a hillside, and we parked the car and we ended up having to sleep the night in the car . . . and in the morning we woke up, we had nothing to clean our teeth with, apart from a bottle of wine, erm . . . and as we looked out onto the hillside, it was magical, the whole hillside was covered in pale blue butterflies, and it was absolutely beautiful and so it was . . . (*fade*)

The strangest place I ever spent the night was in a mud hut in the northern hills of Thailand, in the chief of the tribe's little hut in fact, and in that little hut the whole family slept, and I was a sort of a guest of the family. I was with a walking tour of about five of us, in fact, but we each had a hut that we were assigned to, that we were told to go and sleep in . . . and er . . . it was very, very quiet for one thing outside erm there was a smell of incense there and there were also these little animals that used to run up and down the walls, geckos, I think they're called, and they would catch little flies, but I found that very strange . . . and of course we were sleeping on just the plain floor, just with a, with a sort of a rug but nothing else . . . and that was an unusual and very strange night's sleep.

Unit 6   Oh I do like to be beside the seaside . . .

1   Tuning-in
I decided I wanted something a little different this year, so I went on a tennis holiday, and I paid a lot of money to go to this place . . . and I arrived and I took one look at the courts and I nearly went home, it was just . . . the courts were like . . . er . . . sloping from the front to the back . . . and there were big holes, and the nets were just really ragged. I went to . . . kind of a dormitory type place . . . er . . . and the beds were really narrow and the mattresses were really thin and I was there for five nights and I think I slept for about er five hours one night but that was the most . . . and we got up and we started to take some instruction and they said in the brochure that there would be small classes

. . . well there was twenty people in my class and . . . er . . . I thi . . . I think the instructor spoke to me twice, and basically he said er 'Watch the ball' and 'Bend your knees' and that was what I paid my money for. So . . . er . . . by the end of the week, . . . erm the people I had been beating at the beginning of the week were beating me so I . . . I really don't think I spent that money too wisely.

A: As it was out of season the rooms were supposed to be really cheap . . . that's what they told me . . . it was too cold to swim and most of the things were closed around there so really I was just there for a bit of peace and quiet.
B: When was that then?
A: Oh . . . about three years ago, I think. Anyway, trust me, I caught the 'flu, would you believe it, not surprising as all the heating was off . . .
B: You're joking . . . even in winter?
A: Mm . . . yeah . . . well . . . there was hardly anyone staying there, apart from a few elderly retired people . . . I'm surprised they survived . . . so after I caught the 'flu they probably thought I was going to die . . . bad publicity and all that, so they put me into the bridal suite (*no!*) . . . eh? . . . which was empty but it was heated . . . er . . . I sort of got better, but they charged me double the price for the room.
B: They didn't . . . didn. . . . didn't you complain?
A: No . . . I was too weak . . . I just paid up and left.

Unit 7   Your number is up

1   Tuning-in
(Extract from 'The Magic Flute'.)

Unit 8   How can I get from A to B?

2   The Highway Code
I think it's very important that there is a highway code so that everyone has to drive according to the same kinds of standards and rules. I think, however, in my country, America, there are certain laws in some states that seem a little silly . . . or useless nowadays. Let me say as an example that in many states yet there is still a maximum speed limit of fifty-five miles per hour . . . and in practice, very few people

adhere to that, they go much faster, sixty-five, sometimes seventy miles per hour. New rules to be added? The only thing I can think of is it would be nice, as every state in America makes up its own highway code, that they took more care to make sure that they were more or less the same from state to state so that people who travel across state lines would not have to memorise or be aware of different laws.

I think it's exceptionally important to have a strict highway code but unfortunately, in England, . . . er . . . the police have a very difficult job in . . . er . . . keeping the law . . . and prosecuting people who . . . who . . . go over red lights, who speed on the motorways . . . it's a sad state of affairs. I can't think of anything particularly silly or useless about the rules in our highway code . . . erm . . . sometimes it's inconvenient not to be able to use the horn of the car after eleven o'clock at night . . . erm . . . if you're trying to warn somebody that there could be an accident . . . erm . . . sometimes you need to use it. So that's very difficult. Erm . . . as far as new rules that I'd like to add, I think there should be a minimum speed on motorways because some drivers who drive very very slowly in the inside or sometimes even in the middle lane I think are . . . very very dangerous to other users of the motorways and I think the minimum speed should be forty-five fif . . . well . . . let's say fifty.

5   Car problems
(Poem.)

Unit 9   Hands

4   He's got the whole world in his hands
(Song.)

Unit 11   Crash bang whizz!

3   Loud mouths?
Speaker 1: I think voice is very important in my job because people need to feel comfortable and supported and you know as we're so busy these days I don't always have as much time as I'd like with each person so I have to speak in a simple, clear way, sort of firm but friendly. I don't want them to worry too much so I try to be cheerful as well. Er . . . I really like this job because I like being with people and helping them through difficult times.

Speaker 2: Well, I'd say . . . er . . . speaking clearly is possibly the most important thing . . . erm . . . because, obviously, being in the business of er . . . communicating . . . erm . . . especially with . . . with younger people, you have to . . . you have to get . . . you have to get your message across, this is the most important thing, and . . . if there's any doubt, if there's any doubt about what you're saying then you've failed in . . . in a way . . . er . . . and so I try to make what I have to say . . . erm . . . lively . . . erm . . . because if you just talk in a monotone, people switch off, and if I have a style I'd say it is to be . . . erm . . . sincere . . . erm . . . truthful rather than dictatorial or authoritative . . . erm . . . but . . . I'm always cheerful, I try and create a nice atmosphere in the room . . . erm . . . because as far as I'm concerned if . . . if people like you, and the atmosphere is cheerful and friendly, they learn, they learn more easily, and I . . . I like the job because it . . . it offers variety and . . . and you meet so many different people.

Speaker 3: Well, voices are . . . are important to us, obviously, because it's our primary tool really, it's our primary tool of expression, and if you look at all the different facets of our work, nearly all of them rely on our command of our voices, on our ability to erm . . . to express emotion and thought through the way we use our voices. Erm . . . and it's . . . it's also one of the pleasures of our work is using our voices in the most creative way we can. Obviously, bodies and facial expressions, they're important too, but I think that . . . that the voice is our primary tool . . . and . . . er . . . I really like my job, I think because . . . of the style of life, . . . when it's going well that is, of course . . . er . . . when it's going well I don't think you can beat it, because you're constantly meeting new people, and going to different places and . . . and meeting new kinds of challenges all the time.

4 Silence is golden

A wise old owl
Sat in an oak
The more he sat
The less he spoke
The less he spoke
The more he heard
Why can't we all be like that
Wise old bird?

Unit 14   Please speak after the tone

1   Tuning-in

1) Hello, I hope this message reaches you in time, I'm afraid we'll have to cancel this afternoon's appointment. Doctor Harvey is sick, he's got the 'flu but . . . erm . . . he should be better by next week so if you'll just call me and we can schedule another appointment . . . bye.

2) Hello darling, it's Bob here, I'm just ringing to see if you're going to be free for the latter end of next week for four days . . . we've got a party coming in from Brazil and I need a coach party through the major buildings and the tourist sites in er . . . four of the European capitals . . . now, as I say, it's going to be for four days: the first day's going to be in London . . . erm . . . you know . . . the usual thing. The second day will be in Paris. The third day will be in Madrid and . . . er . . . and the fourth day in Rome, . . . the usual thing. Maybe you can think about this and let me know your availability?

3) Hello, this is Mary Robinson here . . . erm . . . I'm very sorry . . . I'd . . . I'd like to postpone the meeting my secretary scheduled for tomorrow . . . something rather urgent has come up, but . . . erm . . . I'd like to say thank you very much for the script . . . the readers have all said the script is . . . is marvellous. We'd . . . we'd very much like to film it but . . . er . . . unfortunately, er . . . I'm afraid the . . . the costs involved in . . . in the . . . riot scenes on . . . on . . . on . . . Mars, I'm . . . I'm afraid they're going to be far too high. Er . . . however, . . . will . . . please call us again soon . . .

4) Er . . . hello . . . er . . . Steve here . . . erm . . . just ringing to say that I'm afraid I won't be able to come round and repair your shower . . . er . . . because we're still waiting for a . . . for a part . . . er . . . for a washer. So . . . er . . . sorry about that . . . erm . . . sorry we've been so long but . . . erm . . . well, the first part was wrong . . . and . . . er, the . . . second one seems to have got lost in the post so . . . er . . . you know . . . I . . . I'm quite sure that I'll be able to come round within a

week or so . . . er . . . er . . . OK . . . thanks
. . . bye.

4 Community complaints

A: Hello, this is Michael Pearson with
'Community complaints', the spot which
gives you a chance to complain about
anything you feel strongly about. I'm out
today in the high street, and I'm just going
to choose a few people and ask them what
grumbles, what grouses, what things really
annoy them about going around in the
street today . . . First of all, I'd like to speak
to this lady here . . . excuse me, madam,
(*Oh . . . er . . . hello*) . . . hello (*yes?*) . . . I
wonder, do you have any particular
grumbles or . . . or things you'd like to
complain about, things you'd like to get off
your chest?

B: Well . . . to tell you the truth . . . I think it's
very frightening now to go out on the street.
I used to love to come out, you know, and
just have a wee walk round, but . . . (*yes*)
. . . it's so busy now, there's so much traffic
and there's so many people, and it's just so
noisy . . . I . . . I get a wee bit frightened I
have to tell you, and there, and there's these
young people, you know, they just run
around in great packs and they have no
consideration for other people and you just
feel sometimes you might get knocked
down, so I don't think it's as nice as it used
to be . . . that's my view.

A: So you'd like to see better policing perhaps
and . . . er . . . more things for the young
people to do in the city.

B: That . . . that's right, I think it's a shame
that they just have to run round the streets
all the time . . . I . . . I'm sure it's not their
fault . . .

A: Thank you very much indeed . . . (*thank
you*) . . . and now I'd like to ask . . . er . . .
this gentleman here . . . excuse me, sir,
excuse me . . . erm . . . is there anything
you'd like to . . . er . . . to moan about
really, this is . . . er . . . the spot on the
programme where people are allowed to air
their views, to complain about . . . things in
everyday life.

C: Well I'm glad you asked me mate, 'cause I
. . . there is something that I want to
complain about, and that's dogs fouling the
pavement, I mean, have a look at the

bottom of my shoe, there's the, there's the
evidence right there. Now I can't walk out
in the street day by day without suffering
this problem. Now . . . now this is a serious
problem, people shouldn't have dogs in
built up areas, unless they're prepared to
look after them.

A: So you think people should keep dogs in the
country?

C: More in the country, or if they're going to
do it here, they should allocate areas where
they can have dogs and not just let them
foul the footpath . . . it's unhealthy as well
for the kids, think about that.

A: Right, well, thank you very much indeed.
And now . . . (*fade*)

Unit 15 Fire power

2 Camp fires

I remember a bonfire party when I was a child
as being a particularly exciting time. It was a
mixture of fear and excitement. There was
mum and dad's faces, and my brother's, lit up
by the flames . . . and we would hold roman
candles or some other sparklers or other . . .
fireworks in our hands and everything was
aglow with sparks and flames and light in the
darkness, it was . . . magical.

I think the most memorable experience for me
with fire occurred when I was . . . fairly young
and had just come to Europe, and I went to
Germany and I . . . I . . . went to a village in the
country, I was invited to a family's house in the
country in this small village, and at midnight, it
being a Catholic community, we went to
midnight mass, walking through the snow to
this medieval church, all whitewashed inside.
There was no electric light . . . it was all
candles, and I will never forget the images of the
candle flames flickering on those white walls
and the beams of this medieval church and all
of the faces uplifted and singing. It will be a
memory I shall always have in my mind.

Yes, we decided . . . erm . . . my youngest son
was, I suppose about eight, and he wanted a
party at home, his birthday's in August, . . . and
so we decided to have an entertainer, you see,
so . . . erm . . . we looked quite simply in the . . .
in the Yellow Pages for home entertainers . . .
for children, and . . . erm . . . there was this one
that . . . erm . . . advertised himself as being a

fire-eater, you see, so . . . er . . . he said he'd arrive half way through the afternoon and er . . . we'd had the food and everything, and Gavin the fire-eater rang the door bell, and in he came . . . erm . . . we'd had all the food and stuff in the garden . . . it was a beautiful August afternoon, . . . well, as chance would have it, we had the most horrendous thunderstorm, . . . so . . . erm . . . we had to come indoors . . . and he assured us that he could do his act indoors as well as out . . . erm . . . so all the little kids were sitting on the floor and he began his act . . . I mean it was all right, it was quite impressive, . . . but, we'd just had these new curtains put in, and there was one very naughty little boy, who was upsetting this fire-eater, and I think it must just have put him off, because one of the, one of the things he was putting in his throat suddenly caught just the corner of this curtain and . . . and you wouldn't believe how quickly the . . . the whole thing went up . . . and as in children's parties you have these enormous bottles of Coke . . . (*Oh, no . . .*) well we had lots of bottles of Coke around, and, that was the only thing to throw on this curtain at the time and we squeezed all this Coke over the curtain and put it out, but I mean it did avert a very very nasty, er . . . situation. Don't invite fire-eaters to your children's party.

3   Have gun, will shoot

A: Well, Kate, do you think it's a good idea to have guns?

B: Well, I don't think I'd like to have guns in my house but I grew up with guns . . . my father has a gun in our living room, in our . . . in his bedroom, by his bed, and in our car.

A: Well I'd be very sorry to see more guns being used because . . . er I think it just tends to escalate, it tends to . . . if one person has a gun then more people are going to have guns.

B: Yes, I know what you mean . . . besides if somebody is attacking you unless you carry the gun in your hand all the time there's really no way you'd get to it.

C: Can you think of no reasons at all why someone should be allowed to have a gun?

D: Well, I suppose if you live in the country and actually need a . . . a gun for keeping down vermin, or whatever, but certainly in the city . . . erm . . . in fact in almost any place I can't think of any good reason, because . . . I don't think people ought to be allowed to take violence . . . you know . . . into their own hands like that, and so many people are not responsible . . .

C: What do you say to the argument that if everyone else is allowed to carry a gun you have to carry one as well or you're defenceless?

D: Well, that's nonsense because I just think it leads to an escalation of violence.

C: I'm . . . I'm sure it does but . . . but the people would argue nonetheless that if they're walking in a street in New York, and they're walking down the street and someone pulls a gun on them, either they're helpless or they have a weapon to defend themselves and that helplessness, I think, is something which encourages people to get a gun when guns are legal.

D: Yeah . . . I would feel much more helpless if I knew half the population was walking round with guns.

Unit 17   Chuckers and hoarders

4   If only I hadn't thrown it away!

I'm always saying 'If only I hadn't thrown it away' with clothes because I keep seeing things sitting in the wardrobe and think well I haven't worn that for ages and ages, it's silly I'll throw it away, and I do, and then, a year or so later, that colour or that style comes back into fashion and I say 'Oh if *only* I hadn't thrown that away' because I've ended up having to go and spend a lot of money buying virtually the same thing.

I suppose I've become more sentimental about holding onto things as I've got older. When I was in my teens, I saw no point in holding onto things and keeping things for sentimental value or any real reason at all, and I wrote a play when I was about seventeen, and thought it was rubbish . . . it was rubbish, but I threw it away . . . er . . . and I've . . . I would . . . I really regret having thrown that away because it would be a useful kind of record of the way I was thinking at that time, and even if it was rubbish it nevertheless would be nice in my old age to sort of . . . look back on it, and read it, and think . . . that's what I was writing when I was a teenager.

(*Part 1*)
I recently bought myself a new hi-fi system which came in . . . in an enormous box. So I . . . had a friend with me and we took all the . . . all the bits out, and then in my haste to get rid of this enormous box and lots of packaging, I bundled it all together and just put it outside . . . and it was Thursday and it was the day when the dustbinmen come, so luckily they actually took it all away very quickly.

(*Part 2*)
Then we set about putting the plug on and trying to get things to work, and of course everything did, apart from the radio which just made a fizz, and I found out I'd thrown away the necessary wires, that is, in fact, the aerial. So . . . I had a radio that wouldn't work, and it took two months for me to have an aerial sent over from Japan.

Unit 18   Sugar and spice

1   Tuning-in
What are little girls made of?
Sugar and spice and all things nice;
That's what little girls are made of.

What are little boys made of?
Snips and snails and puppy dogs' tails;
That's what little boys are made of.

3   Feminine and masculine
What makes a man masculine? Well, I don't really think it's anything to do with muscles or . . . er . . . hair on the face, in fact I think that's all a bit revolting really . . . erm . . . I suppose you could say it could be somebody who's . . . erm . . . strong in other ways . . . erm . . . strong-minded, decisive perhaps . . . erm . . . knows what they want.

It must have something to do with . . . with physicality, the shape of the person, the way the person stands, a confidence that er . . . that man evokes, and the way he presents himself has something to do with how you perceive his masculinity, I think.

Yes, I think . . . er . . . to make a woman feminine . . . er . . . there's, there is softness, there is er . . . er . . . a . . . physically attractive . . . erm . . . feel to the word 'feminine' erm . . . there's also the mothering thing too isn't there? . . . of . . . of . . . er . . . feminine women . . . erm

. . . have a sort of caring attitude to children and have that sort of . . . er . . . ability to . . . er . . . probably mother great big grown-up men as well.

Well, again I don't think what makes a woman feminine is anything to do with the way they look . . . erm . . . certainly you don't have to have long legs, blue eyes and er . . . er . . . bubbly blond curls . . . er . . . I suppose when I think of the word 'feminine' lots of good things come to mind, all the things that seem to matter . . . er . . . caring, warmth, er . . . openness, . . . intuition, sensitivity, and er . . . I suppose that's what makes a woman feminine.

4   What can I say to the children?
A: Well, it's . . . I don't know . . . (*Mm*) . . . it puts us in a bit of a fix, doesn't it, really?
B: Well, it does because we usually give him what he wants . . . (*yes*) and what he asks for (*mm*) . . . for his birthday, so what are we going to do?
A: I don't know. (*Oh . . .*) . . . what we could suggest to him is that we . . . we give him something like er . . . Action Man, I mean that is a doll, isn't it?
B: But he doesn't want Action Man . . . he wants this teenage girl doll, that is what he wants . . . (*yes*) . . . I mean I . . . er . . . I'm going to ask him what games he thinks he can play with a teenage girl doll, I mean he's only eight . . . (*that's right*) . . . it's a bit worrying.
A: He'll want to show it to people won't he, at school?
B: Well, I feel that his friends are going to make fun of him at school (*mm*) . . . that's one thing (*I think that's very important*) and call him . . . call him a cissy . . . (*I think that's very important*).
A: I think it'll bring more trouble than it's worth. Let's decide not to give it to him.

Unit 19   Zoo story

4   Endangered species
I think the animal I would most like to protect is probably the dolphin . . . I don't know why particularly, except that . . . erm . . . they've always appealed to me, they seem to be really wonderful . . . creatures and . . . er very knowledgeable and intelligent and also extremely gentle . . . and somebody told me a

story once, and, in fact, I've since read about it in the newspaper, which really affected me, which is that fishermen when they're fishing for tuna, erm . . . they . . . they put out really big nets, and quite often they catch dolphins in the nets, and they don't put them back, so, I know it sounds a bit horrible, but it is quite likely that when you're eating a tin of tuna fish that it's got a bit of dolphin in there, so I would like to see something done about that.

I think the . . . er . . . the considerable amount of work that's all being . . . already being done towards protecting the elephant . . . er . . . needs to be expanded even further. The poor elephant is a wonderful, noble beast er . . . , does nobody any harm . . . occasional stories of it charging a village or . . . or . . . whatever but . . . er . . . these are very very rare instances . . . it's a wonderful creature, and simply slaughtered by man for no reason other than . . . fashionable vanity really . . . wanting little bits of elephant tusk carved into funny shapes, it's er . . . a terrible, terrible thing and . . . and it represents the very worst of er . . . human greed.

To the teacher

This book has been written to encourage the development of fluency in spoken English. It is intended for students at an intermediate level of English. To us, developing fluency implies taking risks, letting go safely by using language in a relaxed, friendly atmosphere – an atmosphere of trust and support. Speaking fluently, of course, involves speaking easily and appropriately with others but it carries a further assumption that in simple terms says: 'What you are saying to me is more important than how accurately you are saying it!'

We have endeavoured to offer teachers and students some imaginative slants on fairly conventional and universal themes. It has been our intention to arouse curiosity and interest and also to stimulate the imagination.

The cassette

You will find the materials available on the cassette marked by 📼. The recorded material in this book is deliberately longer and more challenging than that used in *Speaking 1*. We believe that an ability to deal with unsimplified spoken English is a vital accompaniment to the development of spoken fluency. However, in order to avoid overburdening the students' capacities for comprehension, our listening tasks generally require understanding only at the level of gist.

As in *Speaking 1*, the listening materials are of several types: some of the materials have accompanying comprehension tasks; other listening pieces lead the students naturally on to making spoken comparisons with their own experiences or opinions; there are some music-based listening activities and finally, some of the units have recordings of people doing the kind of speaking activities which the students themselves will eventually do. Where listening tasks have specific answers, these can be found in the key. The listening materials in this book contain a variety of native speaker voices and thus provide a rich base for the comprehension of spoken English.

Grading

We have tried to order the twenty units in such a way that the more straightforward ones are earliest in the sequence, but there has been no conscious linguistic grading. Within each unit there are activities which pose varying degrees of challenge to the linguistic resources of the student. Teachers, no doubt, will make selections and adaptations accordingly.

Flexibility

Each unit can be worked through in its entirety where circumstances make that an appropriate option; alternatively, most sections within a unit can be used on their own, perhaps as an accompaniment to a coursebook unit or as a break between sessions focussing on other skills.

Personal themes

Some teachers and students may consider that some of our material has been explored in too personal a fashion. Much depends both on the type of relationship that teacher and students enjoy and also on the approach to language learning that both find comfortable psychologically. In an atmosphere of personal trust, we believe that talking about topics in personal terms strengthens and enriches the quality of social contact in the classroom. More than that, it widens the boundaries of interaction involving the target language in the future.

Involving the teacher

Students are generally interested in their teachers – their lives, their views, their attitudes. We have encouraged the involvement of teachers in the activities in this book so that they can be partners in the interaction as well as facilitators and monitors. Clearly, individual circumstances and teachers will dictate the degree to which the invitation to be involved is taken up.

The teacher as bridge

Fluency materials, especially those that explore personal themes, rely on the skill of the teacher in easing the students into the material and in setting a tone of trust and respect. It is important, in our view, for teachers to create a pathway into the units by using simple activities, mimes, visuals, or questions to elicit spoken language before opening and using the book. The book is perhaps best used after this bridge has been built and the students have thereby become oriented to the chosen unit theme or activity. What is more important is that the students should be ready to pursue the theme and keen to talk about it together. This bridging sequence is a vital part of transferring the initiative, as far as possible, to the students, and of building a positive social atmosphere in which correction becomes the servant of both encouragement and the sharing of ideas, opinions, and information.

Inexperienced teachers

Teachers who have had little teaching experience or little experience of materials like these will obviously be sensible enough to select activities and ideas from this book and adapt them to their teaching styles and to the type of classes and students they have. It is, we believe, unwise to follow the activities too closely in the hope that the book knows best. The book provides a framework only. Adapting materials is an art which teachers are expert at, and we strongly encourage them to continue to develop it.

Students working together

All our units invite students to talk with one another in small groups or in pairs. Being in a classroom learning a language is essentially a social experience and should be memorable, in part, because of the relationships forged during a time of being and learning together. In fluency work one of our aims is to make learners less conscious of their vulnerability in the target language by tempting them to become interested in the people in the classroom. Risk-taking is a natural companion of such curiosity, as far as we are concerned.

Vocabulary

In some of the units we have been generous with the number of vocabulary items. This has been deliberate and reflects our belief that the strength of the contexts and the activities can support enhancement of students' vocabulary, both actively and receptively.

Cultural location

Although our material inevitably reflects our Western backgrounds, we have tried to avoid too many specific references to British or other English-speaking locations. In fact, in several of the units we have asked students to talk about their own environments. This seems consistent with a belief that students can talk more easily and flexibly about places they know well.

We wish you an interesting and fruitful time with the activities in this book and welcome comments and reactions from teachers who use these materials.

BLACK
&WIGHT
FIREWORKS

FIG 1–i BLACK ARROW R3 leaves Woomera to orbit PROSPERO, 28 Oct 1971
(*Commonwealth of Australia*)

BLACK
& WIGHT
FIREWORKS

British Peroxide
Rockets

by

Derek Mack

COPYRIGHT

British Library Cataloging–in–Publication Data
A catalogue record and a copy of this publication are available at the British Library.

First Printing: 2018

ISBN 978-178456-605-0

Published by http://www.fast-print.net/bookshop

Available from – https://www.thegreatbritishbookshop.co.uk

To my unique wife and family
whose affection and tolerance
withstood my self centred career

CONTENTS

ACKNOWLEDGEMENTS ix
PREFACE xi
ABREVIATIONS xii
INTRODUCTION 1
Chapter 1 THE WORKHORSE 3
Chapter 2 I MOVE OFFSHORE 11
Chapter 3 PROOF FIRING at HIGH DOWN 19
Chapter 4 I MOVE DOWNUNDER 25
Chapter 5 BK LAUNCH SITE – Area 5 33
Chapter 6 WHILE THE CATS AWAY – – – – 43
Chapter 7 BK 04 TRIALS – H D & Area 5 49
Chapter 8 BK 06 TRIALS – H D & Area 5 55
Chapter 9 GASLIGHT & DAZZLE + (BK08 saga) 59
Chapter 10 BK 07 TRIAL – H D 63
Chapter 11 BK 09 TRIALS – H D & Area 5 67
Chapter 12 BK 07 TRIAL – Area 5 75
Chapter 13 BK 13 TRIALS – H D & Area 5 (+BK15 Sabot) 79
Chapter 14 BK 16 TRIALS – H D & Area 5 85
Chapter 15 BK 21 & 19 TRIALS – the door begins to shut 93
Chapter 16 THE NEW ERA 97
Chapter 17 THE CORK IS PULLED 109
Chapter 18 BA R0 TRIAL – H D 113
Chapter 19 BA R0 TRIAL – Area5 (& Termination Inquiry). 131
Chapter 20 BA R1 TRIALS – H D & Area 5 153
Chapter 21 BA R2 TRIALS – H D & Area 5 163
Chapter 22 BA R3 TRIAL – H D 169
Chapter 23 BA R3 TRIAL – Area 5 179
Chapter 24 A RETROSPECTIVE OVERVIEW 199
Chapter 25 VIV Le FRANCE – DIAMANT 203
Appendix A BLACK KNIGHT DETAIL 215
Appendix B BLACK ARROW DETAIL 249

ACKNOWLEDGEMENTS

REFERENCES: For those readers seeking a deeper understanding of British rocket history than this work can offer, I commend the following authors and their well-researched publications.

Peter Morton:

- Fire Across the Desert – Comprehensive history of the Weapons Research Establishment at Salisbury and Woomera, South Australia.

Nicholas Hill:

- A Vertical Empire – The History of UK Rocket & Space program 1950 – 1071.
- Black Arrow cancellation – http://www.spaceuk.org/ba/blackarrowcancellation.htm

Douglas Millard:

- Black Arrow R4 – A candidate for materialising the history of technology
- A History of a Satellite launch vehicle and its engines.

– – – – – – – – – –

COVER: Shows three "New Battery" historic gun aprons that denote where the High Down test site once stood high on cliffs above the Isle of Wight Needles landmark.

- Design by: Dion at Moosejam Design. www.moosejam.co.uk
- Aerial picture: Courtesy of Brighton Scenic. www.brightonscenic.co.uk

– – – – – – – – – –

PHOTOS & LINE DIAGRAMS: Each entry is accredited accordingly.
Contains public sector information licensed under the Open Government Licence v3.0.

– – – – – – – – – –

COLLEAGUES & ASSOCIATES:
During my years at High Down and Woomera, it was my privilege to be associated with many talented and amiable individuals. Alas as time reduced our numbers it also blunted my recall of many personal details. To avoid offence by omission or error, I've chosen to sidestep this tricky issue altogether!

x

PREFACE

At 13:39 on 28th October 1971, Black Arrow, a lone UK carrier rocket rose from the South Australian desert to successfully place the Prospero technology satellite into a 346 by 993 mile (557 by 1598 km) earth orbit at 82° inclination.

This event was noteworthy because it was: –

- The only indigenous British rocket & spacecraft combo ever launched.
- Britain's last liquid propellant rocket ever launched since then.
- Tasked to orbit a Client payload after just two qualification flights.
- Fashioned ahead of the modern industrial digital technology era.
- The only HTP rocket to orbit an Earth satellite.
- To mark UK as the first nation to abandon its indigenous orbital ability.

The Black Arrow lineage emerged some sixteen years before Prospero entered orbit when in 1954 its Black Knight predecessor was conceived to investigate earth re-entry issues for the Blue Streak ICBM. With an enviable record of 22 flights free of major mishap, these simply engineered rockets spawned the design, manufacture and operational routines applied to this new satellite carrier vehicle. Ironically, just as launching Prospero drew nigh, a myopic government abandoned the entire program in favour of free lifts on US Scout rockets.

ABREVIATIONS

5A	Black Knight launch pad
5B	Black Knight/Black Arrow launch pad
AC	Alternating current
AOO5	Area5 Operations Offier, Range E,
Area5	BK / BA launch area at Range E
ASM	Armstronge Siddely Motors
BA	Black Arrow
BHC	British Hovercraft, Cowes, IoW
BK	Black Knight
BS	blue Streak
CSMU	Control system monotor unit
CSO	WRE Cheif Safety Officer
CSP	Contractors Standard Precdure
CSSU	Control System Signal unit
DC	Direct Current
DH	De Havilland
DTL	Deputy Team Leader
EC5	Equipment Centre5 at Area5
EEL	Experimental & Electronic Laboratory BHC, Cowes IoW
FCS	Flight Control System
FPS16	Instrumentation Radar tracker
FSO	Flight Safety Officer
GRASS	WRE Range TrackerAquisition System
H&B	Hartman & Brawn
H202	HighTest Peroxide
HMG	Her Majestys Government
HTP	High Test Peroxide

IB	Instrument Building, Range E
ICBM	Inter Continental Ballistic Missile
LO5	Launcher Offier Area5
Mike3	Telemtry Receiver station, Range E
N2	Nitorgen
OISC	Officer In Scentific Charge
QA	Quality Assurance
R&D	Reasearch & Development
R0	BA Maiden Flight (Destroyed)
R1	BA First proving Firing
R2	BA Second proving Firing
R3	BA Prospero Orbital Firing
R4	BA Science Musium exhibit
RAE	Royal Aircraft Establishment
Range E	A missile test range at Woomera
RDD	Rocket Development Department
RF	Radio Frequency
S&S	Systems & Sequence reheresal test
SARO	Saunders Roe, South Australia
SO	Safety Officer
SR	Saunders Roe, Cowes, IoW
TL	Team Leader
TS2	Test Shop at Range E
TS4	Test Shop at Range E
UV	Ultra Violet
WRE	Weapons Reaesarch Establishment
WREBUS - Flight termination radio	
WWII	Second Wold War
X3	Prospero satellite

INTRODUCTION

Having failed to unearth a single first hand account of "launch pad life" during the Black Knight and Black Arrow rocket trials some 50 years ago, I've chosen to recall my time at the Isle of Wight and Australian test sites, assisting with development and firing these unique space vehicles.

So called "Rocket Science" jargon is deliberately minimised and readers may care to recall that these machines were contrived and flown before the "Digital Age" had become common industrial practice.

Chapters 1 through to 5 outline the emergence and purpose of Black Knight, and the participant agencies central to the test and launch operations. Anecdotal snapshots sketch how life unfolded at both sites as operational methods were honed, development hitches were fixed and a new trail was being blazed.

Of 22 Black Knight rockets launched between 1958 and 1965, my part with others who launched eight of them at High Down and Woomera is detailed in Chapters 6 to 15, in the order they were launched (as distinct from their serial number sequence). The close similarity between each rocket occasions a high degree of repetitive detail across these chapters, much of which contributes little to the mood or tempo of the moment beyond risking a degree of reader fatigue. Editing out repetition was considered but resisted since it reduced the need for chapter cross-referencing and one reader's trivia may be of special interest to another. If tempted to skip the odd trial, a scan of "italic paragraphs" and Appendices A & B, should not be overlooked.

Chapters 16 & 17 outline the hesitant birth of Black Arrow; hindered by the wiles of Whitehall and a lukewarm government who managed to loose the General Election just as it committed to the project. The incoming government kept faith and sought financial discipline by applying quarterly extension contracts, which tended to shackle program headway; headway that suffered two serious knocks from an engine test-bed explosion and total loss of the R0 maiden flight. To those directly involved these events were very traumatic but they also served to stiffen resolve across the entire project, which brought good technical rewards from the R1 and R2 trials.

Swayed by Common Market attractions, the next government ended all home grown carrier rocket activity in favour of European and US hardware and decreed that Black Arrow would terminate when R3/Prospero was launched.

With heavy hearts, bruised prides and raised hackles, the last BA launch team readied and fired R3, which confounded matters by unerringly earth orbiting Prospero and mark UK as the first nation to abandon its indigenous orbital insertion ability. These topics are expanded in chapters 18 to 23 – again in repetitive detail.

Chapter 24 recounts BA's final dalliance with the satellite world when Centre National d'etudes Spatiales (CNES) adopted the BA Payload Fairings for their three final Diamant rocket firings.

<u>BLACK ARROW R4</u>: The last example of this fine and simply engineered rocket vehicle of 50 years ago is now on display at the London Science Museum.

<u>DATES:</u> These are given in good faith but must be viewed with caution – it all happed long ago and like my notes of the time, the grey cells have worn thin, so be warned!

<u>PHOTOGRAPHIC QUALITY</u>: As indicated by their poor focus and resolution, these were scraped together from the pre-digital era and are included for historical interest. Security restrictions of the time banned all personal cameras and most official examples are difficult to source these days.

<u>ERRORS</u>: Finally, all opinions and errors expressed herein stand as mine alone.

THE WORKHORSE **1**

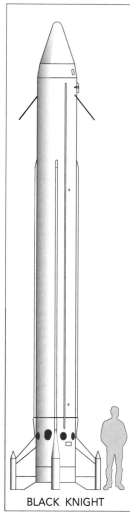

BLACK KNIGHT

FIG 1-1 *(DM)*

As WWII drew to a close, leading world powers concluded that a nuclear deterrent was the "must have" weapon and that German V2 rockets had heralded the preferred means of delivery. Atomic devices of the day were massive and required large powerful rockets to carry them, which prompted the UK to emulate others by opting for a liquid propellant, land based Inter-Continental Ballistic Missile (ICBM) code named Blue Streak. Design and construction of this giant machine was entrusted to the Rolls Royce and De Havilland Aircraft companies overseen by the Royal Aircraft Establishment (RAE). While recognising this as a challenging task for engineering skills of the time, it was also realised that knowledge of re-entry physics would need practical research. Additionally, command and control, integration, qualification and the processes necessary to safely firing large liquid propelled rockets had yet to be established. To address these pressing research tasks alongside the main Blue Streak program, a less complex workhorse rocket was proposed to evaluate re-entry phenomena and act as a pull through to accrue 'Wet' rocket experience. In co-operation with the Saunders Roe and Armstrong Siddeley Motor companies, RAE devised a low development, low budget package, which became the Black Knight series of re-entry research vehicles. Watchwords at every stage of this program were: simplicity, current technology and cautious expenditure.

As originally specified, a 200lb payload was required to enter the earth's atmosphere (taken as 200,000ft) at 12,000 ft per second. Aside from exotic exceptions, propellants fall into two generic groups: liquids and solids i.e. 'Wet' or 'Dry'. 'Dry" designs are simple but hardware and steering methods needed development and 'Wet' propellant knowhow for Blue Streak wouldn't be obtained.

Of the wet engine candidates, the De Havilland 'Spectre' that powered the Saunders Roe SR53 fighter aircraft, and the Royal Propulsion Establishment (RPE) 'Gamma' engine evolved to assist aircraft takeoff, were shortlisted. Ultimately the single chamber Gamma producing 4100 lbs sea level thrust was chosen, possibly to avoid diverting DH effort from their considerable Blue Streak commitment and I guess it offered RAE closer control over the engine development pathway. Four Gamma engines thrust chambers each fitted with swivel trunnions were bundled together cruciform fashion to generate 16,000 lbs of vectored steering thrust. After scanning available resources and consulting specialist agencies, project teams were assembled and requirements for the remaining hardware was formulated.

BLACK KNIGHT SALIENT FEATURES: These are set out in detail in Appendix 'A'.

THE FOUNDING PLAYERS: Four main organisations co-operated to bring Black Knight into existence and man the entire development programme:

ROYAL AIRCRAFT ESTABLISHMENT (RAE): As the overseeing government agency, RAE held overall technical responsibility for engineering, project planning and cost control. The task embraced liaison between UK and Australian government agencies and supervision of all prime contractors. Additionally the RAE designed and built the experimental payloads and resourced telemetry transmitters, command link radio receivers, gyros and S band transponders from the government inventory.

SAUNDERS ROE (SR, >WHL >GKN): Was assigned as lead contractor to flesh out the design and manufacture of each rocket together with all test site and launcher facilities, excluding the guidance tracking installation. The selection of SR was probably influenced by the following factors:

- Current HTP experience (SR53 and SR177 mixed power plant fighter aircraft)
- Established design and build history for low quantity innovative aircraft.
- Well-established R&D facilities and electronic laboratories.
- Potential site for integrated rocket testing existed on the Isle of Wight.
- Medium sized company culture.

The SR responsibilities embraced: -
- Aero and thermo dynamic analysis.
- Structural loading and stiffness analysis.
- Flight and servo control law analysis.
- Airframe design, manufacture and mechanical testing.
- Sub systems integration.
- Handling, transportation and storage logistics.
- Design and conversion of the High Down site.
- Maintenance of static firing facilities at High Down.

- Design, installation and maintenance of launcher facilities at Woomera.
- Storage and handling of propellants at High Down.
- Test process and Trial Plan formulation for High Down and Woomera.
- Rocket integration, development and acceptance trials at High Down.
- Direct support to rocket preparation and launch activities at Woomera.

ARMSTRONG SIDDELEY MOTORS (>ASM>Rolls Royce): Lead contractor for all aspects of engine design, manufacture, type testing and calibration. Later on, ASM evolved the more advanced Gamma 301 engine, spun off from its Stentor engine design developed to power the Blue Steel stand off bomb.

WEAPONS RESEARCH ETABLISHMENT, SA. (WRE): As control and admin authority for the long-range weapons testing facilities at Woomera, 300 miles north of Adelaide, WRE provided the test range, its overall safety and security environment, its tracking and instrumentation complex, recovery services, dedicated workshops, all utilities, road and air transport, accommodation and catering services. Funding was subject to a joint UK/Australian agreement.

DE HAVILLAND AIRCRAFT (DH): With their established weapons trials unit at Salisbury and Woomera being expanded for the Blue Streak program, wet rocket "pull through" experience was provided by tasking DH to man the BK launch trials at Woomera. Additionally, this role embraced installation operation of the dedicated BK guidance system and assisting Saunders Roe (the resident launch system maintenance agency) between trials.

THE UK INTEGRATION FACILITY: With a launch site 12,000 miles away in South Australia remote from design centres, it was soon realised that a dedicated post-production and development UK centre was essential. The facility would enable vertical assembly, replicate all rocket/launcher interface features, and allow static firing tests in a safe and secure environment away from public gaze. A readily adaptable location was found at High Down on the Isle of Wight, on the chalk cliffs overlooking the famous Needles landmark at the Island's western tip; surrounded by open sea on three sides and downland to the east. This ancient gun battery offered numerous reinforced underground rooms, a large water reservoir, public isolation, dense chalk foundations and several cottages to accommodate 24-hour security patrol staff with their families and guard dogs. The site is approached via a dedicated single-lane metalled road along the cliffs from Alum Bay, snaking up a steep incline to The New Battery at the far end. Three semi circular abandoned gun emplacements face northwest across the Solent approaches, some 300ft above sea level. Southwest of the gun positions, an expansive grassy triangle sloping down some 100ft to the cliff edge, formed a natural amphitheatre facing the sea.

This ideal spot would readily accommodate two rocket-test stands; each duplicating the other should one sustain serious damage – a real concern in those early ground breaking days.

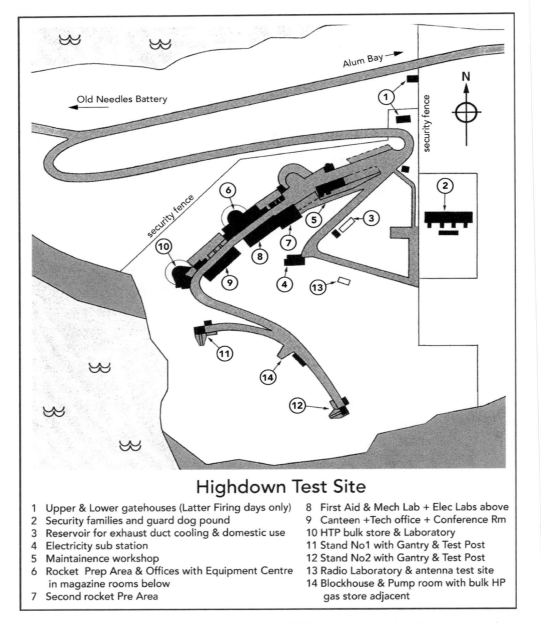

Highdown Test Site

1 Upper & Lower gatehouses (Latter Firing days only)
2 Security families and guard dog pound
3 Reservoir for exhaust duct cooling & domestic use
4 Electricity sub station
5 Maintainence workshop
6 Rocket Prep Area & Offices with Equipment Centre
  in magazine rooms below
7 Second rocket Pre Area

8 First Aid & Mech Lab + Elec Labs above
9 Canteen +Tech office + Conference Rm
10 HTP bulk store & Laboratory
11 Stand No1 with Gantry & Test Post
12 Stand No2 with Gantry & Test Post
13 Radio Laboratory & antenna test site
14 Blockhouse & Pump room with bulk HP
   gas store adjacent

FIG 1–2. HIGH DOWN NEW BATTERY MAP   (D Mack + GKN Aerospace)

As seen in Fig 1–3 and 1–4, civil engineers built test stands at each end of a new 90ft curved roadway terraced across the amphitheatre slope. Midway between stands a blast proof Blockhouse and reinforced Plant Room was built to house safety observers and a large water pump needed to feed coolant to each efflux deflection duct. The old Magazine areas under each gun position ideally served as Firing Control Centre, Recorder Room, Equipment Storage and staff shelters during engine firings. Electrical cabling and water services between Test Stands, Blockhouse and Firing Centre were routed via ducting under the road network. The westerly gun emplacement became the HTP and demineralised water bulk store with a dedicated chemical laboratory. A light industrial building erected over the central gun bay formed a general preparation area, admin office space and give access to the below ground areas.

FIG 1–3. HIGH DOWN LOOKING N/E. Three historic gun aprons just project from the building complex on the left. *(GKN Aerospace)*

Other existing above ground buildings provided a Tech Office, Electrics Lab, First Aid and Canteen facilities. The easterly gun bay remained as a vehicle turning area.

ROCKET DEVELOPMENT Dept (RDD):

Saunders Roe dedicated a project manager to steer design and manufacture activities through the established Company departments at Cowes. To administer the High Down and Woomera test sites and embrace all postproduction activities, a new entity, the Rocket Department (RDD), was formed under a Chief Engineer.

> *Where are the Indians?* Arising from the projects urgency and attractive nature, initial RDD recruitment lured an abundance of aspiring "Chiefs" whose incessant jostle for influence distorted the early evolution of the emerging organisation. As funding constraints became obvious, most of the ambitious empire-builders took flight and department politics were allowed to mature organically as working practices and responsibilities were established. A compact and well-balanced team of twelve sections under the Chief Rocket Development Engineer was the eventual result.

SECURITY GROUP – To provide High Down with a 24-hour security patrol, three company security officers with families and guard dogs were permanently quartered in the refurbished Coastguard Cottages located alongside the boundary fencing.

SAFETY GROUP – Headed by the Safety Officer, the section oversaw all hazardous activities, directed the downs public clearance parties, dealt with all routine personnel matters, organised transport and catering, maintained the First Aid room and handled visitor management. In later years the Safety Officer founded a well respected, WRE approved safety certification course specific to and used by the UK missile industry at large. As activities intensified, three assistants joined him.

SECRETARIAT, SUPPLY AND INSPECTION GROUPS – These sections were supportive to the entire RDD group and eventually grew to about 12 plus 3 based at Cowes.

LAUNCHER GROUP – Resided at WRE Salisbury, South Australia, under a fulltime manager. Eight High Down trained personnel supervised the installation and maintenance of all SR supplied hardware at Test Shop 2 and the launch sites The office liaised with WRE and DH, ran essential telex liaison link with UK, hosted visiting UK working parties and trials teams and kept an extensive drawing and documentation library. In earlier years worldwide telephony was poor and irregular but this office invariably established a project telex service on most days.

TRIALS GROUP – Lead by a Principal Trials Engineer, six personnel evolved Trial Plans, Firing Instructions and Test Procedures; organised Rocket Logbook documentation, co-ordinated static firing and major overall test activities.

To shepherd each rocket through High Down and Woomera testing, a team of four to five RDD specialists were seconded from each technical section and headed by an exclusive Team Leader (TL).

At Woomera the RDD Team leader served as deputy (DTL) to the DH Team Leader and each RDD team member operated as an advisor to the relevant DH section. In this role the DTL task narrowed to focus on detailed preparation of flight hardware at Test Shop and Launcher.

MECH, ELECT, INSTRUM'T & DATA GROUPS – These were the core-engineering specialists who fulfilled RDD's primary role. A Principal Engineer led each section with eight, peaking to twelve engineers and technicians. These sections carried out the detail of all rocket integration, qualification and development activities at High Down. Manning for each dedicated rocket team was drawn from these sections.

MAINTENANCE GROUP – A supervisor and seven mixed tradesmen with a comprehensive workshop serviced the heavy plant and general site fabric, manned an on site fire fighting party and Downs clearance parties.

FIG 1–4   HIGH DOWN INTEGRATION SITE circa 1960   *(GKN Aerospace)*

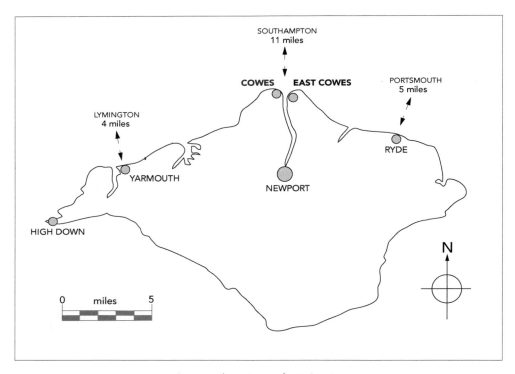

FIG 1–5 The ISLE of WIGHT   (D Mack)

I MOVE OFFSHORE   **2**

Before joining Saunders Roe I'd spent nine years with Vickers Armstrong; the aircraft makers located on the old Brooklands Racetrack near Weybridge, completing an apprenticeship and absorbing experience in the companies Guided Weapons Department.

At a year underage, I began as Shop Boy in the Wind Tunnel Department earning the princely sum of one guinea a week plus a daily lunch voucher. This self-contained organisation boasted design and aero offices along with specialised aero model and instrument workshops needed to support four wind tunnels ranging from a 1ft x 1ft transonic machine to a 16ft x16ft slow-speed monster. The Valiant V bomber was the main topic of study at this time.

My year as Shop Boy was priceless and seminal because it placed amide a team of young enthusiastic research scientists and engineers all keen to spotlight their talents; talents I could never have encounter elsewhere in the factory. As tea boy come gofer I interfaced at all staff levels, soaking up their R&D world and cultivating a lifelong appetite for Aero Research. My mentor, an egalitarian foreman, honed my machine tool skills and left an indelible mark by emphasising self-discipline, self-worth and above all cultivation of a perceptive curiosity.

The apprenticeship proper began with an eighteen-month tour of main factory departments, which all proved informative but very dull. Hard lobbying moved me to Barns Wallace's R&D group where I enjoyed several months with his Crescent Wing team until fate made the next move.

A newly founded Guided Weapons Department urgently needed a small "security classified" workshop where miniature autopilots could be prototyped until their own unit came online, and the Wind Tunnel Dept drew the short straw. The foreman, my erstwhile mentor, insisted that this imposition must gel with his workshop's renowned reputation and tipped me as a suitable contender! This fluky route into the emerging GW industry led into the magic world of servomechanisms, gyroscopes, telemetry techniques and the advanced methods being evolved for remotely guided flight. Two enjoyable years ended as the apprentice agenda took me into a General Technical Office where a chair bound existence was in prospect.

More lobbying placed me in the Flight Trials section where three distinct missile types were prepared and flight trialled: Blue Boar (TV guided bomb), Red Dean (active radar air to air missile) and Red Rapier (pilotless bomber). This engaging work involved autopilot and telemetry servicing, integration of explosives hardware and firing trials across government ranges at Larkhill and Aberporth.

I was taken aback when HMG killed off Red Dean development just as I was joining the programs Australian trials team – my world collapsed in doom and gloom as several months of personal planning had to be ditched.

My time at Weybridge was priceless. Hazards specific to this fledgling industry were revealed and "hands-on" experience with remote controlled flight systems and explosives hardware had been obtained across three widely differing missile types.

Ideas hatched during my Wind Tunnel days had matured to confirm that a pragmatic curiosity was fundamental when meeting most new challenges. Recalling my mentor's caution against early specialisation (A master remains chained in his ivory tower while his student may freely roam), I chose to stay close to the operational side of missile testing for my immediate future.

Several colleagues had migrated to Saunders Roe where Black Knight was in gestation so I followed to dip a toe in the 'Wet' rocket business and test the delights of Solent sailing! As the program advanced over the years I put down Island roots and tied the knot with my brilliant "Island" sole mate who gallantly cared for and groomed our two offspring alone during my Australian campaigns. Like military wives of the time, an airmail letter was our sole link and telephones were reserved for emergencies.

I JOIN THE RDD TEAM –

On a cold rain swept February evening in 1957, I set foot on the Isle of Wight to search out my Dickensian lodgings in Newport, the Island's county town where I found that inhabitants of those times dwelled in a time warp! Even today, local facilities tend to lag the mainland by a year or so, which can be nicely relaxing or very frustrating in equally measures.

I often escaped back up to London and 'civilisation' each Friday evening until a working weekend introduced me to the Island's many wide and varied leisure activities that are far too numerous to explore here.

Having wended my way around the Company premises at Cowes for a week meeting who was who in the Design office, the Electronic labs and the Factory, I finally made it out to the Rocket Development Dept (RDD) at High Down, which lay some 15 miles away on the Islands western tip.

I was immediately spellbound by the rugged solitude and magnificent sea panoramas at this remarkable place. The windswept grassy wilderness inhabited by seabirds and rabbits was often shrouded in mist and rain but became a truly glorious spot on a fine clear day. Mother Nature's power was evident everywhere and I was eager to work at this unique spot on what I felt was going to be a unique project.

Civil engineers had begun construction some months earlier and were finishing off as I arrived. RDD staff recruitment had reached about 40 people, mostly clad in duffle coats and woolly hats as they struggled to coerce stout electric cables through underground ducts; others were in open combat with strange mechanical structures. The Test Stands, Gantries and Equipment Centre consoles for site No1 were in place and connecting them together as a functional entity was the current priority.

The sites remote location prescribed a dedicated bus and canteen services; at peak times, two 52-seat coaches and two canteen meal sittings were operated each day plus a minibus shuttle link with the factory at East Cowes. The minibus remained on site for firing days to serve as emergency transport and a number of site staff doubled as trained fire fighters with an on site appliance.

Winter the months could be taxing, especially when it snowed and the coaches dare not risk the serpentine road climb: everyone gallantly trudged up and down to Alum Bay on foot and seemed to enjoy the novelty because attendance usually remained high. The dispersed nature of the on site test facilities made for patchy communication during a routine day – mobile phones had yet to be invented and the rudimentary intercom points were sited to suit firing day operations only. Consequently, tea breaks and meal times became the regular contact times, where one caught up on the scuttlebutt, progressed activities, sorted out hang-ups and smoothed out ruffled feathers.

One observant wag insisted that tea-breaks displayed an individuals self esteem i.e. some sat down while drinking, others stood up while drinking and some stood drinking from the green teacups reserved for salaried staff, whilst a select few had tea sent to their office on a tray, and some never turning up at all!

As a brand new department with brand new staff at a brand new venue, RDD needed to cultivate networking links with opposite numbers inside and outside the Company. Recalling that personnel at Cowes and elsewhere who had already invested many months of effort on BK, were now getting their handiwork pulled apart by a bunch of longhaired duffle coated know-alls, was not the way to form friends so diplomacy became yet another watchword to observe. In this respect, RDD had gathered a few difficult oddballs who took any opportunity to rub people up the wrong way and aggravate the liaison process.

A particular fellow comes to mind that had previously worked on the African groundnut scheme, frequently raised hackles with his abrupt approach and inane practical jokes. On one occasion the maintenance crew were baffled for a week by a rotten kipper secreted in the Equipment Centre air ventilation system.

In a later incident he covertly ordered five hundredweight of coal to be tipped outside a colleagues digs in the village. But his undoing came when he placed an acetylene filled toy balloon on a live electric cooking ring outside the workshop.

The resulting explosion alarmed the entire site so he had to go. The RAE had a strong motivation to be influential at High Down and feelings were soon mutual as bonds were formed and RDD ultimately became a virtual Farnborough outstation. Growing pains dissolved as the installation phase gave way to site commissioning and staff began to see what was expected as routine began to emerge – but one potentially volatile aspect did rear its head.

> *A serious irritation emerges* – *Recalling that BK was a pull through for Blue Streak and that DH would be running all launch trials at Woomera, problems began to surface. As a large affluent company, DH took advantage of RDD's relaxed visitor policy and flooded the site with highly paid manpower that grew dominant and caused resentment. DH staff came and went as they pleased and splashed generous expenses around the local pubs while moderately paid RDD staff were shackled to a shoestring budget. As they strived to devise test methods, create test gear, carry out rocket acceptance testing and train DH personnel, they were expected to stand aside from the most fulfilling aspect of the entire exercise. As launching agency, DH would claim credit for all successes while the SR designers would shoulder all failures.*
>
> *As matters grew to a climax, the Chief Designers of both companies convened a showdown meeting at a Ryde hotel. While having sympathy with the RDD gripe, I was disturbed by their venom compared with the angelic stance of the DH side. Eventually the DH boss called for order and made his defining declaration: "This program is too important to risk discord, from now on, in all matters concerning Black Knight, both companies will stand shoulder to shoulder and their flags will fly at equal height". This statement calmed the RDD side and predictably, the evening grew friendlier as drinks and refreshments appeared! The extravagant antics of DH staff diminished and their numbers at High Down fell to sensible levels but the salary and expense differentials were never addressed.*
>
> *It must be emphasised that good relationships and the willingness to work alongside their wealthier DH colleagues owed much to RDD's keen enthusiasm for the project. In all except reimbursement matters, the senior managers of both companies vigorously enforced the equality principle throughout the BK and later BA programs.*

Ironically, as time passed, DH staff frequenting High Down and working at Woomera on BK and BA grew more distant from their Blue Streak colleagues and developed a close kinship with their RDD and RAE counterparts. Additionally, due to exceptionally poor subsistence rate for RAE personnel while at Woomera, it became an unwritten rule for all sub contractors to minimise their Mess bar costs.

HARDWARE SHORTFALLS – Efforts at Cowes and elsewhere were myopically prioritised on finalising the first flight rocket and completing the Woomera installation, which left scant time or funds for so called fringe test equipment.

Typically, a means of data logging dynamic engine data from static firings and sub system tests had been under played and RDD sought to correct this and similar omissions by the age old tactic of scrounging, innovation and creative accounting. This process persisted for several years until the reliability and efficiency implications were grasped and partially addressed by Ministry managers.

Most RDD staff proved resourceful and keen to get over every hurdle by fair means or foul, many having served in the armed services where this approach is endemic; fortunately our supervision staff who usually came from the aviation and electronic industries, managed to keep rampant enthusiasm well grounded. A small on site maintenance workshop with skilled tradesmen had been provisioned to maintain the water pumps, electrical power and similar site services. As the main installation work drew to a close, this team of artisans combined their efforts to make the "bare" site installations "user friendly" by adding handrails, lighting, camera mounts, custom stowage's and numerous other practical improvements. All this investment of effort was to pay dividends when trials work began in earnest.

MEASURMENTS GROUP – Having earlier experience with missile instrumentation it was natural that I join the Measurements Group of two engineers and five technicians charged with setting up facilities to calibrate transducers and secure real-time records. The team were an enthusiastic bunch of lively young guys from the mainland who brought a wide range of experience and humour to the scene. If needed, all were prepared to get dirty hands and pursue a problem until it was solved or fully defined – just what was needed in these early days.

As originally planned a Motor Console in each Equipment Centre visually displayed engine pressures to an observer who could terminate a firing if necessary.

As a link between calibration firings at Ansty and those done at High Down and Woomera, an array of similar bourdon tube dial gauges at each site were to be photographed by 35 mm stepping cameras. This "Auto Observer" had yet to materialise so the Measurements and Site Maintenance guys constructed a waterproof cabinet to house the dial gauge array, camera and floodlights close by the Launcher stand.

Each gauge linked to the appropriate engine point via grease filled micro tubing and isolation buffers where HTP was involved. RAE provided an electric 35mm step camera; and RDD ran the remote control circuit back to EC5. The set up worked well and was duplicated later at Area5. It was soon clear that wider data bandwidth was wanted if useful fault diagnoses were to be done. The data list was fourteen engine pressures, 6 efflux duct temps, 12 flight FCS values, 12 timing events, and five cine camera views, all to be logged at various speeds during a 35 second static firing.

Measurements group foresaw that post firing data analysis would need permanent real time analogue data logging at a suitable bandwidth and after steady lobbying 6 Hartmann & Braun four- channel galvanic recorders materialised after persistent requests. These rudimentary devices (See Fig 2–2 below) used an UV light source to trace galvo mirror movements onto sensitised paper – a media that soon fogged up in daylight, which required the traces to be hurriedly pencil over before they vanished forever! A photo fixing processor was eventually added to the setup and Measurements Section devised a set of light tight take up spools for each recorder.

Each engine pressure display on the EC motor console and its related transducer at the Launcher, formed a ratiometric bridge circuit, which was immune to power supply drift. These ideal voltage sources were paralleled off to the nearby Recorder Room (just a cable rack and empty room at this stage!) could tap into.

FIG 2–2 – The ORIGINAL RECORDER set up of H&B ultra violet recorders at HD   *(GKN Aerospace)*

Flight Control System (FCS) voltage data sources were picked off via break-in boxes at the Test Stand and buffered by locally built cathode follower units. Poor funding often led to poor solutions; our rudimentary recorder room lacked a cross patching facility to link recorder channels with incoming data circuits.

Incoming data was connected to specific recorder channels in accordance with defined allocation lists – often re-hashed at the eleventh hour by picky test engineers.

To provide allocation flexibility a crude scheme was devised where all incoming data feeds and recorder channel inputs were terminated on two opposing Chock Block strip arrays where any data source could be quickly linked to any recorder channel required channel allocation insertion of a simple jumper wire.

I well recall a colleague and I burning the midnight oil, tracing faults and making late changes to these links before a Systems & Sequence check next day. Our crude solution did not offer the desirable option of reliable quick changes between test conditions or Launcher sites.

A year or so later when the Gaslight and Dazzle series needed both Launcher sites functional at High Down and Woomera a "patch card module" was installed that used interchangeable preset patch cards, which allowed rapid fault free site swops and allocation changes.

Aircraft gun sight cine cameras loaned from RAF stores were used to capture engine close-ups and situation films. Again, mountings, flood lighting and remote control units were fashioned on site using local resources.

FIG 2–3. HIGH DOWN – FIRST PROTOTYPE LOADING INTO GANTRY NO2. Notice the tank on Test Post roof standing in for a leaky rocket tank   *(GKN Aerospace)*

PROOF FIRING at HIGH DOWN

A series of static firings were required to proof the Test Stand, test exhaust duct cooling, shakedown all site systems, exercise operational concepts, and demonstrate safety arrangements. A non-flight rocket (First Prototype) airframe with an operational engine had been allocated for this purpose.

> *Unfortunately:* The first prototype was also a manufacturing prototype and poor sealing made the HTP tank unfit for use. A very thin skin, stiffened with external stringers attached by discrete fasteners caused numerous leaks, sees Fig A–4 of Appendix A. Continuous electric seam welding on thicker 20swg skins without external stringers was successfully perfected and used on all flight vehicle tanks.

The tank limitation was overcome by installing a commercial aluminium tank on the Test Post roof outside Gantry No2 (See Fig 2–3 above) and rigged with a rocket pressurising system and routed by a 4" diameter thick walled polythene outlet pipe direct to the engine inlet manifold. As an engine running tool only, setscrews instead of steering servos, preset each thrust chamber swivel angle.

I dimly recall, the First Prototype came on site about March '58 and after about 8 days of handling exercises in various transfer configurations in the Preparation Area and on the Transporter, the vehicle was erected in Gantry No2 and readied for firing.

My only contribution to these proceedings was to assist with pressure transducer calibrations, a tedious activity at the best of times and real purgatory in cold weather.

It was about this time that we were privy to a classical installation cock up, which readily demonstrated the RDD ability to solve problems on the fly: –

> *A Party piece!* To start a Gamma engine, its shutdown valve is electrically opened to admit a high pressure HTP shore side supply that spins up the four-turbo pump turbines and opens the HTP stop valves sited on each combustion chamber inlet trunnion. As delivery pump pressures rise they exceed shore side HTP feed pressure and check valves close to bootstrap each turbine to its own turbo-pump output to sustain a continuous HTP feed to each combustion catalyst pack. As described later, hot running begins when kerosene is admitted to the process.
>
> Originally the 5-gallon HTP shore side tank was mounted in a snug and handy spot 20 ft from the rocket engine and linked to it by a two-inch stainless steel pipe that meandered along a winding route, clipped at frequent intervals to handy concrete and metal structures along the way.

When first operated using demineralised water, every pipe clip instantly sheared off as the two-inch pipe straightened out under 350 psi pressure, just like a child's party squeaker and just as entertaining to us onlookers! Within four days, site resources had re-positioned the tank close beside a launcher leg to give a short straight pipe run to the engine.

The long awaited engine firing happened on a bright sunny day; by mid morning the Measurements crew had the Recorder Room system powered up, a few popped UV lamps were replaced, fresh media rolls were inserted, all recorder channels had been spot calibrated and the remote cameras had been loaded with film, harmonised, and idented. We then kicked our heels until the rocket team were ready for the truncated 5-minute count down originally planned for 11:00 hrs. After several delays and procedural hiccups the –120sec Auto sequence was reached and amazingly it ran through to +35 seconds without hesitation. All recorder room events happened as planned and we quickly set to pencilling over the H&B records before they faded away! Not privy to the bigger picture in those days, my impression was that all had gone well and only a few functional queries remained to be followed up.

The Disappointed ones: This first static firing did not please everyone. To the uniformed, the firing was a very big let down because the thunderous noise, immense clouds of smoke and many other fanciful manifestations invented over a glass or two at the local pub, had not came to pass. The slight ground rumble felt on site didn't match expectations at all and their deflation was total when the downs patrol party and villager folk had heard nothing! The local pubs saw much ribbing and colourful advice dished out that evening.

Over the next week or so, further firings were done to check duct cooling at extreme chamber angles, test revised N2 purge system settings and examine turbine response times with pre primed start pipe and transducer capillaries. When these tasks were concluded, the mechanical team began the long and noisy engine drying out process.

AT LAST! REAL PROGRESS WAS POCKETED – On completion of the proofing tasks, the vehicle was removed to the Prep Area and readied for shipment to Woomera around early May to commission the Area5 site.

These early firings had answered important questions: -

- Transportation, lifting and handling methods were satisfactory.
- HTP transfer arrangement OK but better quantitative accuracy was needed.
- Efflux duct cooling and water flow rates were established and found moderate.
- Ground start run up time was good but a proper means of priming the start hose remained to be solved.

- Purge system revealed high delta between static and flow pressures – pipe flow losses need to be reviewed.
- Poor mixture ratio results. A topic dogged by flawed tank volume calibration, which was to persist until precise metering equipment was later acquired.
- Pressure data logging was adequate but capillary priming was needed to eliminate system "ringing".
- The Safety Plan and related operations were exercised and passively proven.
- Public exclusion arrangements were demonstrated – (On firing days, security teams patrolled the Downs to prevent public access west of Tennyson's Monument.)
- Some limitations in procedural routines, communications and documentation were identified.
- Engine drying in saline air conditions was verified.

Repeatedly assured that First flight vehicle (BK01) was imminent invariably proved false due production problems. As site commissioning was concluded a period of refinement and tinkering set in, interspersed with equipment exercises. Measurements Group pressed on with improving hardware and sussing out the inconsistent transducer response times; thought to be related to uncertain priming of capillary pipes from transducer to engine and peroxide buffer units. Some improvement was made but reliability and consistency was never achieved until the Gamma 301 engine arrived some years later. Equipped with its shuttle valves at every engine tapping point, capillary pipe bleeding and pressure step calibration could be achieved without breaking pipe connections.

A huge effort went into calibration and spot measurement of mechanical vibration at various Engine Bay locations. The ultra high impedance semi conductors and integrated circuits common in today's well-defined technology had yet to be marketed in UK and funding limitations led us to improvise crystal accelerometers, construct thermionic capture amplifiers and forever wrestle with line capacitance drift. Arising from these vibration activities, Measurements Group were belatedly tasked to install, setup and operate the rocket's 465MHz telemetry systems. Having worked with 465MHz telemetry systems at Vickers Armstrong, I became involved with these demands until a dedicated section was set up. The flight system and ground monitoring radio receivers were designed and supplied by RAE Bramshott but a fundamental requirement had again been overlooked.

No method of recording a histogram for post firing analysis had been considered so thoughts turned to exploiting a grazing radio sight line that existed between High Down and Bramshott to use their comprehensive recording facilities.

However, the approach proved unreliable and the solution lay between: a suitable reel-to-reel video recorder or a tall aerial mast.

Again, lack of funding and foresight won the day and telemetry at High Down remained only a setting up and acceptance procedure for many years until well into the BA program. After several serious attempts to persuade the RAE of the benefits attached to extracting rocket data via telemetry, it was finally scotched when RAE imposed the maxim: " A flight system must not qualify another flight system". This blinkered view prevented detection of many monitoring faults until the Woomera trial where the full Mike 3 facilities were to hand. Had tele recording been available at Ansty and High Down via transducers of similar bandwidth, direct correlation across all Test Site results and flight results would become possible.

AT LAST! A FLIGHT VEHICLE ARRIVES – Circa mid November '57 the long expected event was at hand. Having demonstrated the ability to organise and conduct static firings, it was now time for High Down to integrate, qualify and clear a flight vehicle for launching at Woomera. Being the debut flight, this trial would rightly be regarded by many as a groundbreaking event but to those who struggled to overcome a serious FCS problem, BK01 would be noted for the long hours and late nights spent between a cold Gantry and chilly FCS Lab running test after test to resolve a serious difficulty; when first functioned as a complete system with all three gyro outer loops connected to the four thrust chamber servo loops running on hydraulic power, the entire rocket structure shook violently until the outer loops were opened. Connecting each outer loop in turn revealed that the roll loop alone, produced a regular low amplitude hum whilst each lateral loop alone exhibited aggressive and lumpy low frequency rumbling, which suggested a relationship with the torsion and lateral bending characteristics of the rockets airframe structure.

> *Structural resonance*: *Referring to Figure, A–18 in Appendix A. The displacement gyros sited up in the Electronics Bay to measure the rockets Pitch Yaw and Roll angles are mechanically linked to the four thrust chambers down in the Engine Bay through the airframe structure. Being a resilient entity, the airframe has inherent bending and torsion resonance modes, which in the BK case lay within the FCS pass band needed for stable flight control. Consequently, airframe excitation by swinging thrust chamber inertias were "felt" by the gyros and fed back to the inner loop servos creates a self-sustaining resonant loop.*

I'd seen similar behaviour at "Vickers" on a short, very stiff airframe that resonated well above the control pass band and easily cured by electronic filtering but this BK situation was a challenge because each natural resonance lay inside the FCS pass band needed to maintain stable flight.

Electronic bench tests were repeated at length, inner loop servo responses were meticulously scrutinised, structural resonance modes were recalculated and analogue computer simulations were revisited. "Experts" were consulted; various structural conditions were tested and time raced by before the problem boundaries were fully mapped. In simple terms, the gyroscopes, FCS electronics, airframe and thrust chamber combination provided a regenerative feed back path that allowed thrust chamber reaction forces to sustain airframe resonances – sometimes referred to in modern parlance as the "tail wag dog" problem.

Because structural loading, stiffness, damping and fixation constraints influenced the resonance signature, a range of conditions starting from empty unpressurised tanks, through to full and pressurised tanks as at liftoff was examined. To address post launch conditions, BK02 airframe was relegated to prototype status and suspended in a "free-free" rig with electric vibrator driven input, at EEL.

The problem was resolved by the following revisions to the FCS installation: –

- Electronic filters added at each gyro signal demodulators to prevent system saturation from unwanted high frequencies.
- Introduction of rate gyros in lateral control loop to damp the first bending modes within the control pass band.

Once re-engineered, further hours were swallowed up retesting the permutation structural configurations.

> *Humour in adversity: This incident captures the forbearing spirit at the coalface in these frustrating days. Many tests on the FCS hardware entailed comparison between laboratory set up and functional performance at the rocket in the gantry. Because we possessed only one set of heavy oscilloscope, signal generator and phase analyser test gear, this and the rocket FCS tray had to be frequently manhandled between the two venues. When asked to shift the gear for the umpteenth time this day, one joker protested by undoing his belt, dropped his jeans and declared "I'm working like an f****** donkey, I may as well look like one!"*

Thrust chamber swivelling forces felt by the airframe are proportional to chamber inertia, swing angle amplitude and swing frequency, plus thrust vector modulation when firing. The combination of these effects was explored at swing frequencies of 5Htz and 10Htz during static firings.

By recording chamber angle and demand angle on four twin beam oscilloscopes fitted with 35mm cameras accurate amplitude, phase and wave shape could be deduced. A Control System Signal Unit (CSSU) with six, gated sine wave generators was built for this purpose and retained as a performance benchmark in all subsequent static firings at High Down and Woomera.

An early learning curve – I often considered why it took so long to resolve this structural feedback snag? As a mere bystander, it seemed to me that the RAE, EEL, RDD and Cowes teams were short on technically informed leadership or too timorous to grasp the nettle. I eventually concluded that lack of trust between fledgling outfits led them to fear reputational damage until a blindingly obvious consensus had crystallised. The magic of collective responsibility, where objectivity and engineering logic trumps the dead hand of blame and financial liability had yet to blossom. Eventually a single-minded, single objective culture grew where candour prevailed, a hallmark that flourished throughout the entire BK/BA programs. A priceless gem discarded for nought when the UK rocket development industry was disbanded.

FIG 3–1   BLACK KNIGHT IN HIGH DOWN GANTRY NO2.
ASM Engine Rep with Yours Truly at the back   *(GKN Aerospace)*

I MOVE DOWN UNDER   **4**

When asked to replicate the High Down engine instrumentation setup out at Woomera I readily accepted and made plans accordingly. Mid Jan 1958 saw all the recording equipment and related drawings dispatched to our SARO office at Salisbury, South Australia. End Feb I arrived at Clyffe Pypard to spend a night with a sprinkling of DH, ASM and RDD engineers before we presented ourselves next morning at RAF Lyneham to board a Transport Command Comet II E's for Adelaide. Unable to recall the actual route, I've listed the stops made over the years.

Akrotiri (Cyprus): A very comfortable and enjoyable stopover.

Luqa (Malta): Spent two restful days relaxing by the sea while an aircraft fault was fixed.

Cairo (Egypt): Another interesting stopover but we were warned never to go out alone! The shopping markets were worth seeing.

El Adam (Libya): The aircraft noise detonated a string of WWII mines in the desert as we approached to land. A very cold night with primitive sanitation – an American colonel reckoned you risked loosing vital parts on the thunder buckets!

Habbaniya (Iraq): Again a very basic RAF base.

Mauripur (Karachi): Like an unkempt farmyard. On first trip out, engines failed to start, luckily a Rolls Royce rep was travelling out to assist Comet servicing at RAAF Edinburgh Field. After unpacking is kit from the hold, he located a "shorting" frayed cable – so off we went.

Khormaksar (Aden): A comfortable stopover with interesting shopping at Crater City but generally a very backward down at heel spot.

Katunayaka (Sri Lanka, then Ceylon): A beautiful tropical paradise, good RAF Mess with snug sleeping quarters and brilliant swimming; was always an enjoyable place to visit.

Changi (Singapore): Probably the best stopover, great food, duty free shops by the score, good B&B and a great place to mix with many ethnic cultures. Always looked forward to.

Darwin (Australian NT): On my first visit, the Australian seated beside me imparted the following wisdom while looking out of the window, "There she is mate, the arsehole of the Empire".

At the airport, health officials come aboard to spray every thing, including us with DTD! In the early days all books and magazines were automatically confiscate as being risqué – presumably for their own use

<u>RAAF Edinburgh</u> (Australia SA), Our final destination. I reached Adelaide in the evening eager to rest a weary head at the Gresham Hotel (corner of King William St and North Terrace, since replaced by a Bank building).

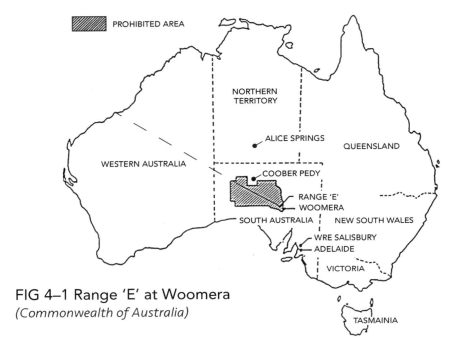

FIG 4–1 Range 'E' at Woomera
(Commonwealth of Australia)

After a day catching up on sleep and laundry and a day touring this lovely city and surrounding hills, I headed out to Salisbury to meet the SARO staff, as Saunders Roe was known out here. A further day was spent meeting various Weapons Research Establishment (WRE) personnel, which included the mandatory security orientation and mug shot routine. The following morning saw me boarding a DC3 for a bone shaking flight up to Woomera.

WOOMERA VILLIAGE –
Founded in 1947, the village lays near the E/W rail line 100 miles above Port Augusta at the head of St Vincent's Gulf, 300 miles north of Adelaide. In those days it was a high security 'closed' village that enjoyed generous funding, able to support 6000 people at its peak.

With 2 schools, three churches, a library, a hospital, Olympic size swimming pool, 3 ovals, a Theatre, Bowling Green and a golf coarse on oiled sand!

Based on its original military format, all single personnel were housed in one of three groups: the Senior Mess, the Junior Mess and the Junior Ranks Club.

As population grew to include families, they lived in individual bungalow homes. In addition to the many village sports clubs, all families were affiliated to an appropriate Mess. All employed personnel worked directly for or were linked in some way with the WRE rocket range activities.

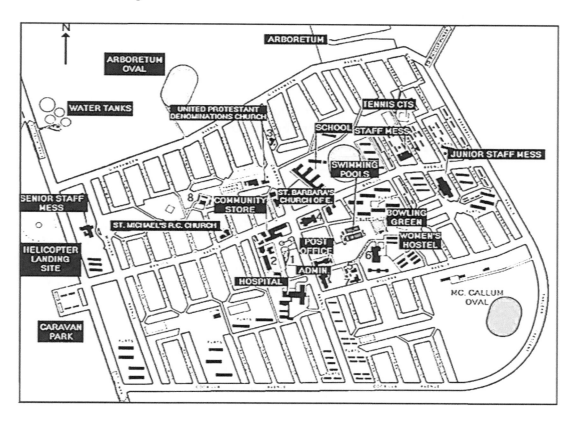

FIG 4–2 WOOMERA VILLAGE circa 1060   (Woomera Board)

The cost of living was low; the weather was usually fine, leisure facilities were in abundance, which combined with the Australian's bent for socialising produce an enjoyable but artificial existence. It was a bad place to stay too long! Many folk I knew over the years became entrapped by the protected unreal tax-free lifestyle and were effectively in a jail and often cursed by alcohol.

THE WRE WEAPON TESTING RANGES –

Weapon testing was allocated to areas dedicated according to weapon type and instrumentation needs e.g. bomb drops, artillery, guided missiles, ballistic missiles etc. Sophisticated guided missiles and high altitude sounding rockets were launched from Range E, the largest and most instrumented facility, located some 30 miles north east of the village and reached daily by bus or self-drive car.

Having an almost unlimited land area, Australian tends to spread facilities far and wide and the expanse between workshops, offices and launch facilities at Range E made wheeled mobility an essential resource.

The BK workshop and offices were located in Test Shop 2, adjacent to the range head complex with its Instrumentation Building (IB) and cluster of smaller launch pads. Due to the potential damage radius the duplicate BK launch pads were located at a lone site 3.5 miles to the SW at Area5.

Lunch and late working meals were provided at a catering establishment about one mile outside the Range E security fence, beside Lake Koolimilka, a dry salt lake that magically spawned fish in the wet years.

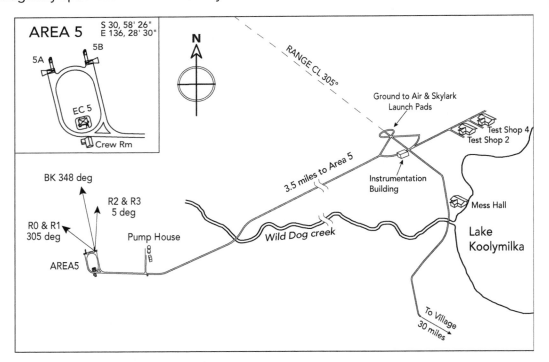

FIG 4–3 – RANGE 'E' & AREA 5 at WOOMERA   (D Mack)

Working outside a BK Trial period required forethought; WRE Security needed to know intended work times, staff numbers, transport and meal needs and if WRE participation was required; failure in this duty would bring matters to a standstill.

I soon found that arranging and satisfying everybody's meals and wheels foibles was far trickier than firing rockets so I usually dodged or delegated this task.

During the early site installation days and between trial actual periods the range could be a lonely place; the few folk around were invariably holed up out of sight with an air conditioner. By contrast, the days surrounding static firings and launch windows became crowded and woe-be-tide those whose logistic needs had been omitted from a Bible called the WRE Trial Plan, wherein almost everything had to be defined.

> *A Lone Ranger:* One of our SARO engineers was a solitary kind of cove who would get submerged in his lonesome task of checking wiring modifications inside junction rooms, behind vast cable racks. His invisibility often meant we drove off to lunch or dinner without him and on several occasions was several miles down the road before it was realised. "Don't forget," notices soon sprung up beside most TS2 exit doors and on car dashboards.

WRE MISSILE TRACKING AT RANGE E – The Range had built up their missile and target aircraft operations at Range 'E' over many years before Black Knight and Blue Streak ever materialised. Activities had included Air-to-Air and Ground-to-Air trials that required extensive electronic and optical tracking facilities along a 50-mile line of fire to capture trajectory and telemetry data and to guide target aircraft. The instrumented area and operational altitude was later expanded to cope with Vulcan bombers dropping Blue Steel stand off bombs, Skylark high altitude sounding rockets and the second generation of air defence missiles. These range facilities underwent further adaptation and major expansion to accommodate the BK, BS and BA beasts.

BK TRAJECTORY – BK made a vertical climb to 19,000ft, where a guidance pilot tilted it 2° down range in line with Area 5 guidance axis; Area5 tracking and guidance continue up to about 350,000ft where engine thrust and directional control ended. Tracking at Area5 continued as a surveillance support function to WRE re-entry acquisition. The head (experimental test body) was detached within seconds of All Burnt and continued climbing ahead of the spent rocket on a free ballistic trajectory path up to apogee heights up to 500 miles before descending into significant atmosphere at 200,000ft and impacting inside a 12-mile circle zone, centred 50 miles down range, 6 miles right of centre line.

BK GUIDANCE TRACKING – The trajectory origin coincided with the EC5 radar/telescope datum. A Flank and Rear optical gunnery tracker provided initial vertical climb data until rocket entry into the guidance radar/telescope beams.

X & Y pilots tilted rocket trajectory 2° down range and maintained its position until engine All Burnt when vector steering ceased. The system was designed by RAE and operated by DH personnel. See Figure A–20 in Appendix A for further detail.

FLIGHT SAFETY TRACKING – To gather substantive independent trajectory data to meet their safety obligations, WRE operated an extensive network of observation sites strung out along the line of fire, and progressively offset laterally to enable observations at increasing altitudes.

- 0 to 10,000ft – Three close in Sykscreen observers.
- From 400ft to limit – Two Optical trackers, X5 and X7.
- From 4000ft to limit – Two Optical trackers, X5 and X6.
- From 10,000ft to limit – Two FPS–16 tracking radars, R38 and R39.

To be effective at high altitudes, some optical & radar sites lay beyond the launch pad horizon and remained blind until the rocket climbed into view. Three Sky-screen units placed to guard pitch, yaw and Instrumentation Building (IB) risks by gauging lateral drift at liftoff. These were simple open sights fixed to view rocket liftoff through vertical wire screens silhouetting the safe flight corridor. The WRE optical X trackers were joystick steered theodolite telescopes that sent elevation and azimuth data to the Range Tracking Centre for triangulation with other trackers and normalisation to the Range Head datum. The FPS-16 radars were high precision tracking instruments that provided angle and range data beyond the extreme limits of the BK flight envelope. Using these data, the Tracking Centre presented real time situation plots to the Flight Safety Officer, displaying rocket altitude and speed, present ground plan position and a predicted walking impact point. The latter plots were overlaid on local terrain maps defining cut down boundaries that protected Homestead settlements, East/West rail line, Woomera village and other Range obligations.

WRE ACQUISITION SYSTEM – This system was originally created to slave Range trackers onto a climbing missile or incoming target aircraft.

For later BK firings the system was enhanced to direct narrow aperture spectral instruments onto an equally small re-entry window some 200,000 ft above, where a tiny object was expected to appear at high speed; a task complicated by brightly glowing rocket debris streaking earthwards on a similar path. The Tracking Centre passed its real time trajectory data to the General Range Acquisition System (GRASS) where it was transposed and fed out to the client sites.

RANGE RECOVERY GROUP – In contrast to over water ranges, Woomera offered a stable base from which accurate observations could be made and offered the potential to retrieve spent hardware for inspection and analysis.

To capitalise on this latter feature, WRE established a very effective Recovery Group, which BK relied on to recover the armoured tape recorder carried in many re-entry bodies, and sundry impact debris for fault diagnoses.

The Recovery Team: A resourceful group of nomads led by a colourful and astute ex RN Lt Commander. Their domain extended hundreds of square miles into the Outback, which they traversed in specially equipped and hardened Land Rovers. Over the years a string of mini depots, tracking sites and watering holes built up about the Range centreline, became their working "havens". Living rough, doing long hours, needed a special kind of hardened self-sufficient individual who enjoyed the wilderness their work offered. BK's impact area was a 12-mile circle, 6 miles right of the centre line and some 50 miles from the launcher.

The terrain varied from broad scrubland OK for motorised square searches, to wooded rocky escarpments only accessible on foot, all prone to flash flooding in the wet times. For an early impact fix, a simple method was adapted from the WRE ballistic camera sites. Six fish eyed Polaroid cameras placed in a circle around the expected impact point with shutters left open minutes before re-entry time the re-entry streak was captured against time lapsed star tracks. Placing all photos on a map and aligning star tracks quickly establish a "Witch's Hat' at the real impact point. This process often delivered recovered items to TS2 by the next morning. When occasional visitors were invited on these nocturnal jaunts the Commander deliberately parked his Land Rover at the expected impact spot, claiming it as safe as anywhere else! Another guy and I joined him for BK08 firing and were in deep discussion after the brilliant short visual re-entry display when the massive shock

FIG 4–4. WRE Range recovery fleet
(Commonwealth of Australia)

wave arrived. As the long rolling thunder laced with sharp crackling sounds played out, our fellow visitor vanished beneath the Land Rover.

The Commander sagely remarked, "The silly bugger's a bigger target under there! Because BK08 Stage2 failed to separate and ignite on this occasion, re-entry parameters were unusual so the Polaroid films were unhelpful.

BK LAUNCH SITE – AREA 5   **5**

As stated earlier, BK potential damage radius consigned its launch facilities to a dedicated area some 3.5 miles SW of the Range Head – a distance that behove you never to leave anything behind at TS2! Like High Down, two identical launch installations, 5A & 5B, stood at ground level above water-cooled exhaust ducts sunk in concrete pits below. Towering above each launcher, the service gantries sat on powered bogies, which moved the structure clear at launch time. Each launcher had a tilting umbilical support mast and a shallow water lagoon to dilute waste HTP.

Below ground a Test Post housed local gas and electrical services complete with

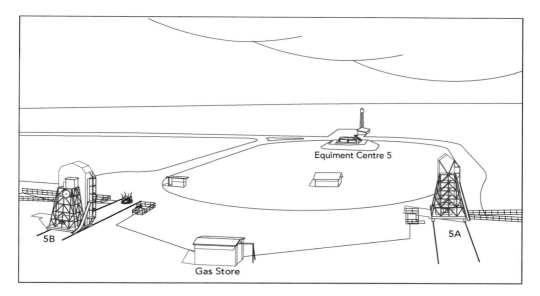

Equiment Centre 5

5B

5A

Gas Store

FIG 5–1   AREA 5 LOOKING SOUTH   *(DM based on WRE Photo)*

control and monitoring facilities to operate the rocket electronic systems free of EC5 dependence. The above diagram (Figure 5–1) depicts Area5 as adapted for the Black Arrow program where the old BK style 5A retained gantry was retained to static fire the Stage2 engine and the 5B Launcher and Gantry was totally replaced to suit the BA Composite rocket vehicle.

As originally constructed for Black Knight, 5B Gantry was identical to 5A as shown, HP gas was purveyed from bottle trolleys and four ex military anti aircraft search lights were deployed to aid sky screen and guidance trackers during the moonless night firings.

EQUIPMENT CENTRE 5 (EC5) –

This is the nearest manned facility to launchers 5A & 5B, standing some 220 yards aft of each pad.   The heavily reinforced concrete structure included closed loop ventilation, hardened periscopic windows and was designed to sustain a full rocket fall back.   It housed 15 to 20 operators with all the monitor and control equipment needed to static fire/launch and guide BK to all burnt.   A resident WRE officer (AOO5) was responsible to the Range Controller (Con1) for all Area5 activities.   From his command position in EC5 he controlled al firing circuit power, interlock overrides, fire fighting services and the communication network, which were all under his lock and key.   His delegate at the Launch Pad was a Launcher Officer (LO5), usually an Australian Artillery Captain, who, with 2 to 3 Bombardiers, oversaw all launcher activities, directly supervised all hazardous tasks and carried out final arming of the rockets ordnance systems.

The remaining EC5 team were all UK contractors except the OISC who was an RAE nominee.   The usual operator compliment is given below but for launch firings, the OISC relocates to the CON1 suite at the Range Instrumentation Building: –

- Area Operations Officer (AOO5)
- Launcher Office (LO5)
- Officer in Scientific Charge (OISC)(Static firings only)
- Team Leader (TL).
- Deputy Team Leader (DTL)
- Engine Engineer (ASM)
- Sequence Officer
- 2 Engine Consol Operators
- 2 Flight Control System Operator
- Telemetry Consol Operator
- 3 Telemetry Histograms Observers
- Extra Services Consol Operator.
- S Band Rader Operator
- Tracking Telescope Operator
- Guidance Supervisor (Launch firings)
- Pitch & Yaw Pilots (Launch firings)

A well-appointed crew room, toilet block, car park and the AOO5 office were sited close by EC5. Some 500yds back along the entry road stood the water tank farm with a hardened pump house able to supply 9500Ltr/min to the exhaust ducts and serve the fire fighting system.

STATIC FIRING INSTRUMENTATION – I now come to the prime purpose of my visit to Woomera: to set up a replica of the "High Down" recorder installation in EC5 and 5A Test Post. Six H&B recorders, four camera oscilloscopes, a Control System Signal Unit and a Kelvin & Hughes event recorder were all positioned on a custom made bench that SARO had premade to my sketches. A scaling and zeroing unit, custom made at High Down, was wired in and mounted below each H&B recorder.

Aided by a DH technician, all the gear was wired to a start/stop controller and data channel patch-board unit at one end of the recorder bench, this in turn was cabled out to the main EC5 junction room to pick up incoming data channels, timing pulses and sequence unit start/stop signals.

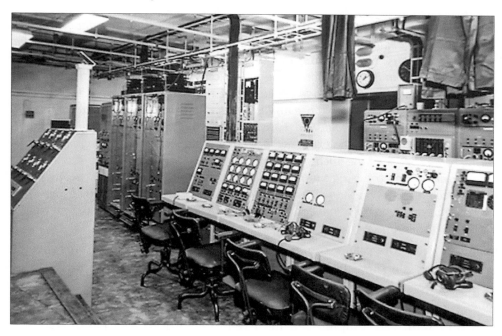

FIG 5–2 AREA5 –EQUIPMENT CENTRE 5 (EC5) AT AREA5
(Commonwealth of Australia)

Out at the launcher each pressure and temperature transducer was locally mounted on a purpose made plate attached to the First Prototype BK engine bay Fin fixing.

This interim transducer mounting pended finalisation of purpose made instrument cabinets mounted on diametrically opposed launcher frame legs.

Each instrument connected to a cable harness that led down via buried metal ducting to the Test Post cable frame below, thence back to EC5.

The Auto Observer gauges were arrayed on one wall inside the Test Post, their oil filled sensing pipes being routed back up to tapping points on the dummy fin, via the metal ducting. I calibrated the overall system by applying ten pressure steps to each sensing point on the dummy fin using a deadweight tester and confirming that each Engine Consol display gauge and Auto Observer gauge agreed to better than 1%. The rest level and displacement of each H&B galvanometer was adjusted to the required scale settings using a similar technique. Thermal sensors were calibrated at two set points using ice and boiling water against a standard thermometer. This concluded the "Measurements" part of my mission until firing time.

> *An Installation Conflict* – About this time a profound dispute arose between SR-UK and WRE concerning the way multicored cables should be interconnect between site installations. Following usual aircraft practice, SR chose to connect all ground electrical equipments by direct point-to-point, single cores between equipments – a lightweight method was well suited to airframe looming but unmanageable for large 18 cored cables. WRE used the method evolved over many years by the telecomm industry, which permanently terminates every core of each 18-core cable to identical terminal blocks mounted on identical main frames at each end using identical colour and number code per core. The method is mirrored at each end of every cable irrespective of distance and location and makes every core available for use. It offers total flexibility to construct or amend any circuit arrangement without disturbance to the expensive permanent site cabling by using single core jumper wires between the open sides of any unused terminal block connection.
>
> The conflicting methods had immense impact on wiring allocation schedules and WRE rejected the SR method outright. A telex war ensued via the SARO office until SR-UK agreed to comply, subject to them retaining control of theoretical circuit design and the "Jumper" schedules.

Meanwhile, to meet the planned trial date, the Woomera installation was racing along and risked descending into chaos if Cowes continued allocating cores and terminals already in use at WRE and visa versa – a Tower of Babel in the making. My long telex to Cowes set out the situation, asked them to restrict their output to "theoretical" diagrams only until we completed a full Area5 cable core and jumper audit. They eventually agreed so I moved to Salisbury where, with two SARO colleagues and a WRE engineer every Area5 cable schedule was vetted and verified to agree with the Cowes BK01 "theoretical" drawing standard and issued a jumper correction list for the deficiencies. These actions were followed up by a physical jumper check at all cable-frames.

From then on Cowes employed the WRE method and converted High Down over to the same system.

> *When experience trumps all* – *When working at the SARO office in Salisbury, we took lunch in the DH dining room and at one such meal, nearing the weekend; were privy to an almighty panic that promised to mess up the fan big time. I relate the tale because it illustrates the importance of having appropriately experienced personnel on the spot at remote 'coal faces' and the need to trust their judgement; they have direct access to the hardware and local circumstances, which shape the facts and possible solutions.*
>
> *Like Black Knight, two firing sites were under construction at Woomera for Blue Streak and the first of two 90ft high service towers was nearing completion. The foreman steel erector who had assembled similar towers at Spade Adam in Cumbria, was checking the completed structure before cladding it, when he realised that two columns in the schedule were swapped over, meaning that the tower had been built back to front so that the side intended to face the launch pad didn't! The program was already months late and this cock-up could add many more, so an inquest meeting was set up for the coming Monday where heads were expected to roll. But the foreman erector knew his business and had to hand hydraulic jacking gear supplied for inserting the rail line bogies later on. Over the weekend he and his crew jacked up the umpteen-ton tower and fashioned a tallow-covered steel table beneath it by using structural steel girders from the unassembled tower. After lowering the 90ft structure onto the table, he attached a bulldozer to each diagonal corner and slid the tower around its vertical axis until it faced the correct direction. Clearly, this man was confident in his own ability and possessed a strong sense of self-preservation. The Monday meeting evaporated and the fan remained intact!*

Because both Salisbury and Woomera were at a distance from the horse's mouth back in UK, local WRE and SARO personnel hungered for any information that threw light on their part of the ship. Being fresh out from High Down, many guys sought me out for a chat, irrespective of my status or speciality (same, same US and French style) – after all, I was from High Down where real BK rocket hardware was being handled and static fired and they wanted to hear about it! I found it refreshing and a touch overwhelming that mature, seasoned missile men were freely discussing their issues with me; unlike UK where a well known maxim usually prevails: knowledge is power so keep all to ones self. I learnt so much from these easygoing men and made many lasting friendships to boot.

> *International Geophysical Year 1957-58* – *This worldwide research program entailed co-ordinated experiments across many countries, all aimed at updating the planets physics data. WRE/UK jointly mounted a series of upper atmospheric probes using the Skylark sounding rocket, which culminated in the consecutive launching of twelve Skylark rockets on a single night.*

If my recall is correct, one failed to reach the launch pad due to preparation snag. The payloads were varied; some spreading brilliant sodium clouds, others loosed fiery beacons, the majority ejected their instrumented packs to descend by parachute. Test Shop 2 had no part in these activities but we worked an unpaid night shift to witness the fun and added to the carnival atmosphere by running a continuous unofficial barbecue for all concerned.

AREA 5 PROOF FIRING TRIALS – May 1958 saw us finalising Area5 to static fire the First Prototype sent out from High Down as reported earlier. As previously explained, this vehicle was just an engine-firing tool provided for handling exercises and to commission the launcher and engine support services. Prior to issuing a fit to use certificate, the site installation needed vetting by WRE firing circuit inspectors who required a Firing Circuit logic map – something I'd not come across, nor had UK judging from their vague reply to my Telex. So after getting a steer from a WRE contact, a SARO colleague and I set to with theoretical diagrams to build a step-by-step cause and effect chart defined the purpose of every relay, every relay contact, arming intercept and event interlock in the Area5 firing circuit installation; a long but fruitful exercise that engraved the network on my mind. The document satisfied WRE and it became a seed for later Area5 certifications.

A week or so later, WRE convened a Preparedness Review where we Contractors presented the Area5 build standard, equipment certification status, plus the Test Procedures and Engine Firing Instructions for a proof firing.

After similar inputs from WRE engineering departments, an authority for Gamma 201 site-proofing firings was issued. During lunch that followed, the WRE Chief Safety Officer enquired how I thought Area5 was shaping up. I felt it was more advanced than High Down at the same relative point because all High Down lessons were embodied and several DH crew had now experienced a firing – things were looking good. Talk turned to the auxiliary HTP tank, which I confirmed was identical with High Down where it had worked well. The installation had pressure tested OK and showed little peroxide sensitivity during training. The chat then turned to social topics with tips on the Australian places I should try to visit during my stay.

All was now approved to begin Gamma 201 static firings at Area5, which as part of the site commissioning process was an RDD/SR responsibility to execute and in this connection fate was about to nudge my career yet again.

As June 1958 threatened, our resident SARO mechanical engineer returned to UK with health problems so this department was thin, then just five days before the first firings, the RDD mechanical engineer who'd come out from High Down with me specifically to complete this task, resigned and flew back to UK!

As the sole RDD engineer remaining in Australia with any static firing exposure, his obligations fell to me and a rapid brainstorming session ensued before the reneging so and so jumped ship. In reality, the situation was not so serious as it might seem; by this time I was no stranger to the Gamma engine or its ground systems, also a laid back ASM representative from UK had arrived and a couple of useful DH chaps had attended firings at High Down.

But lessons learnt long ago in my Vickers days paid off once more; being an inquisitive at every opportunity, broadened experience and slips the shackles of convention. I bequeathed care of the instrumentation system to the DH guy who'd installed it alongside me.

With the DH team we moved the First Prototype rocket out to Pad 5A, hoisted it into the Gantry and secured it on the launcher. As explained elsewhere the rocket HTP tank was unusable so a commercial light alloy tank was set up on a temporary lattice tower beside the launcher, and rigged with an ex-rocket pressurising system as at High down. The auxiliary tank was flushed, blanked off and filled with demin water before being pressure tested and HTP trained.

The next two days were spent connecting, bleeding and calibrating pressure transducers, coupling up and testing the N2 purge plant, filling the kerosene tank and filling the start tank with demin water. When all was ready a Systems and Sequence (S&S) dress rehearsal got underway – this went well the second time around, once everyone understood what was expected. The peroxide tanks were drained of water and everything was now set for tomorrows firing.

MID JUNE 1958 – THE FIRST AREA 5 STATIC FIRING – By 09:30 the WRE HTP bulk carrier was on site and with our keen LO5 supervising, some 4000 lbs of peroxide went into the auxiliary tank without difficulty. Supported by a DH guy, I filled the ground start tank using a large polythene jug and funnel, having loaded it from the bulk carrier peroxide pump bleed off. Then came the more tricky task of to prime the long 2 inch braided flex hose leading up from ground start valve at ground level to the pull off connection up on the rockets engine bay; a dedicated rig for this job was yet to be devised. Again, with help from my DH aid, the pipe was held near vertical while the pull off coupling was unscrewed removed and I carefully fill it to the brim with HTP from my large polythene jug. With the pull off coupling refitted it was stowed into the engine receptacle ready for engine start up.

> Priming the Start Hose: – See Figure, A-16, Appendix 'A' for system diagram. An arrangement for start pipe priming was provisioned in time for the BK01 trial. A vented stowage point to park the engine end of the start hose was fashioned by mounting an engine pull off receptacle high on the launcher structure and piping its outlet away to the site peroxide drain system.

With the start hose plugged in the parking point and a transfer hose connected from HTP pump bleed off to the start tank fill plug, the engine start valve is opened to let peroxide flow until it appears at the parking point drain outlet.

The start hose is now full and the start valve is closed to maintain the prim. The excess start tank content is allowed to flow back down to the fill plug level, via the filling pump drain. Finally the fill point is capped off and the start hose remains in the parking stowage until transferred to the engine prior to firing.

Though it was winter, sunshine made working in the all-embracing PVC suits a hot business and we all lost many body pounds. After hosing down the pad area and disrobing, I did a final walk around checklist – Gas pressures, Auto Observer, Release jack safety pin etc., took leave of the LO5 and cleared away with our guys for a cleanup and commune with nature at the crew room before crossing to EC5 where, after a few words with the motor console and recorder guys, I handed the operations over to AOO5 and Sequence Officer to run the countdown.

Thrust chamber swing angles: The prototype angles were preset by opposing setscrews and as no electrons were involve the FSC console remained unmanned.

After much chit chat with Con1 and others the truncated 10 minute count down began and ran through without hitch, all four thrust chambers reached full pressure within a few seconds and shut down cleanly at +35 seconds as intended. All Engine Consol pressures had settled in their running zones without noticeable hesitation followed by an almost simultaneous transition to hot burning. Later at the launcher no damage other than the usual light flame marking of the efflux duct was evident.

Once HTP was removed and the area was washed down, all gas and electrics services were isolated the Gantry was closed up for the day.

I retrieved the Auto Observer film and drove back to Test Shop 2 to scan the H&B records and get them pencilled over.

There was concern about N2 purge pressure levels because H&B records for two chamber pressures hinted at a slight hedging as they began hot running, never the less spirits were high and the odd bottle of wine appeared at dinner that evening.

N2 purging – See Figure A-17, in Appendix 'A' for system diagram. During the engine start process; turbo pumps force high-pressure HTP through silver gauze catalyst packs at the head of each thrust chamber.

This process liberates large quantities of heat as each peroxide molecule divides into water (H2O) and oxygen (O), manifesting itself as oxygen rich superheated steam exceeding the kerosene flash point. To prevent kerosene entering the chamber ahead of establishing full steam pressure and to keep the fuel burner galleries entirely clear of peroxide products, a vigorous flow of high-pressure nitrogen is maintained through the fuel pathways, burner plate and out into each chamber.

The Fuel valve is an OR device that switches N2 flow to Fuel flow when HTP steam pressure has reached a preset value.

This process is reversed at engine shutdown when steam pressure falls as HTP feed ceases. Without such an arrangement, fuel detonation inside the kerosene burner galleries risks chamber destruction.

The N2 differential pressure between full flow and zero flow must suit the engine operating pressures correctly; N2 flow pressure must give adequate purging while its static pressure must not hinder fuel stop valve operation.

Tests revealed pipe losses between the Test Post regulator and test orifice simulating the engine, were causing an excessive pressure drop. With co-operation from WRE workshop group, the piping was shortened by rerouting and eased with swept bends to bring the zero flow and full flow pressures to acceptable levels.

Two further static firings were done to confirm the revised arrangement and to explore the duct cooling water flows; in conclusion, the Area 5 installation was approved for running Gamma 201 engines. The engine was dried out and the Prototype rocket returned to the TS2.

July 11,1958 I flew home by RAF Comet in five days and was the only BK passenger among twenty odd. I vaguely recall the route as Salisbury, Darwin, Changi, Ghan, Aden, Cyprus and Lyneham.

FIG 5–3   BLACK KNIGHT IN TEST SHOP 2 AT RANGE E
(Commonwealth of Australia)

WHILE the CATS AWAY – – – –   **6**

After a few days leave I returned to find a different set up at High Down. My old Measurements boss had moved on and been replaced by a guy from the Cowes stress office (!) who initially seemed vague on rocketry but proved to be a sound engineer. We were to become good social friends and close colleagues as I eventually rose to Chief RDD Trials Engineer as he advanced Deputy Chief RDD Engineer.

However, the management had covertly stolen "my" Measurements Section while I was abroad sorting out its business and squaring up several major company cock-ups. As Section deputy from the early days, I'd pioneered many capabilities under austere circumstances, lobbied hard for equipment and resources and developed an operational structure by formalising our routine duties. It seemed a shabby reward for spending four months away fixing serious Company oversights at Woomera but it served to recall two well known lessons: Out of sight is out of mind and Who you know trumps what you know but as events panned out, Lady Luck knew a trick or two! The Measurements fiasco put a solid block my promotion prospects via that route so I sought and was granted in October a transfer back to my old discipline of Flight Trials and operational testing.

By now, BK01 had already flown and BK03 was well advanced through the High Down acceptance process, so I was pencilled in as Flight Control System (FCS) engineer for BK 04, due on site sometime in December. The new role entailed qualifying and acceptance testing at High Down before preparation and launch trials at Woomera.

> *The next 13 years: Switching back to flight trials worked out well for me; it brought immense job satisfaction and took me around the World working alongside many accomplished and resourceful people. Over the years I enjoyed having a direct hand in launching eight Black Knights, four Black Arrows, three French Diamantes, six Falstaff solid propellant fireworks (– – – and a Partridge in a pear tree!!) As always, most good things have a downside; other than an occasional short course, further education for itinerant students with uncertain timescales was near impossible until the Open University materialised some years later. Similarly, as hinted earlier, promotion opportunities often fall victim to the 'out of sight' black hole and of equal importance, long-term female relationships became tricky to establish and harder still to maintain.*

Program variables played havoc with personal plans and my tolerant fiancé occasionally took issue when trials took priority, luckily she also recognised the advantage of long weekends and generous free time during thin trials periods.

"Between Times": R&D field trials are often spasmodic and I found it amusing to observe how RDD staff responded during slack periods. Those with narrow imaginations tended to bitch and moan while the inspired types pursued pet practical or intellectual interests. These were many, one guy filled the airwaves with his amateur radio chatter, and another bunch took up cliff abseiling until it was barred for fear losing too many staff! A further group built monster kites, which were hoisted nearly five hundred feet above High Down! I was able to build most of a Go-Kart during one such lull and on a later occasion designed and project managed the build of my first family home; these were good inventive periods when time allowed stimulating discussion among creative people.

Heading for Gantry 2 one sunny afternoon I heard bagpipes loud and clear from a nearby radio but as I turned onto the Promenade, there, high up on the hill stood a fully regaled Highlander facing the sea playing his pipes – he was a post grad apprentice who later gained a professorial chair at a well-founded university north of the border to research wave energy harvesting.

I often felt these "Between Times" as I called them, should be harnessed and applied to the cause, it just needed organising and modest funding but it was not to be until we reached the doldrums period between BK and BA some years later when this available talent was put to good use.

FLIGHT CONTROL SYSTEM ENGINEERING – My attention now turned to the FCS, its hardware and setting up processes. Compared to Red Dean and Red Rapier of my Vickers days, the BK hardware was very enchant – not a single transistor in sight, just power hungry thermionic valves. I guess the tight spend policy forced adaptation from earlier incarnations and compact packaging was not essential in a roomy rocket airframe – never the less, excess weight is lost velocity. Except for the hydraulic actuators and chamber angle sensors located in the engine bay, all FCS components resided on a light alloy fabricated tray resting on rails across the Electronics Bay, at the top of the rocket. The set up included two Reid & Sigrist fully gimballed displacement gyros of enormous size, almost of marine proportions! Despite moderate drift requirements and a modest flight acceleration field, these instruments often exceeded drift limits. Several superior alternatives existed but again the cost conservation hand had chosen from an earlier application.

High-tension DC voltage for thermionic valve electronics and AC excitation for angle pickoffs was derived via motor/generator powered from silver zinc rechargeable batteries. Low tension DC for thermionic heaters and gyro wheels was also sourced from similar batteries.

To avoid battery use during general testing and pre-launch warm up, shore-side DC power was routed into the rocket via an umbilical connector from lead acid batteries in a Test Post beside the launcher.

At minus 40secs in the launch sequence, on board DC loads were switched from external power to the internal batteries, which were then assessed ahead of umbilical ejection at minus 8secs.

All connections between electronic sub units followed conventional aircraft practice using point-to-point single core wiring and multi-pin connectors. Alas, the lack of experience or foresight had overlooked the need for to directly access to each electronic sub-unit to check amplifier gain and balance output settings. The current solution used RDD made "jumper break in boxes" between each sub-unit and the tray wiring – a practice prone to frequent pin mix-ups among the profusion of boxes and excessive unplugging of connectors – a real hindrance to diagnostic activities.

I opted for a radical remedy by replacing tall break in boxes with an intuitive scheme using a single 19" monitor panel that depicted the FCS "black box block diagram" shown in Figure A–18 in Appendix A. By placing single "Banana" sockets on a diagram line linking two black boxes, its function was immediately understood without tiresome references to drawings or pin idents. For isolating the inner and outer control loops for servo frequency response tests etc, the line from each gyro demodulator output was terminated by two separate banana sockets each side of an earth socket; the latter providing a convenient zero point while the outer sockets enabled inner outer control loops to linked when required. All the banana sockets were wired back via multi cored cable to a newly introduced multi pin "diagnostic" connector mounted on the FCS tray, which was permanently wired to each FSC sub unit. Our EEL design office agreed to this new facility once the logic was understood. (I've invariably found that informed engineers usually agree to logical requests when cogently argued) The new monitor panel allowed full FCS access without disturbing a single subunit and avoided the fearsome prospect of inter connection errors. Using site resources and scrounged components, two panels were prepared for the forthcoming UK and Australian trials. The new panel and a bank of recorder buffer units became standard equipment in all Gantries at the Electrics Bay level and were known as Control System Monitor Unit (CSMU). Under the guiding hand of later FSC engineers the CSMU grew into a very comprehensive test set.

Before live launch S&S checks, the CSMU diagnostic lead is replaced by a "Flight Link" plug that permanently liked all sub units for flight. To validate this hardware intrusion, an absolute sense test was evolved ('Rock and Roll' sense test) outlined below and detailed in Appendix A.

With the FCS and hydraulics powered up, the gyros are un-caged and the rocket is manually turned about the release jack ball through a small Pitch, Yaw and Roll angle while the resulting chamber movements are visually confirmed as corrective with respect to the line of fire. For this process, wind brace arms and anti torque lugs are released to let three technicians apply the required rotations; an upper clamp ring that abuts with gantry loading rollers prevents extreme rocket movement.

As stated earlier, BK01 had already flown successfully at Woomera – at least that was the initial conclusion; later analysis revealed that the flight termination system was triggered accidentally and destroyed the vehicle some 30 seconds before all burnt. BK01 used the S band transponder as the duplicate flight termination link and it had triggered on a false radar ghost signal to initiate breakup! Telemetry data confirmed the S band beacon as the culprit and later tests proved it to be prone to false reflection problems. To meet the need for two mutually redundant breakup radio links, a second Command Link receiver was introduced into the Electronics Bay for all subsequent flights.

Because the BK01 flight come close to optimum in all other respects and WRE had satisfied with their ground systems and flight safety arrangements, it was expected that the next firing (BK03) would endorse the design as fit for purpose. Planning for success, BK04 was assigned to release the first functional re-entry test body for a high-speed descent into the upper atmosphere – well that was the plan!

CONTRACTORS STANDARD PROCEDURES (CSP's) – These formal documents were required by WRE for all contractors Hazardous activities carried out at their establishments and formed part of a Trial Plan submitted to WRE ahead of each trial. They cited special precautions, tooling, test methods and the test results required. Each procedure was drafted and proven by RDD staff as an adjunct to High Down acceptance testing before passing on to DH for formatting, RAE/WRE approval and publication. BK01 & 02 trials had proven the utility of these documents in formalising methods, test gear and safety detail so RAE gradually extended them to all trial tasks at Woomera. From then on, creating and checking CSP's was a never-ending way of life for each RDD team member. Having enjoyed writing the original FCS, CSP pack, I became an ardent apologist of the system and drafted many documents for the FCS and Ordnance installations. Compared with to-days IT paradise where computers abound, originating and keeping CSP's current was a perpetual nightmare at High Down and Woomera. After several years struggling with typewriters and Gestetner stencil machines we eventually obtained a Xerox photocopier but charm, persistence and guile was essential to gain access to this locked away treasure!

CSP Drafting: These started out as informal affairs but extreme style variation and excessive technical detail got out of hand – until he was wised up, one author began by explaining how to don your overalls! Such Undue detail undermined operator culpability, blurred objectivity, created bulky documents and a plethora of amendments – remember, no digital word processors in these days.

To bring consistency, I spent much time redrafting and outlining many electrical procedures in consultation with DH and RAE to fix drafting rules. These assumed that users were trained and well rehearsed operators who merely needed an aid memoir for the hazards, sequence of actions and acceptable numeric values.

To illustrate the cynicism caused by excessive detail, I recall one mechanical engineer who'd spent some days writing the start-up procedure for a large trolley compressor used to pre-cool a payload system. He said, "Tell me why I've spent several days covering umpteen sheets of A4 to describe how this compressor should be powered up, when gangers up and down the country just shout "Paddy! Start the compressor" and the compressor starts up"!

"MY" BLACK KNIGHTS – This tongue in cheek claim merely reflects my close involvement with preparing and launching the eight Black Knight vehicles listed in Table 6/I below, the first two as the FCS engineer and the remainder as Trials Team Leader (Deputy Team Leader at Woomera).

TABLE 6/1 – "MY Black Knight's".

Vehicle	Flt No	Stages	Engine	Trial Objectives	Payload
1st Prot	N/A	N/A	201	5A Site Proofing	N/A
BK04	3	Single	201	Payload release	20° Steel cone + Tele
BK06	5	Single	201	Payload Test	10°/40° Ablate + Tape R
BK07	8	Single	201	Payload Test	10° High drag cone +Tele
BK09	7	Two	201+ Cuckoo I	Gaslight	12.5° Eroding cone + Tele
BK13	9	Single	201	Gaslight	10°/40° Eroding cone + beacon +
BK16	13	Two	301+ Cuckoo I	Dazzle	15° Copper cone + Tape R
BK19	18	Two	301+Cuckoo II	Dazzle	17° Copper ball + Tape R
BK21	17	Two	301+ Cuckoo II	Dazzle	15° Copper cone + Tape R

A detailed account of the High Down and Woomera trails relating to each of the above listed rockets is given in the following Chapters. The reader should bear in mind that by definition, one trial is very similar to the next and the repetitive content is prone to become boring. Each rocket trial is described in its launch order as listed above

FIG 7–1   BK01 on Pad 5A. (BK04 appeared similar but boasted a tidier Cannon umbilical connector)   *(Commonwealth of Australia)*

BK 04 TRIALS – HD & AREA 5   **7**

"My" first bird – First as FCS Eng.

TRIAL OBJECTIVE –
- First attempt at Payload detachment.
- First Head re-entry experiment.
- Further burn phase development.

BK04 BUILD –

This single stage Gamma 201 rocket duplicated BK03 in all respects except for the two diametrically sited single explosive bolts and multiple compression spring units set around the separation bay rim. Both explosive bolts were fired by a thrust sensing inertia switch and solid-state delay timer, which let the compressed springs push the Test Body clear. The Head was a 20° steel cone fitted with small solid fuel thrusters to pitch it over 180° and spin stabilise it about the roll axis for re-entry alignment. Several material specimens were carried on the conical surface to assess ablation behaviour, and a 465 MHz telemetry relayed thermal and dynamic behaviour until impact – see Fig A–1 in Appendix A.

BK04 at HIGH DOWN – Late Jan 1959 hardware began to trickle on site. With the FCS modified to avoid the BK01 structural vibration problems and my tidied up test gear as described earlier, setting up the system and functional testing it was settling down to a routine operation. Circuit wiring checks, followed by calibration of Laws relays, motor angle pickoff sensors and their micro-switches concluded the Prep Area airframe testing. Testing moved into the FCS laboratory where each electronic sub unit was set up and both displacement gyros were drift tested. My spare moments were spent brushing up the test CSPs; an ever-present task as these formalised procedures was extended to cover every aspect of the Woomera trial.

Functional testing at the gantry progressed with little technical difficulty, good servo frequency responses were recorded and no evidence of structural resonance could be detected or induced – I recall it being very cold at the Gantry; we worked wrapped in Duffel coats, scarves, woolly hats and gloves and used all the photo floodlights as heaters to keep warm.

STATIC FIRING S&S TEST: This test entailed patching FCS signal data points at the CSMU monitor panel through cathode follower buffer units to the Recorder Room instruments and calibrating the voltage sensitivity of each recorder channel. A full FCS functional test followed with pressurised hydraulics and preset angular demand signals from the CSSU (Control System signal Unit) sited in the Equipment Centre. The FCS was now ready for the Systems and Sequence test, which was a full-scale systems dress rehearsal, carried out one day before each engine firing.

The FCS presented correctly during the S&S and its dynamic behaviour was verified by completing a detail recorder trace analysis.

STATIC FIRING: Following an FCS spot check next morning, the Mechanical crew finalised the engine support systems and had the HTP loaded and cleared away before Lunch. The firing sequence began about 13:30 and ran to +35secs. I gathered that all systems performed well but the Engine guys had concerns about mixture ratio anomalies, poor propellant loading accuracy and the absence of in flight data (the RAE was perfecting level sensing probes to signal discrete HTP tank content levels).

When the noisy engine drying out task ended, the FCS "Flight plug" was fitted and the FCS sensing was demonstrated by a Rock & Roll test as detailed in Appendix A.

Each system was now readied for EMC testing. Non-Haz internal batteries were installed and 30sec load tested before closing up the Electronic Bay. "Feel" checks on chambers and structure for evidence of physical disturbance were done while each electrical system and device was energised and switched to "internal" power before Head separation was initiated. Both explosive bolt circuits were monitored throughout the test for transient pickup using Cossor oscilloscopes. While scrutiny of these tests would be improved with specialised recording facilities, no gross RF or other EM disturbances were encountered.

(DISPATCH TO AUSTRALIA): With the rocket structure returned to the Prep Area, a physical QA audit was done in support of the weighing and balancing procedures. Hardware was crated up for transfer to TS2 by Bristol Air freighter early Mar '59.

First week Mar'59 saw our team of four RDD engineers and myself at RAF Lynham scheduled to reach Adelaide in six days.

BK04 AT WOOMERA: – Monday pm, DH had already unpacked and set BK04 on a floor trolley in Test Shop 2, see Fig 5–3 above. After renewing a few friendships I got stuck into FCS lab setup. BK 03 had yet to fly and was still in preparation out at Area5. Consequently our TS4 phase was worked with a skeleton DH crew – all nice and peaceful.

With two trials now under their belt, the DH team were clearly becoming organised, the Control Lab was nicely laid out with our new "Monitor" panel, all of which aided a smooth FCS checkout. However, gyroscope selection was a problem, of six units held; only two were inside drift limits, two were marginal and two were unacceptable. Checkout at the launcher was straightforward and uneventful, the inner loop frequency responses and related tests shadowed the High Down results.

(STATIC FIRING): S&S check went well and the engine firing next day also appeared to go well with an engine shutdown at +35 seconds.

> *A Steaming Engine Bay: After normal engine shutdown at +35 seconds, significant steam continued to issue from the engine bay despite repeated water deluging so an HTP plumbing failure had to be assumed. If HTP decomposition elevated local temperatures above the kerosene seal limit a potential fire hazard would ensue so the HTP tank must be emptied. A dump hose was always laid from launcher to the water lagoon ready for such a contingency but it would need three mechanics at the launcher for about 5 minutes to connect it to the rocket.*
>
> *The plan was OK'd within our team and put to AOO5 who referred it to Range Control. They passed it to the Chief Safety Officer (CSO) out on a golf course 300 miles away in Adelaide!*
>
> *When the AOO5's phone ring some 2.5 hours into the incident, he surprisingly passed it to me saying the CSO wanted to talk! (Our dealings during the First Prototype firings must have struck a cord with him). After detailing the situation and the apparent stability, we reviewed the plan and who'd be taking part before he spoke with AOO5. The LO5 and nominated crew were released to the launch pad to fit the dump hose and return.*
>
> *After deluging to cool things down, inspection revealed a cracked HTP stop valve casing on one engine. This incident spawned the creation of a remote HTP dump facility controlled from EC5, which SR designed, manufactured and had installed for the next firing.*

Extended heat soakage dictated the engines return to UK for a strip inspection at ASM. When dried out and returned to TS2, the engine bay was detached, crated and dispatched to UK along with most UK team members. Several guys including myself opted to stay as tourists until the new engine returned, so three of us went opal mining.

> *Opal Mining: Some 70 miles north of Woomera brings you to the Andamooka opal fields where a lifestyle unique to pioneer prospectors the world over, began a few generations back. Inhabitants lived a meagre and rough existence, often dwelling in hand dug caves, their days spent toiling with pick and shovel in small low crawl tunnels accessed down narrow vertical shafts.*

Opal occurs in fragile "podge" layers that randomly form in gypsum seams and the first prospectors usually discovered it where the seam broke surface on hillsides. These easier 'finds' were soon exhausted and further access required shafts to be sunk from higher up the hillside.

The area is now pock marked by hundreds of grave like shaft holes among spoil heaps, giving the place of a moonscape appearance. As the workings progress, prime opal 'finds' are removed at the work face and the remaining spoil is hoisted out and dumped in heaps where it is reworked in two phases: Noodle screening was done by the claim owner before he abandoned it for Fossicking by any one with a miners right from the state government (this may have changed under the 1994 Fossicking Act).

As operations moved higher up the hills so shafts grew deeper and became more arduous to sink but market prices also grew until it was viable to use powered machinery and dynamite.

Modern operations now have very large backers and co-operatives who cut drift entrances with full height tunnels and have built specialised for Noodling machinery. These days the area boasts a thriving tourist element with underground motels and many opal retailers.

With two mates, I spent five days there in April '59, staying with three new Australians originating from Austria. They were the first to take a bulldozer with pneumatic power tooling up there to seek their fortune. Within months they realised that sinking shafts for others was more profitable than mining so they added dynamite to their inventory. To house their machinery they'd erected a large corrugated iron shed, ubiquitous to the Aussie Outback, and it was there we laid our sleeping bags beside a giant Caterpillar bulldozer to yarn the evenings away over a few cool beers from the kerosene refrigerator. The entire stay was rugged and relaxing and stood in stark contrast to the formal safety rules used at Woomera. We watched dynamite being fired in six drillings spaced out on a shaft floor, each with a short burning fuse (kept short because of expense)! On the bases that each man would look after himself the firer merely asked if all the machinery was safe before lighting each fuse and climbing up to safety himself. As each shot blew, the firer smiled or cursed as the sound told him of a good deep penetration or an upward blowout. On this occasion only five shots fired so I asked what happens now? His reply was "Finish my fag then pop down and pull it out". He'd never last long at AREA5. These guys had security clearance to use Woomera village for stores, fuel and medical services.

Mid May'59: The refurbished engine arrived and after refitting followed a repeat of the Test Shop check out phase, which took three days. FSC preparation and servo testing at the launcher ran without a hitch.

(STATIC FIRING): See Table A/2 of Appendix A for countdown timing.

A good S&S test was followed by a satisfactory static firing.

Preparation for Launch was now the aim and my task was to oversee removal of test leads, final fitting of the flight plug, repeating the overall sense test and fitting of internal battery packs. After a satisfactory battery 30sec load test and an Electronics Bay checklist, the bay was closed up and pressure tested. Many other tasks such as filling with kerosene, charging the hydraulics, topping up gas bottles and fitting the engine flight nut progressed in parallel.

(S&S FOR LAUNCH): Internal batteries were again 30sec load tested. Sequence unit and interlock override switches in EC5 were crosschecked and sealed and all Stop Action services were proven. This S&S exercise would include all WRE range elements and their operators – an extensive array of equipments and personnel to be co-ordinated.

Initially the S&S sequence ran perfectly through the manual section and the –120sec Auto sequence followed smoothly until –8secs when the umbilical plug failed to eject. While this item had often played up in past, this time failure of the uncage gyro interlock circuit prevented plug ejection. The fault was narrowed down to one gyro but with no serviceable spares available and moonrise only a few days away, another long postponement was on the cards. Work began to wrap things up by draining the kerosene, removing the Payload and the flight batteries.

> *Open Heart Gyro Surgery:* *An in situ drift test at the launcher proved that both gyros did uncage without hesitation but the interlock loop from one unit appeared resistive, suggesting that its signalling contacts were at fault. On this evidence the FCS team proposed the unorthodox step of servicing the wayward gyro in situ at the Launcher. The process of removing a gyro casing and contact cleaning was demonstrated to the OISC in TS2 laboratory and he agreed to try the option provided that he witnessed the process, personnel were limited to two other individuals and still air conditions prevailed.*
>
> *On Gantry level 'E' the FCS tray was extracted, the casing of the errant item was lifted and its cage/uncage action demonstrated to be sound and repeatable. The contacts were cleaned using a watchmaker's burnish, the cage action and interlock function was shown to be OK and the instrument closed up and replaced in the Electronics Bay. Further drift tests and a "Rock and Roll" sense check revalidated the overall installation and we were hot to trot again! A quenching diode was replaced in the ground circuit in case it was failing to nail current spike induced from the ground relay coil inductance.*

Preparation then hummed along as the kerosene tank was refilled and a refreshed Payload was installed.

With new flight batteries fitted and checked a second S&S check was successfully completed and the final launch preparation begun.

My final obligation of the day was attending the LO5 team as they fitted Payload explosive bolt detonators and break up catalyst charges. LO5 cleared the launcher area and armed the break up circuit. This circuit remains safe after arming until the instant of move switches close at lift off.

(LAUNCH): My launch station in EC5 was alongside my DH opposite number at the FCS console. After their preamble Con1 and the AOO5 began the manual countdown at minus 30 minutes with transponder pre-heat. All other electronic systems including the FCS were progressively powered up and the Range verified good telemetry reception. By −4 minutes all operators had closed their readiness switches, which permitted Con1 to initiate the −120sec automatic sequence.

Each event in this phase is interlocked to the previous event; its execute time being selected by the EC5 sequence unit but barred if its preceding event fails to return its confirmation signal.

The engine ground start valve opened at zero time and engine burn commenced; hydraulic pressure rose to centralise all chamber angle and close their zero degree micro switches, when all thrust chamber pressure switches closed they opened a bomb slip that extracted the engine start hose. This final action opened the release jack to give BK04 its freedom!

As the rocket lifts, a loop through one rip plug breaks to signal Instant of Move to all range operators that flight has commenced.

The guidance pilots with their supervisor and telescope tracker are located inside EC5, therefore a quiet discipline must be maintained until their task ends at All Burnt, around +150 seconds. During this time, flight progress may be gleaned from the EC5 telemetry displays and intercom traffic.

BK04 LAUNCH: Lift off occurred at 22:34.5 hours on 11 June 1959. The engine reached its design burnout velocity at +145 sec without evidence of cold thrusting; guidance and control performance was good. Apogee reached 500 miles and good telemetry data was returned throughout. This first re-entry experiment with spin-stabilized separating head was successful. The head re-entered (200,000 feet) at 11,740 ft/sec, telemetry worked through to impact, excepting for a short period at re-entry when ionization interrupted RF. Recovery of the head together with ablation test patches, were achieved.

1959, June 26: Four months after leaving UK, I was back on the Comet bound for RAF Lynham. After a few days at work to sort paperwork etc, I took a week off to mooch around London, then back to the Island for a bit of outstanding boat maintenance.

BK06 TRIALS – HD & AREA 5 | **8**

"My" Second Bird – as FCS Eng

TRIAL OBJECTIVE –

- Repeat of BK05 experiment with high penetration 10°/40° double cone Test Body.
- First use of armoured tape recorder to capture Test Body internal data.
- Payload separation time delay increased to counter engine thrust decay.

BK06 BUILD –

Because BK05 exhibited a severe thrust tail off at "All Burnt" the spent airframe had collided with and wrecked the Test Body Tele aerial, which resulted in a total loss of all internal data. BK06 duplicates BK05 in all particulars except the Test Body separation delay time was extended to 8 seconds.

The Durestos clad Test Body included a drogue parachute to minimise impact damage and pyrotechnic flash units to assist post "All Burnt" tracking acquisition. An armoured tape recorder to log Test Body internal data replaced the usual Telemetry method.

BK06 at HIGH DOWN –

Vehicle hardware arrived on site at the end of August '59, with a planned dispatch by end of September. From the FCS standpoint, this trial held few surprises. All subsystem checks through Qualification to Acceptance testing followed the regular routine and all test results met design requirements. Payload integration and mutual RFI checks were also straightforward and acceptable. After weighing, balancing and packing the vehicle, I made the journey to Woomera once again along with our four RDD team members.

BK06 at WOOMERA –

Test Shop 2 preparation began last week in September 1959 and adhered to what was now a well-established pattern. However, the gyroscope situation again concentrated our minds because only four of the six units were inside acceptable drift rates.

> *Different end games: High Down and Woomera carry out similar tasks on similar hardware with the same diligence and integrity but the former venue always finished up with intact hardware for repeat testing whereas the launch trial ends in a one shot unrepeatable event.*

On occasion, venues lost sight of each other's priorities as they grappled with their own technical issues but what could be irksome at High Down might be a showstopper at Woomera. Such a situation arose when high drift gyros began arriving regularly at TS2.

To ease early supply problems, High Down had permanently held four drifty units for home use and sent the rest direct from maker to user at Woomera. This had three outcomes – High Down was never hindered by drifty gyros, flight units never underwent an ex-factory test before reaching TS2 and faulty gyros became a headache exclusive to Woomera. This state of affairs persisted until DH took the ball directly to the gyro maker who was unaware of any problem. RDD closed this loophole by introducing a defect reporting system to manage all hardware and procedure faults arising at both venues, with a quality team at High Down to rigorously supervise and vet the process.

(STATIC FIRING): It was now autumn and woolly jumper time out at the launch pad; like most desert areas freezing nights are often followed by frosty mornings. The FCS servo tests, S&S check and static firing all went to plan and good results were obtained from all the FSP flight hardware.

Preparation for the live firing was held for several days by high winds and a sandstorm of which we had been forewarned. As a precaution, all vulnerable rocket and gantry test gear areas were carefully cocooned with polythene sheeting and adhesive tape and no serious damage was sustained, just heaps of sand to be cleared away before unwrapping things.

The FCS "Flight Plug" were fitted and verified by a Rock & Roll sense test in accordance with Appendix A. Following internal battery installation I was free to eyeball the tasks being carried out by Telemetry and Mechanical guys. With much leg pulling, the ASM rep completed his 'onerous' task of fitting the "Flight Nut", which toggled the engine start/stop solenoid to remain latched open during flight.

(LAUNCH): A faultless S&S check was achieved before lunch and the rest of the day was taken up with propellant loading, gas bottle charging and final check lists as hatch covers and service panels were closed and secured.

After taking dinner at Kooly we returned to prepare the Gantry for roll back once the LO5 team had armed the payload firing circuits and inserted breakup charges.

Is an armed rocket still safe? Yes, the rockets Breakup and Payload separation circuits embody dynamic intercepts that stay open until Instant of Move in the former case and 5g is exceeded in the latter case. This arrangement ensures that final arming and attendant procedures remain safe until the lift off occurs.

The release jack safe pin was pulled and the pad was cleared for LO5 and his team to arm the Breakup system.

As the evening wore on it grew uncomfortably cold at the Launcher so those of us destined for EC5, stopped at the crew room for a warming brew before taking up our firing positions.

The actual countdown took some time to get under way as various Range sections checked in and the usual last minute hold for a cloud report was obtained. The 28min manual sequence ran down to the −120sec auto countdown and on to engine light up without hesitation for a good lift off.

BK06 LAUNCH – Lift off was at 21:21hrs on 30 October 1959. AUW 13095lbs. A good guidance phase accompanied a good engine performance; all burnt occurring at +147 secs. Trajectory was nominal and a re-entry velocity of' 11,220 ft/sec being achieved at 200,000 ft. Apogee of 450 miles was attained. Even with the extended separation delay, pronounced thrust decay again caused a Test Body collision. The resulting impact deployed the pyrotechnic flashes and parachute on the way up instead during descent. The Head tape recorder functioned correctly and recorded separation and re-entry. The intact tape cassette and eroded ablating cone were recovered. So this trial was a qualified success.

> *Thrust Decay:* Like some earlier flights, ragged shutdown at All Burnt had allowed the spent rocket to catch up and nudge the Test Body.
>
> Gamma 201 engines are four totally independent propellant feed and thrust chamber pathways, each regulated by fixed flow orifices that cannot not compensate for thrust chamber or other in flight variables. Added uncertainties about tank volume calibrations and the earlier OISC's to favour some cold thrusting to use every ounce of propellant, made a clean zero thrust cut off chancy.
>
> A static firing shut down is a cleanly defined process where all four HTP stop valves are closed simultaneously by the Start/Stop solenoid valve, and kerosene flow is snapped off the N2 purging action. In flight "All Burnt" just comes about randomly as each of the four engine systems run dry sequentially. Without a purged shutdown the risk of chamber popping or even exploding due to hot residue propellant mixing is almost certain to generate small and ragged vehicle accelerations. The process presents a dilemma, if Test Body release delay is too short, collision must occur, if it is too long, directional accuracy must suffer. Perhaps a more energetic Test Body separation impulse device is needed.

After this six week launch trial I returned to UK with the team in 23 Nov 1959 and stole a weeks leave before facing up to the grindstone.

FIG 8–1 BK03 ON PAD 5A AS EVENING DRAWS NIGH with distant EC5.

(Commonwealth of Australia)

GASLIGHT & DAZZLE 9

By now the firing program had gathered sufficient re-entry data to meet the Blue Streak design requirements, just two further flights: a high drag geometry and a deep penetration geometry were planned. The future of BK had begun to look gloomy for some time but an exciting new research prospect appeared over the horizon.

It transpires that BK firings to date had revealed two hitherto unexplored physical re-entry features. The first effect appeared in the rocket engine wake as it passed up through the upper atmosphere, and the second was present in the Test Body wake as it re-entered the atmosphere; both effects offered possible methods for detection and defence against hostile ICBM transits.

- The archaic S Band radar used to guide BK repeatedly returned unique echoes from the engine efflux not readily seen with modern higher frequency radars.
- Each Test Body emitted a re-entry spectrum that was totally defined by it's construction materials.

To explore these phenomenon quickly, Britain, US, Australia and Canada collectively set up two consecutive programmes: four "Gaslight" firings using readily available ground observation instruments were to precede ten "Dazzle" firings when more sophisticated US ground instruments had been installed at Woomera.

The re-entry speed of BK would be increased by adding a downward firing second stage – See details Appendix 'A'. Additionally, to meet the specified urgency for obtaining data, the firing rate would be significantly increased, meaning that manufacture, testing and firing facilities would be upgraded accordingly.

High Down received a second preparation area and additional laboratory space to relieve current overcrowding of the FCS, Telemetry and Data Analysis disciplines. Similarly, the congested recorder room was moved into a larger underground space and given a major facelift to increase capacity, reliability and enable quick and reliable cross patching between test sites. The second launch pads (5B and No1) at Woomera and High Down were completed and commissioned and each Equipment Centre and the High Down Blockhouse received switch over patch capability to work two test sites. EC5 recorder installations were also equipped with cross patching and TS2 workspace at Woomera was enlarged.

All these site changes and the construction of a Second Stage BK disrupted the already planned launch program by about three months and revised the launch vehicle allocation. BK08 and BK09 became flight proving rounds for the new two stage configuration while BK07 and BK13 remained as single stages to fly the outstanding Head geometries and complete engine development issues like overheating, thrust decay and propellant usage. With duplicate launch pads now available, BK08 & BK07 followed by BK09 & BK13 were each paired as parallel trials. BK10 & 11 were already built and equipped to do Blue Streak radio system pull through trials for WRE tracking, flight safety and telemetry facilities prior to that projects début firings, and were set-aside until ELDO plans matured.

IS THIS A PROMOTION? Without any serious domestic ties at the time, the RDD Chief Engineer suggested I put my three-year BK trials experience to use as a Team Leader (no mention of a financial advantage!). I opted to prep BK07 and BK09 at High Down in March/April with the launch trials in June and July. Alas, events dictated otherwise when in May, BK08 failed to properly detach its second stage just a week after the RDD team and I arrived at Woomera. To reduce the impact of this mishap on the Gaslight program, the RAE decided to launch BK09 ahead of BK07.

> *Deputy Team Leader: As stated earlier, to provide in field experience ahead of their upcoming Blue Streak activities the DH Company were contracted to man Black Knight launch operations at Woomera. To provide knowledge updating for each Woomera launch trial, the RDD team (Saunders Roe Team Leader with several specialist engineers) charged with shepherding a rocket vehicle through the High Down acceptance trial, was co-opted to the Woomera Launch team. At Woomera, the RDD Team Leader became Deputy (DTL) to the DH Team Leader and each specialist engineer became advisers to the relevant DH section leaders. In practice, the DTL focussed on co-ordinating preparation of the rocket hardware in detail while the Team Leader dealt with overall and exceptional matters, staff management and external interface issues.*

<u>BK08:   THE BEWITCHED ROCKET:</u> The BK Type Proving Vehicle for Gaslight and Dazzle two-stage configuration.

While I took no active part in the trial, I am compelled to include an account of the most bizarre trial in the entire Black Knight history. Additionally I enjoyed watching its re-entry alongside the WRE Recovery Crew beside the predicted impact point.

The rocket vehicle reached Woomera in mid February and was still there as our team arrived with BK 07 and 09, nearly two months later. A weary crew told of their trying experiences and the bewitched nature of their chunk of hardware, which had so nearly caused a catastrophe.

No1 STATIC FIRING – Manually stopped due to P2 chamber over pressure.

No2 STATIC FIRING – Spontaneous shut down at +27secs. Attributed to rip plug chatter, engine function was deemed acceptable (*Was this the onset of Y1 bootstrap problem seen later*).

FIRST LAUNCH ATTEMPT – Sequence ran correctly, engine ignited on time but shut down within seconds for no obvious reason. A launcher inspection team were astounded to find the start pipe had ejected and the release jack jaws wee wide open, everything else being correct. Event recorder analysis confirmed all events had functioned correctly and on time, stop action had not been initiated and the IoM signal had flickered ON indicating the rocket had momentarily lifted before engine shut down. On the spot investigation concluded the "Engine Start/Stop Valve" had not been latched-up in the flight mode yet the "Flight Nut" was correctly fitted. (Was this the same Y1 bootstrap problem encountered later?)

> *The Engine Start/Stop Valve:* The aborted launch symptoms suggested a latch up failure of the Start/Stop solenoid valve. The engine start up cycle would begin normally when the shore side "Start" voltage opened The Start/Stop vale and the ground start HTP source was admitted to the engine system. When chamber thrust was sufficient, all pressure switches closed to eject the start-hose and open the release jack.
>
> As the rocket lifted, the braking rip plugs removed the shore side "Start" voltage from the Start/Stop valve causing it to close without its latch-up facility. This action vented all four HTP stop valves, which shut down all thrust chambers.
>
> A full description of the Start/stop solenoid valve and its workings is given in Fig A–14, Appendix A. This incident exposed a hitherto unrealised flaw regarding engine start and release jack timings. Before this incident, shore-side "Start" voltage was applied to the Start/Stop valve "Open" solenoid at zero time and held until +35 secs as required for Static Firing timing. For all future live firings, the "Open" solenoid was voltage reduced to a 2sec pulse at –4secs and release jack arming was inhibited until +4secs, giving an unlatched valve a 6sec window to drop out and safely shut down the engine.

Application of ground start HTP remained at zero time to retain the normal engine light up time base. A scan of CSPs revealed only one stop valve function test was done: a) without the "Flight Nut", and b) during the test shop phase.

Luckily, the resulting lift displacement was less than that needed to disengage the wind brace arms, else the Rocket would have toppled over! Similarly, had the failure sequence occurred with a 301 engine and its retracting release jack, the outcome would have been total destruction – unthinkable visions of some early V2 and US on launcher disasters become vividly to mind.

The "Engine Start/Stop Valve" was replaced and a further static firing was done.

No3 STATIC FIRING with new Stop/start valve – All Y2 pressures rose very slowly.

SECOND LAUNCH ATTEMPT – Auto stop action at +10secs. No combustion pressure interlock, assumed due to Y1 failing to bootstrap. Strip inspection of Y1 self-feed system failed to reveal any reason.

No4 STATIC FIRING – With start tank pressure increased from 350 to 450psi, Y1 took 3sec to begin self-feed.

No5 STATIC FIRING – Repeat of previous firing, Y1 failed to self-feed, Y1 system examined again but nothing was found to explain why.

No6 STATIC FIRING – Repeat of previous firing, start pipe ejected at +10 secs; Y1 was not self-feeding so it stopped running.

The engine was removed and sent to Ansty for examination but the only report I've been able to unearth offered no explanation for the behaviour.

Sanity returned to this trial with the replacement engine; a super static and live firing followed but the BK08 gremlin was alive and well because the second stage failed to separate properly. A truly desperate trial that drove the OISC at one point to telex RAE saying, "What am I to do with this most unfortunate rocket?"

BK07 TRIAL at HIGH DOWN | **10**

'My' Third Bird – First as TL

TRIAL OBJECTIVES –

- High drag Test Body using a bluff 10" radius heat shield nose on 10° frustrum.
- Test Body heat transfer and dynamic data retrieval via 465MHz telemetry.
- Kerosene run-out sensing.
- Fin pod lamps for visual tracking beyond all burnt.
- Revised anti slosh baffle in HTP tank.
- Detection of base bleed airflow cessation.
- Establish engine bay thermal environment.
- Flight-test of a thrust augmenter experiment.
- UA Experiments: Geiger counter, Scintillation counter and Sporadic E probe.

BK07 BUILD –

Was similar to previous single stage Gamma 201 vehicles plus additional equipment listed below for the trial objectives listed above:

- Kerosene end: Telemetry probe fitted in tank sump as a calibrated near end point.
- Thrust cessation investigation: To establish engine bay thermal profile a number of pressure and thermal sensors placed at strategic points around the bay to map local conditions.
- Base bleed airflow cessation: Six large engine bay bleed holes were closed off by inward opening, lightly sprung doors, each with telemetered proximity sensors.
- Thrust Augmenter: (See Figs A–25 & A–26, Appendix 'A'). A low cost experiment to explore thrust harvesting at higher altitudes. A 2ft tall titanium cylindrical cuff or skirt, fitting around the engine bay was arranged to descend below thrust chamber exit plane on pre-tensioned guide wires, late in the burn phase. Constriction of the over expanded exhaust plume by with the titanium skirt might extract extra thrust. Reflective heat shielding was added around the thrust chambers to limit thermal reflection back into the engine.
- Upper Atmosphere Experiments (UAE): To extend BK's utility and support general research, universities were invited to fly lightweight experiments.

These were located inside the separation bay where their data output utilised telemetry channels that became redundant from main stage functions at All Burnt.

BK07 AT HIGH DOWN –

The TL role: Extended my personal interest to all features of BK07 preparation and testing, which I took to mean close attention to all systems activities, be they in laboratory, Prep Area, Gantry or elsewhere, and at the risk of occasionally being a thorn in the side of the odd sensitive individual!

All hardware including Test Body was on site mid March 1960. The standard Prep Area checks progressed without undue difficulty or delay except for the additional engine bay instrumentation that took almost two days to clear due to sensor numbers and poor accessibility.   Each sensor was spot calibrated, position mapped, photographed and identity traced back through to the telemetry histogram.

Each base bleed door was easily fitted by quarter turn 'Dzus' fasteners and telemetered by non-contact reed switches.

Surprisingly the thrust augmenter hardware proved easy to assemble and repeatedly deployed without fail, a surprising performance for such a "Hairy" looking device.

(GANTRY 1): With the Rocket erected, propellant tank sight glasses and level sensors were calibrated and the HTP tank pressurisation system was functionally exercised.

Loading propellants: The volumetric capacity of each tank is calibrated by logging tank liquid level versus filling pump meter readings, using demineralised water or kerosene. Short removable sight glasses sized to measure the upper portion of each tank are fitted and calibrated during these tests and used again for every propellant fill. Fluid density and temperatures is spot checked at the start and end of each run. The telemetry level sensing probes are also calibrated during this process.
Using the fill pump metering as a calibration source was a worry because fluid density, viscosity and pressure head are all variables known to influence the linearity of a simple impeller pump. See Appendix A, Section11 for more detail.

Frequency response of each thrust chamber servo and the overall stability margins were tested and found satisfactory. No evidence of structural feedback could be detected or induced with propellant tanks empty, full and or pressurised.

The FCS overall sense test with "Flight Plug" fitted was carried as detailed in Appendix A was shown to produce corrective servo responses.

The Thrust Augmenter was installed and held retracted by two diametrically positioned bomb slips, several deployments were successfully carried out before it was secured in the retracted position.

The Telemetry team now took tenure of the vehicle to set pressure transducer rest levels and do the tedious trace audit from all measurement sources back to the histogram display in the Equipment Centre.

This elaborate task took time and required the participation of all vehicle systems techs to apply dynamic stimulus at each telemetered source; two voltage-scaling anomalies were unearthed and corrected.

Connection and calibration of the static firing ground based pressure transducers and the Auto observer that had been in hand for several days, was concluded. The N2 purge and engine start system static and flow rates were set up, vehicle gas bottles were charged and propellant transfer rigs were readied for use. All test cell cameras and flood lighting were harmonised and tested.

Our Safety Officer team ensured the reservoir water level was adequate, the fire-fighting system was functional, the Downs clearing party were told off and arrangements for the visitor influx was attended to.

(STATIC FIRING S&S DAY): – See Table A/2 of Appendix A for sequence times. This dress rehearsal exercises personal, systems and procedures prior to static firing by running a full count down with a dry rocket and a water filled ground start tank. Today's test was successfully achieved by 12:15hrs and a firing was set for 14:00 hrs next day, a convenient time for the usual RAE and other visitors to travel down to the Island.

Final tasks for the day were filling the rocket kerosene tank and inspection of recorded S&S results.

(STATIC FIRING DAY): Measurements team loaded their recorders and cameras and spot calibrated each recorder channel. The Safety Officer had deployed his Downs clearing parties from early morning and his on site team supported the HTP filling activities at the launcher. By midday all rocket gas bottles had been topped up to 4000psi, the rocket had been filled with 3200lbs of HTP. Ground start HTP tank and the start hose were filled and primed   When all was washed down and the pump rig removed, a top to bottom checklist inspection was made before all personnel except a safety watch were stood down for lunch.

After a final spot check of all gas pressures, the HTP tank was sealed, the engine start pipe was plugged in as Siet2 was cleared finalised checklists were passed to the Safety Officer in his Blockhouse and I headed up to the Equipment Centre.

After a word with the console observers and the OISC, I passed operations over the Safety Officer who gathered in all readiness reports before arming Site 2 firing circuits and clearing the Sequence Officer to run the 30-minute countdown.

Following the 28 min manual power up of all rocket electrical systems, the 120sec auto sequence ran cleanly to time zero; all thrust chamber pressures rose to hot running level by +2 to 3secs and shut down cleanly at +35secs.

First reports confirmed a successful burn subject to analysis of recorded results, assessment of propellant usage and a physical inspection of each thrust chamber.

When all propellants were drained, the engine drying out crew began their noisy overnight vigil – a 20-hour exercise that pumped hot air through the engine HTP piping and catalyst packs.

(RFI/EMC TESTS) – Over the past few days all Internal and Haz battery packs were packed and charged, fuse head "puffers" for simulating explosive detonators were wired up in the Pre Area.

A fully prepared Test Body was installed and functionally proven as serviceable. Command Link receivers (with flight aerials), and an S Band transponder were installed and functionally tested. All Non Haz and Haz internal batteries were installed and puffers" were connected in place of the Test Body explosive bolts and continuity tested. When all access panels were closed up to offer representative aerial ground planes, the Haz batteries and "puffers" were armed.

RFI/EMC testing begun by progressively powering up of each electrical system in discrete steps, during which each vehicle and Test Body system, and each separation "puffer" was monitored for evidence of electrical pickup. As stated before, this time eating activity will require rationalising to cope with the proliferation of Haz circuits if as hinted BK were to get an upper stage. Finally, bridging and releasing the thrust sensing inertia switches fired off the Test Body separation puffers. On this occasion all operations passed off correctly and no evidence of interference was encountered.

Over the past few weeks the Data Analysis office and RAE engineers had been busy reviewing each of the rocket system performance records to assess BK07 fitness for launch trials. The formal RDD/RAE fit for purpose meeting it was agreed the BK 07 should be released to Woomera to commence launch trials.

The Test Body and Main Stage were removed to the Prep Area were the latter was balanced, weighed, crated for air freighting to TS2 Woomera first week of May 1960.

The team and I now regrouped to carry out the BK09 High Down trial before taking it and BK07 for consecutive launch trials at Woomera.

BK09 TRIALS – HD & AREA 5　　　　　**11**

'My' Forth Bird – Second as TL

TRIAL OBJECTIVES:

- Second BK two-stage proving flight.
- Test Body - 12.5°ablating cone with armoured tape recorder.
- Second firing in the Gaslight series.
- UA Experiments: Sporadic E probe.

BK09 BUILD –

This two stage Gamma 201 vehicle was a duplicate of BK08 in all respects except that the upper stage separation system now embodied full redundancy (seemingly inspired by the BK08 failure but was a long-standing upgrade installed before BK08 had flown).

STAGE 2 – The GA and operation of the upper stage is detailed in Figs, A–8 & A–9, Appendix 'A'.

> _Explosive bolts_ – Hitherto, BK vehicles used single ended explosive bolts severed by a single detonator and single firing circuit. As described in Appendix 'A', using double-ended bolts with twin cutting detonators, one above and one below the structure separation line enhanced reliability. The entire firing circuit, batteries, arming and initiation components were also duplicated above and below the separation line and isolated from each other such that operation of either detonator in each explosive bolt would effect structural separation. See Fig A–23 Appendix 'A'.
>
> _Inertia switches_ – These devices were used for two purposes: sensing cessation of engine thrust and dynamically arming ordnance circuits. Previous BK's used single switches crudely mounted on the airframe by a single simple "P" clip around their cylindrical casing. The revised arrangement as described in Appendix 'A' now use duplicated switches housed in accurately machined clamps as a sub-assembly with pre-wired, plug ended fly leads. This arrangement allowed each switch to be installed and wired up in laboratory conditions before fitting to the rocket structure. See Fig A– 22 Appendix 'A'.

BK09 AT HIGH DOWN – All hardware except the Test Body had arrived on site by April 1960, for a planned airlift to TS2 early May. With the Second Stage came a proliferation of ordnance hardware, firing circuitry and extra handling requirements.

Only mass simulated explosive stores were used at High Down, so qualification focussed on proving component interfaces and accessibility along with electrical continuity, insulation, cross circuit isolation and RFI isolation. It was anticipated that WRE authorities would show keen interest in the new hardware and scrutinise our documentation with care. To ensure these aspects were adequately addressed a new RDD subsection was formed and tasked to provide a connector access panel for wiring checks and a service rig for test fire the Gas Separation Unit (GSU). The brief also embraced unique handling gear; tooling and draft test procedures together with a trained technician to compliment each RDD rocket trials team.

Before the Sabot, Phillips gauge, inertia switches, firing battery packs and lanyard canister were installed in the Adaptor Bay, each were individually wiring checked; a tedious task of continuity and pin-to-every-other-pin insulation tests. This time consuming test not only verified that hardware had been wired up correctly but importantly ensured that no extraneous electrical pathways or loops existed; the exercise was concluded without fault. Finally, all Adaptor Bay items were installed and functionally tested.

Routine Prep Area work on Stage1 and its removable sub assemblies progressed in parallel without difficulty; only the Sporadic E experiment needed attention and procedure drafting.

(AT GANTRY 2): With the vehicle now erect on the launch stand, each sub-system was installed and functionally tested as team members pursued their well-versed routines. Since my last trial, the method for measuring propellant tank volumes had been vastly improved. The Kerosene sight glass and sump probe were now calibrated by a swept volume-metering pump certified to better than 1%! A similar arrangement became available for HTP tank calibrations when pump makers turned with a water compatible unit about four weeks later. Judging from the filling crew and data analyst's comments this kit was the crème de la crème. Without doubt it was a significant step towards getting accurate mixture ratio measurements.

The FCS tray was installed and functionally readied for inner loop response tests while the shore-side hydraulics were prepared and the trunnions were flooded. A good FCS sense test was concluded by lunchtime – See Appendix A for test detail.

Stage2 assembly to the mainstage began by hoisting the Adaptor Bay, Sabot and dummy Test Body as one pre-assembled package, before fitting the dummy Cuckoo motor and an actual GSU.

> *Fitting the Cuckoo igniter:* To avoid hoisting a live Cuckoo with a live igniter installed out at Area5, a 10" high workspace extension rig was devised to fit on the Adapter Bay.

This served to secure parking spot for the Cuckoo motor to keep it stable and provide an access space for the LO to fit his live igniter. When fitting was complete the Cuckoo with igniter was raised to unship the spacer rig before being lowered and secured on the adapter bay.

APRIL 1960: BLUE STREAK IS CANCELLED! Rumours abound and the impact on BK is uncertain. Whispers have it that BS might become the mainstage for the ELDO project.

The overall rocket structure was now close to full build, less liquids, ready for the FCS inner loop frequency response tests and structural stability margin tests, which produced results little different from the single stage results. To bring rocket mass up to near lift off condition, kerosene and demineralised water was loaded in the propellant tanks and FCS outer loop stability margins were again assessed – no ill effects from the taller structure were apparent.

(STATIC FIRING): See Table A/2 of Appendix A for countdown detail. Both the S&S and next days Static Firing ran through without problems except that the propellant mixture ratio again remained outside tolerance compared to Ansty – so the question still remains, is it an engine variance or measurement anomaly?

(RFI/EMC) – When the engine was dried out, preparation for RFI/EMC testing began, which involved a full strip down and rebuild of Stage2 in order to service Test Body batteries and tape recorder etc.

As outlined before: This test searches for electromagnetic interference between electrical systems and the absence of trigger currents at the various ordnance detonators. All electronic systems and electro mechanical devices were exercised on internal power, as if operating during flight, with all door panels and aerials fitted and extraneous test gear like the CSMU and the umbilical plug removed.

All Stage1 systems were powered up followed by a –120sec launch sequence to zero time. Stage2 separation was initiated by bridging Stage1 thrust sensing inertia switches to fire explosive bolt puffers and operated the gas thruster at low gas pressure. Stage2 descent sequence was initiated by bridging the Phillips Gauge to fire the puffer's simulating Cuckoo, Sabot and Test Body explosive bolts. Telemetry and oscilloscope records were taken throughout these activities. Good results were obtained and every technical facet of these checks proved acceptable with no evidence of extraneous electrical pickup. The process of synchronising operators to initiate discrete actions at the rocket against the flight time base while others try to complete observations and do detailed measurements was fraught and untidy.

Many repeat sessions were necessary before all results were secured – As mentioned before this test requires rationalising.

Stage2 was dismantled and returned with the mainstage back to the Prep Area for balancing, weighing and a QA audit.

With an inhibited engine and tank desiccant breathers fitted, all items were crated for airlifting out to Test Shop 2 mid May 1960.

BK09 AT WOOMERA – The team made Adelaide 14 May 1960 and I arrived 21 May, a day before BK08 was expected to launch; that team had struggled for weeks with a strange engine fault as outlined in Chapter 9 earlier. Hopefully their new engine will lift the beast more than the few millimetres of their first attempt. As described earlier in Chapter 4, I was able to watch this vehicle re-enter with WRE Recovery Section out at the impact site.

> *BK08 & Gaslight: This rocket was bewitched to the end; with its new engine it performed well up to All Burnt then failed to let go of Stage2! To reduce the time impact on the Gaslight program it was decided to launch BK09 ahead of BK07.*

With BK07 & 09 hardware plus BK08 team, TS2 floor space, laboratory space and office space were at a premium; hardware and people were everywhere.

(TS2 TESTING): During the next two days, our DH & RDD team working with the MAO & LO5 pair managed to test and certify the Haz circuits fit for flight. LO5 then moved on to supervise live Cuckoo motor and live Sabot preparation over at the Range E Magazine area.

Check and calibration of FSC, Telemetry and Transponder systems progressed alongside Mechanical testing on Engine start/stop valve, tank and electronic Bay vent valves and the hydraulic installation. The Mainstage was readied for transfer to 5B.

(LAUNCHER 5B): When erect at 5B, the Mainstage HTP tank pressurising system was functionally exercised. Engine trunnions and shore side hydraulic service were prepared for FSC inner loop frequency testing and overall sense testing as per Appendix A. Telemetry and Command Link systems were functionally tested. Setting up, calibrating and exercising the engine ground support services continued.

(STATIC FIRING): See Table A/2 Appendix A for countdown timing. A good S&S test was followed by a routine propellant transfer and normal static firing; all engine pressures having settled at design values within 3secs, good pressure records were obtained. However, two days later the OISC wanted a second firing to resolve a mixture ratio concern. (Was he catching the BK08 bug?) The repeat burn exhibited an identical light up response and similar pressure levels but this time the mixture ratio was much nearer the Ansty values; me thinks number crunching must have gone astray first time. The engine was dried out and examined while it's ground pressure transducer piping was stripped off and sent for cleaning.

Live firing preparation now began in earnest with a formal FCS sense test. The upper clamp ring was fitted, the FCS "Flight Plug" was inserted to replace the CSMU diagnostic connector.

Shore side hydraulic power was applied and a clear demonstration of correct thrust chamber deflection with respect to the Range firing line was demonstrated.

> *A fanciful thought* – *I often compare the next section of our trials to the opening night of a theatrical production where talented specialists unite and seamlessly ply their skills to bring a real-time first night performance to life and on time. Alas, our "show" is often late and can never be encored!*

Meanwhile the Test Body was being re–batteried and undergoing instrument reset to pre-launch status at TS2.

The imminent assembly of Stage2 with its live ordnance stores restricted EC5 and Launcher 5A personnel to the 8hr shift discipline.

(STAGE2 JOINS STAGE1): With Test Body positioned in its handling stand at the foot of but to one side of the 5B gantry hoist, the "live" Sabot and Adapter Bay were placed over it and secured by two single ended explosive bolts; the pad crew took a "Smoko" while LO5 inserted and wired up the two bolt detonators. When the Sabot lanyard had been coupled the complete assembly was hoisted to level 'F' and secured on BK09 Separation Bay by four double-ended explosive bolts. Again, the upper Gantry floors were cleared while LO5 inserted and connected the bolt detonators. Finally the Cuckoo motor "work space" rig was set atop the Adaptor Bay ready for motor installation tomorrow.

(LIVE CUCKOO MOTOR): The motor arrived early at 5B, was hoisted and settled down on the "work space" rig while LO5 inserted and connected the igniter unit. As the motor was raised clear, the "work space" rig extracted and the motor was lowered and secured to the Adaptor Bay with multiple hex headed bolts.

LO5 and team fitted all Haz battery packs and load checked them. Finally, the Gas Jet Separation (GJS) unit was shear pinned to the Cuckoo venturi and electrically connected. The local fairings around GJS would be attached and secured at the final gas bottle charge prior to launch.

> *VIP visitors:* *Those keen on eyeballing a two stage BK had been coming out to Area5 in dribs and drabs ever since we got to the launcher. However, once the live Cuckoo motor appeared the area became a lonely place – as one wag put it "can find a joker to grab a rope end when needed".*

> *Life's Clever Dreamers:* *Once in a while one comes across the odd individual who seems detached from the real world. I stumbled on one such very talented instrumentation engineer happily plying his magic inside the Electronics Bay.*

He was using an Avometer with its batteries still installed and totally oblivious to the electrically sensitive explosives being handled on the gantry floor above his head – so he was smartly banished back to TS2 with a flea in his ear!

Stage1 Nonhaz battery packs were installed and 30sec load tested on "Internals". As each pre-flight task was progressively 'finalised', section leaders with their witness, (usually the DTL and or the TL) gathered to audit flight hardware status, every detail, every plug and socket, every service fastening, every pressure or voltage setting was agreed and noted on a formal master checklist, a process that would continue in the background until we cleared the Pad for the launch countdown.

The ground start tank was watered, vehicle gas bottles and hydraulic accumulator were charged. The "Flight Nut" was fitted and the start/stop solenoid "latch" function was proven.

(LAUNCH S&S TEST): See Table A/2 Appendix A for countdown timing.

Wintertime: Being late in the month, sunset came early and moonrise phase was creeping up, which prescribed an early launch slot at around 19:00 hrs. To meet this slot an extra early morning shift was arranged to get the S&S check done with Range services by morning "Smoko"

A good S&S was put to bed and as hoped, tonight's prep got going early and eagerly. The Kerosene tank was filled to capacity; the pad area was cleaned down, the remote dump arm was exercised and the HTP transfer gear was set up. Alongside these activities, propellant temperatures, densities were selected and sight glass levels were calculated and agreed with the OISC. After a crew room cut lunch, the kerosene load was trimmed down to launch level and HTP was loaded in the rocket and ground-start tanks by mid afternoon. All loose items were dealt with, all except the final arming access panels were closed up and the Gantry was generally readied for roll back before the pad crew left for dinner at Kooly. The LO5/Stage2 team and I got back from Kooly promptly to final arm Stage2 and insert the breakup catalyst capsules.

Sight glasses were removed to seal the rocket tanks as the Gantry floors and doors were folded back. When prompted from EC5 the Gantry was rolled back and locked down to reveal BK09, a condemned innocent standing as Joan of Arc did waiting for the fire to start! Pad 5B was cleared of all personnel to let WRE carry out radio transmission tests.

The HTP start pipe was connected, its bomb slip was cocked and all Test Post gas pressures were turned on.

The release jack safety pin pulled and presented to LO5, we all retired from the pad.

Strolling back to the crew room, the weather looked fine, no cloud, no moon, just a very gentle breeze; things were looking good.

(LAUNCH COUNTDOWN): As DTL, my EC5 interests now extended to all console operators excluding the guidance team.

I joined the TL and AOO5 on the observation area over looking the consoles, for my first chance to watch a BK lift off through the periscopic windows.

As the clock ticked down and each event presented correctly, tension in EC5 grew and time crept slower and slower until zero time. Just as the engine was initiated, I turned towards the launcher window and watched for AOO5's "Instant of Move" light, and a truly magnificent sight unfolded.

> *Lift Off*: *BK09 slowly lifted away with a relentless purpose, only a major calamity could stop it. Without the vast smoke clouds produced by LOX engines, these lovely bad boys just brandished a stack of clearly defined shock diamonds under each thrust chamber as modest evidence of the power now sending this object of our efforts to its destiny. It was soon lost from view above the window frame – would the engine burn to full time, would the upper stage release properly and make its mega death dive, would the Payload detach, would the lanyard survive? – We'd get good idea soon. I turned to watch for All Burnt at the telemetry display, and then Sporadic E switched, on telling me Stage2 had parted! We all trooped outside to watch for Cuckoo ignition and the re–entry trails, which proved spectacular, minute and short lived – we learnt later from the recovery crew that the Test Body had managed to partially destroy itself!!*

(BK09 LAUNCH RESULT): Lift off was at 19:35 hrs on Tuesday 21 June 1960. AUW 13739lbs. A good mainstage burn ended at +149.5 sec, no noticeable thrust tail.

Apogee was 301 miles, Stage2 fired at the correct height to reach a re-entry velocity of 15000ft/sec. Test Body recorder logged re-entry data down to 80,000ft where the Body casing broke up following violent oscillations a second or so earlier. Gaslight instrumentation acquired good data and a remnant of Test Body outer cladding was recovered together with an intact tape recorder cassette. The Sporadic E probe also recorded data. Test Body instability was attributed to a cladding detachment. Both stages performed 100% but the Test Body anomaly reduced the experiment to a qualified success. My first shot as DTL was fulfilling and edifying, aside from initial hardware delivery all come together well, CSPs', test gear, test teams at both venues were up to the task. These guys now worked cohesively and knew their trade well.

The RDD team and I remained at Woomera to continue the BK07 launch trial.

FIG 11–1 SINGLE STAGE BLACK KNIGHT ON PAD 5B, one winters day.
(Commonwealth of Australia)

BK07 LAUNCH TRIAL AREA 5   **12**

22 June 1960. BK07 had been receiving drip feed attention at TS2 as and when the BK09 work allowed. Most of the FCS, Tele instrumentation and radio laboratory setting up tasks had been completed and the MAO/LO5 certification were soon cleared. FCS, Tele, Engine and Airframe tasks were concluded over the next five days without notable difficulty.

(LAUNCHER 5A): By end of day one, BK07 was standing erect on the launcher and all electronic trays had been installed and functionally exercised.

We'd not been forewarned of a heavy rainstorm that swept in overnight to drench the rocket and its test gear; the simply clad Gantry was no shield against wind driven rain. When such rare events happen at Woomera, numerous mini lakes and umpteen puddles appear to make a red muddy bog that soon spreads everywhere, woe betide those who stray off metalled surfaces.

Once all visible water had been mopped, sponged and wiped away from the rocket and test gear at every Gantry level and Test Post, the team set about assessing the damage by running insulation checks on the electronic systems. Numerous faults were found at the vehicle, especially at break down connectors inside the shrouds running along the rockets external skins between engine and electronics bays.

A great deal of time was spent with hot air blowers and air jets to remove all trace of moisture but the high impedance circuits stubbornly refused to come good.

> *Wonders will never cease*: On an earlier visit to EEL at Cowes I'd been shown an aerosol product, which they claimed (and demonstrated) would cure most moisture insulation faults so I asked for several cans' be included in the TS2 spares kit. With crossed fingers I rang TS2 stores who sent a can out pronto.

Neither the crew nor I believed it would be any good but like magic, within minutes of a few squirts the resistance values began climbing and all was soon back to normal, which assured me of free beer that evening! We eventually had things got back on the track doing FCS frequency response tests and a telemetry functional audit of all inputs with Mike3 at the Range reception centre. The thrust augmenter was fitted and repeated bomb slip deployments functioned well.

(STATIC FIRING S&S TEST): See Table A/2 of Appendix A for countdown timing. Preparation of the engine, its ground support gear and instrumentation systems progressed in parallel. Soon after lunch a successful S&S test was concluded. Kerosene was loaded, demin water was drained and the engine and ground support systems were rigged and gassed up for tomorrow's static burn.

(STATIC FIRING): Scheduled for 13:00hrs. After a pad wash down and dump arm test, LO5 called in the bulk carrier and the specified HTP loads were transferred the rocket and starting tanks. As final checklists were concluded, the pad was cleared and I joined the EC5 team to cross check with each consol jockey and watch a short telemetry record run with Mike3 before things got going. The countdown sequence ran to engine light up without hesitation, all pressures rose smoothly and stayed at correct levels until a snappy shutdown at +35sec yet again! As always the pad crew assumed success and made ready to dry the engine over the next 12hrs. But concerns about mixture ratios took hold and as talks of a second firing gathered strength and pad crew gloom grew until deeper analysis persuaded the OISC that a repeat burn was unwarranted and the drying got under way.

> *A background anxiety: Having now been closely associated with static firing a number of Gamma 201 engines at High Down and Woomera without encountering any serious problems I'd developed a respect for their consistency. From start-up acceleration, through hot running transition and settled burn pressure levels to the snappy shut down at + 35 secs, each engine had shown near identical behaviour – even to the repeated mixture ratio issues, overheating worries and thrust tail off artefact. However, our history of trouble free engine burns and successful launches was getting a tad unsettling, when was the law of averages going to seek redress?*

(LAUNCH PREPARATION): The Rock & Roll sense test came next, which it may be recalled is done to demonstrate that FCS control of each thrust chamber with the "Flight" plug fitted is corrective with respect to the firing line. This convoluted exercise as detailed in Appendix A, passed off successfully but took us into the early afternoon before the flight Test Body could be loaded. With fully charged batteries the ugly bluff nosed Test Body was secured and system tested via EC5 and Mike3 by end of today's play.

With good weather forecast for the next few days, arrangements were made to retain the Adelaide commuters for a working weekend to meet an early S&S test on Monday July 25th with a launch slot that evening.

Internal batteries were fitted with a 30sec load test before check listing, closing up and seal testing the Electronics Bay at 10psi. Gas bottles were charged, the engine solenoid valve "Flight Nut" was fitted and "latching" function was verified.

(LAUNCH S&S TEST): See Table A/2 of Appendix A Sequence timings.
The test passed off without fault.   While Tele records were perused the rocket kerosene tank was filled ready for trimming when final loadings had been decided.

> *OISC Allowance:*   Most had their personal fine-tuning factors for propellant loading, all aimed at getting the longest burn time with the least cold running. Aside from temperature and density tolerances, calculations are confounded by two main uncertainties; the historic lack of confidence in the HTP tank volume calibrations and the in-flight mixture ratio profile.
>
> But the uncertain thrust decay at All Burnt was now a troubling factor. While my loading calcs agreed with his on this occasion the OISC settled for 0.5% (6lb) kerosene over fill, betting that a hot shutdown would be cleaner.

Close after lunch the Pad crew were ready for HTP filling but were kept on standby pending a pre–planned VIP visitation. They arrived an hour late and lingered with no sense of urgency, our HTP transfer before dinner was under threat.   Clad in PVC suiting the loading crew froze in the cold afternoon breeze until our LO5 decided to apply his diplomatic skills: –

> *Launcher Officer (LO) diplomacy:* These guys were appointed by WRE to oversee all launch pad activities and supervise all hazardous operations. I found these Australian Artillery captains very friendly and easy to work with due to their unique laid back style (One of them spend several enjoyable weeks staying with my family back on the Island during his High Down posting).
>
> On this occasion a party of VIP's were to eyeball BK on the 5B pad after lunch and clear it promptly to enable HTP loading and final arming ahead of launching that evening. Predictably they arrived late, the HTP bulk carrier had waited several hours to come on site; our 8-hour shift time was being squandered and the visitors seemed oblivious of the situation. Finally, the LO5 stepped forward and announced in a commanding voice "Everybody listen up! We are going to load HTP. All those senior to me should leave the launch area now – the rest of you will f*** off immediately!" Needless to say, all visitors vanished whichever cap they wore.

With propellants loaded and adjusted the area was hosed down ahead of dinner at Koolymilka. Afterwards, the cooled rocket gas bottles were finally topped up and capped off.   Pre-launch checklists were completed as LO5 armed the Test Body separation ordnance and inserted the break up capsules before we rolled back the Gantry and locked down. Finally, after checking Test Post gases and HTP dump arm, the start hose was connected to the engine and its bomb slip was cocked before I pulled and passed the release jack safe pin for LO5. The crew and I cleared the pad and LO5 and armed the break up system. In EC5, I checked with console driver and moved onto the dais while the countdown was on hold for the usual Met assessment of upper atmosphere winds.

When the count did start it was stopped at −20mins by EC5 for an S band transponder failure. A hold for this temperamental item was a worry; the moon phase would soon begin, cloud fronts were mounting; missing tonight's slot heralded a long delay.

> _Being prepared:_ In true "Boy Scout" tradition, the guidance team "happened" to hold a spare transponder in EC5 so launcher access was immediately sought and obtained to change it. With the LO5 team along to disarm the break-up system, I drove two guidance techs and a mechanic out to 5B. The Techs removed the fin pod's nosecone to unplug the beacons power lead, while the mechanic and I unshipped the pod from the fin to lay it sideways for beacon extraction from below. Just as the Techs had secured the new beacon into the pod, Con1 called for an update – he'd already warned that moonrise was just two hours away so time was the real issue. I knew him well and realised he couldn't be kidded so with the pod still laying on its side, the long beacon power lead was quickly connected, which enabled me to call EC5 to "start transponder pre-heat" then tell Con1, "will clear back to EC5 in six minutes". The pod was soon reattached to fin and its nosecone was secured as the beacon began its 35min preheat. We were back in EC5 12 minutes after leaving, followed by the LO5 team a few moments later.

This countdown ran through to engine ignition and lift off without further ado. Apparently the guidance pilots dealt with a lively spell at one point but all ended up correctly.

(BK07 LAUNCH): Lift off at 21:25 on Monday 25 Jul 1960. AUW 13371lbs. Engine, one chamber ran cold for 3secs seconds. All Burnt at +148.5 sec, Apogee was 330 miles. Later analysis of thermal measurements defined the heat flux profile during ascent and base drag flow ended +85 seconds. Tele recorded thrust augmenter deployment but I assume it perished because I've never been able to find any data about its behaviour. The Test Body detached cleanly but separation and spin thrusters failed to ignite, causing the Head to re-enter at high incidence, good telemetry and re-entry data was secured. The fin pod lamps were seen beyond engine burn and Kine theodolite tracked well beyond. All UAEs worked.

The team and I returned to a sunny UK in early August 1960 after a nine-week Down Under campaign. Just in time for a spot of sailing and boat maintenance.

BK13 TRIALS – HD & AREA 5   **13**

"My" fifth bird – Third as TL
TRIAL OBJECTIVE –
– Test Body –

- High penetration double cone devised to elevate ablating nose heat input.
- Test Body with a tracking beacon, armoured tape recorder and wake camera.
- Payload separation delayed further to counter engine thrust decay.

– Rocket investigations:

- Confirm cessation time of engine bay airflow.
- Measure engine bay thermal conditions.
- Measure engine bay pressure distribution.
- Flight-test of second thrust augmenter.
- UA Experiments: Ionic composition probe, Galactic radio noise receiver.

BK13 BUILD –

This single stage Gamma 201 rocket replicated BK07 in all respects except the Test Body, which used a revised geometry and carried an armoured tape recorder in place of telemetry, a low power acquisition beacon and a rear facing cine camera to record re-entry wake detail.

BK13 AT HIGH DOWN –

Began week one in Nov 1960 and scheduled to conclude week two of Dec 1960.

Being similar with BK 07, the team were very familiar with all aspects except for the UAE's and payload detail so only a few extra CSP's were needed – great joy! The Woomera annual shutdown occupies six weeks from mid December, so this trial was held over into the New Year.

> *Telemetry v Static firing records: A long-standing concern regarding comparative accuracy between telemetered and ground-based pressures measurements was resolved during this trial. Direct comparison between ground based and telemetered instruments can only be made from static firings at Woomera where full Tele recording facilities are available and such studies had revealed 2 to 3% systemic bias between the systems. Meticulous investigation cleared the ground system so the witch-hunt turned to the telemetry system. To measure pressure, 465MHz telemetry used variable inductance transducers that form intrinsic elements of the oscillator modulating the RF transmitter.*

Initially it was difficult to understand how the tuned circuit in the laboratory transducer calibrator was dissimilar to the flight setup until it was remembered that only the latter case was sequentially multiplexed. Checking the dynamic behaviour of each setup revealed marked differences between the modulator "Q" values, a quality parameter relating to selectivity, damping and agility of a tuned circuit. The introduction of multiplexing with a revised calibration modulator ended the controversy.

The full schedule of testing was completed without any noteworthy problems or delays, just one engine firing was needed and the system RFI/EMC test satisfied all acceptance requirements. After the final weighing and CG checks the crated hardware was dispatched for TS2 during week one of Dec 1960.

BK13 AT WOOMERA –

January 12, 1961 saw our team back at a very busy TS2, because BK14 and team had also arrived. With both Area5 launch pads available for use the OISC had visions of handling two trials in parallel. Alas, the last week of January saw the only occasion when two Black Knights stood side by side, BK13 on 5A and BK14 on 5B, because BK14 developed an engine problem that delayed its launch until early April.

(STATIC FIRING): Our trouble free progress suddenly ended when an HTP tank reaction forced us to reverse the filling process to investigate why. The ambient temperature was in the high 30's, so some HTP activity was expected till cold oxidant cooled the tank. But this persistently high noise level from the HTP tank was outside our experience so it was drained and flushed with demin water. An HTP training routine begun using dilute peroxide for three hours, followed at a higher strength for two more hours. Twelve hours later the tank checked out as OK – As described below, contaminating debris was the culprit and WRE was able to reclaim the contaminated HTP by re-filtering.

HTP Training: Components in contact with HTP are fabricated from compatible materials and receive meticulous etching and training treatments but complete absence of impurities at cut edges etc cannot be guaranteed. BK tank skins used Alclad a copper/aluminium core with an outer layer of pure aluminium but the cut edge problem remains. By steeping in dilute HTP, small catalysing impurities build an oxide coating to form an isolation barrier. Dilute peroxide slows the process but avoids a thermal runaway risk. On this occasion, a highly reactive remnant from a gas bottle thread seal was recovered in the flush water and shown to cause a violent reaction of 250ml of HTP within 40 sec, which shot a column of super heated fluid tens of feet into the air! Subsequent investigation established that the gas bottle makers invariably employed lead sealing discs between bottle and its connection union.

Following the above distraction another good static firing was put in the bag.

(LAUNCH PREPARATION): This began at TS2 by fitting the Test Body with fresh batteries, loading tape and camera cassettes and fitting orientation pyrotechnics. A functional test cleared it fit to fly before being moved out to launcher 5A and hoisted to BK13's separation bay where it was secured by two diametrically opposed explosive bolts. A final functional test via EC5 confirmed that all was well at the sharp end. LO5 and team installed all Haz batteries (engine solenoid, Break Up, and Test Body separation) before inserting and connecting the two Test Body explosive bolt detonators.

Non-Haz system batteries were fitted in the Electronic Bay and 30sec load tested before a final M3 readout of Tele channels confirmed all systems were up and running correctly.

(LAUNCH S&S TEST): After a WRE radio transmission test, a pre-launch S&S test with all Range services was successfully concluded before lunch. While waiting for approval of the system records, kerosene was loaded.

FIG 13–1   BK13 on pad 5A with BK14 on pad 5B in the background.

(Crown copyright)

Check lists were progressively cleared during the afternoon as each service hatch was closed off and the Electronics Bay was sealed and pressure tested.

During dinner at Kooly, jet stream worries were the gossip but the OISC sensibly chose to ignore the rumour as we retuned to Pad 5A.

With final HTP and Kerosene temperatures taken, numbers were crunched, kerosene tank level was trimmed and HTP was loaded; sight glasses were detached and both tanks were sealed and catalyst capsules were inserted. Gas bottles were topped and Test Body pyrotechnics were armed before the Gantry was rolled back about 20:30'ish. After a final check of Test Post systems, I pulled the release jack safety pin and cleared the pad for LO5 to arm the rocket breakup charges.

Back in EC5, we learnt that the jet stream was OK, so after my usual yak with the console jockeys and the to and fro between AOO5 and Con1, a faultless the count down ran down to Time Zero. As the engine fired up and IoM was signalled I again revelled in watching another BK rise majestically off the launch pad.

> *Jet Stream Winds: These broad 'rivers' of wind that snake violently across the upper atmosphere at 200 mph or more, can present problems for the FCS as the Rocket passes up through them. To maintain heading attitude in this region, larger thrust chamber angles are demanded, which in the extreme would cause loss of control if a chamber reached end stops or an amplifier saturated. When jet streams are in the area, balloon soundings are done and analysis made to ensure that safe margins are maintained.*

BK13 LAUNCH – Lift off was at 22:17 on 07 Feb 1961. AUW 12813lbs. Good engine performance with All Burnt at +149.5 sec, Apogee at 301miles and a Re-entry speed of 10870 ft/sec.

Payload separation, orientation and spin up worked perfectly this time but finger trouble had struck yet again, a timer in the Test Body had been incorrectly set causing a tape recorder and camera early start up and mistiming of all on board re-entry records.

Engine Bay thermal measurements were again recorded and base bleed flaps shut at +92 seconds. All level sensor probes were recorded. Electronic flashes were seen but tracking lamps were not. According to Telemetry, the thrust augmenter deployed but again as for BK07, no mention of behaviour is available; maybe it just perished! Good rocket, bad Test Body.

The team's return to UK after seven weeks of warm Oz summer to a High Down midwinter took a week or so of adjustment.

A REAL 36" BALLS UP

SABOT TRIALS at Larkhill, circa Mid 1961.

BK15 was to carry aloft a 36" diameter hollow sphere of high purity copper, to serve as a datum shot for the panoply of Dazzle spectrometers on the ground at Woomera. To secure a debris free re-entry the spent rocket would be turned end for end after All Burnt by firing small lateral thrusters. When facing downwards the copper ball would be propelled clear by a powered sabot, tethered back to the rocket by a deploying lanyard. My only contribution to this exercise was to conduct sabot function trials on the Larkhill artillery range, near Salisbury

The Sabot Test Rig: *The Sabot was a light cylindrical structure, 36" diameter by some 20" high. The upper rim formed a padded cup in which the Ball seated, both being secured to the rocket structure by a central explosive bolt. Many small solid fuel thrust units were mounted around the Sabots lower rim, splayed outwards to thrust through the Ball's CG. A centrally connected lanyard ran back to a stowage canister in the rockets separation bay.*

To examine dynamic behaviour a full scale Sabot and Ball assembly was rigged on a custom made stand set at 45°QE on the concrete launcher apron at Larkhill. During our preparation, building contractors who were laying cement to extend the apron took a keen interest in our antics and persistently ribbed our "space" efforts. We knew the sabot flight would appear tame when fired and were dreading their response. When the button was pressed everything worked perfectly, the Ball and Sabot assembly rose in a long gentle arc, When the Sabot was halted by the lanyard the Ball detached and continued up to some 200ft or so before curving back to earth about 800ft down range, and bounced several times before coming to a stand still – after a pregnant silence, loud applause and ribald cracks about our chances of reaching orbit any time this century filled the air! Mugs of canteen tea all round!

FIG 13 – 2   BK16 at HIGH DOWN   Note the neat canon umbilical
connector plug right of centre.   (GKN Aerospace)

BK16 TRIALS – HD & AREA 5 | **14**

"My" sixth bird – Forth as TL

TRIAL OBJECTIVES:

- Two stage Dazzle research series.
- 15° Copper cone with armoured tape recorder.
- Stage 2, C Band tracking beacon for re-entry acquisition.
- First proving flight of Gamma 301engine.
- First proving flight of transistorised FCS.

BK16 BUILD –

In addition to replicating BK09 this vehicle was flight type approving a new propulsion unit and an updated flight control system: –

Gamma 301 Engine: *Comprised four state of the art thrust chambers and other major components derived from the ASM developed Stentor engine used on the Blue Steel stand off weapon. The HTP/Kerosene propellants yielded 19,000lbs sea level thrust. See Figs A–10 & A–11, Appendix 'A' for further detail.*

Flight Nut: This bane of every ASM Rep was no longer needed. The latching function of the start/stop solenoid valve was now negated for static firings by an external gas actuator, not fitted for launch firings.

Solid State FCS: Just as the original thermionic FCS had been engineered before the semi conductor age, so this transistorised version materialised just as the integrated chip became vogue. Never the less, it was robust and thermally stable and very user friendly. Significant weight saving resulted from simplified power supply needs and the consequent reduction of battery packs.

Revised Tethering: It is an unfortunate fact that most advances often bring unwanted baggage. In this instance the new 301 thrust chamber trunnion axis was some 8 inches higher above the nozzle exits than the 201 chambers, which set the tether ball and release jack claws high up between the chambers. The resulting loss of annular clearance of chambers around the release jack required the jack to retract down as its jaws were opened. For further detail see Appendix A,

Servicing: To capitalise on lessons learnt in BK's early days when attention to servicing access had been limited, the BK16 RDD team had shadowed pre-production development at Cowes, Farnborough and Ansty to influence operational features.

By mid 1961 several visits to Ansty and the FCS mock up at EEL Cowes had secured the following servicing easements:

- Shuttle valves introduced at all engine pressure tapping points to allow bleeding and pressure calibration without system intrusion.
- Externally accessible instrumentation bays in engine bay structure.
- Access to every internal battery pack without disturbing adjacent equipment.
- Manual operation of separation switches in 'assembled structure' condition.
- Electronics Bay internal layout revised to avoid inter-system servicing conflicts.
- FCS sub units oriented to permit replacement and adjustment without tray removal.
- Numerous pipes rerouted to assist servicing and inspection.

BK16 AT HIGH DOWN –

Stage1 delivery was stalled at Cowes waiting for an engine to finalise electrical looming and forming final pipe connections. Without the benefit of today's CAD, the pipe route and interface from tanks to engine was hand patterned against real hardware before production, acid etching and HTP training could begin – a time consuming chain of events using actual hardware as the interface gauge.

To cater for the piecemeal delivery and installation of flight components, Cowes QA co-operatively arrange on site final vetting of effected flight hardware installations. This approach enabled RDD to steel a march on devising new test procedures, checking test rig interfaces and identifying snags that required early design office attention. Advanced delivery of the new FCS equipment complete with a full set of sub units allowed the FCS crew a two–week head start before Stage1 delivery.

Stage1 complete with engine finally arrived late in March 1962, minus some HTP pipes due the last minute etching failures. The delays due to missing hardware during the Prep Area phase caused more disruption and time loss than any test related problems. However, once all hardware was to hand and properly installed, the improved access and reliability of the new FCS and engine began to pay off; many operations were now much quicker and could be done without collateral disturbance to adjacent systems.

(AT GANTRY 2) – Once the uncertain Prep Area period was concluded, Stage1 was erected in Gantry1 for routine propellant tank pressure tests and volume calibrations. Stage2 with an inert Cuckoo was assembled to Stage1 ahead a satisfactory inner loop frequency response test session. The overall FCS sense test as detailed in Appendix A then held everything up for half a day to complete. Telemetry setting up and source auditing then followed.

Connection and calibration of ground pressure measuring transducer rolled along in the background like clockwork via the new shuttle valves.

After installation and testing the Command Link and S-band transponder, preparation for the Static Firing began. The new engine boasted two turbo pump gearboxes equipped with lub oil systems that needed filling and flow checking.

(S&S TEST) See Table A/2 of Appendix A for sequence time. Setting up and functional checking the engine ground support services (ground start and N2 Purge systems and the new failsafe gas actuator) were satisfactorily completed. On closing the final checklist I headed to the Equipment Centre where the many extra visitors far out numbered our usual firing team. As a good omen, the S&S test ran without fault. Charging vehicle gas bottles, replenishing gearbox oil, loading kerosene and draining the Start tank finished up today's activities.

(STATIC FIRING) – With fair weather forecast the Downs Clearance party got away early and tasks at Site1 began by washing down the area, rigging for HTP transfer and loading the vehicle and ground start tanks, which we managed to conclude and cleared away by lunchtime. The firing sequence was entered about 13:00hrs and ran as planned to +35secs with a good engine performance. All pressures rose to hot running level within 2sec and remained stable throughout. This was the best engine burn I'd ever witnessed with all pressures and propellant usage coming very close to Ansty figures; a really gratifying outcome for everyone associated with this new hardware; a quantum leap.

(RFI & EMC TESTS) – Stage2 was removed and sent to the Prep Area for Test Body battery servicing. All none Haz internal battery packs were installed in Stage1 and 30sec load tested. Next day the Test Body with Adapter Bay returned to Gantry2 and Stage2 was assembled the Dummy Cuckoo motor and flight Nosecone pack. All Haz batteries were fitted and load checked, and all "puffers" were connected and armed. As carried out on earlier trials, the RFI and Flight Sequence test proved a protracted and disjointed affair so a revised routine was adopted.

Flight Timing Hitherto; each in flight event was functioned at its designed flight time – a manageable method on single stage vehicles with only one Payload firing circuit. The many flight events of two stage vehicles became intractable when many timed runs were needed as separation switches, delay timers and a Phillip's gauge were manually functioned and tricky RFI measurements and puffer observation were carried out. Either a dedicated time sequence run was required for each flight event or each flight event was executed as a discrete action in the correct in flight order without using a clock. Once the principle was understood and demonstrated the OISC agreed to drop the flight time based method. This arrangement formalised the process without hurried oscilloscope measurements and multiple repeat actions and was easily achieved in reasonable time with less frayed tempers or repetitions.

Following the RDD/RAE fit for purpose review at High Down, Stage2 and Stage1 were dismantled and returned to the Prep Area for Balancing, Weighing and inhibiting for transferring by air to Woomera circa end June '62.

As the team and I wended our way to Woomera once again, I risked offending the fates by thinking that the omens pointed towards a good launch trial!

BK16 AT WOOMERA –

All hardware reached TS2 during week one of July 1962. It was noticeable that MAO's (Missile Acceptance Officers) were adopting a more formal and stylised approach to missile circuit checking, no doubt a spin off from the more complex bird over at Area6. At least two WRE engineers plus the LO, plus our own guys swarmed over Stage2 to vet the Haz circuits with meticulous care. Wire routing, clipping, continuity and core to core and core to frame insulation was checked. I found this independent scrutiny of the finished build very reassuring. As might be expected they also showed a keen interest in the new Gamma 301 engine.

> _Cynical thinking!_ I often wondered if Blue Streak did derive real operational benefit from BK at the trials level. It was clear that WRE had gained much but little seems to have crossed the great divide at DH; presumably senior managers drew confidence from our earlier launches. While the BS team had an open invitation to view BK activities, I wasn't aware of any reverse arrangement for TS2 personnel – maybe security served as the barrier. Some years later when I was involved in warhead space exposure trials, very little head profile similarity existed between the actual heads and those flown on BK. No doubt the underlying science carried across but as a cynic I've often felt that "Need to know", "Self Protection" and "Inter-department rivalry" diluted the synergy that might otherwise be achieved. A well-established bureaucratic penchant for power is to monopolise knowledge!

Six days after arrival at TS2, Stage1 was moved out to launcher 5A and Stage2 was soon built up with a functional Test Body and a mass simulated Cuckoo motor to work our way through the subsystem testing. All checks ran smoothly until it was found necessary to roll back the Gantry for C band transponder interrogation checks with the FPS16 Range radar at Red Lake; all co-lateral work was suspended while monitor leads and gear was stripped off the vehicle and all Gantry floors were folded before it was rolled clear. This intrusive exercise will need rationalising if this transponder becomes a regular feature, e.g. a simple gantry transfer aerial was wanted.

> _A mature Launch team:_ Most Woomera tests had become routine, flight hardware was more user friendly, personnel were well experienced and shortages were exceptional. Hardware integration in UK had tightened up and supply channels were well established. All core CSP's were field proven and right test gear was to hand.

(S&S AND STATIC FIRING) – Table A/2 of Appendix A details sequence timing. This test and the engine firing mirrored the performance at High Down; a quick acceleration to hot running across all pressures before settling to uniform steady values before a clean instant shutdown – nevertheless, all metaphorical fingers will remain crossed!

It was now time to confirm the launch slot but early weather forecasts were unsettling. During winter, weather fronts often came in seven-day cycles for two to three days so it was not unusual to run preparation up to the S&S test then face day-by-day waiting until battery life intervened. On this occasion a longer bad spell was predicted so the OISC put off S&S testing till Thursday with launch options that night, Friday night and Saturday night as an outsider.

> *Launch Slots:* These are negotiated with the WRE Range Controller who merges requests from all range users to declare a weekly/daily trial programme and it behoved one to establish and preserve an honest record in these dealings. A BK trial is expensive to mount, many range sites are involved many miles down range all needing extra personnel flown in, fed and bedded down from Salisbury. Committing to these logistics together with the inevitable wage tally cannot be undertaken lightly. By establishing a record of frankness and honesty, an OISC may expect, and usually got WRE indulgence when an unexpected spanner in the works up ended his well laid plans.

With most remaining tasks now time tied to a distant S&S test, work at the launch pad slowed to a make do and mend session. The mass simulated Stage2 was stripped down to release the Sabot for Imp installation at the Range Magazine, where the flight Cuckoo motor was already unpacked and processed ready for use.
The FSC "Flight Plug" was fitted and validated by a Rock & Roll sense check per Appendix A. Upper Air Experiments were batteried up and cleared for flight.

(LIVE STAGE2 ASSEMBLY) – From now on the existence of explosive stores at Area 5 will limit all personnel to a maximum shift time of eight hours on and ten hours off.

> *Cuckoo Igniter:* As mention several times elsewhere, it was preferred to hoist the live Cuckoo to Gantry level 'F' without an igniter fitted. This was achieved with the aid of a 400mm high "workspace" frame temporarily added to the Adapter Bay to form raised interface for the Cuckoo motor. With the motor parked on the frame it was held still and stable on the hoist while the igniter was fitted and connected. The motor was lifted to remove the "workspace" frame before being lowered and secured on the Adapter Bay.

With the Test Body and transit stand under the 5A Gantry hoist, the live Sabot and Adaptor Bay was secured to it using two single ended explosive bolts.

The LO5 now inserted and connected both detonators because of access limitations later on. When the Sabot Lanyard had been coupled, the complete assembly was hoisted to Gantry level 'F' and secured on Stage1 by four doubled ended explosive bolts that again had eight detonators inserted and connected to avoid later access problems. The GSU unit was now anchored to the Cuckoo nozzle by three special shear pins.

All gas bottles and the hydraulic accumulator were charged and the kerosene tank was over filled to stand overnight.

(S&S FOR LAUNCH) – Thursday AM the Electronic Bay battery packs were installed and 30sec load tested and the engine start tank was filled with demin water. Gearbox oil flow was run and replenished and the hydraulics was rigged for shore running.

Pre Flight checklists would now continue on an opportunity bases right up to clearing the pad for launch. The S&S rehearsal was delayed an hour to replace an errant Telemetry transmitter and check channel rest levels before re–sealing the Electric Bay. A good S&S was achieved by mid afternoon but as feared, tonight's launch was called off due to cloud overcast.

(LAUNCH FIRING) – Started very chilly so the obligatory battery checks were delayed until the day had warmed them up around lunchtime. All Haz batteries were fitted and load tested. Gearbox lub oil was flow tested to drench the gear train and the HTP dump probe was set up. By mid afternoon all vehicle gas bottles and engine hydraulics had been charged and the area was prepared for HTP transfer. With peroxide and kero temperatures to hand, the OISC agreed to load without any frig factors so after the kero was trimmed down the HTP bulk carrier came on scene.

The HTP filling and area wash down was completed and the LO inserted the breakup capsules before we broke for dinner. On our return, all gas bottles were finally topped and sealed, LO5 armed the Stage2 explosives before we rolled the Gantry back to reveal BK16 in all her naked ready to go glory. Once the WRE radio transmission tests were over, the ground start pipe was connected and the Final Actions Checklist covering Launch Pad, Test Post and Rocket were given one last scan before removing the release jack safe pin and passing it to LO5 for safe keeping. As LO5 armed the break up circuits we headed for the Crew Room to clean up, down a coffee and crossed to EC5 where I yarned with each the console driver before joining the TL on the dais.

As Con1 and AOO5 concluded their various exchanges, the count down started; time dragged its way down zero, which seemed to arrive suddenly without interruptions and liftoff soon followed.

Like previous launches: I was gripped by BK16 as it slowly rose with gathering pace, to leave our care forever and play out her fiery destiny. Despite the phallic appearance I have always viewed these chunks of hardware as feminine. No doubt Freud would have a view about that!

(BK16 LAUNCH) – Lift off at 21:09 on Friday 24 Aug 1962. All Up Weight 13787 lbs. All burnt at +128.3 sec, Apogee of 356 miles, re-entry velocity 14,600 ft/sec.

Telemetry good: all engine pressures, engine bay temperatures, control system parameters and guidance data returned good records.

The university experiments were telemetered and functioned. All aims of this trial were achieved. The Gamma 301 engine was impeccable and the transistor control system behaved as well in flight as it did on the ground.

Stage2 ignition and Test Body separation occurred as planned. FPS.16 radars at Red Lake and Mirikata tracked the C band transponder to give good acquisition data and verification of flight events e.g. upper stage lift off, spin and Cuckoo ignition. The head tape recorder captured re-entry dynamics and temperature data and the Dazzle circus had secured plenty to chew on – a very rewarding trial and all concerned must be commended for a job well done.

I remained at Salisbury till mid September to read flight records and attend the WRE post mortem meeting. After ten weeks of Australian spring, I headed home to a chilly autumn. All told I'd spent five months fulltime nursing and burning midnight oil with BK16, plus the last two months at Woomera – It has been a long spell and will be really good to be home again.

FIG 14–1   TWO STAGE BK ON PAD 5B WAITING TO GO.   Floodlit by searchlight
units used to aid optical trackers at lift off   *(Commonwealth of Australia)*

BK21 & 19 TRIALS – the door begins to shut | **15**

Late in 1962, our departmental boss left to join an American company and the subsequent reshuffle moved me up to Chief Trials Engineer, which extended my sphere of concern to all RDD trial activities at High Down and Woomera.

The cyclic nature of trials work often left staff lightly committed and I decided we should begin an update and review of our operational control documents, which had grown up piecemeal like Topsy over the years and needed to be streamlined and harmonized. Most operational guys are biologically averse to paperwork, just keeping CSP's current and completing checklists being their only concession to this view. Eventually they were persuaded that the historic record was all that remained after a rocket was fired and an unstructured shambles was worse than useless. Gradually the Vehicle Build Standards, Trials Plan, Test Procedures, Firing Instructions and Vehicle Log Books were revised to dovetail with each other. By the end of 1962, the BK launch tally had reached: –

- Eight Single Stage rockets powered by the Gamma 201 engine.
- Four Two Stage rockets powered by the Gamma 201 engine.
- One Two Stage rocket powered by the Gamma 301 engine.

Aside from the early mixture ratio and thrust decay issues, the rocket had performed as specified and had never suffered a catastrophic first stage failure, a brilliant record when set against any comparable project – each bird except BK01 had always burnt close to its allotted duration. In addition to testing re-entry body specimens and researching re-entry physics, the program had supported considerable rocket vehicle and HTP engine development. Operational weaknesses in systems and support equipment had been largely eradicated or tamed and the additional upper stage had significantly elevated re-entry speeds. Propellant loading accuracy had been maximised and the Gamma 301 engine brought consistent flight mixture ratios; uniform thrust decay and has not shown any over heating. The simple robust engineering, easy accessibility and moderate power supply needs of the new solid-state FCS had proved a breeze to service; gyroscope rejection was now an exception. On the guidance side, work was in hand to automate the ground piloting functions.

With their long pedigree in unmanned aircraft the command link receivers had never caused a moments concern. The magic-fingered guys who set up the S band tracking transponders were now adept at finding each unit's sweet spot. Such improvements reflected in the pattern of trials activity, which was smooth and almost predictable; only the weather and unrelated outside factors remained variable. Occasionally a technical fault grabbed the spotlight for an hour or so but the gentle mantle of a well-oiled machine soon prevailed. The Blue Streak rocket had now become an ELDO first stage and space aficionados of all colours were striving to provide it with large satellite capability. The schemes invariably coupled Blue Streak with upper stages yet to see the light of day, implying frightening price tags. An alternative study aimed to capitalise on existing technology with a "BK" like demonstrator for smaller satellites; about mid 1962 I began shadowing this topic at our Design Office, EEL and the RAE. Meantime Bk21 and 19 had to be fired.

BK21 TRIALS AT HIGH DOWN & WOOMERA:
"My" seventh bird – fifth as TL.

TRIAL OBJECTIVE:
- Two stage Dazzle research series with a 15° copper cone.
- Up rated Gamma 301 engine.
- Cuckoo II upper stage motor.

BK21 BUILD –
Build and experimental role closely matched BK16 so the Trials Plan, CSPs and related documents required minimal attention.

BK21 AT HIGH DOWN –
All hardware had arrived on site by early Feb 1964. Preparation and system installation tests were carried though without undue difficulty; a good Static Firing and faultless RFI/EMC check concluded the qualification program.

BK21 AT WOOMERA –
March 13, 1964 I reached TS2. The Test Shop phase was routine and systems installation checks at the gantry together with the static firing were unexceptional. Launch preparation also proceeded to plan and for once the weather was benign.

BK21 LAUNCH –
Lifted off at 20:32 hrs. April 21 1964. AUW 14106 lbs, All burnt +121.3 secs. Apogee was 404.6 miles, with a re-entry speed of 15000ft/sec. The upper stage functioned correctly, Cuckoo ignition was good but sabot lanyard parted. Good Dazzle observations were reported and Tape cassette was recovered – another good flight. I returned home May 10 after a nine week trip.

BK19 TRIALS AT HIGH DOWN & WOOMERA:

"My" eighth bird – Sixth as TL

TRIAL OBJECTIVE:

- Two stage Dazzle research series with a 17" diameter copper sphere.
- Gamma 301 engine up–rated to 21,000ib thrust.
- Cuckoo II upper stage motor
- Sabot with 4 IMP X's.

BK19 BUILD –

Except for the Test Body design, the vehicle Build Standard and experimental role mimicked BK21 and the Trials Plan, CSPs and related documents read across with few amendments.

BK19 AT HIGH DOWN –

Began mid May 1964 and took four weeks to complete. The established format was followed and nothing unusual was encountered.

BK19 AT WOOMERA –

I reached TS2 24 June 1964; again both the Test Shop and launcher phases were straightforward. First launch slot was cancelled due to very cold and poor weather conditions that persisted for several days.

> *A tongue in cheek chat:* During dinner at Woomera senior mess, a visiting RAE Space Dept VIP extolled the merits of mechanical timers versus electronic types – our table suggested that solid state devices with zero moving parts must be more reliable and he countered that electronic timers failed to retain the status quo when power was lost and went on to elaborate RAE research on the topic. When asked about reliability statistics for the development hardware, with a mischievous look he replied, "Goodness me, as yet no hardware existed but the principle was sound and reliability was the design engineers problem". So we emptied our glasses and departed to the snooker room

BK19 LAUNCH –

Lifted off at 02:45 hrs, August 06, 1964, AUW 14187 lbs. All burnt at 122.8 secs, Apogee at 374 miles, re-entry speed 15900ft/sec. Upper stage and Test Body separated correctly and Dazzle ground stations saw a debris free re-entry. All head remains were recovered – another good flight.

On returning home from Woomera 10 August 1964 after an eight week tour, my efforts were now directed towards finishing the bungalow begun a year earlier – my long–suffering fiancee and I planned to marry in November, a dead line I had to meet without fail.

A VERY REGRETABLE ACCIDENT: Around this era our hierarchy felt useful publicity might be had by staging a High Down open day. RAE endorsed the idea subject to keeping classified features under raps. All hands were set to tidying up the Site and scheming exhibits, several were nominated as tour party guides whilst others would be placed at strategic spots to explain things.

The day arrived to sunny weather and all events ran well until early afternoon when a serious accident intervened. A simple procedure intended to demonstrate seemingly passive HTP was quickly aroused to violence by adding a catalyst, had resulted in a small serious detonation; serious because several members of the public took shrapnel wounds and an RDD technician was severely injured. The poor guy was directly over the blast point and took the full impact, which shielded many onlookers. He was rushed to hospital with a badly damaged leg, eye and hand, and remained very ill for some time but his strong constitution pulled him through and despite a permanent gammy leg and the loss of two fingertips, he recovered well and remained an active member of the BK/BA trials teams until the program ended. In common with most accidents, the enquiry identified several aggravating factors like: spectator proximity, inappropriate test vessels, and the concrete demo surface. Inadequate clean up between demo cycles may also have been a contributing factor. Needless to say, open days were taboo from then on.

THE BK DOOR BEGINS TO CLOSE – – – – WILL BLACK ARROW OPEN ANOTHER?

Times were a changing as they say, the BK era would end when BK25 flew next year. The rumoured engine size upgrade using the Stentor large thrust chambers to continue Dazzle experiments at higher velocities were scotched when UK dropped all interest in having a home grown deterant. RDD's continued existance along with the other project participants would now depend on Government endorsement of Black Arrow as UK's small satillite carrier rocket.

Black Knight's headline record was:

- 22 launches – 14 Gamma 201 & 8 Gamma 301.
- No catastrophic failures.
- Max apogee of 500 miles.
- Re-entry Body design data secured.
- Rocket efflux radar signatures discovered and researched.
- Re-entry physics spectral phenomena explored.
- Significant rocket hardware developed at moderate cost.
- A mature design, manufacture and operations co-operative.

This history combined with a moderate financial record and proven reliability of Gamma 301 engines, was a cast iron down payment on a 'budget' sized satellite launcher program, should secure a UK seat at the world's Space industry club until better times return.

THE NEW ERA

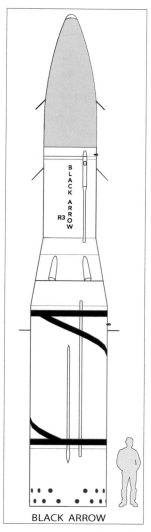

BLACK ARROW

FIG 16-1   *(DM)*

Ideas for a UK satellite launcher of some ilk were being promoted before the concept of a small payload rocket vehicle took hold. After a stream of studies by a variety of space advocates, the RAE with Westland (>Saunders Roe) and Bristol Siddeley Engines (>Armstrong Siddeley) proposed a three-stage small satellite launcher based on the back of Black Knight facilities and proven engineering. Whitehall inertia delayed Julian Amery's ministerial approval of the project expected late 1964 but the Tory government lost power in the October general election. Though keen to embrace "White Hot" technology, financial concerns obliged the new Prime Minister, Harold Wilson, to review all nonessential spending, which put the whole Black Arrow program on the back burner once again. Early in 1965, three-month holding contracts were initiated to retain much of RAE Space Department, engine development at Ansty and some exclusive industrial teams.

With no National Space agency or enthusiastic Government to crystallise policy, uncertainty allowed Whitehall freedom to manoeuvre, procrastinate and revise. The Treasury persuaded RAE to cut type-proving flights from 6 to 4 firings, a chancy plan with little room for error. The original aim gradually added complexity to each new firing, progressing from a Stage1 burn only through to an orbital demonstration before lofting a client payload on shot 6. This classical path advanced test objectives with least risk and kept journalist hawks at bay until shot 6 when airworthiness was proven. While a four shot plan might bring a mature design to the launcher earlier; it fell far short of the potential risk levels practiced by comparable programs.

These risks were spelt out at the highest government level but ignored when reliability was tabled as a reason for cancellation.

As the next chapters explain, the program was eventually authorised with a given launch date target of January 1968, with the Treasury still hedging it's bets by retaining three monthly contracts until program cancellation in 1971. I suspected this as an endgame option for UK's rocket industry. Having been party to blowing large sums on Blue Streak in its various guises, the UK "Space Lobby" kept doggo instead of urging government to lay foundations along with France and India in readiness for a dawning Space bonanza that would surely follow the growing digital technology.

THE ADDITIONAL PLAYERS –

Added to the existing Black Knight team (RAE, WRE, Westland, Rolls Royce and DeHavilland) the following companies were enlisted for the Black Arrow task.

FERRANTI – Devised and supplied the Attitude Reference Unit (ARU), a cut down version of their small military inertial navigator.

BRISTOL AEROJET – In conjunction with RPE Westcott, designed and manufactured the: spin- table thrusters, the Siskin stage separation thrusters and the Waxwing apogee motor.

EMI – Configured and supplied the 465Mhz telemetry transmitters.

MARCONI – Designed and built two Prospero Satellites and staffed the satellite launch support crew at High Down and Woomera.

THE BLACK ARROW FEATURES:

The design objective was to insert a 132lb payload into a 300mile circular earth orbit using a two-stage variant of the well-understood Black Knight rocket plus a bespoke solid propellant apogee Stage. The dominant hardware features together with the flight corridor and trajectory diagrams are set out later in Appendix 'B'.

THE TICK OVER YEARS –

Before Fred Mulley's go ahead in 1966, cost limits kept BA activities at Westland, WRE and elsewhere to planning, design and self funded preparatory tasks in order that the meagre government funds could focus on engine development, RAE research, Bristol Aerojet and Ferranti. As High Down activity moderated, RDD staff dwindled and effort was confined to defining possible engineering and operational issues. Unlike the early BK days, RDD was now a mature campaign-hardened group with inventive engineers, green-fingered artisans and proven problem solvers.

Bearing in mind that Computer Aided Design (CAD) and such like had yet to come over the horizon, RDD were sought out to mock up prototype assemblies and devise solutions to tricky three-dimensional constructs.

Over the years several like–minded RDD engineers and myself had tamed many BK design foibles and were determined that our collective knowledge must be applied early in the BA design phase while change was still feasible. After reviewing candidate subjects, a study list was agreed and work began to define the issues, explore ways and means, and feasible cost solutions. BK experience had shown that finance for such topics would be overlooked in the larger scheme of things so a substantive cost plan was prepared with all the ducks put carefully in a row.

My particular interests came within the following collective studies:

Detonator Shielding	Data recording	Test gear
Airframe rigging	Servicing access	Stage3 separation tests
Trial Plan format	RUSPs	Engine testing

DETONATOR SHEILDING – BK firing circuit acceptance tests at High Down were designed to prove that RF and switched inductance fields did not induce currents that exceeded the "zero fire" threshold specified for each detonator/igniter type. Compliance was simply demonstrated by fitting "Match Head Puffers" to simulate the bridge-wire fuse of each detonator/igniter and discretely applying the appropriate radiating sources. Ever mindful of safety, WRE upped the game on all new projects by reducing acceptable induce current levels by a factor of 1000.

The bridge-wire electric initiator, ("Match Head"/"Puffer"/"Detonator"/"Igniter") uses a very short length of high resistance wire (the bridge) immersed in a bead of thermally sensitive incendiary compound. Whilst the design is inherently tolerant to low energy inputs due to its very low ohmic resistance, demonstrating compliance with the new requirements was a challenge. The initial approach was to search industry for a device that would quantify very low energy levels at a bridge-wire. After this fruitless quest, effort was put into constructing a device that would relate "Puffer" temperature to bridge-wire current. Careful insertion of a miniature thermister bead inside the incendiary compound close to the bridge-wire of a live "Puffer" might be a possible solution if it was totally enclosed within a thermal and EMC shield. After modelling several options, the version outlined in Fig 16–2 below was calibrated for temperature rise versus a range of bridge-wire currents and shown to be an effective if fragile RF pickup sensor.

Total screening for the entire rocket firing circuit installation was ruled out for weight and sustained integrity assurance reasons.

While resolving the screening issue of our new pickup sensor, a simple remedy to the whole EMC screening problem emerged, each detonator or igniter is invariably housed within a metallic casing that forms a ready made local screen.

By fitting such enclosures with ceramic bead feed though RF filters, the general firing circuit outside each casing could remain unscreened.

The principle was easily demonstrated by simultaneously exposing two 20ft long, parallel unscreened firing circuit pairs to EMC fields from transient inductive sources and a 465Mkz telemetry transmitter. Both of the test pairs were terminated with screened RF pickup sensors, only one of which included the RF bead filters.

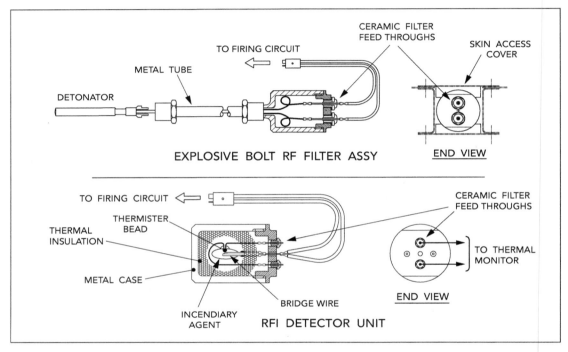

FIG 16–2   EXPLOSIVE BOLT RFI FILTER & DETECTOR UNIT   (D Mack)

As predicted, the unfiltered pickup unit registered a recordable thermal rise whereas output from the filtered circuit remained undetectable when exposed to RF fields in excess of the BA environment. It was concluded that local shielding with filters would easily meet the new WRE requirement and it only remained to design a suitable screened envelope for the explosive bolt detonators, see Figure 16–2 above.

Physical examples and sketches of the revised detonator/igniter casings were circulated to the Cowes Design Office, RAE and Bristol Aerojet; ultimately 43 of the 50 detonator/igniters installed in Black Arrow were protected in this way.

Random searches using the pickup sensor technique were carried on each rocket ordnance devices, excepting the Satellite and Payload fairing separators and ACS gas valve, which allowed a reduced safety margin due to their zero debris output.

DATA RECORDING – Three areas came under consideration plus a total revamp of the High Down Recorder Room to embrace BA requirements and streamline operations. See Figure 16–3.

(a) ADDITIONAL DATA CHANNELS – Pressure and voltage recorder channels would increase from 14 to 24 and 20 to 44 respectively, almost 100% capacity uplift. The Measurements guys were anxious that money should not be wasted on renewing the primitive and aged H&B recorders so an industry wide trawl was mounted to seek suitable modern alternatives. Hitherto it had been routine to annotate, photo fix, copy and present a "First Look" assessment to the RAE within an hour or so after each firing, before they travelled back to the mainland that day.

FIG 16–3   HD RECORDER ROOM AS EXTENDED FOR BLACK ARROW.   The original H&B UV recorders are seen on the RH wall with the new recorder suit on left hand wall. Tele recorder and site patch card are LH out of frame   *(GKN Aerospace)*

To keep this arrangement with increased channels for Black Arrow RDD proposed dividing data channels into two categories, (Cat1) essential acceptance data and (Cat2) fault diagnostic data, the former being processed immediately and presented to RAE on firing day as usual while the latter would be mailed within 24hrs.

If, on firing day a particular Cat1 data channel revealed a problem, related Cat2 data would be processed immediately to assist fault diagnosis. Unfortunately the RAE was unable to agree on a definition for each data category so this innovation fell at the first hurdle.

(b) RECORDER REDUNDANCY –The lack of surplus recorder channels risked the need to repeat firings and squander engine life whenever a recorder failed to function. Modern recorder reliability would reduce this risk but not eradicate it. RDD proposed duplicating important channels but again like (a) above, the RAE were unable to define a duplicated channel list.

(c) CORRELATION ACROSS TEST SITES – Engine pressures measured during calibration at Anstey and qualification firings at High down and Woomera, plus the flight data, were mostly done using different transducer types with various bandwidths. The Auto Observer that is installed at each venue to compare static firing behaviour uses "dead beat" bourdon gauge instruments and sequential photo stills, which cannot capture dynamic behaviour. On site fault analysis and resolution of the BK08, Y1 bootstrap problem might have been possible with higher data speed.

In an attempt to provide comparable measurements across all venues and solve the capacity and redundancy concerns raised in (a) and (b) above, RDD proposed recording the telemetry transducer outputs alongside each existing measurement system. Flight pressure transducers that already reside in each engine bay could be installed at Ansty and remain with each engine wherever it went to log data at a common bandwidth via a standard multiplex modulator/demodulator and recorder unit. By this means standardised data would be obtained from engine calibration through qualification firings and on into flight. The arrangement offered conformity across the venues and partially resolved the recorder channel redundancy issue at High Down and Woomera. But the RAE could not be encouraged to agree the data categorisation mentioned in (a) above. After selling the idea to our Chief Designer, RDD made a formal presentation to the RAE who rejected it on the narrow grounds: "That a flight system must not acceptance test a flight system", a trite response, which laid bare a weak grasp of this serious issue without offering an alternative solution beyond sticking one's head in the sand!

I'm again reminded of that profound negotiating principle: never attempt to present a topic head on, always find an oblique circular approach. However, the value of these proposals did eventually permeated to some degree because funds were discreetly secured for a multiplexer, modulator/demodulator and suitable recorder at High Down, which RDD integrated using "Tween trials time" manpower.

This allowed High Down records to be directly correlated with Woomera ground and flight results. Alas, where a closed mind prevails full synergy is rarely achieved; Ansty was never equipped to read telemetry transducers and High Down/Woomera ground recorder capacity was doubled any way. No attention was ever given to the recorder redundancy issue.

TEST GEAR REQUIREMENTS –

The study group liaised at length with various flight equipment providers like such as: RAE, Ferranti, EMI, EEL, WRE and later on Marconi to identify their servicing and accessibility needs.

(a) SPECIALISED TOOLING –This topic embraced proprietary test meters, gauges, portable test sets and specialised hand tools not normally seen as standard hand tooling. Additionally, each RDD laboratory assessed what interfacing aids were required to exercise, calibrate and set up their various electronic and mechanical sub assemblies.

(b) PREPARATION AREAS – The expansion of Haz circuit content and doubling of routine system testing that arose from two vehicle stages gave cause for concern. If test time, error rates and connector wear and tear were to be minimised, purpose made connector access would be necessary and I drew the short straw to specify this requirement.

The chosen scheme used three overhead cable ducts extending out from the workshop wall, placed and sized to drop test cables down to mate with the Stage1 and Stage2 airframes lying on floor trolleys below. At the vehicle end, each cable terminated with vehicle matching connectors. Each cable was routed back to wall mounted 19" panels where each core terminated at Banana sockets arrayed and idented to mimic their Stage connection source, or connected to meter displays as appropriate. To accommodate test gear and associated paperwork, a long desk surface with drawers below similar to modern kitchen units was provisioned below the panel arrays. High Down and TS4 workshops were equipped with identical setups.

(c) CONTROL SYSTEM MONITOR UNITS – The CSMU's located at each Gantry level 'E' required extensive alteration to suit Stage2 FCS together with an additional version at Gantry1 and 5B for Stage1 FCS. The configuration of these units were specified by the RDD, FSC lab in conjunction with EEL.

(d) MECHANICAL SYSTEM SERVICING – RDD engineers and workshop resources procured or renovated assorted pressure test rigs, handling gear and specialised setting up tooling to mate with the revised ground and rocket mechanical systems.

(e) SEQUENCE PROGRESS DISPLAY UNIT – I took the opportunity to remedy a longstanding irritation of mine by seeking the introduction of a central Sequence Display panel to indicate progress of the 120sec auto count down in each equipment centre. If a countdown Auto Stopped, it was important to localise the reason without undue delay, a task that currently required decoding an unfriendly Teledeltos spark recorder before the problem could be bracketed.

A suitable wall display devised in conjunction with Cowes DO, illuminated as each sequence event was initiated and its associated interlock confirmation occurred. This informative display became useful to operators and visitors alike at High Down and Area5 Equipment Centres.

SERVICING ACCESS – As manufacture drawings came to hand, RDD staff vetted each flight system installation for realistic servicing access and adjacent system disturbance. As mentioned earlier, CAD with its 3D modelling goodies was a thing of the future; 3D visualisation invariably remained iffy until full-scale hardware appeared when all but essential changes could be entertained. RDD made much use of cardboard and adhesive tape and were encouraged to keep designers aware that servicing was crucial to success – a delicate diplomatic process eased along by the good rapport established over the BK years.

TRIAL PLAN STRUCTURE – Placing a satellite in orbit entails co-ordination with extensive Woomera Range stations and remote worldwide agencies that remain obscure to those at the Launch Pad. For these expensive resources to be economically reserved for tracking, interrogating and harvesting data from in flight hardware their preparation must be lock–stepped with the rockets prelaunch progress. To this end, headway towards the launch window needed to be robust and meticulously planned. Weather conditions and technical issues will always be a variable but Woomera Met forecasting was usually good for 36 hours ahead so the main challenge for trial managers was awareness and control of technical progress. After much discussion and head scratching, RDD structured a launch Trail Plan format that subdivided all TS2 and Area 5 activities into five main phases: Stage1 Test Shop, Stage2 Test Shop, Stage2 5A, Composite vehicle 5B and Live Firing 5B and devised a daily plan for each phase. The satellite authority, formulated and piggy backed their Payload preparation on this Launch Vehicle plan. Working back from Time Zero, every activity was time analysed, grouped into work packets and mapped on a daily graphic that showed time scale, task relationships and synchronising rules at each point in the Trial.

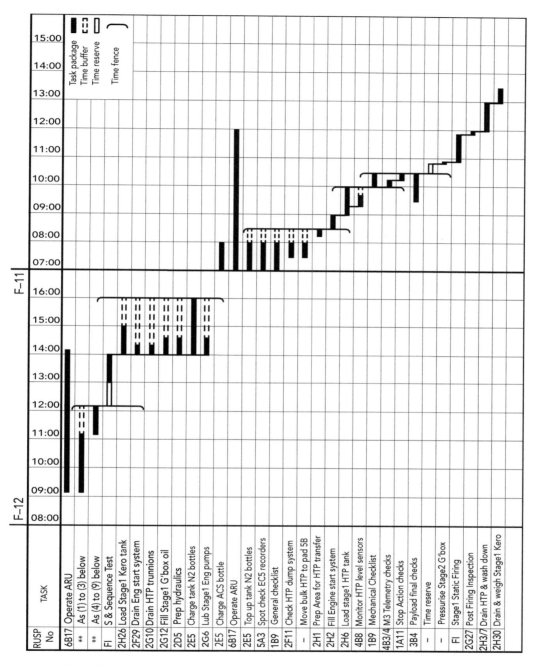

FIG 16–4   TYPICAL DAILY TRIAL PLAN FORMAT   *(D Mack)*

In the earlier phases where time was less critical, each work packet could stretch to several hours but as a static firing or launch firing approached each work packet time was defined in fractions of an hour. To graphically convey these relationships with buffer times and deadline fences in a real time frame, a variation of a critical path diagram was evolved, See Fig 16–4 above.

After much iteration to minimise conflicts, each packet was sketched out in RUSP (see below) format and farmed out to the RDD specialist sections to flesh out and agree with hardware designers before passing to DH as drafts subject to RDD trials proofing. The final 36 hours of Live Firing preparation was obviously most crucial so each deadline sensitive packet with hazardous content was identified in 15–minute increments and arranged with deadline fences and time reserves. Hitting a deadline fence ahead of packet completion implied a knock on time delay, which, after local assessment might have to be passed on to the outside world. Due to the hazardous content and need to coordinate with several Range facilities, the same philosophy was applied to static firing windows in the Stage1 and Stage2 phases and aspects of the Composite Assembly phase.

STAGE 3 SEPARATION DYNAMICS – To investigate design issues relating to interface geometry, spring impulse sizing and timing delays contributing to Stage3 separation events, the mechanical test section of EEL was tasked with a full-scale boiler–plate free fall study, which I managed to join as an observer.

A dummy Waxwing motor and Payload were mocked up to replicate actual inertias in the six degrees of freedom. Live ordnance was used to rotate the spin-table, sever the Manacle Clamp and detach the Payload – no other explosive elements were involved. The entire assembly was suspended from the Balloon Shed roof at Cardington, which provided nearly a 200 ft of freefall. High-speed cine cameras filmed each drop and calibrated nylon ropes arrested the test hardware before impacting the ground. Because the full sequence took up most of the available height a number of simple dead weight drops were done to size the arrester ropes and resolve camera issues. Despite these precautions, the first drop destroyed the camera sited directly below the descending assembly; a risk avoided later by sacrificing a 45° mirror. It was soon found that rope stretch was not constant and varied with ambient temperature that could not easily be held to close limits so an impact cushion was devised. Initially, an inadequate sand heap was tried as a buffer, followed by a light alloy crush tube extending from the test specimen. Finally a light alloy sheet placed atop the sand heap proved successful once its thickness was sized to match the crush tube.

The Onlookers: Such tests invariably attract a few eyeballers and a couple of guys were heard to remark at the cleverness of being able to exactly line up the "diameter crush tube with the 4" hole in the impact sheet every time, failing to understand that the descending tube pierced its own hole!

Once these rig details were resolved, a series of successful tests explored spin Imp numbers and sizes using two payload masses, several separation spring rates and timer delays. The time delay between firing the manacle clamp and payload release was telescoped for the test to suit the available drop distance.

RANGE USERS STANDARD PROCEDURES (RUSP's) These replaced the CSP's (Contractors Standard Procedure) of the BK days. While the title change grew from WRE Blue Streak activities and was applied to all new WRE programs, their content and format remained very similar to CSP's. With a proliferation of explosive devices in multiple rocket stages, WRE required the "User" staff to be qualification as Range Users Explosive Officers (RUXO's) to work alongside their Launcher Officer crews. The RDD Safety Officer at High Down ran a WRE approved course to meet this standard, which was soon opened to UK industry at large.

AIRFRAME RIGGING – The Engine bays, Stage1, Stage2, FCS Tray etc., were all constructed in individual diverse assembly jigs.

While the interfacing between each structural unit was simple and did not present a complex tooling challenge, High Down offered the only vertical assembly facility in the UK so it fell to RDD to verify overall alignment and devise a means for doing it.

Stage3 comprised a series of machined circular elements that needed no further checking beyond the machine shop inspections. The Spin Table offered the obvious Stage1/Stage2 datum plane interfacing Stage3 with the added advantage of rotation. A downward facing tool-room telescope with cross wires mounted on a beam projecting radially from the Spin Table rim allowed the entire airframe to be viewed and mapped with a stick micrometer. The Cowes Tool Room devised and constructed this rig, which was manacle clamped to the spin-table. Alignment between the spin-table rotation plane, ARU mountings and each thrust chamber swing datum was established using a standard Tool Room inclinometer.

ENGINE CALIBRATION at ANSTY – Several fact-finding visits were made to Ansty to explore Gamma 8 and Gamma2 engine hardware with particular regard to servicing routines, access and special tooling.

The Gamma8 engine as described in Appendix B, was two 301 engines with paired chambers trunnion mounted in cruciform to provide the thrust vector steering pioneered on Black Knight.

Viewed from below, all thrust chambers were grouped closely around the release ball, which left much of the 2-metre diameter bay unused. This confinement ensured that all thrust chamber efflux footprints remained inside the existing BK exhaust duct diameter. Good internal access was affected via several large service hatches and two externally accessed compartments dedicated to electrical gear and pressure transducers.

The start/stop solenoid valve was revised to delete the "Flight Nut", whose function was replaced by an external gas actuator, actuated by a shore-side pressure source and only fitted for static firings. To protect against accidental loss of actuating gas pressure, an in flight termination Haz battery will always be fitted to energise the shore side Stop Action circuit.

The ground start and N2 purge feeds now used self–sealing lift off couplings, and extensive drain/bleed facilities were provided.

The Gamma 2 (Stage2) engine as described in Appendix B used two fully gimballed 301-type thrust chambers, which boasted kerosene cooled nozzle extensions to improve the high altitude expansion ratio. Informed attention had been given to servicing access of this very compact assembly.

A self-contained engine start and N2 purge system resided in the disposable Inter Stage Bay between the Stage1 & 2 structures.

These very useful visits provided the insight needed to configure test procedures, settle on test gear design and servicing tooling needs and go some way towards optimising the preparation trial plan well before hardware appeared at High Down

RF AERIAL MOCKUP – The immovable High Down gantries structures presented very effective Faraday screens, which made realistic free-free RF aerial testing impossible. Routine transmissions between ground stations in the Equipment Centre or RF Lab were achieved via parasitic transfer aerials to pass RF across the gantry cladding.

To do credible radiation pattern testing and EMC studies, RDD designed and built a full-scale vehicle mock-up for examination of aerial performance for various configurations and lines of fire.

This rig also served to research Wrebus compatibility with the proposed Black Arrow RF installations. As reported elsewhere, any loss of RF sensitivity while Wrebus is operating in Fail/Fire mode, will trigger vehicle destruction. The mock–up was arranged to lay horizontal to aid equipment access and fitted with a hoist to raise it into the vertical test position.

THE CORK IS PULLED | **17**

Mid December 1966, some 13 months after the last BK flew, government extended their three-month financing contracts to all BA Contractors who then raced into the long awaited BA manufacture and modification program. To deal with the new vehicle, many existing technical facilities at High Down and Woomera required alteration or replacement, which had stalled for to lack of hardware. RDD staffing levels had drifted down to a core of about 80 folk across all grades and activities had been restricted to planning, research and strip down tasks until this 'go' was given. As April 1967 arrived major engineering parts for the launcher, Gantries and Equipment Centres at both venues begun trickling in. Site No1 and Launcher 5B were adapted to accept Stage1 for all Composite vehicle operations and the alternative sites were rigged for Stage2 static firings.

Alterations at the Stage1 site were extensive: launcher framework was fully dismantled to insert an azimuth girder ring needed for various lines of fire was reassembled with a revised centre cruciform and over hung wind brace pivots. Additionally, site 5B received a tall Stage2 HTP dump arm.

Cladding on High Down Site1 Gantry needed attention after a ten-year exposure to saline air and was replaced as necessary; the load bearing structure was reinforced to meet the higher lift loading and a localised roof extension was created to accommodate the taller rocket nose structure.

The 5B Gantry was barely adequate for BK and a total redesign. The cladded area was replaced by a larger more enlightened design, devised and constructed under supervision of SARO, Australia. The floor footprint was doubled at all levels by moving the clad sidewalls out to the limit of the existing bogie chassis; this allowed enclosure of all stairways, inclusion of an equipment service lift and offered space for new electronic equipment racks needed to service the additional rocket and satellite systems. An escape route was provided via fireman's pole to ground from floors B, C and fireman's pole plus slide chute to ground from floors D, E, F and G. Apart from an inquisitive interest, my primary remit at this stage was to bid for certain structural features on the upper floors to install a Clean Room I'd become involved in planning with Marconi and the Cowes design office for later more sensitive payloads.

Structural adaptation of Site No2 and 5B to suit Stage2 was relatively minor. An interstage-mounting frame replaced the centre cruciform of the BK launcher and the wind brace arms were discarded; no major changes to the gantry tower were necessary.

All Test Posts underwent a major rewire with revised priming consol panels. Gantries at both venues were equipped with new Control System Monitor Units (CSMU) to service Stage1 and Stage2 as appropriate.

Revised higher capacity systems to purge and start engines were installed and piped in at Sites 1 and 5B. To meet increased gas flow and volume demands new permanent bottle stores and compressor houses was constructed between the gantry towers at both venues.

Equipment Centre layouts were rearranged to make way for a Stage2 engine consol, ARU rack, C band and Doppler console and a Payload monitor console by moving the sequence Timing Unit into an adjacent room. RDD Measurements Section was deeply involved in an extensive revision of the Recorder Room facilities and similar arrangements were in hand at Area5.

TEST SHOP 2 FIRE –

April 1967 saw a disastrous fire in TS2 air-conditioning system that totally destroyed the entire building and its test equipment. This set back might well have doomed the entire Black Arrow program but for WRE's positive approach in reshuffling other programs to make TS4 available. In some respects this was helpful since TS4 was larger and big enough to embrace the proposed Satellite clean area that had yet to be installed.

RDD TRIALS TEAM SQUADS – As BA trials were now becoming an ever-stronger probability, the RDD trials office and I set about devising a Trials Operations Plan, structured along the lines outlined earlier. This process led on to define the skills and number of personnel required by each team to shepherd a vehicle through qualification at High Down and launch trials at Woomera. Each team must now include the following disciplines drawn from the various RDD sections on a rotating basis:

    Team Leader (Deputy TL at Woomera)
    Mechanical Engineer
    ARU/FCS Engineer
    Telemetry/Instrumentation Engineer
    RUXO Engineer
    Wireman (drawn from EEL at Cowes)
    Documentation/Spares clerk

Team members would be required to attend Woomera for the duration of each launch trial. Implications of the 8hr–working rule that surfaced during the R0 trial led to the addition of a second Deputy Team Leader to supervise the night shifts necessary during final launch preparation phase.

Additionally, each test venue would have the benefit of a visiting Ferranti (ARU) and Rolls Royce (Engines) engineers. The RAE and the specialist payload contractor would provide full manning for their operational areas.

TARGET DATE FOR BA TRIALS –

The four shot development program imposed in Feb '65, specified a first launch date of Jan 1968, an ill considered choice because the WRE Christmas shutdown meant that Woomera staff vanished to the four winds until mid February. The earliest possible launch attempt would be three months later in mid April'68. A practical plan was hatched to get Stage1 to TS4 by mid Feb'68, after a six weeks sea journey and a twelve-week trial at High Down, starting mid Sept'67. But as always events were to prove otherwise when a catastrophe disabled engine progress at Ansty. Research engineers had spent several months grappling with a catalyst performance issue when, on the brink of success a thrust chamber exploded and took much of the Test Cell with it. This devastating incident halted engine delivery for eight to nine months while chamber design was revisited and re-type tested.

However, a silver lining adorns most dark clouds and this one masked significant conversion delays at High Down and Woomera due in part to the inhibiting quarterly contract shackles; in the event all sites were very well prepared when a rocket did eventually arrived.

The following chapters will outline the many operational events that attended the R0, R1, R2 and R3 trials at High Down and Woomera.

FIG 17–1   PART OF BK & BA TANK WORKSHOP AT COWES   *(GKN Aerospace)*

R0 TRIAL – HIGH DOWN | **18**

"My" ninth bird – Seventh as TL

TRIAL OBJECTIVES:

- Black Arrow Maiden flight.
- Line of Fire 305° (Northwest).
- Stage1 – Prove Gamma 8 burn, Flight Control and Stage2 release.
- Stage2 – Prove separation, Gamma 2 ignition and burn.
- ARU/FCS performance.
- Inter–stage and Payload Fairing discard.
- ACS performance.
- Stage3 – Spin up and release.
- Stage3 – Payload release.
- WRE – Prove launch facilities, RF systems, Flight tracking & safety.

BUILD STANDARD:

All Stage elements were configured with an inert Waxwing Sage3 motor. The Payload was a Boilerplate Telemetry instrumented package designed to capture Stage3 and Payload separation dynamics.

TRIAL OUTLINE:

The notional trial plan given in Table B/4 of Appendix B indicates a nominal 63-day lapse time from Stage1 receipt at High Down to the UK shipping date ahead of the six-week sea passage to Adelaide. Being a first of type, R0 attracted a crop of developments tasks e.g. FCS structural stability, Spin Table mock-up, Post liftoff inter-system EMC tests and proof of Detonator shielding and FCS stability documents. These factors taken with late hardware delivery inflated Stage1 lapse time at High Down to a total of 74 days.

The key milestone events are listed below and fully described in the paragraphs that follow.

D – 64   Stage2 erected in Gantry 2
D – 62   Stage1 erected in Gantry 1
D – 50   Stage2, Static firing
D – 44   Stage2 erected on Stage1
D – 38   Stage3 assembled on Stage2
D – 32   Stage1, Static Firing

D – 29   FSP tests
D – 22   RFI tests
D – 10   Acceptance review
D0   Stage1 dispatched
D+17   Stage2 cleared for dispatch

END NOV'68 – An Attitude Reference Unit (ARU) arrived at High Down and was set up on a geodetic reference plinth in the Flight Control System (FCS) laboratory. Under the guiding hands of a visiting Ferranti engineer, RDD FCS engineers spent several weeks mastering the special powering up and calibration routines required for this sophisticated hardware.

The ARU alignment routines:
As detailed in Appendix B, two distinct procedures are used: –
Simple 2hr alignment: By omitting the gyro drift calibrations, this truncated less accurate routine is used when running the ARU in support of collateral system testing e.g. S&S tests, Static Firings, Internal Battery tests and general FCS testing etc.
Precision 12hr alignment: Entails thermal stabilisation, E/W and W/E gyro drift calibration and max accuracy heading alignment. It is used to set the FCS datum and the rocket airframe heading before surveyor verification checks and setting the launch Line of Fire. High Down operations found that rocket mounted 12hr ARU runs became excessively extended because small structural disturbances arising from parallel working activities prolonged gyro settling time. By running the 12hr routine overnight (typically 20:00 to 08:00hrs) this problem was minimised.

EARLY DEC '68: (ARU/FCS) A crucial development milestone arrived when the ARU and FCS electronics were first united, a long overdue exercise delayed by late FCS delivery. As the awaited moment arrived, inquisitive onlookers crowded the laboratory glass partition to witness the historic event – interest was so intense it resembled a pedigree livestock "mating" session without the mess! Alas, an underlying problem was found; with all units connected and powered up, 'noise' appeared across all FCS sub-units. Several days testing with EEL engineers on hand unearthed an obscure resistive earth loop between the FCS and ARU power packs. The FCS items were returned to EEL where they were to remain undergoing modification until the New Year.

Stages1 & 2 were still bogged down at Cowes awaiting engines while we at High Down had many urgent Stage2 issues to explore that merely required a Gamma2 engine as a structural element. Ansty offered their mock-up engine to let Cowes finalise system interfaces and speed delivery to High Down but the tactic failed at our end because the kerosene extension nozzles turned out to be simple single skinned space mock-ups.

The resulting mass and inertia values were not acceptable for servo frequency response tests so effort was diverted to the Haz circuit installation.

As the nerve centre and source of all timing, steering, tracking and flight termination events, Stage2 featured in almost every operational routine from subsystem level up through to overall qualification. The stage also embodied the lion's share of the ordnance elements and circuitry that mechanised most in-flight events. Classified as Hazardous circuits, these installations required certification by WRE approved Range Users Explosive Officers (RUXO's). Because our Safety Officer was WRE approved to train and qualify RUXO personnel for the UK industry at large, we had the competent personnel.

EARLY DEC'68 – (STAGE2). Arrived complete with mock-up engine and the three-day RUXO haz-circuit checkout began. Unlike the plethora of connector boxes that dogged BK early days, our Prep Area now boasted fixed panel displays presenting every interstage connection on an array of pictorially displayed test points. The tests entailed point-to-point continuity, point to every other point continuity and point to airframe insulation resistance, which took time to do but the absence of any stray conducting paths was ensured.

The FCS crew took possession of the rocket vehicle to calibrate thrust chamber swing angle sensors (AC and DC pick offs and zero switches); servo Laws relays and the ACS jet valves. The Tele crew followed to pad and calibrated the inductive pressure transducer installation, checked thermal sensors, propellant level sensors and aerial standing wave ratios. Weaving through this hive of activity the Mechanics inspected all pipe routing, clipping, bonding and joint integrity, measured the set points of breather valves and confirmed the action of each solenoid valve. The Inter-Stage Bay was set up in Gantry2 where the Gamma2 start and N2 purge systems where pressure and flow tested.

Useful progress was also made at mocking up the Spin Table hazardous circuit installation. When accepted by Cowes Design office, parts were ordered and drawing revisions were put in hand. Final assembly and wire up might be possible within four weeks.

> _Spin Table Mock-up:_ See Fig B-10 in Appendix 'B'. To create a balanced disposition of the hazardous circuit hardware festooning the Table while providing workable access to battery pack and arming plugs for final arming, the Cowes Design Office enlisted High Down to "mock up" a suitable layout using the RO hardware.
> All mechanical rotating features had already been engineered and manufactured; just the Haz circuit hardware, cable routing and clipping were needed.
> When a balanced and accessible arrangement had been resolved, redundant breakaway pathways for timing signals from Stage2 to Spin Table and on to the Waxwing motor were devised.

These comprised two-miniature multi pin pull away connectors mounted on two diametrically opposed spring-loaded trailing arms that attached to structure below the Spin Table on self-aligning pivots.

The miniature four-pin socket on each arm aligned horizontally and tangentially with a mating plug slung beneath the Spin Table itself. When unlocked and rotated, the Table pulled each connector apart to let their trailing arms spring down clear of the rapidly rotating gizmo above.

Simple, vertically aligned single pin pull-off connectors formed dual circuit pathways from atop the Spin Table across the Manacled Vee band joint to the Waxwing motor. These parted as the multiple compression springs gently push the Waxwing clear as a Spin Table delay timer fired the Manacle Clamp explosive bolts.

MID DEC '68: (STAGE2) When the Prep Area tasks stalled for lack of hardware, the Stage was moved out to Site2 and set up on the Interstage Bay to calibrate HTP tank sight glass and level sensor volumes, using metered pumping with demin water as employed on BK. The lenticular kerosene tank was small enough to fill via a weighed transfer churn. The lone sump level-sensor was calibrated by flooding it then slowly draining to the sensor trip point. The remaining contents were then drained back into the transfer churn and weighed.

Both propellant tank pressurisation systems were functionally tested with full liquid levels to confirm leak tightness, followed by an empty pressurisation to verify gas storage bottle capacity. Both systems settled correctly around 20 psi with no wet or dry leakage detected

(STAGE3) We now devoted time to gather experience at assembling this stage and fitting the Payload Fairings. Using a custom lifting harness, the inert Waxwing motor was easily hoisted and secured on the Spin Table. Similarly, an SSB and dummy Payload provided by RAE were attached without difficulty to the inert Waxwing, but hoisting and attaching each Payload Fairing proved a much more tricky business; a delicate operation that called for careful handling and the creation of a custom handling and lifting rig.

Handling Payload Fairings: The fairing design and operational features are fully detailed under Section 7 in Appendix B, and only summarised here in relation to the handling problems mentioned above. The fairing assembly divides vertically into two lightweight clamshells fabricated from magnesium alloy, a stiff, strong and light but brittle material, prone to cracking when locally overloaded. Each half fairing was provided with two threaded inserts located about one third from the nose end to serve as hoist points but these easily pulled out under normal handling loads. This problem and the general workshop handling needs was resolved by creating a light alloy tubular "strong back" frame to served as stowage cradle, general handling aid and hoisting frame.

These frames fastened to each half fairing via the original lift points (now reinforced) plus two additional points lower down beside each main hinge unit.
These frames remained attached to each fairing half from factory through to pre-launch time. To impart a more sensitive "feel" when lifting and attaching each fairing to the Stage2 structure, a light hand operated two-drop pulley hoist was introduced between main hoist hook and handling frames.

CHRISTMAS: After studying the expected weather conditions it was decided to leave the Stage2 & 3 airframes assembled in Gantry1 over the holiday period. Operations were suspended Friday Dec 20th until Wednesday 1st Jan, though several guys came in randomly to quietly square paperwork (or was it to escape a hectic domestic scene often prevalent at these times).

Both Stages were "put to bed" by disconnecting all external test cables and test piping, and transferring all removable electronic trays etc to the laboratories, closing up hatchways and fitting propellant tank desiccant breathers. Copious plastic sheet and Duck tape was applied against direct water ingress. The usual 24-hour on–site security patrol would remain and I made frequent visits to check that all was well.

NEW-YEAR: Belatedly advised that a functional Gamma 2 engine was arriving within several days our attentions switched to this possibility – pity the whisper hadn't circulated before the Christmas break! After stripping away all plastic shrouding the Payload Fairings, Stage3, Stage2 and the Interstage were broken down and returned to the Prep Area.

(Authors Note. Where an asterisk is given against the following day idents, the value may be in error due to scrappy notes and an even scrappier memory)

D*–77: (STAGE1) (CIRCA MID JAN'69) – Arrived on site complete with a functional engine – would we be burning diesel at last? A few HTP pipes still remained at Cowes being pickled and trained but we had plenty to do without them.
Stage1 Prep Area checkout progressed fitfully over the next 12 days, as staff became free from the Stage2 critical path.

D*–77: (STAGE2) (CIRCA MID JAN'89) – The operational Gamma2 engine arrived along with both FCS electronic packs, which now ran happily with the ARU, and the last of the Spin Table mod kit came to hand.
The Gamma2 engines were changed over and the RUXO, FCS, Tele and Mech crews worked co-operatively over Stage2 to revalidate the disturbed systems. Conveniently, the EEL wiremen managed to complete the Spin Table assembly and wiring as Stage2 became ready for Gantry 2.

D*–64/60: (STAGE2) – Was returned to Gantry 2 where propellant tank and pressurisation tests were again carried out.

Before adding Stage3, the overall structural alignment and the ARU mounting pad levels were measured against the Spin Table rotation plane using a purpose made telescope, stick micrometer and tool-room clinometer; all results fell well within design tolerances. Spin Table static friction and rotational freedom were then assessed before locking it at flight orientation. To complete Stage2 structural build for the approaching FCS stability tests, the dummy Stage3 units (Waxwing, and Payload) and SSB were secured on the Spin Table and enclosed by the Payload Fairings.

D*–62: (STAGE1) – Was moved to Gantry1 and set vertical by trimming the Wind Brace arms to achieve a horizontal plain across the separation bay explosive bolt housings. Propellant tank volume and level sensor calibrations then followed. Tank pressurisation tests were put off until the EC and Blockhouse services could be patched over to Site1 after the Stage2 static firing at Site2.

D*–59/58: (STAGE2) –The FCS circus now set up camp with their test gear as the Mechanics readied the engine for servo running using shore-side hydraulics and flooded the trunnions with Kero and demin water to lubricate the seals.

> *Inner Loop frequency responses:* The two gimbal mounted Stage2 thrust chambers were servo controlled to direct thrust ± 10° in Pitch and Yaw and differentially in Roll, as demanded by the ARU/FCS. To maintain flight path and achieve a precise and stable vehicle attitude for orbital insertion, exacting rapid servo response is essential, a behaviour that is assessed by measuring the sinusoidal waveform, amplitude, linearity and phase lag of each servo across a defined amplitude and frequency range.

Frequency response testing dragged on for nearly two day's while several repetitions and procedural refinements were explored together with demos for the RAE before all was pronounced fit for use. ACS trigger settings, jet axis allocation and sensing were also tested and found correct.

As the opportunity presented, C Band beacon, WREBUS Rx and the Telemetry system was installed and functionally checked via vehicle and gantry transfer aerials. As usual, several scaling and related anomalies were found and corrected in some tele channels.

D*–57: (STAGE2) – To explore aligning the ARU when mounted in the structurally flexible rocket, the Switch On Unit (SOU) and Alignment Unit (AU) were made ready. The platform was installed but after an hour or so the crew found that airframe movements induced by parallel routines exaggerated the gyro settlement times. Co-operatively the ARU crew decided to run their 12hr precision tests overnight (Saturday) to work in undisturbed conditions.

The above arrangement became the modus operandi whenever accurate alignment was required.

D*–56/53: (STAGE2 FCS STABILITY) – With the ARU aligned, the FCS and ACS Pitch, Yaw and Roll channels were balanced and harmonised accordingly.

Finally, with hydraulic pressure applied, Stage2 outer loop structural stability margins were explored with tanks empty, tanks full and tanks pressurised. No evidence of instability was encountered or could be induced.

In readiness for the upcoming static firing S&S check, N2 purge and engine start systems were setup and flow checked through test orifices, and the gearbox Lub system was tested, drained and replenished.

D*–55/53: (STAGE1) – At Site1, it now became Gamma8's turn for inner loop servo response testing so trunnions were flooded and shore side hydraulics were rigged for running. Servo tests were completed and found satisfactorily as and when the FCS guys found time away from their Stage2 activities.

Telemetry inductive rest levels were trimmed and voltage channels were progressively cleared as the systems being monitored became operational. Doppler beacon was fitted and proved to be functional. Many Stage1 tasks were now held pending availability of EC, Blockhouse or Recorder Room facilities when the critical path activities at Site2 were concluded.

D*–52: (STAGE2) – Effort now exclusively focussed on the Gamma2 static firing. Support services like the exhaust duct cooling; fire fighting and deluge, Equipment Centre facilities and Recorder Room functions were being routinely brought to an operational state. Each vehicle system and the associated recorder services were fussed over until finalised. Stop Action services, Sequence Console timing and Interlock Overrides were checked and sealed.

The Kerosene load required later was weighed and stored to be temperature conditioned ready for the firing.

D*–51: (STAGE2 S&S TEST) – See Table B/6 of Appendix B for countdown times
Everyone with an operational role during the firing will now rehearse the process in a coordinated time sequence that would result in engine ignition if propellants had been loaded.

In line with BK practice, the BA S&S test was undertaken 12hrs ahead of firing time.

The day began with avid activity around Gantry2, in the Equipment Centre and the Recorder Room.

Telemetry, C–Band and WREBUS were spot-checked and the FCS was exercised via the Control System Signal Unit (CSSU) using shore hydraulic supplies.

Engine HTP start bottle was filled with demin water and all gas bottles were charged to 4000psi, N2 purge backup and Fail/Safe gas lines were attached.

When all was ready at Gantry2 I moved to the Equipment Centre (EC) and conferred with each console observer before passing the count control to the Safety and Sequence Officers. Some 15mins into the count, the Recorder Room called a "hold" to quickly fix a spooling jam up; the –120sec Auto sequence then run through to +35secs to complete a good S&S test; a rewarding result considering the last time was 3 years ago.

All initial reports positive so kerosene was loaded and gas bottles given an initial charge ready for tomorrow.

D*–50: (STAGE2 STATIC FIRING) – A dull dry day carrying a slight breeze. The S&S records confirmed all systems were on the money and the ARU was still running sweetly and pointing in the right direction – the Downs Clearance Party had already sallied forth so we will be static firing today!

Test Cell and Safety Officer team donned PVC suits, washed down the area and loaded some 2000lbs of peroxide in the Stage2 HTP tank and approx 5lbs in the Interstage engine start tank. A lub oil flow check wetted the gearbox; N2 purge was functioned and the vehicle hydraulic accumulator and gas bottles took a final top up. After a further area wash down and final check on Test Post gas settings, the checklists were closed and the Gantry area quarantined for lunch.

> *Engine Fail safe/fail fire modes*: It may be recalled that like the BK gamma 301 engines, the Gamma2 required a shore-side gas operated actuator to inhibit the Start/Stop valve latch function during static firings. As a backup against loss of shore-side gas source, a flight shutdown battery was always installed so that the engine could be halted via the shore side Stop Action/Flight termination circuit.

Count down was planned for 13:30, which allowed the Downs Clearing parties time to finish a sweep back to the safe distance boundary (a North/South line through Tennyson's Monument) and let non participating site staff, especially the canteen crew, get cleared up and settled in their shelter positions. Along with the test cell team I checked all gas pressures, scanned for unsecured items and checked the rocket hold down bolts before leaving the Gantry. EC was stuffy and crowded with many visitors squeezing into our tiny standing space. After a final word to each console observer and a nod from the OISC, I checked the room at large before handing over to the Sequence Officer (SeqO).

As the SO armed his Gantry 2 firing circuits at the Block House he cleared the SeqO to begin the count down. All systems powered up and presented correctly to enable all "Readiness" switches closed by –3 min.

The −120sec Auto sequence ran down without a pause; all tanks pressurised, cooling water pressure interlocked, N2 purging started and zero time arrived. All engine pressures reached hot running values inside 2 to 3secs and remained firm until dropping quickly to zero at +35 seconds.

This tight, well-orchestrated behaviour reflected the continuous development this engine had undergone since its Blue Steel origins. The mixture ratio came in at 8.1 and Auto Observer readings closely matched those at Ansty. As all concerned were satisfied with engine performance, an overnight engine dry out was put in hand ready for Stage3 removal next morning. However, high spirits were dashed next day when a serious engine issue came to light; kerosene lab samples from the engine drain vessels revealed particle contamination and further flushing confirmed that tiny black wax like impurities had entered the engine – making it mandatory for a strip inspection back at RR, Anstey.

> *Stage2 Fuel Filling error:* Re-enactment of the fuelling process revealed that proper precautions were not taken to prevent contamination of the open transfer churn from Gantry hoist debris. Operations were revised to: –
>
> (1) Always displace the hoist away before removing the churn lid.
> (2) Clean the churn lid before its removal.
> (3) Flush the churn with clean kerosene immediately before use.
> (4) Over fill the required churn load by a gallon or so, before leaving it covered to thermally condition over night.
> (5) Drain down to required weight through a screening filter.
> (6) Confirm filter is free from contamination.
> (7) Transfer fuel to the rocket tank via the screen filter.

To retain progress, the OISC agreed to continue the trial as planned by assembling the Composite vehicle, completing the Gamma8 static firing and Vehicle Qualification tests to release Stage1 on its six-week sea passage on time. A Stage2 engine refit and static firing repeat would easily be managed during the 4–week interval before it was flown to Woomera.

Over the weekend, the Equipment Centre and Recorder Room were patched over to Site 1 and checked using the Electrically Similar Vehicle (ESV)

D*–44/40: (STAGE2 MEETS STAGE1) – Our mechanical team were now adept at shuffling rocket structures about; by evening Stage2 was atop Stage1 in Gantry1 and all interstage electric connectors had been proved continuous.

All three tank pressurising systems were functionally tested; the ARU, FCS and RF equipments were progressively reinstalled and checked out as operational. All telemetered data channels had also been proven serviceable.

D*–39: (FCS SENSE TEST) –

> *This test*: Proved absolutely that all steering torque sources were acting in harmony with a polarity that would bring an ARU error demand to zero. The process applied Roll, Pitch and Yaw angular demands (as sensed by the ARU) to Stage1 and Stage2 thrust chambers (using hydraulic power) and the ACS jets (using gas pressure).
> Operators positioned about the rocket, witnessed thrust chamber and gas jet response as two mechanics physically applied small angular inputs to the airframe. See Appendix B for full process detail.

With the ARU 2hr aligned earlier, this elaborate exercise was carried out with correct results. As a bonus, it was noted that no structural instability was evident at any time during this fully active FCS test; all sensing waveforms remained flat and free from structural buzz or servo chatter.

D*–38: (ASSEMBLING STAGE3) – For FCS stability testing, the rocket vehicle mass was approach that of a Composite vehicle mass at launch by the addition of Stage3. Prior its installation the Spin Table rotational freedom was spot checked with six dummy Imp thrusters fitted; sticktion and running torques were examined before locking the table at the flight orientation. Loading the dummy Waxwing motor and fitting the SSB then followed. Both Stage3 pull away umbilical cables were trailed clear of the Spin Table rotation path before being connected to the SSB and secured to it by light breakaway tie wires.

> *Stage3 umbilical shambles*: Two diametrically opposed cables each ran from below the Stage2 Spin Table rotation plane, up past the projecting Spin Imps and to pull away connectors on the SSB sited atop the Waxwing motor. Each cable connector was held to its SSB socket by a light fuse wire tie, intended to break when lanyard pulled by the adjacent Payload Fairing as it ejected away from the rocket. The arrangement lacked precision and failed to constrain the floating cables as they meandered past the "castellated" Spin Table assembly. The actual route became totally invisible as each Fairing half was closed up. Being obscured by each Payload Fairing half, reliable visual inspection of this haphazard electrical installation during final assembly was impossible – later established to be the direct cause of Fairing ejection hang-ups encountered on the R1 & R2 firings.

When the fully batteried X0 Payload was hoisted to level 'F' and secured on the SSB it was functionally tested via the Equipment Centre console and cleared serviceable; these tests were repeated after the Payload Fairings were fitted, which had become a well-understood and fluent operation by now.

> *The X0 Payload*: This non-orbiting instrumented package was equipped to telemeter Stage3 and Payload separation dynamics. An on site RAE team serviced this unit throughout the High Down and Woomera trials.

D*–36: (FCS STABILITY TEST) –

About Structural resonance: Reaction forces from swinging thrust chambers at one end of a flexible rocket structure, excites bending and torsion resonance modes that are sensed up top by the ARU, that forms an oscillatory loop by causing further chamber swings. If resonances lie within the FCS pass band and are self-sustaining they must be eliminated to avoid loss of flight control due servo damage or electronic saturation. After the BK experience early FCS design studies and included suitably scaled rate gyros to damp the natural modes and notch filtering to cut the higher Stage1 lateral modes. See Fig B–17 in Appendix B for Block Diagram. All "On Launcher" mass and stiffness conditions were explored during R0 qualification trial at High Down to confirm the design assumptions.

This development type test was applied to R0 only at High Down only to confirm FCS design study findings. As outlined above, all three stages, including the Payload and Payload Fairings were assembled to closely match the pre-launch build excluding the internal batteries, ordnance stores and a few service hatch covers. Four structural conditions were considered: Unpressurised and pressurised tanks, dry and full tanks. The 2hr ARU power up routine was used throughout these tests and no evidence of instability was found or nor induced during these tests.

D*–35: (STAGE1 STATIC FIRING PREP) –

Static firings: Are carried out at High Down and Woomera to demonstrate engine performance and repeatability when: –

1. *Propellants are being fed from the rocket tank system.*
2. *Integrated in a lightweight "flexible" airframe.*
3. *Interfaced with the rockets FCS inner loop hardware.*
4. *Constrained by the launcher structure.*
5. *Being served from the shore side launch pad facilities.*

The Composite Vehicle static firing at High Down closely emulates a Launch Firing so constitutes a major milestone towards rocket qualification and release to Woomera. It was expected that static firings at Woomera might eventually be omitted as confidence in engine behaviour was gained.

The Vehicle build standard would differ from the 'Launch" condition as follows:

- CSMU monitor cables remain connected.
- Stage2 HTP tank is filled with demineralised water.
- Ground pressure transducers are connected to the Gamma8 engine.
- All live ordnance stores are omitted.
- Only the Stage1 engine shutdown Haz battery is fitted.
- Some service hatches remain open.
- Release jack is a non-operational device.

For the S&S only, vehicle power supplies switched to internal batteries at –40secs and the umbilical plug ejection was inhibited and overridden. To limit consequential waste of engine life, manual Stop Actions were kept to engine and FCS services only from time zero to +35 secs during the firing sequence; all other system faults being allowed to run and be resolved post firing. Setting up engine support services, pressure logging recorders and completing the ever-present checklists were all brought to operational status by close of play today. ARU power up and alignment began at midnight and should continue until post firing.

D*–34: (COMPOSITE S&S TEST) – See Table B/7 of Appendix B for count down timing. Additional to the usual visiting engineers, site facilities were stretched today by several senior parties from RAE, Rolls Royce and Cowes.

All final checklists were wrapped up and the ARU was fully aligned by midday and a very satisfactory Composite S&S test was concluded soon after lunch. All electronic systems powered up correctly and remained running from internal battery supplies. First look analysis of recorder results were approved so Stage1 Kero tank was filled to thermally stabilise for tomorrow.

D*–33: (FIRING CANCELLED) – Firing postponed due bad weather – rain and high winds lasted throughout the day but a better situation was forecast for tomorrow.

D*–32: (COMPOSITE STATIC FIRING) – Overcast but less wind and rain was an intermittent drizzle. The Downs Clearance parties set forth at 08:10 and Measurements guys tended their gear, securing fly leads and shooting film indent boards etc. All gas bottles were charged, an oil flow run drenched the gearboxes and checklists were paused while 7550lbs of peroxide was transferred to the vehicle HTP tank and 26lbs to the start tank. When all was cleared away we each headed for our preferred feeding spots.

After a final Launcher safety check and word to Safety Officer, I joined a very crowded and stuffy Equipment Centre. Each console and the OISC confirmed their readiness and the count down sequence began. All consoles "Cleared" early, the 120sec Auto sequence was stated on time. My new display panel was informative to all as each event was initiated and was followed up by the confirmed signal. As zero time arrived my concentration zeroed onto the motor console; by +1.5secs all four propellant deliveries had leapt up to their line value, to be immediately followed by eight combustion pressures, which rose in line like a well trained team and remained solidly at line value until the fall to zero at +35secs. Yet another Static free of interruptions, are we testing lady luck too far? Record analysis confirmed it was indeed a copybook run. When the HTP systems were deloused and a good engine inspection was done, engine drying out was put in hand.

D*–29/25: (FLIGHT SEQUENCE FUNCTIONAL TESTS) –

Test Purpose: To confirm that the FSP and vehicle Haz circuit systems will function as one. Many operators stationed at disparate vehicle locations to close switches or witness events as they occur. The Equipment Centre is fully manned to run the minus 120sec auto sequence and tend the FSP, ARU, Tele, Doppler, C–Band and WREBUS consoles. RUXO observers are posted to witness "Puffer" events at Stage1/Stage2 separation area and again later at the Stage3 events. Technicians' are stood by to remove Payload fairings and FCS crews are positioned to verify Pitch over programs, Gain changes, ACS initiation and WREBUS modes.

The ARU is re-alignment between each run. From Table B/3 of Appendix B it is seen that the FSP program divides into three sections: Section One is started at –10sec by the EC Auto sequencer, Section Two and section Three are each started by bridging Stage1 and Stage2 All Burnt inertia switch sensors. Since FSP timing accuracy is established during laboratory tests elsewhere, these tests merely prove that FSP events and vehicle Haz circuit responses occur in the correct sequence order and delivers a minimum firing current to each ordnance device at about the right time.

The –120sec countdown sequence and vehicle build configuration remains as described above for the Composite Vehicle S&S test plus the following: –

*   Payload (X0) batteries recharged,
*   All Hazardous circuit batteries are fitted and armed.
*   Puffers (with RFI filters) are connected in place of all detonator/igniters.
*   All in-flight arming inertia switches are bridged to simulate 'Armed'.
*   Thrust sensing inertia switches are bridged by push button switches.
*   All non-launch ground cables & pipes are removed.
*   All major hatch covers are fitted.
*   Haz battery and detonator arming plugs are fitted.
*   EC sequence unit starts FSP Section 1 at –10secs.

FSP Section1: Initiated at –10secs.
FSP Section2: Initiated by Stage1 All Burnt sensor.
Following removal of the Payload Fairings:
FSP Section3: Initiated by Stage2 All Burnt sensor.

All events were seen to function in accordance with Table B/3 of Appendix B.
This trying test was brought to heal by running each FSP section as separated consecutive sequences and stage-managed accordingly. Even then two days were to slip before all was satisfactorily put to bed.

D*–22/18: (EMC/RFI TESTS) –

Test Purpose: To confirm that all flight electrical systems remain from cross system and ground based Electro Magnetic interference, with particular emphasis on both flight termination WREBUS receivers.

WREBUS modes: Each receiver has two FSP time selected modes:
FAIL FIRE – Rocket destruction is triggered by the loss of a constantly transmitted SAFE signal by both receivers.
FAIL SAFE – Rocket destruction is triggered by the reception of a transmitted DESTRUCT signal by either receiver.

The Flight Safety Plan operates the Fail Fire mode only as the Payload Fairings are being ejected in case of possible WREBUS aerial damage. Therefore it is essential to prove that both WREBUS Rx are not desensitised by any rocket or ground based RF source during the Fail Fire mode. The immovable metal High Down Gantry is an effective Faraday cage, which limits free-free RF conditions so these tests merely indicate issues to be fully pursued at Area5 where the 5B Gantry tower is withdrawn and all Range RF sources operational at launch are radiated.

Before running the test, each WREBUS receiver, C–band beacon and Telemetry transmitter in Stage2 and the Doppler set and Telemetry transmitter in Stage1 were functionally proven to be serviceable via their respective flight aerials.

Vehicle structure was configured closer to flight build by removing all extraneous test cables, hoses and pipes and fitting the Payload Fairings. Recharged non-Haz internal battery packs were replaced and given a 30sec on load test ahead of closing off the Electronic and Equipment bay service hatches. WREBUS radio sensitivities were established and monitored as each ground and rocket electronic service was successively powering up. When all systems were running, rocket services were switched to the internal batteries and the umbilical plug was ejected. At no point did the sensitivity of either WREBUS receiver diminish nor did any other service experience cross system interference. The Payload Fairings were removed and RFI testing as detailed above was repeated with the same results.

D*–15/14: (DETONATOR SHIELDING) – These were development tests confined to R0 at High Down only to demonstrate compliance with WRE requirement for EMC pickup at each electric detonator did not exceed 0.001 of the NO fire threshold.

Earlier RDD research: established that a fully shielded detonator connected to the firing circuit via low pass feed through filter beads, remained free of EMI emanating from all Rocket Vehicle radio sources down to the required level.
Compliance with WRE requirements was demonstrated by noting low-level temperature rise at one of each type of detonator housing, with and without filters. An instrumented electric match head (or puffer) had been devised by RDD to detect the very small thermal rise involved. See chapter 16.

Using five unfiltered Match Head RFI detectors (see Fig 16–4), ten measurement runs was made at one chosen detonator connection in each group of ordnance circuits e.g. one Siskin, one spin Imp etc., All major access hatches closed and each RF source was radiated/interrogated sequentially via their flight antenna. All unfiltered pick up levels recorded were less than 0.001 of the Fire threshold. WRE agreed to waive these tests on later vehicles subject to reassessment when EMC sensitive build modifications were made.

D*–13/12 (LOG BOOK WORKING WEEKEND) – As the trial drew to a close this period concentrated on confirming that all Rocket Log Book, RUSP and QA Certification paperwork was up to date for the Fit for Purpose review meeting.

D–11: (COMPOSITE VEHICLE) – Stage2 & 3 stripped down and returned to the Prep Area piecemeal.

D–10: (R0 FIT FOR PURPOSE REVIEW) – Flight components and subassemblies were shown to be: approved supplier QA released, within life limit and calibration. All electronic sub units were "Burnt-in" and QA cleared at EEL, Cowes. For each system listed below, the High Down Acceptance trial had confirmed interfacing and functionality as listed: –

1. Stage2 engine started by Interstage system and served from rocket tanks.
2. Stage1 engine started by ground start system and served from rocket tanks.
3. ARU, FCS and ACS functioned during Stage1 & 2 engine static burns
4. Telemetry system functioned during Stage1 & 2 engine static burns.
5. FSP, WREBUS, C band functioned during Stage1 & 2 engine static burns.
6. Payload and SSB function during Stage1 & 2 engine static burns.
7. FSP functionality with ARU, FCS, WREBUS & flight event Firing Circuits.
8. EMC between all flight and ground systems.
9. Servicing accesses.
10. Ground command, control & monitoring services.
11. Handling and hoisting arrangements.
12. Launcher system support services.
13. Preparation documents and tooling.

Note ** Item 1 above to be repeated after Stage2 engine change

The relevant Design Authorities had witnessed each major test and their outcomes were progressively published and reviewed at the RAE monthly Project Panel. After discussion, it was agreed that R0 was fit for purpose and, subject to a successful static firing of Stage2 replacement engine it would be declared Airworthy. Stage1 was cleared for immediate sea shipment to Adelaide.

D–10 TO–4: (STAGE2 ENGINE) – With the replacement engine already on site the contaminated Gamma 2 engine was replaced and returned to Ansty. Disturbed Telemetry, FCS and firing circuit systems underwent revalidation checks before the completed Stage2 was prepared and moved to Gantry 2.

D–9 TO–1: (STAGE1) – Returned to Prep Area for final QA inventory audit preceding balance and weight tests. The engine was inhibited and propellant tank desiccant breathers were fitted. Vent valves and open pipe ends were sealed or filtered off, access port covers and hatches were fitted with a full complement of fasteners. Crated up for sea transportation.
The Equipment Centre and Recorder Room were re-patched to Gantry2 and ESV checked and the Interstage bay was mounted in Gantry 2 ready to receive Stage2.

D–3 TO 0: (STAGE2 RETURNS TO GANTRY2) – The OISC agreed it was unnecessary to involve the ARU, rate gyros, WREBUS, C Band units and entire Stage3 for the static firing, just the FCS and Telemetry systems were required to control chamber angle and confirm satisfactory operation of the engine pressure transducers.
The inner loop servo frequency response tests were rerun and found satisfactory.

D0: (28 MARCH 1969 STAGE1) – Dispatched to the Docks en route to TS4.

D+3 TO+7 (STAGE2 S&S AND STATIC FIRING): Both exercises passed off uneventfully, engine performance matched that obtained at Ansty and the FCS servo system functioned correctly. All recorded data agreed with design values, the engine was dried out after a full post firing inspection gave it a clear bill of health.

D+10 TO+17 (STAGE2): Returned to the Prep Area for balancing, weighing, QA auditing and inhibiting before being pallet loaded and moved to Luton for air freighting to Adelaide. Alongside this work, the Payload Fairings, electronic trays, battery packs, ARUs, gyros, RF equipments and numerous loose items were inspected and crated up together with a host of service spares, also ready for air freighting.

D+21 Logbooks were closed up and RDD team headed for Adelaide via Luton airport.

Author's comment: This had been a long arduous trial due mainly to hardware shortages and consequent deadline pressures. Aside from early teething and some prototyping issues, the rocket vehicle and ground systems presented few design or service accessing problems. To address the relentless work arounds caused by hardware shortfalls and minimise their impact on program target dates, the team put in long hours and many weekends – my final ten weeks just smeared by without one day off! Anticipating a Woomera campaign of at least eight weeks, I was running into serious obligation territory with my long-suffering wife, confused offspring and aggressive cat!

With the paperwork finalised and Vehicle Logbooks closed, our team of seven stalwarts (Mech, ARU, FCS, Tele, RUXO, Wireman and myself) took a few days off before heading Down Under via Luton Airport, courtesy of Monarch Airways. I was very comfortable with this RDD team; their skill and dedication was well proven throughout this trial and camaraderie was strong. Together with a competent Rolls Royce and Ferranti engineer and a seasoned if rusty DH crew (most being ex BK guys), all lead by a well plugged in and sociable OISC, the outlook boded well.

FIG 18–1   R0 STAGE 2.   BALANCE & WEIGHT CHECKS at HIGH DOWN.
Note a scale reader perched in the roof and yours truly idling on the right.
(GKN Aerospace)

R0 LAUNCH TRIAL – AREA 5 19

24 APRIL'69: Flight scheduling quirks took me and the team to Adelaide five days early after jet lag was slept off, we went sight seeing around this lovely area before being security processed by WRE, Salisbury and flying up to Woomera to settle in to our Senior Mess accommodation.

TRIAL OUTLINE: Stage2 arrived by air 5th May '69, followed by Stage1 on the 15th May'69.

The trial was based on the notional plan set out in Table B/5, Appendix B, with adjustments for week ending dates, late deliveries and additional tasks. Key events are listed below and fully described in the paragraphs that follow.

F – 33	*Stage2 to Area 5A*
F – 28	*Stage1 to Area 5B*
F – 25	*Stage2 Static Firing Aera5A*
F – 22	*Stage2 assembled on Stage1.*
F – 18	*Stage3 assembled on Stage2*
F – 15	*X3 (A) loaded on Stage 3*
F – 14	*Composite RFI test*
F – 11	*Composite vehicle Static Firing5B.*
F – 6	*Flight Waxwing motor fitted*
F – 5	*FSP Tests*
F – 3	*Fitting Ordnance Stores*
F – 2	*X3 (F) loaded on Stage3*
F0a	*Launch aborted FSP did not start*
F0b	*Cancelled due weather*
F0c	*Cancelled due cloud*
F0	*Launch*

F–57 (or thereabouts): Collected the self drive mini bus and took RDD team out to Range E, to renew old friendships and inspect TS4 – all very new to us since the incineration of TS2. BA test gear layout almost identical to High Down and our guys easily settled in with their DH section leaders. The Team Leader and I had worked many BK trials together; I would be focussing on detail preparation, assembly and functional testing of all, non-Payload flight hardware.

F–52 to 51 (WEEKEND)

F–46: (STAGE2) Uncrated TS4. After a physical inspection all loose subassemblies (FCS trays, Tele trays etc) were passed to their dedicated labs. Two ARU units had arrived several weeks earlier and hours of running by the Ferranti specialist engineer had checked each unit thoroughly and brought the DH crew up to speed.

F–45 to 44 (WEEKEND)

F–43: (INTERSTAGE BAY). Set up on 5A static firing stand, pressure tested and flow checked using demin water via a test orifice. The N2 purge installation was similarly tested. When drained and dried the assembly returned to TS4 to await arrival of Stage1, expected on F–39.

F–43 to 41: (STAGE2). Inductive transducer installation, propellant level sensing system, temperature sensors and the numerous voltage monitor channels were all confirmed as functional. The FCS crew continuity and insulation tested all non-Haz wiring before calibrating thrust chamber feedback pickoffs, DC pickoffs and limit switches

F–41: (STAGE1). Arrived at Port Adelaide and due at TS4 on F–39.

F–40 to 39: (STAGE2). MAO (WRE Missile Acceptance Officer) with LO5 (WRE Launcher Officer) and our RUXO team got busy by certifying all small items like arming plugs, the flight and spare FSP units and installed all inertia switches. A detailed inspection of the Haz wiring installation began and continued until held pending completion of the Interstage Bay / Stage1 checks.

F–39: (STAGE1). The stage was Unpacked at TS4 and Inspected. When the Inter-Stage Bay was attached and structural interfacing was verified correct, the MAO/RUXO crew tested and certified the Haz wiring and physical components. Interstage Bay was removed and assembled to Stage2 for completion of the Stage2 MAO work.

Gamma8 engine solenoid valve operation and integrity was confirmed the preparation advanced along similar lines described above for Stage2 but at a slower pace due manpower priorities. Following lunch, the commuters and tourists with the MAO headed for Woomera airport en route to Adelaide.

F–38 TO 37 (WEEKEND)

F–36 to 34: (STAGE2) With Interstage Bay fitted the MAO finalised his Haz circuit examination with an FSP functional run, his fit to fly ticket sent our spirits soaring. Gamma2 engine solenoid valve operation and integrity was confirmed.

Area5 installations: I stole time to catch up with changes at Area5 and acquaint myself with who was who out there these days. EC5 interior looked much like the BK days, just the new ARU rack, revised console panels and 'my' sequence progress panel. The new gantry tower at Launcher 5B was a vast improvement on the old BK structure, which still remained at 5A for Stage2 static firings.

No more obstructions for an unwary head or narrow access ways; it was what a working area should be and clearly owed much to the large ELDO tower at Area6. Maintenance of Area5 sub systems fell to mix of WRE, SARO and DH staff according to their contractual remits. The mandatory site clearance tests before releasing for Trials use were well advanced and should finish on time.

F–33 TO 32: (STAGE2). With the Interstage Bay attached, the stage was moved out and erected on the 5A static firing stand. Propellant tank pressure gauge and firing circuits were electrically checked while tank gas bottles were charged to 4000psi. Operation of Kero and HTP tank pressurising systems went well with both settling close to 20psi and free of leaks.

Parallel tasks of connecting, priming and calibrating engine pressure gauges and Auto Observer gauges would be ongoing for several days. Validation of the many telemetry voltage channels also progressed as each vehicle flight electrical systems were installed and functionally tested. Engine systems were rigged for servo running (i.e. trunnions wetted and Kero hydraulics rigged for ground running) and Gearbox lub oil flow checks were completed as the FSC electronics and rate gyros were installed and setup. Unusually, the frequency response tests took time and drifted over to Friday AM. All results were satisfactorily and put to bed by a cautious crew before flying down to Adelaide for the weekend.

F–31/30: (WEEKEND)

F-29: Everyone appeared refreshed by the weekend in Adelaide. All general tasks and rigging up the ARU ground equipment were complete by mid afternoon. Stage2 would now be off limits until ARU calibrations were concluded AM so it was a "make do and mend" day in TS4 and EC5

ARU alignment: As mentioned in the High Down trial, two options are provided: –
A quick 2hr nominal alignment to support collateral system procedures e.g. general FSC sense tests, Internal battery load tests, S&S tests, RFI tests and the like.
A 12hr precision alignment used when zeroing FCS/ACS balances, theodolite checking and setting the launch Line of Fire. As the title hints, this long process is easily aggravated when the gyros sense small physical disturbances via the rockets airframe.

F–28 TO 26: (STAGE1). Was move Stage1 out and erected on the 5B launch pad but general progress was hindered due lack of EC5 services and manpower, which were prioritised to critical path activities on site 5A.

Telemetry, Doppler and connection of engine pressure gauges all made slow progress. The Gamma8 trunnions were wetted, hydraulics were rigged for ground running and the FCS crew found time to complete good inner loop frequency response tests.

F–28: (STAGE2) The Control System Signal Unit (CSSU) in EC5 that applies a set program of frequency demands to the servos during static firings, was run through the FCS and recorded at EC5.

The Tele system, WREBUS and C Band beacon were functionally tested with their respective ground stations via gantry transfer aerials.

At EC5, data recorders received fresh media, sub-sequencer timing and interlock overrides were verified and sealed, and all Stop Action inputs were exercised. Communications and timing services with Range Instrumentation Building (IB) were confirmed. During these two days the following mechanical systems were prepared for use:

- N2 purge and ground start feeds were connected to flow test orifices.
- HTP start tank was filled with demin water.
- Gearbox lub oil was replenished.
- Kerosene load was weighed and set aside.
- Duct cooling water flow was checked.
- Fire fighting service was tested.
- Rocket gas bottles were charged up.

F–26: (STAGE2 S&S TEST) See Table B/6, Appendix B for countdown times.

This dress rehearsal before the static firing was fixed for soon after lunch, so it was convenient to start a 2hr ARU run up as the dayshift began.

As the gas bottles were topped and sealed, the launcher actions were concluded as I vetted Test Post services, closed off the checklist and headed for EC5 for a short confer with the console jockeys and TL. After the AOO5 was given our readiness, he conferred with LO5 before clearing Range Control Officer (Con1) to begin the countdown. After a few Range holds, a faultless countdown followed. Positive reports from all sources let us make ready for tomorrow's firing by gassing up all vehicle bottles and filling the kero tank. The HTP tank and trunnion water was drained. The ARU crew would do a 2hr alignment ahead of the morning shift tomorrow.

F–25 (STAGE2 STATIC FIRING): A fine autumn day and gentle warm breeze, just right to suit up for HTP handling, (Ha, Ha). 5A was a buzz with WRE staff and our guys completing their final tasks and checklists. Engine start water was drained off, gearbox was "wetted" by a flow check and drained, lub tank was replenished and clean drain collectors were set in place.

Gas bottles were charged and HTP tank sight glass was fitted. While WRE staff finalised their cameras and set up the fire fighting and duct cooling water service, we rigged the HTP dump probe and clobbered up in PVC suits, which prove tolerably warm in the autumn sun but freezing when wet in a windy shade.

After an Area wash down the LO5 called in the HTP bulk carrier and peroxide transferring was set up; WRE staff handled the tanker pump and delivery hosing and our crew tended the rocket interfaces while LO5 presided and kept AOO5 in the picture.

2000lbs of peroxide was transferred without notable out-gassing rumble or sight-glass bubbling – always a concern at first filling in case of contamination. The Interstage start tank received 5lbs of peroxide via a portable dispenser unit. After a further wash down I ran through the final checklist, including the Stage2 and Interstage Bay hold down bolts!

Following lunch, gas bottles were finally topped and sealed, propellant tank breathers were closed and Test Post gas settings were noted as with the LO5 crew we cleared 5B. After a Crew Room visit, the endorsed checklists were passed to TL in EC5, where after a nod from each console operator we were ready to fire.

When Con1 got the show on the road, all vehicle subsystems powered up without incident and the –120sec auto sequence ticked down faultlessly with events responding on time. By plus +2 secs all engine pressures had reached nominal values, sitting sweetly and rock solid through the CSSU program until diving to zero +35 sec.

Engine behaviour mirrored that at High Down: delivery pressure rise instantly followed by the chamber pressures that remained stable until a clean collapse at shutdown – lovely stuff! The DH guys who'd not seen these Gamma engines running were impressed by their clockwork response, I commented, "wait till you see a Gamma 8 burning!"

With all remaining peroxide unloaded, the drain vessels were screened and gauged before washing down the area. While waiting for approval of the EC5 and Mike3 records, the previously charged up ACS gas system was leak checked and functionally activated via the CSMU. By late afternoon the records were cleared and the ARU watch team were at last let off the hook.

F-24/23: (STAGE2 – A WORKING WEEKEND) – EC5 services were patched across to Site 5B and ESV tested. Gamma2 post firing inspection and drying out was followed by a detailed leak inspection of the ACS installation.

F-22 TO 21: (STAGE2) – Was moved across to 5B and set up atop of Stage1. Interstage continuity and insulation checks followed. Pressurisation system tests on all three propellant tanks were free and regulated at design pressures.

Functional spot checks of Tele systems and FCS accompanied preparation of ARU ground equipment at 5B and EC5. Over at the Range E magazine, work commenced on assembling and testing of the various detonator and igniter units.

F–20: (FCS SENSE TEST) –

Demonstrates: that all control steering torque sources act in harmony with a polarity that would bring ARU error demands to zero. The process applies Pitch, Yaw and Roll angular demands (sensed by the ARU) to Stage1 and Stage2 thrust chambers (using hydraulic power) and the ACS jets (using gas pressure). Many operators are involved in the Equipment Centre and positioned about the rocket to observe thrust chamber and gas jet function, and to physically apply airframe angular inputs. See Appendix B for full process detail.

With the ARU 2hr aligned ahead of day shift start, this elaborate exercise was completed smoothly and correctly and all airframe constraints were restored by mid afternoon. It was noted that no structural instability was encountered during this fully active FCS test; all sensing waveforms remained flat and free from structural buzz or servo chatter.

F–19 (ARU ACCURACY & AIRFRAME ALIGNMENT) – The wind brace arms were adjusted to bring the Spin Table surface level within 0.1°, and a 12hr ARU precision alignment was carried out overnight to complete airframe Line of Fire checks.

The ARU 12hr alignment: Includes three successive phases: thermal stabilisation, gyro drift calibration and gyro compassing onto the Line of Fire. The latter two phases involve long gyro convergences that get prolonged by small structural disturbances. Hence the ARU team's preference for conducting this process overnight to avoid halting parallel daytime vehicle work.

With the ARU accurately set on the Line of Fire, the airframe roll (azimuth) angle was physically trimmed (by adjustment of the anti torque lugs) to bring the ARU roll synchro output to zero. Actual airframe roll angle was then theodolite confirmed against a local pre surveyed upright. The FCS and ACS systems balances were adjusted to zero.

F–18 (STAGE3 BUILD):

Three reasons: To assemble Stage3 at this time:
- *To warn of any RFI problems ahead of final build.*
- *To expose the Payload to an engine burn environment.*
- *To provide a rehearsal for DH and LO teams*

The Payload Fairings was hoisted and stowed at Gantry level 'F' and were together with the Spin Table and its support structure were vacuumed cleaned and tack-wiped.

The inert Waxwing motor was hoisted to level 'F' and secured to the Spin Table. During SSB fitting procedure the LO5/RUXO's did an access assessment for fitting and connecting live igniter and head cutting charge planned for later rocket builds.

The two diametrically opposed pull away umbilical cables were lightly secured to the SSB sockets by weak tear away wire ties.

> *Heath Robinson is alive and well!* See the High Down trial for a detailed description and critic of this installation. Disposition of the unfettered cables and lanyards are not visually verifiable during Fairing close up, a situation that must risk proper operation of the Spin Table and Payload Fairing ejection process.
>
> (A suitably engineered installation did not materialise until R3, see Fig B–7 Appendix B for more detail).

The entire level 'F' area and vehicle assembly above the Payload Fairing attachment line received a further clean down ready to receive the X0 payload.

Alongside the above activities, Doppler, C–band and WREBUS units were installed and interrogated by their respective ground stations via flight antennas.

None Haz internal battery packs from TS4 were installed and given a load test by powering up and switching the associated systems and doing a 30sec switch over to internal power.

F–17 TO 16 (WEEKEND)

F-15 (X0 MEETS R0 for an RFI TEST): The fully prepared and batteried up X0 payload arrived at 5B inside a dedicated trailer. After hoisting to level 'F' and secured on the SSB, it was powered up via EC5 and functionally cycled while Mike3 recorded fully acceptable Tele data.

General preparation for the approaching RFI tests included, fitting and securing all main hatch covers and preparing the Gantry for tomorrows roll back.

F-14: (COMPOSITE RFI). As planned, RFI testing was expected to span two days. All vehicle electronic systems were powered up and pronounced serviceable in conjunction with their respective ground stations, and a good internal battery power supply test was achieved. With the wind speed checked as acceptable, the Gantry was rolled clear to reveal an "embarrassed" R0, looking naked without Payload Fairings.

> *Radio Frequency Interference (RFI):* To avoid departure from the approved flight corridor, Black Arrow carried duplicate WREBUS radio receivers specifically designed by WRE to initiate the rockets termination system if both links were lost or individually if the FSO deemed it necessary. Either action stops whichever engine is thrusting, neutralises Waxwing thrust, detonates unfired ordnance and catalyses any remaining HTP.

The above action reduces the rocket to inert scrap with little lateral velocity, gently descending to impact within a footprint inside one of several predefined dump areas.

Both WREBUS radio receivers were located in Stage2 electronics bay, each working on a unique reception frequency. Both receivers were equipped to function in Fail/Fire mode or Fail/Safe mode, either of which being FSP time selected during flight.

The Fail/Fire mode initiated flight termination when both radios failed to receive a constantly transmitted "Safe" signal from the Range Head.

The alternative Fail/Safe mode initiated termination if either radio received a unique "Destruct" signal from the Flight Safety Officer at the Range Head. Black Arrow flew in Fail/Safe mode except for the Payload Fairing ejection period (+151.2sec to +210sec), when Fail/Fire was FSP selected in case one or both WREBUS aerials were compromised. Using a Fail/Fire period made it essential to prove that WREBUS reception remained unimpaired by any RF field radiated from R0 or WRE range source, with and without Fairings fitted.

The test began by operating each WREBUS Rx and the Range Tx's to establish basic receiver sensitivities. Then each Range RF ground station was in turn brought on line, followed by all the rocket flight systems.

Finally, the vehicle systems were switched onto internal battery power and the umbilical plug was ejected. No loss of Wrebus sensitivity was detected nor did any vehicle system experience interference in this configuration.

Because this satisfying result was achieved by lunchtime we pressed on with setting up the second test condition by fitting the Umbilical plug and Payload Fairings fitted. See Fig B–9 and Section 7 of Appendix 'B' for Fairing details.

Using a lightweight hand operated double fall hoist hung from the main hoist, to provide a sensitive 'Feel', each half Fairing was raised, aligned and gently set into place and secured on the Stage2 'break-hinge' points and hand held half open while the SSB cable lanyards were attached. When all was secure and the ubiquitous check list was complete, each Fairing half was closed against the other, link pinned and tensioned up. As the Gantry rolled clear, R0 stood fully dressed, as it will at lift off. Lady luck smiled again today by providing interference free results. After Gantry replacement all systems were stood down at the end of this successful day.

Connecting, priming and calibrating the Gamma8 ground instrumentation system now able to begin and would continued along with the engine support services needed for the coming firing. The Gamma2 chamber harness was installed (a device suspended within Stage1 separation bay to prevent each thrust chamber from flopping around during Stage1 burn).

F-12 (COMPOSITE STATIC FIRING S&S): Table B/7 Appendix B for countdown timing.

Another busy morning at the launch pad for WRE and our crew as all systems were brought to S&S readiness. The ARU had been adequately aligned during the early hours.

Stage1 hydraulics was rigged for ground running and the FCS was powered up, balanced and CSSU demand checked. Engine lub system was flow tested, drained and replenished while the engine start system was filled with demin water and gassed up.

Back in EC5, the sub-sequencer and override switch panel were set up and sealed and Stop Action services were exercised. Propulsion pressure recorders were spot calibrated and the Auto Observer camera located in Test Post 5B was loaded and remotely tested.

By midday all vehicle gas bottles were at pressure, the N2 purge and engine start test orifices had been fitted and the N2 failsafe feed connected.

As all launcher tasks except the final checklist were wrapped up, packed lunches were taken in the Area5 crew room.

After eating, final checklist was revisited, Test Post gas settings were noted, each wind brace and anti roll lug and the release jack safety safe pin were all given the once over before we cleared the Pad.

Inside EC5 everything was S&S ready, after my usual yarn with each console operator and a checklist perusal with the OISC and TL, AOO5 cleared Con1 to start the time count.

Each system powered up and presented correctly, the −120sec auto sequence start was held off for several minutes while a Tele channel issue was clarified with M3, the Range reception station. Once underway, all auto sequence events and their interlocks also presented on time. After appraising the recorded data the OISC confirmed we would static fire next morning. Kerosene was loaded to thermally stabilise overnight, trunnions and ground start tank were drained of demin water, the ground start and N2 purge feeds were rerouted from test orifices to the engine connections and the HTP dump arm was installed and exercised. By evening all was set fair for tomorrow.

F–11: (COMPOSITE STATIC FIRING): Weather outlook was good. EC5 carried out their routine firing circuit and stop action checks; sequence timing and interlock override settings. Range engineering primed exhaust duct cooling and deluge water services. The Gamma 8 gearbox was wetted by a lub oil flow, clean drain collectors were positioned and Test Post systems were gassed up. The release jack 'safe' pin, wind brace arms and anti roll lugs were again security checked and the 5B launch area was cleared of all unwanted equipment and washed down ahead of HTP handling.

The HTP bulk tanker was called in and LO5 supervised the transfer of 7400lbs and 26lbs into the Stage1 and ground start tanks respectively and a peroxide primed start hose was connected to the engine lift off connector.

As the tanker cleared away, a further area wash down was followed by cut lunch of weary looking sandwiches taken in the crew room.

Vehicle gas bottles got a final top up, propellant tank breathers were sealed, and Test Post gas settings and release jack safe pin status were noted as the LO5 cleared the area. Back at EC5, after a chat with each console operator I passed the signed checklists to the TL and OISC and AOO5 armed the 5B site as he cleared Con1 to begin the countdown. All electrical systems powered up and displayed correctly and Range RF stations reporting satisfactory reception.

For some reason external to EC5 the -120sec auto sequence was held up for several minutes but it eventually got going and ran to +35sec without fault. By plus +1.5secs all propellant feeds were at line pressure and closely followed by the eight thrust chambers, which rose in lockstep to stay rock steady at hot burn pressure until collapsing to zero at +35 sec. This burn replicated the rapid start up, uniform steady level and clean shut down experienced at High Down and Ansty – another brilliant Rolls Royce performance!

All propellants were removed, the ACS gas pressure was measured in case the firing had induced leakage and the vehicle was secured for the day. After a scan of the firing records, the non–Adelaide weekenders adjourned to the village for a few well-earned ice-cold ones and a shower before enjoying a contented team dinner at the Senior Mess.

F-10to9: (WEEKEND) – Gamma8 engine was dried out and post-static inspected while various engineers analysed the firing records.

F–8: (X0 & DUMMY STAGE3 REMOVED). Both Fairing halves were unshipped and stowed at level 'F', X0 payload was unloaded and returned to TS4 for servicing and new batteries and generally made ready for launch. The SSB and Dummy Waxwing were also removed and sent to TS4. In preparation for tomorrow's airframe and FCS checks, the ARU 12hr Line of Fire alignment was carried out overnight.

F–7: The first task today was a rigorous check of FCS and ACS following the Static Firing with insertion and proving of Stage1 & 2 "Flight Plugs". The above tasks were followed by adjustment of the airframe Roll (Azimuth) position to bring the ARU synchro output to zero, by trimming the torque lugs. A theodolite comparison with a pre-surveyed vertical confirmed these settings as correct. The upper and lower thrust chamber angles were then trimmed to zero using shore side hydraulic power after removal of the Gamma2 chamber harness.

Using the pressurised vehicle gas bottle, all ACS trigger settings were also zeroed. Finally the Gamma2 chamber harness was re-installed

F–6: (LOAD FLIGHT WAXWING) – The Spin Table area was vacuum cleaned and tack–clothed and the inert flight Waxwing motor was hoisted to level 'F', rotationally aligned and manacle clamped to The Spin Table, then fitted with the SSB. Both Payload Fairing halves were readied for the FSP testing tomorrow. Both kerosene tanks were overloaded to enable a trim down when propellant temperatures are assessed at loading time.

> *Inert Flight Waxwing:* Unlike the dummy Waxwing used hitherto, the inert flight item embodied haz wiring and had been physically prepared to ensure dynamic balance and electromagnetic neutrality.

F–5 to 4: (FLIGHT SEQUENCE TESTS). This required three FSP test runs: the first using an FSP simulator was followed by the spare FSP, and finally with the nominated flight FSP unit.

This test confirmed a satisfactory firing pulse reached each group of ordnance arming plugs, operation of the ARU, FCS, ACS and Wrebus (pitch turn over, control gain change, ACS initiation and BU Fail modes). Each half Fairing was held open to access the SSB and Spin Table during each test. The ARU was re-levelled and various Haz circuit-switching elements were reset for each run. Finally, with the flight FSP reset to zero, a status test was done to verify that all switching elements within the vehicle Hazardous and Break Up circuitry had been restored to correct pre-launch condition.

Payload Fairings were removed for tomorrow's Stage3 ordnance fitting,

F–3: (FIT ORDNANCE STORES) – From here on a continuous 8hr rule will remain in force until Lift Off or trial cancellation.

The LO5/RUXO team installed fresh Haz batteries, load testing each one via the arming sockets. Commencing at Stage3, the explosive devices listed below were progressively installed, electrically connected, tested for continuity and insulation via the relevant arming sockets: –

- Fit & connect 4 Payload Fairing pyro separators.
- Fit & connect 2 Satellite pyro separators.
- Fit & Connect Waxwing pressure Tx, motor igniter and a head cutting igniter.
- Fit & connect 3 Manacle Clamp explosive bolt detonators.
- Fit & connect 6 Spin Table Imp thrust units.
- Fit & connect 2 Spin Table unlock gas charges.
- Fit & connect 2 ACS frangible pillar detonators.
- Fit & connect 16 Stage2/Interstage explosive bolt detonators.
- Fit & connect 16 Stage1/Interstage explosive bolt detonators.
- Fit & connect 4 Siskin separation rockets with igniters.

The flight termination catalyst capsules are not inserted until each hosing is proved to be leak free following HTP loading on day F-0).

A long final checklist running through to launch time was begun; Section Leaders collectively examined bay interiors as service accesses were progressively closed off and secured.

F–2 (FLIGHT X0 MEETS R0) – As non-haz flight batteries were being installed and 30sec load tested, the flight ready X0 payload arrived at 5B. When hoisted and secured on the SSB, it was function check via EC5 and M3 who OK'd all data as fit to fly.

The DY Fairing was mounted on Stage2 and secured via the break away hinges and the weak pull away lanyard was attached to the adjacent SSB umbilical cable. When check listed, the fairing was held closed while the UY Fairing was similarly processed. Lastly, each pair of pyro separators were linked and drawn together via their in-built turnbuckle, to preload the DY and UY Fairings against each other. (*The fairings will have to be swung open again to enable SSB and Spin Table final arming, during the final overnight launch preparation.*)

Preparation of engine systems included: rigging Stage1 hydraulics for ground running, replenishing gearbox oil bottle, charging ACS and propellant tank gas bottles. Filling Stage1 trunnions and ground start tank with demin water and removing the engine fail-safe gas actuator. Stage2 HTP dump arm was erected, aligned functionally tested.

> *WRE Prep:* Alongside these rocket activities, numerous Range Authority ground systems were being setup and tested in and around Area5, EC5 and the Instrument Building (IB) and out along the numerous observation stations strung out along the 305° line of fire towards Talgano in Western Australia.

The final 12hr ARU integrity run begun during the evening and would continue though the night ready for the mid morning S&S test tomorrow; if all goes to plan, it will remain running until the end of flight.

F–1: (LAUNCH S&S TEST) –See Table B/7 of Appendix B details the countdown timing scheduled to begin at 10:00hrs. Unlike static firings when activity is dominantly centred on Area5, Con1 and Mike3, this launch firing will involve extensive Range Authority facilities like the Data Services Centre, the numerous optical and radar tracking stations, the Flight Safety services, plus Telemetry and Doppler resources strung out along an extensive flight path. To ensure all these facilities are up and running smoothly before committing to the main S&S, an event that commits the rocket and Area5 to hazardous non-reversible actions, the Range exercises its systems using two pre S&S clock runs labelled Part A, B.

Part C is the main event involving Area5 and all Range systems working in unison on a common time-base and purpose. Except for specific rocket radio transmissions and the ever running ARU, no other vehicle or launch pad systems are operated during Parts A & B.

Needless to say, no liquid propellants are present, no vehicle ordnance is armed and the release jack remains safely pinned throughout. The Gantry is not rolled back and transfer aerials are employed to aid vehicle aerial transmissions.

For Part C, all rocket gas bottles were topped up, Test Post gas systems were on, the exhaust duct cooling water was primed and Stage1&2 propellant tank pressure systems were armed. The ARU remained aligned on the Line of Fire.

Part B was scheduled to end soon after 10:00hrs but it ran to midday before part C got started. With vehicle and launcher services all hot to trot and checklists closed, I moved into EC5 where all positions were manned as per a static firing except the OISC had relocated to Range Head control centre at the IB.

An extended AOO5 and Con1 opening patter fronted the manual countdown, which eventually progressed normally and all rocket electronic systems were pronounced serviceable well before Con1 initiated the -120sec Auto sequence.

All timed events at the launch pad responded correctly and engine initiation would have occurred; intercom reports from all Range services appeared satisfactory so the OISC confirmed his intention to launch next morning.

Out at 5B the umbilical was refitted followed by a check on all electronic systems. Stage1 gas bottles were recharged and unused Stage2 gas bottles were checked for pressure loss. Water was drained from trunnions and engine start tank. Stage2 Electronics bay hatch fastenings were finalised and pressure tested.

Stage1&2 HTP dump arms were functionally checked, Gamma2&8 gearboxes were wetted by lub flow checks, drained and replenished; Stage1 & 2 hydraulic accumulators were pressurised and set up for flight.

By 14:00 hrs I'd run out of my 8hr haz shift and retired to TS4 to spend 30mins going over the propellant loading calculations with the OISC before heading back to Woomera village.

The final approach to launch would begin at 02:30 when HTP was loaded and then continue over night through the final arming routines until the 08:00hrs launch slot tomorrow so I aimed to be back on shift at 01:00.

After a shower and snooze I enjoyed the calm of a Senior Mess dinner and chat with old WRE buddies up for the firing; the Chief Safety Officer entertained us by relating antics of one ELDO team; to avoid using their LO for every haz system test, one European outfit had secreted their own duplicate set of all arming plugs!

F0: (FIRST LAUNCH NIGHTSHIFT) – I was back at Area5 by 00:30 to witness both Kerosene levels being trimmed down by a few lbs, inline with figures agreed earlier in TS4. With HTP sight glasses fitted and the area washed down, LO5 supervised as HTP was transferred into the Stage2, Stage1 and both engine start tanks.

Both vehicle tanks remained audibly passive and their temperature plots were flat.

Launcher access was limited for an hour or so while LO5/RUXO team load tested and armed each haz battery before no volting and loop checking each explosive store as the arming plugs were inserted. The mechanical crew were on hand to open one Payload Fairing half for access to SSB and Spin Table arming sockets; the SSB cables appeared to be properly set before revisiting the checklist and closing up.

Finally, all Fairing spring keepers and handling frames were stripped off and stowed for possible later use.

EC5 were now pacing our actions to remain in sync with Range progress and they agreed an early Crew Room breakfast courtesy of the TS4 multi skilled store man made sense.

Whispers of jet stream problems emerged but a phone call quashed the rumour. Eventually, as HTP tank sight glasses were removed each tank was sealed off to breath via the differential vent valves. Exhaust duct cooling water was primed and the Gantry was readied for roll back as the LO5/RUXO's progressively inserted, connected and loop tested the six catalyst capsules at their respective HTP tank housings. Bulk N2 gas was applied to Test Post room 'A' systems, Stage1 engine start pipe was connected but the release jack safe pin remained in situ until LO5 began clearing the area. When OK'd by AOO5, LO5 armed Stage2 break up system and the Gantry was run back and locked down.

Stage1 break up arming is accessed from launcher level and would be held off till area clearing time.

> *Ordnance safety: I may have explained this before. When live Ordnance and Break Up systems are armed, they still remain inherently safe because the former circuits require the closure of 5g inertia switches, and each Break Up circuit requires closure of the Instant of Move switches at rocket lift off.*

As the launcher was cleared, two DH sections leaders and I did a final sweep around Pad and Test Post before presenting LO5 with the Release Jack safe pin.

At EC5 the monitoring team were loafing around in thought or quiet conversation. I settled at my usual spot beside the TL and AOO5, where we overlooked all monitors and had a clear view of 5B launcher.

PRE LAUNCE SEQUENCE: While waiting for the action to begin I reflected on the road we'd all stumbled along to reach this point.

Aside from persistent supply snags, teams at both venues had worked well together; each person knew their slot and how it fitted with each other. At this point an intercom saying Stage1 Telemetry was u/s suddenly yanked me out of my revere. We soon established that direct rocket access was needed so a 1.5-hour hold was requested and granted for the following rework plan: –

- Insert the Release Jack safe pin,
- Disarm Stage1 BU system,
- Return gantry to the rocket,
- Disarm Stage2 BU system,
- Remove Stage1 equipment bay hatch cover,
- Service the fault,
- Clear back for transmission test,
- Close up hatches.
- Retrace trial plan actions back to the launcher evacuation point.

This took a team of six plus the LO5 crew at the launcher. The AOO5, LO5 and OISC were briefed and the rework plan was approved. By 08:00hrs all had been fixed and we were back on track with a serviceable rocket but a Range tracking problem now tested our nerves until WRE came up with a workaround. Finally, the EC5 team and AOO5 gave a green light to Con1, who did a last check with all WRE positions before beginning the 30-minute count down.

BACK ON TRACK: (LAUNCH SEQUENCE): See Table B/7 Appendix B. The now familiar manual sequence advanced without interruption as all rocket electronic systems were cleared fit to fly and Con1 started the automatic –120sec sequence, which also progressed correctly until minus nine seconds when the rocket's FSP failed to start!

> *Ultimately Traced* to a ground circuit wiring error, which only appeared when the Release Jack Safety Bar was closed, a condition not permitted in the S&S test. WRE corrected the wiring fault.

Regrettably, investigation and rework ran well beyond the launch slot, which was reset to F0, same time next day (Wednesday). All was made safe by inserting the Release Jack safe pin, disarming all Haz circuits and removing HTP from both stages and their start systems. The aligned ARU would continue running for the next launch sequence. While the faulty ground circuit was being fixed, the Electronics bay was opened to reset the FSP and test a –10sec restart from EC5 that followed successfully.

A few ARU watch keepers joined us for a staggered Kooly lunch before we hit the village to shower and relax at civilised evening meal before tonight's performance – I had a slight concern because the weatherman was looking long faced at dinner.

F0: 25 JUNE (2ND LAUNCH NIGHTSHIFT) – By 02:00 the night crew and I were back at 5B setting up to transfer HTP to the rocket and engine start tanks before aiding the LO5/RUXO team with Stage3 final arming and cat–capsule insertion.   As 05:00 approached a clear sky came with the dawn; maybe the weather johnnies got it wrong after all.   Preparation run like clockwork and spirits were high until EC5 delayed our Gantry roll back – was cloud in the offing after all?

As the normal 5B evacuation time passed, Crew Room odds were shortening as EC5 instructed us to "make safe".   When these unrewarding make–safe tasks were done it was back to TS4 for a planning session; the OISC had been advised of uncertain weather until 28th June so he reset the Trial back to F–1 for a repeat S&S on 27th June. This allowed many of the shift crews to enjoy a rest day and enabled an un-hurried reworking of R0 back to flight readiness.   It also let WRE get bulk HTP temp down to preferred levels and me catch up with my laundry mountain!

All Stage1&2 non-Haz batteries were replaced with the TS4 stand by set and 30sec load tested.   A fresh set of Haz batteries were prepared for replacement during final arming and X0 batteries were conditioned in situ.

F–1: 27TH JUNE: (REPEAT S&S) – The day shift repeated their F–1 work as described above for 23rd June.

The ARU had been restarted before dawn; all vehicle gas bottles were given their first charge.   This time S&S Parts A, B and C were concluded promptly: by mid afternoon the OISC was able to confirm his intention to launch next morning at 08:00hrs so the night crew and I retired to the Village to qualify for our 10 hrs off duty.

F0: 28TH JUNE (3RD LAUNCH NIGHT SHIFT) – Back on site by 01:00hr to find both HTP dump arms had been set up by a helpful day crew; so we togged up and worked through the clean down and HTP transfer routines for filling both vehicle tanks and engine start systems.

Stage1&2 gearboxes were wetted, hydraulic accumulators and vehicle gas bottles were topped up and sealed off.

Around 02:00 general launcher access was halted while LO5/RUXO's replaced and armed Haz batteries, armed the ordnance stores, which required Payload Fairing assistance as set out earlier.   When 5B access was restored, HTP sight glasses were removed, tanks were sealed, cat–capsules were inserted and the Gantry was readied for roll back.   Being again ahead of plan but too early for a Kooly breakfast, we again feasted on the DH store man's culinary creations in the Crew Room.   Around 06:00 bulk N2 gas to Room 'A' was applied, the N2 purge, engine start and release jack system pressure settings were verified, and the HTP start hose was connected to the engine feed point.

As AOO5 cleared LO5 to arm Stage2 BU system, we followed up with Gantry roll back and lock down. A final checklist scan preceded removal of the Release Jack 'Safe' pin as we cleared the pad and LO5 armed Stage1 BU system.

After a wash and tidy up in the Crew Room I joined the EC5 team. Having enjoyed their wholesome Kooly breakfast, the EC5 team were in buoyant mood and rearing to get R0 on its way. I took my usual spot with the TL and AOO5 for the familiar countdown; all vehicle systems ran up correctly and the −120sec auto sequence followed after a short Range delay. Tension grew as the count progressed and each second seemed longer as zero time approached. While I'd watched many Black Knight launches, I could barely control my breathing as I turned towards the launcher and waited for the IoM light − Lift off!

(LAUNCH) WHAT HAD GONE WRONG? R0 was in real trouble slowly cork screwing back and forth as it cleared the launcher; a permanent fault seemed to exist as it continued to roll back and forth while climbing out of view from the window.

Turning back to the telemetry screen − all chambers were up to pressure and swinging end to end in Roll. A closer look suggested one pair might be marginally out of step and slamming end stop to end stop. Could the airframe survive this treatment until all burnt?

Intercom chat ticked off the altitude as we all waited for 10,000ft to exit from EC5. Outside I saw R0 twisting upwards until the Payload Fairings seemed to deform as a barrel roll began and became end over end tumble. The engine had stopped and a wake of propellants traced out R0's tortured path upwards before starting its descent. Over the intercom the Flight Safety Officer warned he would initiate termination at 9,000ft, then counted down to that point. We all rushed back inside EC5 for shelter and watched the desert light up as R0 exploded. Moments later a lone thunderclap marked the end of nine months full time dedication and seven years of scheming. Like so many others I felt shaken and at a loss until pragmatism kicked to think out a likely explanation for this dreadful event − it had to be a chamber angle feedback problem because hydraulic actuator was driving the chamber end to end when the amplifier input changed polarity, yet telemetry had shown the feedback pickoff was functional so where did this fault lie?

POST LAUNCH: The normal post launch routine was to aid the OISC in formulating his post launch communiqué so I drove over to IB on autopilot where the TL and I outlined our thinking on the failure process. Loss of angular feedback to one steering servo forced the cyclic roll accelerations, which probably wrecked the lightweight magnesium alloy SSB structure. This would let the X0 Payload loose inside the nose Fairings. Dynamic instability induced tumbling that disrupted engine propellant feeds.

All officials and visitors were very conciliatory and the Flight Safety Officer was almost apologetic, though in an aside he admitted it was gratifying to know the termination system was so effective! He also stated that this mid air bang was biggest ever experienced so close to the Range Head. WRE provided the OISC with a recovery helicopter to reconnoitre the remains and he invited the TL and I to join him. Apart from many small fragments, the only recognisable items from the air were a few thrust chambers, gas bottles; the Waxwing denuded of its efflux nozzle and a very crumpled but apparently complete, X0. On flying back to Woomera, we landed at the golf club where a stiff reviver was taken before a taxi drive back to the Mess. After a shower I slept until dinnertime – needless to say, a blighted atmosphere dominated the evening.

HOME TO UK: A crestfallen RDD team departed for UK on 30th June while I remained until 3rd July to attend the post mortem meeting at WRE Salisbury – ironically, a bomb hoax at Adelaide airport added to the teams frayed nerves.

I arrived back to a sombre atmosphere at High Down. Black Knight had never met a disaster like this, yet now on the brink of our "new" venture we were facing this unimaginable disaster; the impact on the future program was unimaginable.

To befriend my long-suffering family again I stole a week off and though a well-earned holiday together somewhere was needed, a bit of R&R time in our sunny garden had to come first.

My next few months at High Down were shared across the following activities:

- Assisting R0 enquiry panel at adhoc sessions and monthly review meetings.
- Integrating R0 RUSP updates into R1 documentation.
- Supporting the current R1 qualification trial.

ENGINEERING REVIEW PANEL – A Panel set up to indentify the cause and define a remedy following the loss of R0 was later extended to review every aspect of the Black Arrow design, manufacture, QA and operational procedures. The panel comprised several sub panels, each chaired by a senior RAE engineer and populated by 6 to 8 specialists drawn from Contractors and RAE departments as appropriate. This root and branch investigation was to continue its work for many months and would maintain a watching brief throughout the remaining program.

R0 – MAIDEN FLIGHT POST-MORTEM – I assisted the panels working on ARU, FCS, ACS, FSP, Hazardous circuit systems and RUSP documentation topics. Because R1 qualification was imminent, priority was given to identifying the failure sequence and prescribing a suitable remedy.

As suggested at the post trial communiqué meeting, the enquiry confirmed that the R0 malfunction began when a Stage1 thrust chamber servo was deprived of trunnion angle feed back at, or soon after the engine ignition/shock at release jack retraction. The vigorous back and forth cyclic roll motion was initially tolerated and Stage1 may have reached all burnt if the X0 had not broken loose within the nose fairings, probably due to SSB structural collapse. The dynamic disturbance induced vehicle tumbling and interruption of propellant flow to the engine.

> *Physical details:* Each of the four servo control amplifiers receives trunnion angle data from a dedicated 2.6Khz rotational transducer. These items are enclosed inside a sealed plastic casing, which is cemented into a light alloy housing fastened to the outer trunnion forging of each thrust chamber pair by a single cap head screw. A fork ended torque arm (that is clamped by a single cap head screw) rotates each transducer input shaft by engaging with a peg mounted on the thrust chamber outer shell. Each fork end is furnished with an anti chatter leaf spring
> The enquiry concluded that clamp screw failure or fork-end disengagement would not have resulted in the clean regular square wave pattern observed on telemetry.
> The internal coil windings of each transducer connect through four threaded studs that secure swaged ring tag terminations of a four–core screened fly lead.
> The entire connection assembly with fly lead outer sleeving is potted into the alloy housing using silicon resin, Thiokol doped to reduce brittleness.
> The Motor Bay electrics box, where all local circuitry is configerated. From here, the wiring passes through a further breakdown connector as it enters the cable conduit running up the HTP tank wall to the Inter Tank Bay and eventually plugs into the Stage1 Flight Control System pack. Wiring within the pack routes the feedback data to the appropriate demodulator, which removes the 2.6Khz carrier and feeds the resulting analogue signal to the relevant servo amplifier and telemetry sender. All wiring is high temperature insulated and uses a mix of high temp solder and swage jointing and printed circuit techniques.

Telemetry indicated that three motor angles had cycled correctly in phase with the vehicle roll angle, while the forth pickoff indicated a motor flopping end stop to end stop as vehicle roll angle changed sign; a clear indication that this servo was not getting feedback data. Because telemetry data was sampled at the feedback pickoff demodulator output located on Stage1 FCS electronic tray, the circuit break must lie between the demode and servo amplifier input. Engineering in this area is a mix of swaged connector pins, individual wiring cores, a summing resistor and printed circuit tracks. Additionally, micro-switches set at ±1° swing angle of each motor pair are chained with thrust chamber and hydraulic pressure switches to open the release jack, ergo the fault began after release and may have been implemented by the 0.23g shock at liftoff.

To guard against this physical sensitivity the Review Panel specified that Stage1 & 2 FCS packs must undergo a rigorous "Burn In" using thermal, vibration and ageing profiles defined by RAE.

While the above findings absolve the downstream wiring the Panel proposed to introduce full circuit redundancy between the FCS trays and the motor bay servos.

The following remedial actions were applied to Stage1&2 installations:

- Transducer reference voltage revised as a ring main feed and routed via opposing HTP tank conduits together with paralleled signal outputs to their respective FCS trays.
- Laws relay wiring paralleled up each diametrically dispose cable duct to the FSC tray.
- Improved cable hardening of the feedback transducer fly leads.
- Revised routing and clipping of wiring within the Motor Bay with minimal cable tying to prevent locally induced strain overloads at terminations.
- FCS tray and subunits: defined cable tying to avoid induced termination strain loads and easements provided for thermal expansion.
- Printed circuit design review to ensure adequate insulation spacing and track width.
- Exclusive use of swaged connections where possible.
- Revised "Burn-in" procedures for all feedback transducers, FCS electronic sub-assemblies and tray assemblies.

PAYLOAD FAIRING STRUCTUAL STIFFNESS – As part of the above general review the entire BA airframe hardware was carried out over the next six months without finding the need of more than refinements. However, towards the end of 1969, detailed studies of the R0 destruction sequence suggested that Payload Fairing edge member stiffness was marginal.

Reinforcement devised to reduce edge member deflection and improve registration engagement between fairing halves was to cause the postponement of R1 launch until the New-year.

R1 & R2 SSB UMBILICAL CABLES: Investigation of the partial Fairing hang-ups experienced during both these flights concluded that entanglement of one or both SSB umbilical cables with the Spin Table assembly was the likely cause and a full Spring loaded swing arms were introduced for R3 to restrain each cable and ensure they safely retracted and stowed below the rotation plane of the Spin Table. See Appendix B for details.

FIG 19 –1   BA STAGE 2 AND PAYLOAD FAIRINGS.   *(GKN Aerospace)*

FIG 19-2   HIGH DOWN GANTRY 1 WITH BLACK ARROW INSTALLED.
A feint Needles Lighthouse lies off to the left.   *(GKN Aerospace)*

R1 TRIALS – HD & AREA 5 | **20**

Having played a background role during the R1 trial at High Down, I now joined its RDD team to cover the prelaunch night shift duties as DTL2 at Woomera – the last minute workload and 8hr rule make this essential whenever launch recycles occur. This obligation was expected to arise around mid November, which will come along soon enough.

The failure of R0 meant design type approval and WRE objectives remained outstanding. The role change required vehicle interface alterations for the revised line of fire. Additionally, detailed improvements to the FCS installation stemming from the R0 enquiry were also embodied.

R1 QUALIFICATION TRIAL AT HIGH DOWN:

Prompt decisions by RAE and an intensive effort at the Cowes factory converted R1 back to the R0 line of fire standard, which enabled a hardware drip feed to reach High Down from the last week in July onwards; additional Enquiry Panel changes were being installed right up to R1's dying days at High Down.

Qualification testing followed the R0 pattern but EEL remedial holdups piled pressure on meeting a November launch date. Delays were just being stemmed until a weld corrosion fault turned up in several high-pressure gas storage bottles. These custom made lightweight items used light weight ultra high strength Maraging steel that required a specialised welding technique known to have stress corrosion issues. No spares were available before the Stage1 shipping date so replacement was deferred to Woomera and the High Down program continued using restricted pressure levels and limited inflations. Eventually, the hindrances diminished and two good static firings were followed by satisfactory FSP and RFI tests, each with straightforward preparations.

This hasty trial was concluded by early September when Stage1 was shipped by sea to the antipodes, followed by the remaining hardware flying out a few weeks later.

R1 LAUNCH TRIAL AT WOOMERA: (My tenth Bird – 1st as night shift DTL).

12th Nov'69: I arrived at Adelaide and flew up to Woomera next morning to reach TS4 just after a successful Stage1 static firing so it was promising for a 26th Nov launch but RAE Space department halted the trial on 21st Nov to investigate a Payload Fairing structural problem observed during R0's limited flight.

Inside each channel section that reinforced the vertical split line of each half fairing, registration spigot and fork fittings were set at intervals to maintain profile alignment under flight loadings.

A study of R0 photographic records together with a design review of fairing stiffness and aerodynamics revealed that structural deflection could reduce tongue and fork engagement to marginal levels. Consequently a means of increasing edge member stiffness and restoring engagement was in preparation.

> *Fairing air pressure balance – To be an effective aerodynamic fairing and protective shield for delicate Payloads, silicon rubber lip seals were used to limit inflow through the vertical joint line between fairing halves. To equalise internal and external air pressures as the latter fell away with altitude, the joint around the fairing base line where it meets the Stage2 structure is left unsealed to act as a balancing path. Aerodynamic studies revealed that as the bow shock wave moved aft with increasing rocket velocity, it could block the base line balance path, which elevated differential pressure and structural deflection towards the fork/spigot engagement limit. To ensure structural integrity for the R1 firing, special deep engagement register pairs were provided and metallic doubler strips were added to the joint line channels to increase stiffness.*

New parts were air freighted to TS4 and easily swopped but shimming and axial adjustment of each spigot axial proved tricky. Each spigot was secured to the edge member channels by eccentric threaded studs, which enabled fine adjusted between fairing edges. Setting entailed closing, measuring, opening and resetting until an acceptable compromise between skin edge alignment and fairing pull open resistance was obtained. This activity required both fairings to be mounted upright in TS4 and a resourceful DH mechanical team came up trumps by constructing a dummy base frame to imitate the Stage2 fairing interface.

Launch preparation restarted as November ended but a persistent FCS fault caused a launch date slip to 10th Dec'69. Apparently the fault in question had cropped up several times before and should have been taken more seriously because it was eventually localised to an insulation weakness in the Stage1 FCS gain change unit. As a potential flight risk, a protracted design investigation ensued at EEL Cowes, which remained unresolved as time collided with the December launch date.

Accordingly, launching was postponed until the New Year because the coming festive season included WRE's annual Range shut down that ran on until the end of January. Stage1 & 2 structures were returned to TS4, desiccant tank breathers were fitted and all electronic trays and similar gear was stored in the TS4 labs.

11th Dec 1969: – The RDD team and I flew down to Adelaide airport to board the "Yellow Bird of Paradise" (a yellow liveried Britannia aircraft of Monarch Airways), which took us through Changi for shopping then safely on to UK and our families for a welcomed Christmas.

RESTART OF R1 LAUNCH TRIAL:
24th Jan'70: The RDD team arrived back at TS4 ready for whatever R1 and SA weather could come up on the intended launch date of Wednesday 18th Feb '70.

I fell fowl of a Monarch seating famine, which cut things fine because I didn't make it to TS4 till Monday 16th Feb! An anxious DTL met me off the aircraft at Woomera to say the S&S test had been good and I'd be running tonight's pre launch shift! Fortunately the flight out from UK had stocked me on sleep.

It was still summer time when the arid Australian desert can easily pipe up to between 42°C and 45°C in the shade on hot wind days. The TS4 evaporative aircon struggled to keep things tepid but out on the launch pad our only salvation was to drink plenty of water laced with salt tablets to hold off dehydration; EC5 was the favoured bolthole at such times with its very thick walls and robust aircon system.

F0: (Pre Launch Night Shift, 18th Feb '70): The overnight crew and I reached Area5 by 01:00 to find a patient ARU team tirelessly watching over their charge.
The day shift had helpfully fitted and seal checked the Electronic Bay doors and attached the many small skin covers over explosive bolt and Fairing hinge accesses. It was 34°C as we donned our PVC suiting for HTP filling – we were going to loose a few body lbs tonight! While the crew washed down the pad and prepared for HTP transfer, I perused the DTL/OISC propellant load calcs and assisted adjustment to the Kero tank contents. When all was ready, LO5 supervised HTP transfer to both vehicle tanks and both engine start sources. As expected, elevated tank temperatures caused pronounced and disturbing tank sounds that gradually settled down as thermal stability was established. With the HTP bulk carrier cleared away and a further wash down, the LO5/RUXO team began arming the Stage3 ordnance with the aid of two Mechanics to unlink and hold open the UY half Fairing for access to the Spin Table and SSB arming facilities. Reclosing presented the usual concern about SSB cable routing and their potential to tangle with the Spin Table – it was impossible to inspect their routing effectively as the Fairings were reclosed.

Light use of narrow gaffer tape went some way to control matters.

Fairing handling frames were removed and all spring keeper pins were extracted and placed in safekeeping.

> *SSB umbilical cabling:* This inadequate set up was reported at length during the R0 trial. Two diametrically opposed substantial fly leads that originated below the Spin Table rotation plane, trailed freely up past the projecting Spin Imps to reach the SSB positioned above the Waxwing motor. Each cable connected with an SSB pull out socket where it was retained by fuse wire ties intended to shear when yanked by a lanyard from the adjacent Payload Fairing half. The lanyard was also "weakened" by more fuse wire ties near the SSB connection where it was intended break away with each fairing half as it ejected clear of the rocket.
>
> No provision existed (beyond minimal use of gaffer tape!) to constrain the free cable as it dangled from SSB down to its Stage2 entry below the Spin Table. Limited physical and visual access made setting lanyard length and cable route a guesswork exercise. A visual checking as each Fairing was closed was impossible and unrealistic in a 1g-gravitation field. This most serious problem could directly impact on Fairing separation.

With Stage3 arming concluded the LO5/RUXO team moved their ministrations to the Interstage, which embodied the remaining none BU ordnance items and kept them busily arming until 05:15 or thereabouts. The Gamma2 engine, its start system, the thrust chamber harness and numerous associated items were visually confirmed fit to fly fore closing up all Interstage Bay service hatches.

Dawn arrived with an abundance of thick high cloud, so Gantry roll back was delayed in favour of eggs and bacon at Kooly. Cancellation came as we returned so our delousing routines for disarming and removed HTP swung into action yet again – who said Woomera enjoyed good weather?

F0a: (Repeat Launch Nightshift, 19th Feb'70) – Using the routines outlined above, R1 preparation progressed during the night without incident or undue haste. The high temperature proved our only hindrance during the HTP transfer and washing down routines. PVC suit removal and a tepid shower restored a degree of comfort.

While Stage3 Haz circuit arming and associated Payload Fairing work progressed up on Level 'F', tasking around the launch pad oil wetted all gearboxes and connected the engine Start and Purge feeds. The launcher area and all Gantry levels were scoured for lose items as the ever-present final checklist were worked through.

After an early breakfast, all gas bottles got a final top up and seal off. We were up to plan as a warning of developing cloud was quickly trumped by the Range who sought a 24hr delay due to a tracking system problem. The pad team again moved into de lousing mode by disarming the ordnance hardware and unloading the HTP tanks and start systems.

Back at TS4 it was established that a repeat launch attempt was on for tomorrow.

F0b: (Repeat Launch Nightshift, 20th Feb'70) – As we returned to Area5 at midnight we would be repeating F0 tasks as detailed earlier.

After loading the HTP and washing down the action moved to assisting the LO5/RUXO team with the Payload Fairings for Stage3 arming, prepping the gantry for roll back after Interstage was armed and the catalyst capsules fitting.

Meanwhile, as HTP dump arms, Engine Start and N2 pull offs were being finalised, clearing and securing all loose equipments left us eager for Gantry roll back. EC5 promptly agreed when asked so LO5 armed Stage2 Breakup system.

With R1 denuded of the Gantry, Pad 5A was cleared of personnel for final radio transmission checks while the crew and I went hunting for a meal. (Yes, you guessed it, Crew Room sandwiches again) Our last checklist items around the Test Post and extraction of the Release Jack safe pin followed as we cleared 5A, hopefully for the final time, and LO5 armed the Break Up system.

Following a quick EC5 debrief, I retired to the Instrumentation Building roof to enjoy what I hoped was going to be a good launch to watch from afar but fate decreed otherwise when the ARU Monitor in EC5 took Stop Action at –2secs; "lower deck" thoughts prevailed all round.

When the Haz circuit and propellant systems were made safe, our night team and I returned to the Village, leaving the day shift to replace vehicle internal batteries, research the ARU fault and to catch up on the numerous system rework tasks.

> *ARU prelaunch monitor:* Once the AU has concluded a 12hr calibration and Line of Fire alignment, it holds the cluster level and effectively "locked" to the Earth gravity vector and rate of rotation at the launch latitude. To examine ARU health, as zero time is approached, the AU is disconnected at -40secs, which returns cluster loyalty back to inertial space. The resulting cluster 'drift' is displayed on velocity meters fed from the ARU via the Engine Bay rip plugs to a purpose made display at the EC5 ARU rack. On this occasion one meter flickered between –7 to –5secs, which left the operator no option but take stop action. After a root and branch investigation of the ARU on the TS4 plinth, and the EC5 velocity display, both flight and ground equipment hardware were found to be fault free and the gremlin was traced to and repeated at a poorly adjusted rip plug connector.

Servicing Payload internal batteries entailed Payload Fairing removal and sending X1 back to TS4 during the above ARU witch-hunt. These activities plus routine R1 rework tasks, doubtful weather, some WRE rework items and two intervening weekends, pushed the next S&S Tuesday 3rd Mar' 70.

F0c: (Repeat Launch Nightshift, 3rd Mar'70) – Back on shift working again, our well-rehearsed overnight team worked methodically through the allotted tasks almost without prompting.

HTP transfers and Haz system arming seemed to gently sail by until we were kicking our heels waiting for the Gantry roll back call. As I remember, the day dawned with a fine clear sky and promised a hot day as we took breakfast in the Crew Room.

When Gantry roll back was sanctioned, LO5 armed Stage2 breakup system and all floors were stowed before R1 was revealed again in its fully assembled glory and 5A area was cleared for WRE radio transmission testing. We returned to complete the final checklist items, apply gas to Test Post systems and pulled the release jack safe pin, hopefully for the last time (why do I keep thinking this!). After a quick EC5 debrief with the DTL and TL I again headed to the Instrumentation Building to await events.

From the intercom exchanges I understood the count was progressing correctly, zero time came and steam clouds from the exhaust water rose to surround R1 as it leisurely left clear the pad at 06:45. Gathering pace it climbed as if on rails until lost to the naked eye.

4th MARCH 1970 – R1 launch results: Initial indications suggested that all Stage1&2 systems had functioned correctly, performance of both engines had exceeded predictions and the Payload was accurately popped into the Indian Ocean as planned. All Stage1&2 telemetry data was recorded but the Payload signal was intermittent during the vital Stage3 spin up and separation; Stage2 Tele verified the event but retrieval of dynamic data at separation was marginal.

Without exception, everyone celebrated through to the early hours, including many of the Village residents who were delighted by our success. Later analysis from range cameras threw doubt on a proper fairing ejection, just one half being seen to fall away for certain at the right moment. This surmise was confirmed many weeks later when a second fairing half was recovered up range and ballistic analysis traced release back to Stage3 spin up time, suggesting that the ill conceived SSB umbilical cabling had held it in tow until severed by ignition of the Spin Imps.

After a ten-week campaign our weary but contented RDD team flew home on various flights Dec12 to 15. We all came home from the tail end of a pleasant Ozzy summer into a really cold UK spring. Sleeping off jet lag didn't go well with the family who were keen to be up and doing to get the garden ship shape!

The PAYLOAD CLEAN CELL planned for 5B:

Liaison with Marconi, Portsmouth had fleshed out an acceptable environmental boundary for X3, (Prospero), the satellite due for launching on R3 sometime in 1971. The means of isolating this sensitive hardware from the rigors of South Australia's desert required an early study of Gantry 5B upper floors to shake out the implications. During spare moments from my R1/R2 trials at Woomera I concluded it was feasible to create a lamina flow enclosure at floor levels F and G that would meet BS 5295 class "G" filtration standard (later replaced by ISO6, equating to FED STD 209E 1000). Such facilities use copious pre conditioned air at low pressure and low flow through HEPA filters located across the entire ceiling area of the cell to form an 'air piston' constantly sweeping down through the work area and vented away at floor level. Airflow pressure, venting and leakage resistance would be chosen to maintain a cell pressure at 0.02 to 0.2 inches of water. The required filter size would readily suit the Gantry geometry and achieve acceptable particle counts within 20 to 30 minutes of closing the cell and a suitable count meter should be provided for this purpose.

The Gantry structure and Area5 climate made efficient cell thermal insulation and exhaust air recirculation very complex to engineer and expensive when reckoned against the intermittent duty cycle and periodic use profile. A brut-force option using a dead loss air circuit and over-sized aircon plant with moderate cell insulation was selected.

The interior of gantry levels 'F' and 'G' were remodelled to create an enclosed dust free central cell as outlined in Figure 20–1 below. The cell walling was lined with fireproof panelling, secured by flush fixings and finished with white easy clean epoxy paint to offer a smooth low-volatile surface. The existing Gantry front doors were draft and particle sealed by a removable fire resistant fabric curtain, retained to the doorframe verticals by boltrope guides as employed on yacht masts. The roof area immediately below the hoist beam was engineered to accommodate two rectangular HEPA filter units; one placed each side of the hoist beam centre line and spanning the Gantry front to back depth. Each filter unit was mounted on slide rails that allow them to be moved apart for hoist operations. Integrated sealing on each filter unit (possible backed up with Duck tape) limited air loss when closed up. Venting flaps sized and weighted to suit the prescribed airflow and back pressure were installed at cell floor level to maintain airflow and distribution. An elasticated fabric collar closed off the annular gap between rocket and floor kicking strip.

During "Clean" operations, a portable bench hurdle positioned to limit direct passage between the level 'F' stairway and the clean cell, and to served as a gowning bench when donning and discarding bunny suits.

The right hand wall included a visitors viewing window to observe interior operations without gowning up. A door in the left hand wall gave access to the emergency escape route and served as storage area for specific to cell gear e, g, vacuum cleaner, laundered bunny suits and the front door curtain.

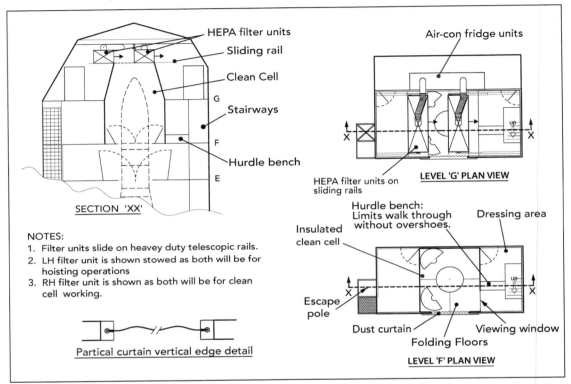

HEPA filter units
Sliding rail
Clean Cell
Stairways
Hurdle bench

SECTION 'XX'

NOTES:
1. Filter units slide on heavey duty telescopic rails.
2. LH filter unit is shown stowed as both will be for hoisting operations
3. RH filter unit is shown as both will be for clean cell working.

Partical curtain vertical edge detail

Air-con fridge units

LEVEL 'G' PLAN VIEW

HEPA filter units on sliding rails

Hurdle bench:
Limits walk through without overshoes.
Dressing area

Insulated clean cell

Escape pole

Dust curtain
Folding Floors
Viewing window

LEVEL 'F' PLAN VIEW

FIG 20–1   THE GANTRY 5B CLEAN CELL AT LEVEL F AND G.   (D Mack)

The Gantry external open structure behind level 'F' was extended upwards to level 'G' to accommodate the aircon plant and restore access to the higher level. The aircon plant comprised three large refrigerant compressors and two air handlers that include pre-filters, fans, evaporators, air heaters and control gear. Each HEPA filter unit included variable speed fans in plenum chambers to adjust the lamina flow velocity. The main air handling and conditioning plant was designed and supplied by a company specialising in clean room installations.

To maintain acceptable thermal conditions inside the nose fairing after Gantry roll back and prior to vehicle lift-off, a 3" diameter flexible hose line was routed up the Umbilical Mast from a nearby cooler trolley, to a pull away port in the fairing skin structure.

Disconnection was accomplished by pull wire; and bomb-slip operated drop weight activated from EC5.

The complete setup was operational for the R3 trial when I experienced the cells utility and found it met the intended purpose surprisingly well but would benefit from detailed intention to improve ruggedness of the opening/closing features but program cancellation negated these ideas.

The launch pad crew regarded the cell as paradise zone at the height of summer!

I was pleased by the engineering standard achieved by Salisbury SARO team who had resolved on the spot many details of the final installation.

FIG 20–2 X1 PAYLOAD – MOUNTED ON THE SAT SEP BAY (SSB)
(poorly focussed original picture)   (*Crown copyright*)

R2 TRIALS – HD & AREA 5　　**21**

As with the R1 trial I remained in support behind the scenes until launch time at Area 5 when I joined the team as overnight Deputy Team Leader (DTL2) to assist the final launch preparation phase.

R1's non-orbital flight along the Range Centreline had proved successful despite the delayed detachment of one fairing half. All other aspects of BA flight performance had been demonstrated and engine performance of both lower stages had exceeded expectations. Of equal importance, WRE had confirmed their ability to track the flight path effectively, maintain flight termination control and retrieve telemetry data. Consequently it was confirmed that R2 would be firing north with a live apogee stage to potentially put the simple X2 boilerplate payload into orbit.

R2 HIGH DOWN QUALIFICATION TRIAL:
The vehicle build duplicated previous rocket builds with the following additions: -
1.　X2 beacon satellite.
2.　Stage3 with a live Waxwing apogee motor.
3.　Stage2 umbilical and HTP dump connectors sited to suit the NW firing line.
4.　ARU alignment parameters adjusted for new firing line.
5.　C Band aerial re-positioned to suit new firing line.
6.　Payload Fairing structure with reinforced edge members.

EARLY MAR' 70 – All vehicle hardware had arrived at High down to undergo an eight-week period of qualification. The static firing of both Gamma engines was satisfactory and achieved without difficulty. The overall RFI tests using X2 (Orba) payload, with and without fairings fitted were also successful; no system disturbances were noted and both WREBUS receivers remained free from RFI.

Stage1 was released for shipping to Adelaide early in May'70 but lack of available cargo space was to delay departure by some four weeks. Stage2 and Payload fairings were flown out forth week July '70.

R2 LAUNCH TRIAL AT WOOMERA:
I arrived in Adelaide on Wednesday 12th Aug' 70, but remained at SARO, Salisbury to clarify 5B clean cell details before flying up to Woomera on Monday 17th.

We were now being housed at the ex ELDO Mess, a great pretentious utilitarian and characterless hotel built during the heady Blue Streak days. It was modern and comfortable enough with good facilities and en suit bedrooms but the public rooms were too large and austere and lacked the character or cosy "Lived in" atmosphere of the Senior Mess.

Despite Stage1 shipping delay, the trial had made good progress; Stage2 had been successfully static fired and was mounted on Stage1 at Launcher 5B preparing for RFI testing. Stage1 static firing was scheduled for 21st Aug with a launch window beginning 1st Sept or thereabouts. As I arrived the SSB and X2 satellite were being mounted on the inert Waxwing ready for freestanding RFI checks. Each test passed off without any evidence of WREBUS desensitisation or intersystem EMC problems.

Towards the end of August the Gamma 8 static firing came up with good results, which cleared the way to prepare for launch.

In common with most desert areas, mid winter at Woomera often brought fine, clear sunny days with really cold nights and predictable weather fronts that often carried just enough rain to reduce all unsealed surfaces to a red sticky mud. The weather men seemed confident of a dry launch day with clear skies and WRE were equally certain that all northerly tracking and radio receiver stations on the new firing line would be ready to go on 1st September.

F–8: (PRE LAUNCH PREPARATION) Saw Stage3 stripped down and X2 returned to TS4 to be batteried up and made flight ready. The Spin Table was physically exercised, locked and confirmed to be level before the immediate structural area was meticulously cleaned ready for the final Stage3 rebuild.

F–7: (FINAL ARU/FCS/ACS ALIGNMENT): Overnight, the ARU had been 12hr aligned on the Line of Fire. The dayshift trimmed the airframe roll angle to bring the ARU roll synchro output to zero then confirming zero thrust chamber angles and ACS jet nulls using shore-side hydraulics and a vehicle gas supply. The WRE surveyor verified the ARU azimuth datum by a theodolite check over the local plumb bob vertical.

F–6: With live explosives present at Pad 5B from today, the 8-hour working rule was in force and nominated team members will operate in two-shifts as workload dictated; I joined the night shift crew as DTL2.

The live Waxwing motor was hoisted to level 'F', rotationally aligned and secured to the Spin Table by Manacle clamp, the SSB was secured on top.

The two umbilical cables from Stage2 were carefully draped clear of the Spin Table and secured to the SSB by a single strand of 5amp fuse wire.

The SSB Umbilical Saga continues: As criticised on every BA trial to date, the two substantial fly leads that emanate below the Spin Table run freely up and plug into the SSB to carry shore side Payload control and monitoring facilities via the rockets umbilical and rip plug interfaces.

Prior to Stage3 separation, both cables must be pulled from the SSB and cleared down below the Spin Table rotation path. Hitherto, a lanyard from each Payload Fairing half is intended to pull its adjacent fly lead from the SSB by shearing fuse wire ties at the SSB, as the fairings swing open towards the 40° ejection angle. The outer end of each lanyard is also intended to shear from the Fairing at a weakened point as it is ejected clear from Stage2. It is expected that the free end of each fly lead will trail aft freely until Stage2 "All Burnt" when zero gravity will allow them to drift randomly – all this cleverness by courtesy of Heath Robinson.

Primary design failings:

(a) During initial assembly, the length of each lanyard must be adjusted to exert enough "snatch" to break the SSB fuse wire without degrading the Fairing swing open impetus before 40° is reached – a tricky three dimensional task that is difficult to access and set up precisely.

(b) With the Fairings fully closed for flight, the fly leads and lanyards drape down onto the Spin Table assembly where entanglement risk cannot be visually assessed.

(c) The set up risks further compromise each time the UY fairing is partially opened to access the Spin Table and SSB arming plugs.

The above concerns may explain the delinquent fairing behaviour on the R1 trial. A full redesign is hand for R3. See Section 5, Fig B–6 of Appendix 'B' for more detail.

All Haz batteries were installed and connected ready for tomorrows Flight Sequence Programmer (FSP) testing. Both kerosene tanks were over filled for later trimming.

F–5: Three FSP test runs were a satisfactory using: the simulator, the spare FSP and the flight FSP. Each test entailed operation of ARU, FCS, ACS, and WREBUS systems plus the Haz circuits for: Stage2 separation, Gamma2 start, Inter-stage bay separation, Stage3 separation, Fairing separation and SSB Payload delay relays – a long taxing process that would benefit from rationalisation.

F–4: Consequent on yesterday's FSP runs, the physical status of all switching elements in the Hazardous Circuit system were tested and verified to be correctly set at pre-launch readiness prior to installing all non BU ordnance stores tomorrow (The BU capsules remain unfitted until HTP filling has proved them leak free).

F–3: (FITTING ORDNANCE) A long working day for the RUXO and LO5 teams as they replaced all "Hazardous Circuit" batteries and installed the following live ordnance stores:

Fit & connect 4 Payload Fairing gas separator units.

- Fit & connect 2 Satellite gas separator units.
- Fit & connect 1 Waxwing pressure Tx, 1 igniter & 1 head cutter charge.
- Fit & connect 3 Manacle Clamp explosive bolt detonators.
- Fit & connect 6 Spin Table Imp thrust units.
- Fit & connect 2 Spin Table unlock gas charges.
- Fit & connect 2 ACS frangible pillar charge.
- Fit & connect 16 Interstage explosive bolt detonators.
- Fit & connect 16 Stage2 explosive bolt detonators.
- Fit & connect 4 Siskin separation rockets with igniters.

F–2: All Non Haz internal batteries were fitted and 30sec load tested. Gearbox oil and hydraulic systems for both Gamma engines were checked and serviced and all vehicle gas bottles were charged.

The flight ready X2 satellite was hoisted and secured to the SSB and electrically connected through Stage2 to shore side services. After completing X2 functional testing via EC5, the Payload Fairings were installed, check listed and closed up; the UY half would be partially reopened later to access Stage3 arming plugs.

Stage2 and Stage1 HTP dump arms were erected and functionally tested.

> *Saved by Uncle Sam:* *Personnel move between Village and Range E by using WRE self-drive cars, self-drive minibuses or scheduled bus service. To prevent vehicle misuse, all self-drive vehicles are over night parked at a vehicle depot about two miles outside the Village, usually reached during normal working hours by shuttle bus, taxi service or thumbing a lift – all extremely difficult processes outside normal working hours.*
>
> *To reach the depot for my 01:00 nocturnal stints took time to roust out a taxi then drive back to the village to pick up my kit. After three nights of this pantomime I took to parking off road alongside my billet. Within two days I was summoned to the Area Superintendent's office – top administrator for the entire Woomera establishment.*
>
> *The great man gently lectured me at length on the misuse of self–drive cars and Tax Payers money. As I began to explain my problem, a high ranking US military officer burst into the room, excused himself to me and addressing the Superintendant by first name, told him that WRE were delinquent in not providing twelve of the twenty odd self–drive cars pledged to his project. Therefore he'd ordered the deficient vehicles from an Adelaide car hire firm who were driving six up in the morning with the rest to follow the day after. His parting shot was "I trust no security or other admin hurdles will stall these arrangements" and left.*
>
> *After a moments thought, the "Great Man" said "I think we'd concluded our business Derek, a Village parking permit will be issued for the duration of your trial!*

F–1: (PRE LAUNCH S&S DAY) – Engine start tank was watered, N2 purge was flow tested, internal non haz batteries were 30 sec load tested as all gas bottles were topped up and checklists were progressively closed off. Good progress had been achieved as our Adelaide "Tourists" returned before lunch and ready for the three-part S&S test, which was successfully concluded by mid afternoon.

F0: (LAUNCH DAY NIGHT SHIFT) – Prior to our midnight shift, the TL advised that all systems had come through the S&S with flying colours but persistent cloud cover had become the next worry. He also confirmed that all vehicle gas bottles were pre-charged and the Electrons Bay had been closed up and seal tested it at 10psi. They had also installed the Stage2 HTP dump arm so a gentle nights work was in prospect.

As the crew washed down and prepared for HTP filling I checked over the load calculations against the actual propellant temperatures and had both Kerosene loads adjusted. All donned in PVC suits, LO5 moved in the HTP bulk carrier and both vehicle tanks and the engine start systems were filled without difficulty – the really cold night ambient ensured a docile process.

While the Pad area got a final wash down the UY Payload Fairing was partially open to let the RUXO/LO5 crew access to the Spin Table and SSB for arming Stage3 Haz battery and detonators. When concluded the Fairing internal checklist was revisited, closed up, re-linked, and re-tensioned before the pyro separator collets were armed.

Lastly, all keeper pins that kept the Fairing push open and hinge ejection springs at bay were removed and the handling frames were unshipped.

The RUXO/LO5 team moved their interest to arming the Interstage Bay services and inserted Stage2 and Stage1 HTP tank catalyst charges.

A final gas bottle top up and sight glass removal led to a coffee break until EC5 cleared us to arm Stage2 BU and roll back the Gantry – just around 05:30 as the sky began to clear. The start and purge pipes were connected, HTP dump hoses were hooked up and duct-cooling water was primed. Gas pressure was applied to Test Post room 'A' services and the release jack safe pin was pulled and handed to LO5. On closing the final checklist we cleared the Pad as LO5 armed Stage1 BU circuits.

After a quick crew room visit, the endorsed checklists were handed over in EC5 and I casually drove over to Instrumentation Building to await lift off.

The 35minute sequence began around 07:00 and ran down to –120secs without hesitation, after an uncertain dwell the Auto sequence was started but stopped at –35 seconds when the Gove station went U/S. I hit the ground running and drove back to EC5 to learn that today's attempt was scrubbed. The overnight team and I set to, to re-safe the vehicle by disarming all Haz circuits and removing HTP before we hunted for breakfast.

I was back in the village by midday, took lunch and went to bed, at dinner that evening we learnt that Gove was up and running and a further launch attempt was on for next morning.

F0a: (2ND SEPT – LAUNCH RETRY NIGHT SHIFT) – The night crew and I reached Area5 at midnight to turn the pre launch preparation handle one more time. Because all vehicle batteries were good for two more days, the Electronics Bay remained sealed, the Kerosene load remained unchanged and the daylight guys had charged up the vehicle gas bottles so we were being let off lightly again. Our immediate arming tasks duplicated last night's activities at a more leisurely pace and Gantry roll back came as 08:00 arrived with a clear sky and just a whisper of wind.

When Stage1 BU system had been armed, the release jack pin was pulled and we left the Pad area once more. I again headed for the IB via the crew room and EC5 to surrender the endorsed checklist. The countdown eventually began around 09:30 and ran straight through without interruptions.

LIFT OFF at 10:04 on 2nd Sept 1970.

From the IB roof, lift off looked normal, clean and gentle. I moved inside IB to watch the Tele displays: Stage1 flamed out on time and Stage2 separation appeared normal but the Gamma2 stopped burning some 13 seconds early, which scuppered Stage3 chances of reaching orbital velocity. Stage3 had spun up and separated and the Waxwing had fired to dispatch the Payload on a long falling path into the sea.

Good radar and optical tracking was obtained throughout most of the flight and telemetry reception was exceptional.

Some concern was again noted regarding the nose fairings, only one half was definitely seen to have ejected; a day or so later recovery evidence confirmed that the second half had remained attached until the spin up event – much the same as R1. Tracking records also indicated marginal ACS stability towards the end of flight – might be due to an open hung up half fairing?

Subsequent analysis revealed that a pressure transducer residing in the Electronics Bay to monitor tank pressure with respect to external ambient pressure had sprung an internal leakage path to the Electronics Bay +10 psi internal pressure. The false atmospheric datum that resulted, regulated Stage2 HTP tank pressure at 28psi instead of 20psi, which lifted the tank relief valve to spill and deplete the gas storage bottles before all burnt time.

This trip was a quick one of four weeks. I flew home with the RDD team on 13th September, intent on some "me time" with the family before taking up the reigns as R3 Team Leader – even the family cat now takes fright when I turn up!

R3 TRIAL – HD 22

Having identified why R2 Gamma2 engine shut down early and why R1 & R2 Payload Fairings failed to deploy properly (see explanations below) it was time for R3 to do BA's first orbital insertion with Prospero as the client Payload.

R3 HIGH DOWN QUALIFICATION TRIAL: (My Twelfth Bird – 8th as TL)

OBJECTIVES
- To place the X3 (Prospero) Satellite into earth orbit.
- Line of Fire – 7° 25' East of North

BUILD STANDARD: All functional elements necessary for orbital entry were implemented and operational, plus the following additions:
1. Revised X3 umbilical mechanism (see note below).
2. Optional C–Band aerial (see note below).
3. Revised ACS gas filter.
4. Amended ACS trigger law.
5. Reinforced Payload Fairing edge members.
6. Cooling air input port added to Payload Fairings
7. X3 satellite transfer aerials added to Payload Fairings.

Loss of R2 HTP tank pressure: *Stage2 HTP tank pressurising system resides inside the Electronics Bay, which itself is vent valve regulated to remain 7 to 9psi above external ambient pressure. An external pressure reference pipe to the HTP tank regulator also serves a differential pressure transducer monitoring tank pressure. Test simulations established that this transducer had harboured a leak path to the Electronics Bay internal pressure, which elevated HTP tank regulation enough to open the tank relief valve and spill gas to deplete storage bottles early. The resulting loss of head caused HTP pump cavitation and loss of oxidant delivery to all thrust chambers.*

Spare part testing was central to unearthing this fault since all spare transducers were found to have a similar leakage path. To prevent further occurrences, the reference pipe skin port will be tested for no gas outflow during the Electronics Bay pre flight seal test at +10psi. The remaining tank pressurising systems are immune from the above problem because they reside in totally vented compartments.

Revised X3 umbilical mechanism: It was finally concluded that the SSB umbilical fly lead set up had caused R1 & R2 Fairing hang up problems.

Section 5 and Fig B–6 of Appendix B describes the new arrangement using two lightweight spring-loaded support arms to carry the fly leads clear of the Fairing and Spin Table mechanics. As each half fairing swings open towards its ejection angle, the spring-loaded arms are freed to swing down and become locked well below the rotation plane of the Spin Table hardware.

C–Band aerial polarisation: The walking impact trace obtained from R2 displayed a pronounced path distortion near the Beresford railroad stop. Extensive line of sight modelling regarding the axis relationship between ground and flight antenna at this trajectory point concluded the anomaly was a polarisation artefact. Analysis hinted that a circular polarised rocket aerial may improve or even eliminate this "Beresford Wiggle" but ongoing investigations were to delay final resolution until the Woomera trial.

TRIAL OUTLINE: Following a protracted strike at Rolls Royce, Stage2 did not reach High Down until early May '71, with Stage1 arriving six days later along with the Payload Fairings. The trial was intended to follow the general pattern prepared for R0 (Table B/4 at end of Appendix B), adjusted for week ending dates. Key milestone events are listed below and described in the paragraphs that follow.

D – 49   Stage2 erected in Gantry 2
D – 44   Stage1 erected in Gantry 1
D – 36   Stage2 Static firing
D – 34   Stage2 erected on Stage1
D – 28   Stage3 assembled on Stage2
D – 23   RFI tests
D – 19   Stage1, Static Firing
D – 16   FSP tests
D – 12   Acceptance review
D0   Stage1 dispatch
D+3   Stage2 cleared for dispatch
D+22   BLACK ARROW PROGRAM IS CANCELLED.

D–61:(STAGE2 + INTERSTAGE) – After a detailed physical inspection and QA audit the RUXO, Telemetry, FCS and Mechanical crews were free to work through their detailed wiring, calibration and functional tests. Meantime, electronic and mechanical sub assemblies were given detailed checkouts and calibration in the various specialist Test Labs. Beyond minor adjustments no noteworthy problems were encountered.

D–60/59: WEEKEND

D–55:(STAGE1 + INTERSTAGE) – Stage1 arrived together with Payload Fairings. A physical inspection preceded fitting the Interstage Bay for RUXO, FCS and Tele testing. On conclusion, the Interstage was moved to Gantry 2 for pressure and flow testing of the engine start and purging systems.

D–53/52: WEEKEND

D–49/47:(STAGE2) – Moved to Gantry2 and erected on the Interstage for propellant tank volume and level sensing probes calibrations preceded tank pressurising functional tests.

D–46/45: WEEKEND

D–44/40:(STAGE1) – Moved to Gantry1. Testing was limited to locally controlled activities because Equipment Centre (EC) and Recorder Room (RC) were patched to Site 2 for Stage2 static firing. Gamma8 trunnions and hydraulics were rigged for servo running, FCS pack was installed and functioned from CSMU and Test Post facilities. Frequency response tests were completed as and when staff availability allowed – good results obtained.
Propellant tank volume and level sensors were calibrated; DC ground instrumentation was connected to the engine shuttle valves begun and will continue for several days.

D–44/43:(STAGE2) – Gamma2 engine and hydraulics were rigged for ground running. Dummy Waxwing motor was installed, FCS tray fitted and functioned via the CSMU; good inner loop frequency responses were obtained. ARU installation and 12hr alignment followed overnight for an accurate alignment.

D–42/40:(STAGE2) – FCS was connected and harmonise to the aligned ARU outputs. Telemetry, C–Band and Wrebus receivers fitted and functionally checked.
The Gamma2 engine prepped for S&S test – gearbox lub oil flow test – start tank filled with demin water etc.

D–39/38: WEEKEND

D–37:(STAGE2 S&S DAY) – Equipment Centre and Recorder Room were fully staffed and powered up with recorders being spot calibrated and camera ident shots. All vehicle and Site2 systems checklists were closed as systems were finalised.
After lunch a fault free S&S sequence run through without noteworthy incident. Immediate reports were good so in anticipation of good Recorder Room readouts kerosene was loaded ready for tomorrow

D–36:(STAGE2 STATIC FIRING) – When general preparations and Downs Clearance Party tasks were concluded, the Safety Officer and Mechanical team loaded Stage2 HTP tank and engine start bottle with HTP.

After a site wash down and loose items check, vehicle hold down bolts were vetted. Following lunch, a final status check on the engine support systems and gasses closed the checklist, which I deposited with the SO at the Blockhouse.

In the Equipment Centre I checked each console driver and the OISC before passing operations to the Sequence Officer who got the clock ticking soon after 13:30. As zero time came, both propellant feeds and two combustion pressures almost climbed in unison to hot running level where they stayed until +35 secs. Following sounds reports from all involved, engine drain collectors were removed to the Lab and HTP systems were drained and washed down.

D–35:(STAGE2) – The internal engine inspection was satisfactory and engine drying out was arranged for tonight. After studying all the firing results, data analysts and systems engineers declared a satisfactory bill of health.

D–35:(STAGE1) – An early start saw the Equipment Centre and Recorder Room services patched over to Test Site 2 and Electrically Similar Vehicle (ESV) checked by mid afternoon. Stage1 gas bottles were charge and a good HTP tank pressurising test was achieved by close of play, having had to replace a leaking pressure transducer.

D–34/33:(STAGE2 MEETS STAGE1) – All Stage3 elements were removed and returned to the Prep Area. Stage2 was dressed with handling gear and transferred across to Site1 with attached Interstage Bay.

Stage-to-stage electrical continuity and insulation testing preceded arming and functional tests of Stage2 tank pressurising systems via the Equipment Centre. The Electronics Bay service doors, vent valve and datum port were all pressure tested at 10psi.

Wind Brace arms were trimmed to level the Spin Table and Stage2 FCS trays were installed and functioned ready for checking with the ARU. The Tele team pressed on with their ongoing audit of vehicle monitor sources as each subsystem became functional.

D–32:(WEEKEND) – ARU installation time – it is now well recognised that ARU 12hr accuracy tests are impractical alongside parallel vehicle activities; small structural movements extend gyro convergence times. ARU installation, calibration and alignment begun around 18:00hr and is expected to conclude around 06:00hr tomorrow morning.

D–31:(WEEKEND) – As expected, ARU was aligned and ready for use by daybreak, when its Roll synchro output was brought to zero by rotating the vehicle airframe angle. Actual vehicle azimuth was theodolite confirmed with the local survey vertical. The FCS was run up and harmonised with the ARU outputs.

D–30: (FCS SENSE TEST) –

> *As explained previously*, this test is done to demonstrate absolutely that all steering torque sources work in harmony and in a polarity that will bring the ARU error demands to zero.

The elaborate procedure involves fully active ARU feeding Stage1&2 FCS, both operating on shore side hydraulics and using ACS gas pressure. Many operators are involved both at the Equipment Centre and positioned about the rocket vehicle to observe thrust chamber deflection and gas jet function while the airframe is physically rotated through a small angle about the release ball: see Appendix B for full test detail. The airframe position was restored to give zero ARU synchro outputs.

Back at the Prep Area the Marconi X3 team were setting up their monitor caravan, a biggish bit of kit for the available area. Cabling was connected the EC main frame to en route to the rockets umbilical connector; a satellite radio link aerial was also rigged up on the Prep Area roof.

D–29:(FAIRING VOLUME CHECKS) – After completing Spin Table torque and swept freedom checks, the X3 cross section template was clamped on the Table and each half Payload Fairing was in turn checked to allow the required clearance with the Payload and its aerials. Final locking of transfer aerials positions is left for the launch trial at Woomera.

The Doppler unit, C–Band beacon, Instrumentation batteries and WREBUS radios were installed and functionally tested and followed by a full Telemetry read out across all Stage1 & 2 flight systems.

D–28/26:(STAGE3 ASSEMBLY) – The inert Waxwing and SSB were Manacle Clamped to the Spin Table. Both SSB umbilical arms were raised and kept connected to the SSB by Red Flagged keeper pins.

D–25/24: WEEKEND – The "A" model satellite (nominated as flight spare) was now fitted for the coming RFI tests. Being the first fit of an actual flight Payload, the process was carried out step by slow step to familiarise RDD, HD, X3 and LO5 personnel with the detail and verify the RUSP accuracy. Snugly protected inside segmented panelling, the sensitive cargo was hoisted up to level F and secured on the SSB with two inert pyro collet separators. The X3 team then ran their communication and functional tests and expressed satisfaction with the results; X3 would stay inside the protective panels for the "Fairings Off" RFI tests fixed for tomorrow.

D–23:(RFI LESS FAIRINGS TEST) – The test is carried out with all vehicle systems and airframe structure assembled to closely resemble flight standard, less explosive stores and propellants.

RFI test purpose: Demonstrates that no radio frequency fields that emanate from the vehicle or related ground installations are detrimental to the proper operation of all vehicle systems, with special emphasis on reception sensitivity of both WREBUS flight termination receivers. The screening, reflectivity and parasitic effects of High Down's metallic and immovable Gantry make it impossible to operate in realistic free-free conditions or field densities.

Therefore High Down testing is merely indicative of issues that may arise under actual operational conditions at Woomera. The rocket assembly is built up to closely match that pertaining at launch, excluding all ordnance stores and attention is given to present the 'flight' vehicle antenna with realistic ground planes by fitting all local access panels.

Back at the Prep Area, the vehicle internal battery packs had been prepared. Each silver zinc cell underwent a charged and on load discharge cycle before being wired into a battery pack. A further charge/discharge cycle was applied ahead of the final charge for flight. All Non-Haz battery packs underwent a 30sec "Internals" operation running its related vehicle system load.

Throughout the RFI test, WREBUS receiver sensitivity was continuously monitored as each rocket and ground based RF source was progressively energised and proven operational. All none RF electrical EMC functions were then activated before switching the rocket systems over to internal battery power. Ejection of the Umbilical plug was followed by Stop Action to shutdown all vehicle systems. With all systems inert, WREBUS function was again assessed.

None of today's tests revealed evidence of any RFI problems. Tomorrows test will be carried out with Payload Fairings fitted.

D–22: (RFI WITH FAIRINGS TEST) – Marconi removed the X3 protective panels and RDD carefully fitted both Payload Fairing halves and secured them together. Marconi X3 communication tests proved satisfactory and the RFI testing described above was repeated with similar results except that X3 transmitters caused a noticeable disturbance to WREBUS Channel 7. Efforts to understand the reason were frustrated by the absence of suitable monitoring equipment and Gantry influence on RF fields. However, these results gave a clear heads-up warning for the Woomera trial where realistic operational conditions and test gear will be available.

D–21: (COMPOSITE S&S TEST PREP) –See Table B/7, Appendix B for sequence timing. As remarked elsewhere, the Composite vehicle static firing is the nearest approach that High Down ever gets to the live Launch sequence conditions.

ARU 2hr alignment began before dawn and barring incidents would continue running through the Static firing.

Stage1 gearbox oil was topped, all vehicle gas bottles were charged, Stage2 propellant tanks were filled with kerosene and water as applicable and Stage1 hydraulics was set up for ground running.

Finally, a CSSU program was run through the FCS and recorded. With an engine Haz battery fitted and Fail Safe gas applied and operation of the engine shutdown solenoid was demonstrated.

D–20: (COMPOSITE S&S) – At the Equipment Centre, sequence timing and override switch settings were checked and sealed, all Stop Action inputs were exercised, Recorder and remote camera media was loaded and spot calibrated.

Clean engine drain collectors were positioned, exhaust duct cooling water was primed and the engine shut down battery and tank pressure circuits were armed.

The S&S run began around 13:30 and –120sec Auto sequence ran to +35secs without interruption. Internal "switchover and Umbilical eject occurred on time, all console operators reported correct behaviour and all Recorder channels were captured.

Stage1 kero was loaded while engine trunnions and ground start tank were drained.

The "Switch to Internal Power" and "Umbilical Plug Eject" sequence channels were disabled and overridden to minimise Stop Action sources during engine firing.

With promising weather conditions we set up for a Gamma8 firing after lunch tomorrow.

D–19: (COMPOSITE STATIC FIRING) – Engine hydraulics were pressurised, both gearboxes were wetted by an oil flow run, N2 purge and start feeds were reconnected to the engine.

By morning tea break, the Recorder Room, Telemetry, X3, RF, ARU and FCS guys had completed their system spot checks and closed their final checklist. After an OK from the Downs clearance team the Safety Officer oversaw HTP transfer to Stage1 and engine ground start tanks. After a final area wash down and a sweep for unsecured items, we dispersed for lunch. After lunch, all vehicle constraints and the release jack were security checked; Test Post system pressures were noted and the final checklist was initialled. I cleared back via the Block House and washroom to the Equipment Centre, which was tightly packed with visiting engineers from the RAE, Rolls Royce, Cowes and elsewhere. After a quick yarn at each console and the OISC, the Sequence officer began the count down.

All vehicle electrical systems powered up correctly and –120sec Auto sequence started. As each event and interlock responded, zero time arrived and all pump delivery pressures were up on line within 2secs. All eight chamber pressures then rose as one and remained steady without any detectable deviation until falling quickly to zero at + 35 secs.

All reports were positive, X3 was unaffected by the experience and everything appeared to be on the money. HTP delousing and wash down was begun and arrangements were made to dry out the engine overnight.

CALAMITY – The post-firing inspection found throat erosion damage in several thrust chambers. This hot topic continued for several days until it was agreed to continue as planned before returning the engine to Ansty for repair. This allowed Stage1 to be shipped to Australia by sea on time, less the engine; an airlifted replacement would reach TS4 with no impact on the planned launch timescale.

D–18/17: WEEKEND.

D–16 to 15: (FSP TESTS) – See Table B/3 in Appendix B for FSP timing.

As found during the R0 HD trial, running each of the three FSP sequences individually and consecutive eased manpower management and co-ordination considerably.

> *FSP IN SITU TESTING: These functional tests are run to prove FSP/Vehicle system compatibility, and show that adequate firing current reaches each activation device in the correct order. Live match head puffers simulate Igniter/detonator devices and all haz batteries were fitted and armed*
>
> *ARU, FCS and ACS systems are run to verify the pitch over programs, gain changes and ACS initiation. Both WREBUS receivers are also monitored to confirm fail/fire mode switching. Three test runs are involved; the first using an FSP simulator, followed by the flight and spare units. Each run covers the three FSP timing sections i.e. Section1 is started at –10secs, Section2 stared by bridging the Stage1 all burnt inertia switch and Section3 is similarly start at Stage2 all burnt. The tests are concluded by a test sweep through all switching devices and time delay units to ensure they have been properly reset to pre-launch status.*

This test involves observations and actions that extend to all Stages and needs the co-ordination and detailed attention of many participants. Several rehearsals were carried out with the FSP simulator rehearsals. The first flight FSP run was aborted due a procedural error but the repeat and following run using the spare FSP were both accomplished without fault.

Selected igniter/detonator locations were chosen to search for evidence of low-level RFI using special instrumented puffers to record thermal rise while each Tele transmitter; the C-band beacon and Doppler units are operated discretely. No evidence of EM pick up could be detected.

D–12: (ACCEPTANCE REVIEW) – Test data for this purpose had been amassed and continually assessed throughout the trial, analysed record results were published in reports integrated in the vehicle log books. Progressive assessment over several months reduced this exercise to consideration of specific hot topics.

The review concluded that R3 was fit for purpose subject to caveats relating to: WREBUS/X3 RFI behaviour, Fairing transfer aerial locking, C band aerial polarisation and the Gamma8 engine refit.

D–11 to10: WEEKEND

D–9: X3 satellite returned to the Prep Area and forwarded to Marconi, Portsmouth. Stages1, 2 & 3 were stripped down and returned to very congested Prep Area.

D–7 to 0:(STAGE1) – After a QA inventory audit, Stage1 was balanced and weighed prior to removing the faulty Gamma 8 engine for rebuild. Airframe less engine was crated up and released for sea passage to Woomera on 7th July '71.

D–6 to D+2:(STAGE2) – QA audit, balance and weigh, inventoried, inhibited and prepared for air palette transit circa first week in July.

THE BOMBSHELL: July 29, 1971, HMG terminated the Black Arrow project but graciously allowed the R3 trial to continue through to launch!!! The team and I left UK for Woomera on 16th August '71 disheartened but with determined mindsets

FIG 22–1 R3 STAGE2 AT HIGH DOWN – Yours truly in the hard hat. *(GKN Aerospace)*

FIG 22–2 GAMMA 8 ENGINE – Shown with heat shields & 3 turbine exhausts removed. *(Crown copyright)*

Fig 22–3 GAMMA 2 ENGINE *(Crown copyright)*

R3 TRIAL – AREA 5 **23**

The RDD team and I arrived at Adelaide on Friday 20th August '71 and flew on to Woomera on Monday reaching TS4 after lunch.

Like us, the DH guys were very crestfallen at the project's unfitting demise. Even though we'd all lived with this possibility for some time, the inept timing came like a smack in the face as we each strived to make British rocket history.

Our OISC, a well–seasoned RAE campaigner and a real "team man" whom I'd been pleased to work alongside over many trials, was clearly ill at ease. Calling us together to share his thoughts, he praised everybody for their dedication during the BK and BA campaigns and voiced his concern for those having to face an alternative livelihood irrespective of R3's pending performance.

He regretted HMG's lack of interest in Space research and humbly asked for our traditional commitment one last time; success would please us all and may even alert Whitehall to a world wide growing Space industry.

It was clear the RAE and this OISC in particular, were pulling out all the stops to make for a successful end to the series. The stronger RAE contingent in numbers and talent than ever before were to join with senior design engineers from each major contractor to man a daily Review Panel vetting each days progress and exposing technical issues – why did we never have this level of support before. It was so reassuring to know that each days preparation results would get unhurried consideration; in the past the basic trials team had run testing, review results, devised solutions, write up daily diaries and compiled log book entries, while struggling to get our fickle beast fit for flight – judge, jury and hard pressed executioner all in one!

> *The CNES method:* In the following chapter I relate my time working on the French Diamant program with Black Arrows nose fairings where an open forum review panel sat in constant session throughout each trial, vetting the technical detail as each preparation procedure was completed. All unoccupied trials staff (a rare animal on our trials) was invited to sit in and contribute or just observe and learn at these inquisitions.

R3 – WOOMERA LAUNCH TRIAL: (My Twelfth Bird – 8th as TL)

TRIAL OUTLINE: *Stage2 arrived by air 26thJuly'71, followed by Stage1, less engine on 17th Aug'71. The replacement engine turned up on 31stAug'71.*

The trial plan was based on the notional plan set out in Table B/5, Appendix B, adjusted for week ending dates and additional tasking. Key events are listed below and described in the paragraphs that follow.

F – 48	Stage2 to Area 5A
F – 39	Stage2 Static Firing at Area 5A
F – 38	Stage1, replacement Gamma8 fitted
F – 32	Stage1 to Area 5B
F – 26	Stage2 assembled on Stage1.
F – 20	Stage3 assembled on Stage2
F – 18	X3 (A) loaded on Stage 3
F – 15/13	Composite RFI search
F – 11	The Composite Static Firing
F – 9a/9b	Further RFI research
F – 6	Live Waxwing motor fitted
F – 5	FSP Tests
F – 3	Explosive Stores fitted
F – 2	X3 (F) loaded on Stage3
F – 2a/2b	Final RFI tests
F – 1	S&S for launch – aborted due vehicle faults
F – 1a	S&S for launch repeated
F0	Launch

TRIAL DETAIL:

F–60: (STAGE2) – Unpacked and waiting at TS4.

(STAGE1) – Unpacked and waiting at TS4, less engine.

F–59/58: (WEEKEND)

F–57: (INTERSTAGE) – Removed from Stage2 and set up on site 5A for engine start and N2 purge pressure and flow testing.

F–57/54: (STAGE2) – Inspected, FCS, Tele, C band sub units moved to calibration labs. ARU's lab tests had begun a week earlier. Non-Haz wiring and FCS inner loop components were continuity tested and calibrated. Two AC pickoff arms were found to have marginal drive peg engagement at extreme trunnion angles. All four locations were fitted with replacement arms manufactured at Salisbury with 0.1inch longer fork tines.

F–53: (STAGE1) – The Interstage Bay was attached to enable completion of the MAO/LO5/RUXO Haz circuit certification. Setting up checks on Telemetry installation.

F–52/51: (WEEKEND)

F–50/49: (STAGE2) – MAO/LO5/RUXO examined and certified two FSP units, all inertia switches, arming plugs and the isolation plugs ahead of their detailed inspection of Stage2 Haz wiring installation. With Interstage Bay returned and fitted the MAO/LO5/RUXO Haz wiring certification was concluded and followed by FSP simulator runs to show the MAO the operation of each in flight event.

During a Payload Fairing assembly check, several spigot and fork lateral registers were found to "bottom" before the cup and cone registers adjacent to each gas separation unit were fully seated. The cone fittings were re-shimmed and re-locked.

The C-Band aerial was replaced by a circular polarised version as mentioned in the HD trial following detailed analysis of the so-called 'Beresford wiggle' problem by DH.

F–49: (STAGE1) – The refurbished Gamma8 engine arrived today; less an HTP tank to pump inlet 'O' ring! UK asked to airmail the replacement pronto.

F–48: (STAGE2) – Transferred out to site 5A where the engine will be static fired. Telemetry electronic trays and associated sub units were installed and functionally tested; systemic inductive transducer drift was encountered and corrected by replacing the tele sender.

Both propellant tank pressurising systems to were armed and functionally tested; one in/out vent valve was replaced due to leakage.

F–47: (STAGE2) – Ground system pressure transducers feeding the EC5 motor console displays and analogue recorders were connected to the engine tapping points, primed and calibrated, a routine that would continue for several days ahead.

FCS trays were installed and set up to measure inner loop frequency response tomorrow and the engine was also readied by rigging shore side hydraulics and flooding trunnions with kerosene or demin water as appropriate – a leaking 'O' ring seal at one kero pump inlet was replaced.

F–46: (STAGE2) – Friday, routine working dried up around mid afternoon to let commuters catch their flights to Adelaide.

Inert Waxwing was loaded for later FCS stability checks. Good servo frequency responses were completed soon after lunch. All was now ready for ARU installation and alignment testing scheduled for Monday.

Stage1 engine refit still held for a missing 'O' ring seal; an urgent gee-up signal was made to UK.

F–45/44: (WEEKEND)

F–43/41: (STAGE2) – ARU mounting pads adjusted to remove a slight rock before installing the unit. A 12hr power up, calibration and alignment session was accomplished without difficulty.

> *ARU alignment:* As described elsewhere, high precision alignments are carried out to confirm ARU accuracy or set the Line of Fire before launching. During this process Gyro drift calibration and gyrocompass convergence may take up to 12 hours, or more if wind or other physical disturbances intruded. To limit disturbance conflict from day shift activities it became routine to begin 12hr precision alignments around 18:00 to 20:00hrs and continue over night to 06:00to 08:00 hrs next day. By contrast, simple 2hr alignments were usually adequate for many related system tests.

The FCS and ACS outputs were zeroed to the accurately aligned ARU outputs before these systems were powered down.

At EC5, Sequencer timing and Overrides were set up and sealed, and Stop Action inputs were exercised.

Operation of Gamma2 stop valve was demonstrated using failsafe gas line and internal Haz battery. All gas bottles received an initial charge, gearbox oil system was topped up and Purge backup feed was connected. Pre S&S checklists were worked through, Interstage upper and lower down bolts were torque checked and the duct cooling water system was primed.

F–40: (STAGE2 S&S CHECK) – See Table B/6 Appendix B for Countdown timing.

A 2hr ARU alignment began at dawn would remain running through to completion of the Static Firing. Good Tele reception and commutation was confirmed by M3 at Instrumentation Building.

EC5/Range Stop Action procedures were verified. Engine start tank was filled with demin water and all vehicle gas bottles were topped to final pressure. As final checks drew to a close, propellant tank pressuring circuits were armed and Test Post settings were logged before I repaired to EC5 where everyone was hot to trot.

After the usual CON1 and AOO5 interchanges, the manual count ran correctly but the Auto sequence was interrupted due failure of exhaust duct cooling water (unforgivably attributed to a time patching error) and a loss of bulk N2 gas supply (attributed to relief valve lift). After deliberation it was decide to lower the bulk pressure by 300psi and rerun the sequence.

The second S&S ran to full time and all indications were good except N2 backup supply pressure to the Interstage-start and purge system fell too low during the run.

N2 Purge fault: It transpired that a transient-damping orifice (or 'snubber') used to aid main flow pressure stability had been incorrectly sited, which caused excessive flow pressure swings to lift the bulk store relief valve and diminished bulk pressure. With the 'snubber' correctly located, the system functioned without error.

However, because low N2 purge pressure presented a risk of thrust chamber damage, the OISC had the WRE bulk store pressure reduced by 300 psi and the relief valve blanked off. The diameter of the back up link pipe between ground system and Interstage was also upgraded.

Apart from several telemetry pressure and voltage channel level anomalies all EC5 recorders confirmed that all systems had otherwise functioned correctly. The Tele faults related to ACS pressures and ARU parameters, the former being a transducer malfunction while the latter were interpretive errors resolved by improvised testing. Kerosene was loaded, gas bottles were given an initial charge and the HTP dump line was exercised.

F–39: (STAGE2 STATIC FIRING) – Gas bottles were topped and sealed. During gearbox oil checks, it was found that a drain collector held 30cc of unexplained oil. This arose from failing to drain the gearbox during repetitive oil flow runs. Sequence Officer event logging was arranged to couple drains actions with each flow test.

LO5 called in the HTP bulk tanker from standby at Area5 pump house and peroxide transfer operations began. While the day was pleasantly warm it proved miserable inside PVC suits as HTP was transferred to the vehicle tank and engine start bottle without undue hassle. After washing down and stowing all loose items, the Interstage hold-down bolts were rechecked and the tank pressure-arming plug was inserted as personnel cleared the Pad.

Back in EC5, after a checklist scan with TL and a brief word with each consol operator, the AOO5 kicked off the countdown with Con1. The manual actions preceding Auto sequence run through without incident; –120sec Auto sequence began on time and reached zero time also without incident. Both thrust chamber pressures rose rapidly behind the pump deliveries and sat steadily at line pressure until falling to zero without apparent hesitation at +35secs. Good reports all round cleared the Pad team to drain off HTP and deloused the site. A following engine inspection confirmed that all was well.

The usual commuting weekenders made haste for the airport.

F–38/37: (WORKING WEEKEND) – The missing HTP 'O' ring had arrived so a DH, RDD and Rolls Royce working party helpfully opted to fit the replacement Gamma8 to Stage1 and dry out the Gamma2 at 5A.

F–36/32: (STAGE2) – Ground instrumentation pipes were stripped of and sent for cleaning.

The vehicle was dressed for transporting across to 5B. All electronic trays and similar sub units except the chargeable battery packs were to remain installed.

ACS System worries: Post static firing tests and data from UK tests revealed the following concerns: -

1. The LY ACS jet failed to function due to a failed wire termination inside Stage2 motor bay. Detailed checks of the Gamma2 and Gamma8 motor bays by our RDD wireman rectified one instance of localised tight loom lacing and another of inadequate lacing, which were rectified and retested as necessary by the RUXO, Tele and FCS teams.

2. Arising from High Down records, the Pitch ACS revealed a trigger point random variation that local testing confirmed and the unit was replaced.

3. A partially blocked bleed orifice had caused ACS ring main pressure instability. After intensive pipe cleaning, a new orifice and numerous fault free operations over several days, the system declared fit for flight.

4. The ACS HP gas bottle had a small but significant pressure loss during the firing; no definite cause was found but to minimise risk, it was agreed to permanently remove the thermal relief valve before lunch.

Due to the above interventions, the Review Panel agreed to recheck ACS integrity by operating it during the upcoming Composite Static Firing.

F–36/33: (STAGE1) – With the new engine fitted, MAO/RUXO Haz-circuit testing and Telemetry checks swung into action alongside the FSC tasks as staff became free from Stage2 operations. EC5 was switched across from site 5A to 5B and functionally checked out using the Electrically Similar Vehicle (ESV), ready to receive Stage1.

F–32: (STAGE1) – Vehicle was moved out and erected on launcher 5B. The routine long-winded task of connecting, priming and calibrating the many DC ground pressure transducers got underway. All Tele transducer rest levels were verified.

F–31/30: (WEEKEND)

F–29: (STAGE1) – Hydraulic trolley rigged for shore side running and trunnions flooded for inner loop working. FCS pack was set up via CSMU and the frequency responses of four inner loop servos measured and found good without difficulty.

F–28: (STAGE2) – Planned transfer to Stage1 cancelled due high wind speeds.

F–27: (STAGE2) – High winds continue to prevent transfer to 5B.

F–27: (STAGE1) – Gas bottles charged up and HTP tank pressurised from EC5; no leakage found and pressure settled to the correct level.

General preparation and functional testing of mechanical ground systems (N2 purge, engine start etc) progressed.

F–26: (STAGE2 MEETS STAGE1) – Winds finally abated to let Stage2 be moved across to 5B and erected on Stage1. All electrical interconnects between Stages were tested. The wind-brace arms were adjusted to level the Spin Table and the ARU mounts were confirmed to agree.

> *A Butt Connector fault*: Gave concern until it was correctly adjusted. These obscurely placed items require experience fingers to insert and secure.

Stage2 tank gas bottles were charged ready for tomorrow's tank pressure tests.

F–25: (STAGE2 at 5B) – FCS was connected to CSMU; powered up and functionally checked out as OK. ARU alignment and monitor gear was checked out in EC5 ready for alignment tests over the weekend. Kero and HTP tank pressurising functioned via EC5. (Kero tank inward vent valve replaced earlier was now leaking so a spare was sought from UK.) The hydraulic system was rigged for shore side running. Telemetry services across all stages was functionally tested and found serviceable.

F–24/22: (WEEKEND – ARU PRECISION TESTS) – 12hr alignment began around 19:00hrs and ended next morning after trouble free drift calibrations and Line of Fire alignment. However, when the rocket structure roll position was physically trimmed to reduce the ARU roll synchro to zero, a 5' theodolite error resulted. The ARU azimuth error was identical next day and WRE surveyor reaffirmed the plumb bob accuracy, so ARU and AU were returned to TS4 for an on plinth assessment.

> *ARU TS4 plinth tests*: The ARU checked out perfectly on the TS4 plinth. However, in particular conditions an AU constant voltage source did exceed limits. After repair a full scale ARU acceptance test proved all was satisfactory.

When returned to the rocket at 5B, the ARU aligned correctly at 7°20' (true) and an integrated system test with the FCS was achieved without further ado.

With the rocket vertical the longitudinal accelerometer Tele channel was reset to zero.

F–21: (FCS SENSE TEST) –

> *This test s done*: to demonstrate in absolute terms that all control steering torque sources are harmonised and act in a polarity that will bring the ARU error demands to zero.

This elaborate procedure involves fully active ARU feeding Stage1&2 FCS, operating with active hydraulics and ACS gas pressure. Many operators are involved at EC5 and positioned around the rocket vehicle to observe thrust chamber deflection and gas jet function, and to physically apply airframe angular inputs. See Appendix B for full process detail.

The ARU was aligned before dawn, vehicle upper clamp ring had been rigged and all required personnel were in position.

The FCS (with hydraulics) and ACS (with gas) were brought on line and the rocket was physically stimulated in Pitch, Yaw and Roll in turn while the response of all thrust chambers and jets were observed to respond correctively in relation to the line of fire.

F–20/19: (PRE–STAGE3 ERECTION ON STAGE2) – The clean cell was opened to admit Payload Fairing halves and satellite template gauge to level 'F'.

- LO5/RUXO crew fitted six inert Spin Imps for clearance testing.
- Satellite template was Manacle clamped on the Spin Table and the SSB swing arm was hand held upright as the 'DY' Fairing was installed.
- Spin Table with template was swept around inside fairing to demonstrate the clearances (the SSB swing arm limiting template rotation to approx ±160°).
- Two aerial transfer loops in 'DY' Fairing were seen to clear the template by 5cm.
- 'DY' Fairing unshipped and stowed. Above tests were applied to 'UY' Fairing.
- 'UY' cooling feed was aligned and ejected before Fairing removal.
- The Table and supporting structure vacuumed and 'tacky' clothed inside and out.
- The inert non-flight Waxwing motor was hoisted to level 'F' rotationally aligned and Manacle clamped on the Spin Table.
- Gantry hoist was parked, the clean cell was closed to purge down over night.
- The SSB was secured on the Waxwing and both umbilical arms were raised, plugged in and retained by Red flagged pins.
- The X3 ground control and monitor equipment was exercised, all vehicle RF (Telemetry, Doppler, C–Band and WREBUS) systems were transmission checked with their respective WRE ground stations. As these tasks advanced the related service hatches were temporarily fitted to offer representative ground planes.

  My RDD college, the DTL2: Arrived today to manage our prelaunch nightshifts. Until then he will usefully assist RUXO activities in the magazine area where he can exercise one of many strings to his bow.

F–18: (X3A) MEETS R3) – In calm wind conditions, the X3 transfer caravan was drawn up under 5B hoist before morning "smoko".

To isolate this tender device from the Australian desert and hoist cable debris, X3 journeyed from the TS4 Clean Room to Gantry 5B Clean Cell atop R3, enshrined within a shell of bespoke segmented panels. As X3 gently rose to level 'F, the Clean Cell roof filters and entry doors were parted to admit the hoist and its precious cargo. Within twelve minutes, X3 had been secured on the SSB and the Cell was closed and purging down towards controlled conditions – a slick operation.

Working from EC5 and TS4 satellite control facilities, the Marconi team completed a detailed checkout of X3 (A) by mind afternoon – in time to catch the weekend Adelaide flight.

F–17/16: (WEEKEND)

F–15: (RFI WITHOUT FAIRINGS) –

> *The Formal RFI test:* This is scheduled to occur later as part of the pre launch preparation. But High Down testing indicated possible X3 transmission problems for WREBUS so these precautionary tests were arranged to establish the true situation.

As the weekend wonderers returned, all concerned noted the gusty conditions, which luckily eased below the R3 freestanding limit by lunchtime. With the Gantry rolled back R3/X3 were handed over to the green-fingered RF specialists who try as they might were unable to detect any WREBUS desensitisation!

The Gantry was replaced around the rocket, clean cell was closed and purged down ready for the X3 team to disrobe their precious hardware and oversee the BA team as they fitted and closed up the Payload Fairings.

> *Perceptive Teamwork:* This was the first occasion that X3 and BA crews had worked in close harmony inside the confined clean cell. The fluent and timely way the guys worked seemingly as one around the sensitive hardware owed much to each individuals perception, common purpose and skill set.

The RUXO/LO5 team took advantage to watch activities via the observation window and assess what they'd be up for during their final arming phase.

F–14: (RFI WITH FAIRINGS) – Retracing yesterdays testing now found a serious WREBUS channel 7 desensitisation but further research was halted due to rising wind speed that decreed R3 needed Gantry protection.

F–13: (MORE RFI TESTING) – As RFI testing continued, one X0 transmitter was isolated as the offending source but the physical reason was obscured by the sporadic behaviour.

To retain the Composite Static Firing slot and provide head scratching time, RFI testing was suspended. Results so far confirm that X3 (F) flight satellite must be RFI tested before launch. See day F–9b for a more complete understanding of this fault.

F–12: (COMP STATIC FIRING S&S). See Table B/7, Appendix B for countdown timing. The ARU was aligned well before dawn. EC5/WRE Stop Action, timing sequencer and M3 Tele reception checks were followed by C-Band and Doppler interrogation tests.

To backup a loss of fail/safe gas line pressure the engine shut down Haz battery was fitted. N2 purge and engine start test orifices were fitted. The gearbox lub oil was serviced, vehicle gas bottles were topped up and the start tank was filled with demin water.

As I headed via the Crew Room to EC5 it was nearing 10:45; everyman and his sidekick seemed to be present. All consoles were double manned, visiting engineers from the RR, Ferranti and Marconi and the OISC with two of his aides had all joined the show. After the customary exchanges, AOO5 armed the 5B firing circuits and CON1 ran the clock for the manual actions. All systems powered up and presented properly and all consoles signalled, "Ready" by minus 4mins, which freed CON1 to start Auto-Sequence as −120sec arrived. The count auto stopped at around −30secs due to an absence of ground start tank pressure.

> *A Test Post fault:* Gas supply cock had seized at half open. Following its replacement a successful S&S test was concluded one hour later.

The initial overview of results confirmed that all systems were good for a static firing tomorrow. Stage1 kero tank was loaded, trunnion and start tank water was drained and a loose item sweep made.

All vehicle bottles were gassed up, Stage1 HTP tank sight glass was fitted and the HTP dump arm was tested before calling it a day. The ARU remained running overnight.

F–11: (COMPOSITE STATIC FIRING) – Being Friday, the Adelaide commuters and many UK visitors fretted about the weekend flight out, so the "escape committee" negotiated an extra early start for today's activities. The 5B Pad opened for business at 07:30 for a static firing sequence at 11:30 with lunch at 13:00 to reach the airport by 16:30. Contentment invariably prevails once meals and wheels have been assured!

Oil flow testing wetted both engine gearboxes and the hydraulic system was set up for hot running. With PVC suits donned, the pad was hosed down LO5 called in the peroxide bulk carrier – a very warm wind was going to make things hot and sticky.

As HTP transferred into Stage1 tank exceptionally loud rumbling noises arose so filling was paused until things settled down – the unseasonably hot day presented a hot vehicle tank. About fifteen minutes later when all was quiet, Stage1 HTP tank and engine start tank filling was concluded without further concern. Once the bulk carrier was removed and the area was washed down we eagerly stripped off our PVC suits and hosed each other down.

> *Progress Logging:* To keep EC5, TS4 and the Range aware of launch pad activities, progress of each procedure (RUSP) was routinely called over to the Sequence Officer in EC5 who maintained a running log and cued TS4 personnel when needed at 5A or 5B. LO5 and AOO5 ran a similar reporting link with Con1.

Working the final checklist, setting out clean engine drain collectors, removal of loose items and verification of wind brace arm and anti roll lugs security completed the teams 5B tasks – as the area was cleared, the release jack Safe pin was confirmed safe and the tank pressurisation arming plugs were inserted.

After a Crew Room stop I found EC5 just as full as yesterday. The countdown began routinely and yet again progressed free of interruption to zero time; by +1sec all propellant deliveries were up at line pressure, and closely followed by eight chamber pressures that seemed to rise in regimental lockstep as they transitioned to hot running. Each value remained solid until shutdown at +35secs.

From console evidence, the engine and supporting systems had performed perfectly. The ARU rack reported a 'sticking' roll synchro meter that was unrepeatable after several realignments.

The post firing inspection revealed that LPO thrust chamber had developed a small crack or slit at the throat of one cooling tube. The fissure was small and well defined; after a very detailed examination and a study of the data records, RR and the Review Panel concluded that the tube was not blocked and the increased coolant spilling at the fault site would ensure adequate cooling well beyond the flight burn time.

F–10/9: (WEEKEND) – The Gamma8 was dried out and a few dedicated individuals resisting the Adelaide call to do a relaxed search of all R3 and X3 (A) records harvested from the static firing.

> *Author's note*: Where extra days are introduced to embrace extra or unforeseen tasks, they carry the previous days ident plus an 'a', 'b' or 'c' cipher

F–9a: (RFI TESTS CONT'D) – The data analysis activity over the weekend confirmed that all static firing results were satisfactory and a refreshed Adelaide crew returned to our RFI problem by repeat testing to confirm that the F–14/13 test results still pertained.

With X3 transmitters radiating, both payload Fairings were partially opened to access the transfer loop aerials and an understanding of our problem gradually dawned as each hinge-mounted loop aerial position was fiddled with alongside its X3 aerial. Moderate alteration of loop aerial proximity to its X3 aerial revealed that the X3 transmitters were very sensitive to VSWR (Voltage Standing Wave Ratios) variation and measurement checks now galloped along to define the extent of this issue. Fairings were removed, X3 protection panels were refitted and the Gantry was rolled clear to allow further dissection of the various waveforms.

By mid afternoon the Gantry had been restored and the Payload Fairings were refitted for tomorrows RFI exercise.

F–9b: (RFI TESTS CONT'D) – Good progress was now being made, the interference pathway had been identified, the mechanism was understood and a cure was in the making.

X3/WREBUS RF interference: X3 Satellite embodied two similar RF transmitters operating on adjacent frequencies and sharing the same four element aerial array. To provide RF transmission through the metallic nose Fairings, each Fairing half carried two external monopole aerials that connected to internal parasitic loops sited beside to each X3 aerial element. Testing showed that X3 (A) transmitters emitted spurious frequency components when their aerial VSWR was marginally elevated, an effect easily induced by the proximity of each transfer loop to its X3 aerial. The apparent intermittency of the WREBUS desensitisation arose from the spurious X3 frequency components, which drifted back and forth across the receiver's narrow reception aperture – a feature that had been hampering investigations so far.
The second WREBUS receiver remained untroubled because the spurious frequency components lay outside its reception window. After careful adjustment of loop aerial positions and stiffening of their physical fixings, the VSWR was reduced well below the level where clean transmitter outputs were reliably obtained and WREBUS desensitisation was reliably eliminated.

F–9c: (RFI TESTS CONT'D) – Today's testing confirmed the finalised loop aerial installation with Fairings fitted and Fairings removed so all was now set to resume launch prep.

F–8: (STAGE3 REMOVAL) – X3 (A) was dressed for transportation, lowered into its caravan and returned to TS4, followed by the SSB and Inert Waxwing motor.
The Clean Cell was closed up for the detailed cleaning of Stage2 upper structure and Spin Table. The latter had a final dynamic check before being locked in flight orientation and the whole assembly was enclosed under dust covers to await Stage3 pre flight build up from day F–6 onwards.
A routine Electronic Bay sealing test found yet another faulty HTP tank pressure transducer (of R2's short burn infamy) was leaking via the external datum pipe and was replaced. Preparatory to tomorrows FCS/ACS detailed balance checks, the ACS gas bottle was charged and shore side running was rigged for Stage1 & 2 hydraulic systems; the ARU was aligned overnight onto the Line of Fire.
Back at TS4, all Haz batteries were charged and packed ready for the upcoming FSP checks.

F–7: (ARU/FCS FINAL SETTING UP) – An ARU synchro output of zero degrees confirmed correct airframe azimuth with the Line of Fire before Stage1 & 2 FCS underwent an exhaustive balance checks prior to replacing the CSMU diagnostic connections with the Stage1&2 FCS "Flight Plugs". With hydraulic power applied to both Stages during these checks, all thrust chamber trunnion angles were confirmed to be at zero degrees.

The ACS was similarly scrutinised and zeroed before all systems including ARU were powered down.

The Stage2 thrust chamber harness was fitted to avoid in flight flopping until servo hydraulic pressure appears with engine ignition.

Alongside the above activities the RUXO crew rigged up the Haz circuit monitor gear required for tomorrows FSP functional tests.

Stage2 flight Kero load was weighed up and stored under cover overnight.

F–6: (SATURDAY, LIVE WAXWING LOADING) –

Stage1 & 2 Kero tanks were marginally over filled ready for trimming down to flight loads later.

> *8hr RULE:* *The presence of explosive stores at Area5 from now on will require all personnel operating in the vicinity to work the 8hr ON/10hr OFF rule. This restriction was managed by nominating personnel who needed access and allocating them to one of two shifts with the late or overnight shift only being invoked when necessary e.g. usually the final overnight prelaunch preparation.*
>
> *The ARU watch keeping team worked a separate shift pattern were also subject to the 8hr rule. While I remained with the day shifts, overnight shifts were looked after by our DTL2 from High Down.*

The Live Waxwing motor (less igniter) was hoisted to level 'F', rotationally aligned and secured on the Spin Table by the Manacle Clamp. With the clean cell reclosed, the SSB was secured atop the Waxwing and both umbilical arms were raised to connect with SSB and be Red Flag pinned in place.

Alongside these activities the RUXO/LO5 installed all vehicle Haz batteries preparatory to tomorrows FSP testing.

F–5: (SUNDAY, FSP TESTING) – See Table B/3, Appendix B for FSP timing and events. The ARU was 2hr aligned ahead of the day shift.

Using the FSP simulator, a sequence program was initiated at -10secs from EC5 and successfully run through to X3 separation and all initial conditions were reset for the following test. With the ARU re-levelled a second sequence was satisfactorily run using spare FSP. The process was about to be repeated using the flight FSP unit until Telemetry reported an incorrect mark/space ratio from the FSP running indicator.

After resetting and fitting the spare FSP it now exhibited a faulty resistance reading; caused by a damaged resistor inflicted earlier by a test procedure error. After repair and re-fitting a perfect flight sequence run was obtained.

During the above tests the FSP "running" interlock in EC5 was again unacceptably irregular, yet its pulse source at the console display performed perfectly. The offending electronic black box was returned to TS4 for examination.

F–4: (HAZ CIRCUIT STATUS CHECK) – Following yesterday's FSP runs, the datum settings of each switching and time device in the rockets Haz Circuit system was examined and proven to have been reset to pre launch status, ready for explosive store installations tomorrow.

The action of Stage1 and Stage2 engine shutdown solenoid valves and the ACS solenoid valve were proven to be in pre-flight mode.

F–3: (FIT EXPLOSIVE STORES) – LO5/RUXO team installed and load tested fresh Haz batteries via the arming sockets. Commencing at Stage3, the explosive devices listed below were progressively installed, electrically connected and loop tested for continuity and insulation via the relevant arming sockets: –

- Fit & connect 4 Payload Fairing gas separator units.
- Fit & connect 2 Satellite gas separator units.
- Fit & Connect Waxwing pressure Tx, motor igniter and a head cutting igniter.
- Fit & connect 3 Manacle Clamp explosive bolt detonators.
- Fit & connect 6 Spin Table Imp thrust units.
- Fit & connect 2 Spin Table unlock gas charges.
- Fit & connect the ACS frangible pillar detonators.
- Fit & connect 16 Stage2/Interstage explosive bolt detonators.
- Fit & connect 16 Stage1/Interstage explosive bolt detonators.
- Fit & connect 4 Siskin separation rockets with igniters.

Fitting the flight termination catalyst capsules is deferred until HTP has been loaded to prove each housing is leak free.

F–2, AM: (LOADING PROSPERO) – Variable wind conditions had persisted for several days and were forecast to continue through to the weekend. With a 30ft/sec wind speed limit on hoisting operations, we gambled on loading the satellite during a "dawn lull".

In the event a very gentle breeze rewarded us early birds as we hoisted X3 (F) up to level 'F' and secure it to the SSB free from hassle. With the cell reclosed the Marconi team were able to conclude their functional checking by midday.

F–2, PM: (RFI LESS FAIRINGS) – Blessed with a gentle breeze again, the Gantry was opened and rolled away from R3. As expected for this test condition, no WREBUS interference was found from any RF source.

With the Gantry back around R3, the clean cell was purged down and Marconi removed the X3 covers and applied their cleaning process. When both half Fairings were attached, a careful position and security check of each loop aerial with respect to its X3 partner was observed as each Fairing half was closed.

The umbilical swing arm keeper pin cords were trailed out as each half came together for tensioning up; the pins would remain un-pulled until final Fairing closure after Spin Table and SSB final arming.

A short spot check on WREBUS behaviour inside the Gantry suggested that X3 (F) was less VSWR sensitive than the 'A' model; all fingers were crossed for tomorrow.

F–2a (WORKING WEEKEND – RFI WITH FAIRINGS) – To frustrate the wind demons, the team mustered again at 06:00 but a dawn calm failed to materialise. As the clock slowly crept up to midday the wind hovered above our exposure limit. After lunch our deputy OISC agreed to drop the limit to 25ft/sec; by mid afternoon a fluctuating anemometer was spending more time below than above the new limit so the bullet was bitten and the Gantry rolled clear. When all vehicle RF systems were ready for a step-by-step power up, WRE stood ready in their monitor van and RF ground stations. To everyone's great relief both WREBUS receivers remained entirely free from RFI. Gantry replacement and clean cell purging ended today's assignments and the joint X3/Stage3 teams relaxed over a merry evening meal at the ELDO.

F–2b: (WORKING WEEKEND – S&S PREPARATION) – Launch preparation now intensified. ARU integrity testing and final alignment rituals begun before midnight – it should now remain running through to Lift off and beyond.

With the ARU on the Line of Fire for launch, Stage2 chamber harness was removed, the FSC/ACS electronics were powered up together with Stage 1 & 2 shore side hydraulics to re-affirm thrust chamber and ACS jet datum status. Stage2 chamber harness was refitted.

All instrumentation dry batteries were tested and the None Haz internal battery packs were replaced and 30sec load tested. The final Electronics bay service hatches were check listed, closed up, pressure tested and the datum reference port was proved leak free.

Meanwhile, X3 (F) successfully underwent a series of test routines to exercise all its operational modes.

Both engine gearbox Lub systems were flow tested/replenished and the HTP dump arms were erected aligned and remotely functioned from EC5.

The EC5 sub sequencer patching and override switch settings were verified and sealed. All Stop Action inputs were exercised.

F–1: (PRE LAUNCH S&S) – Ground start tank was watered, N2 purge flow pressures checked, all vehicle gas bottles were charged and tank pressurisation systems were armed. Exhaust duct platforms were removed and cooling water Valve 199 was primed.

The Release Jack safe pin was replaced by the 'No Retract Safe Pin' to let the jack to open but not retract!

Following a short transmission from each Tele sender as requested by M3, the master checklist was closed and Pad 5B was ready for this very important S&S test, which is divided into three consecutive parts: –

Part 'A'   is a clock run devoted to WRE specific instrumentation and flight safety systems dispersed throughout the Range complex.

Part 'B'   includes all WRE and rocket RF transmission systems.

Part 'C'   is the full-blown countdown where all R3, X3F, 5B, EC5 and WRE systems and facilities participate the launch countdown rehearsal together.

As Part C grew imminent I joined the Team Leader and AOO5 in EC5 to watch events; the OISC and his team were now stationed at the Instrumentation Building (IB) over at the Range Head area.

When the count did get underway, it ran to plan until ARU release at –40secs when an unacceptable Roll velocity was noted.

The count was allowed to continue until it Auto stopped at –8secs because the Umbilical plug failed to eject: this required 30min to fix the plug fault but imposed a 60min delay to recharge vehicle gas bottles.

During a local clock run to check the umbilical repair, the illusive FSP interlock problem reappeared by failing at +4secs yet its source at the EC5 console monitor confirmed correct FSP operation remained so until auto stop action at +10secs.

A second clock run with the FSP interlock overridden failed to initiate the Release Jack – we were now collecting a new fault with each clock run!

The ARU monitoring problem: During a launch sequence, velocity meters in EC5 (which reach the ARU in Stage2 Electronics Bay via Engine Bay rip connectors) are observed to assess ARU health. At –40secs the AU is disconnected to observe free ARU behaviour as the Earth turns beneath it. The high Roll velocity seen in this S&S did not attribute to a real physical rotation nor could it be repeated. In situ testing was inconclusive so ARU, SOU and AU were all replaced with an overnight precision and Integrity check before the installation was declared fit to launch.

The 'faulty' ARU checked out later at TS4 with flying colours and its earlier malfunction was attributed to the exceptionally high temperature of 42°C that prevailed at the launch pad. Prelaunch alignment and the part played by the AU during the countdown sequence are described in Appendix B.

The Umbilical plug problem: The solenoid release pintle had seized due moisture ingress and was replaced. The incident exposed an omission in Area5 pre-trial testing and EC5 pre S&S check.

FSP Interlock problem: This signal originates inside an electronic package that measures a pulse mark-space ratio emanating from the FSP drive motor within the rocket.

The unit resides in EC5 to serve a console display and generate a closing contact in the launch interlock chain. The visual display had never failed through out the trial but the associated interlock function was a frequently offender. To avoid a false Auto Stop action at engine light up it was decided to rely on the console display for FSP integrity and manually override the interlock as engine ignition was initiated at – 4secs.

Release jack circuit problem: This system is the last action in a long chain of safety intercepts and functional interlocks. An extensive investigation verified the engineering and physical conditions were sound and without fault so it was concluded that failure lay with the adhoc interlock override set up devised for the improvised clock runs. The system was shown to function correctly during all subsequent clock runs.

NOTE: For S&S tests a special release jack 'Non Retract Pin' is used to let the jack jaws open but for obvious reasons prevent its retraction.

Resolving the ARU problem and re-validating collateral disturbances while working the 8hr rule imposed a significant time burden but as events were to prove, poor weather dictated a program revision that repeated the S&S test on Wednesday 27th for a launch on Thursday. ARU 12hr precision alignment would again be run overnight ready for FCS/ACS datum checks and prelaunch preparation per F–2b and F–1 above being picked up tomorrow.

Stemming from this re-plan, WRE co-operatively agreed that nominated personnel needing to exceed 8-hrs may work two additional hours at TS4 on non hazardous tasks, providing the 10 hours off range was maintained. This concession enabled Section leaders to keep abreast of the re-cycle routines, attend review meetings and manage staffing continuity

F–2b: (S&S PREPARATION) – Following yesterday's intense activity and overnight work by the ARU team, today centred on revalidating the ARU/FCS combination as per F–2b above, plus a 30sec load test on the Non Haz internal batteries. All engine and ground systems were revisited and checklists were reopened.

F–1a: (REPEAT PRE-LAUNCH S&S) – Today's preparatory tasks as described earlier in F–1 above progressed without incident.

Haz batteries were replaced less those inside the Fairings (will be replaced along with the SSB pack when the Fairings are opened for final arming).

By mid afternoon all three S&S parts were concluded, just one small hold up in Part B while WRE resolved an RF intrusion on the WREBUS frequencies.

The Review Panel vetted the telemetry records and I went over the propellant loading calculations with the OISC once again before heading back to the Village about 17:00 wondering if R3 would get off the launcher this time?

After a shower and a few hours shuteye I joined a very upbeat Satellite team at dinner who were certain Prospero would be in orbit tomorrow. I resisted raining on their parade but we still had some way to go. I made bed with an alarm call at 05:00.

F0: (OCTOBER 28TH 1971 LAUNCH DAY) – It dawned cool with crisp clear sky often seen on a South Australian spring morning. As we drove 30-miles out to Range E, the sun rose to uncover a light mist hanging between the shallow hills.

The countdown was due to at 13:00 hrs; R3's final preparation had begun in earnest at midnight when the overnight crew trimmed the kerosene loads and filled both HTP tanks to suit the engine mixture ratios. Arming the ordnance systems in each stage would have followed and been completed before dawn while the ARU plodded along on its nonstop task. The many smaller preparation tasks to engine and associated ground system should now be nearing completion.

I began at 07:00 hrs to get an hour with the night DTL2, who advised that all tasks had gone well and were about 15 to 25 minutes ahead of plan.

(11:00 Hrs) – The Clean Cell and Gantry were opened up and rolled clear to reveal R3 standing proud as the last of her type; her red painted nose fairings resembling a giant lipstick! 5B was cleared for radio checks between R3 and the various range installations. Around this time the ARU seemed to throw a wobble by displaying more erratic velocity readings. With the recent ARU history this caused consternation until the penny dropped; without gantry protection R3 was exposed to a gentle westerly breeze and Karman Street vortex shedding was inducing a very small structural sway, which a dutiful ARU felt and correctly expressed them as earth velocity changes – problem over!

(12:15 Hrs) – R3 was ready to go, the flight termination system had been armed and the release jack safety pins were pulled to let it open and retract when required.

I drove back the 800 metres to the Crew Room to wash and take a moment or two before crossing to EC5.

The Team Leader and each console jocko were primed and up for it and waiting for the Range Authority to finish their final routines.

> *To recap:* *The 30min Launch sequence has two phases: the first 28 minutes covers manual powering up actions while events in the last 120 secs are applied automatically by a central sequence timer with progressive interlocking events. The former phase will tolerate time 'holds' but the final phase has only one of two outcomes: launch or abort.*

The countdown started close on 13:00 hrs and all EC5 indications were OK and remained so when Con1 called his 10min hold at −5min to assess cloud cover.

Rocket systems remained good as Con1 restarted the manual.

I listened contentedly as the Range readiness reports streamed in until I noticed that the apogee telemetry station up at Charters Towers in Queensland remained silent. As −120 secs approached tension climbed − without the apogee station this sequence must stop. Suddenly, around −3 minutes a cheerful voice came over the net saying "Charters Towers ready!" (*Shades of a famous Ceil B DeMill epic anecdote and unprintable comments did the rounds.*)

As the final 2 minutes progressed, each second got slower and slower until suddenly it was time zero; I turned from the telemetry displays to watch for IoM on AOO5's console, which lit up by +4secs.

LIFT OFF (13:39:29 OCT 28, 1971) − Finally! Through the periscopic windows the long awaited scene unfolded as R3 gently left the launcher, balanced perfectly on eight clean jets with no hint of roll or lateral motion. Accompanied by exhaust duct steam clouds the defining stack of bright shock diamonds within the transparent blue jet from each thrust chamber − the trademark of these lovely engines was always impressive to see in action.

The captivating scene soon vanished above the window frame so my attention switched to events playing out on the telemetry displays and the intercom.

EC5 personnel were kept inside until +60secs when the vehicle was too high to see detail with a naked eye so I stayed to watch the telemetry monitors.

Stage1 burned correctly until +130 seconds, Stage2 engine sparked up on cue and burnt till about +245 seconds. Before this, at +180 secs the payload fairings departed successfully. This was nearly too much accept as each event followed the script.

ZERO (+510 SECONDS) − Charters Towers reported a successful apogee event − meaning that Stage3 had fired, a momentous event had actually happened! But did the Waxwing point in the right direction? Had Stage3 spun up? Had Prospero safely separated? Many things may yet have failed.

I returned to TS4 to prep for the post launch communiqué at +1 hour.

The Satellite Team were ecstatic; piling praises on us for delivering their precious hardware into orbit. They'd followed their telemetry in detail and were convinced the job was done and dusted but we veterans had been here before only to find success wither as mature data came to hand; we tempered our spirits and wondered if celebration or commiseration would dominate the ELDO bar tonight?

LATER (14:20 HRS) − A message came over from Fairbanks, part of the global satellite-tracking network, "We have an operational 137Mhz signal passing overhead".

This was it, despite six drip-fed years BK/BA engineering was vindicated and unbridled emotions broke loose. We had shown that despite feeble Government and bureaucracy interest Britain was able to handle high tech tasks.

After the communiqué meeting I returned to the Village and took a shower before joining the massive rave up going on at the ELDO Mess. Every man and their sidekicks were hard at it, from the taxi and bus drivers through to very senior members of UK and Australian government agencies. However, efforts to prolong the mayhem next day faltered as reality penetrated enfeebled minds – Black Arrow would never fly again and we'd be chasing after new occupations.

Despite being Britain's only indigenous satellite carrier, the success of R3 marked the dynasty's end. Hard won and paid for wet rocket technology was now lost to he nations engineers along with a peerless close collaboration between the scientific civil service and industry. Technical accuracy and budget issues dominated the teams' collective conscience throughout all levels, from design through to the coalface. Irrespective of each employer's diverse remuneration terms many real fellowships were formed and Prospero will girdle the Earth to mark their endeavours for many years to come.

FIG 23-1   PROSPERO
(Crown copyright)

NOVEMBER 1ST.: Along with the rest of our RDD team I flew home with a feeling of great relief and a troubled mind for the future. It was wonderful to see my family again, and be unburdened from outstanding rocket pressures.

I was saddened at our employer's attitude as we return; they had no doubt celebrated the projects great achievement but it seemed to us "coal face" folk that we came after the Lord Mayor's Show and were now a surplus embarrassment.

A proportion of ex BA staff were retained for an alternative Woomera based program but the majority faced finding alternative occupations – not an easy task on the Isle of Wight!

A RETROSPECTIVE OVERVIEW **24**

Peroxide rockets:

Visionaries of the period saw Black Arrow and its HTP engines as a progressive step towards low cost carrier rockets suited to smaller satellites expected to emerge from the dawning digital era. Just as the BA Gamma 2 & 8 engines evolved from the Blue Steel Stentor small thrust chamber (6,000 lbf thrust) so the Stentor large thrust chamber (24,000 lbf thrust) and related propellant feed train, was being adapted in those long gone days by Bristol Siddeley as their PR27 four-chambered engine (100,000 lbf thrust).

With such hardware potential in the pipeline it was not excessively expensive to foresee that BA's current low earth orbit payload could be doubled or even approach 350lbs if launched nearer the equator as the Russians now do with Soyouz from Frances Centre Spatial Guyanais (CSG) Kourou site. Moreover, unlike Woomera's sole northerly orbital line of fire, CSG offers many orbital options and benefits from a daily air link and 14-day sea link with Europe.

High Test Peroxide:

HTP is a low fuming oxidant easy to manufacture, handle and store at normal ambient temperatures. The outstanding hazard is an inclination to be catalysed by all organic and most inorganic materials excepting a few specific metals, glasses and plastics that have undergone specialised cleansing. While Specific Impulse (240sec) is modest, a high specific density (1.28) favours compact airframes.

A reviving interest in this propellant combination in recent years dwindled due to the lack the necessary facilities and skills!

Who killed Cock Robin?

While Black Arrow enjoyed Black Knight technical virtues it also inherited its deep-seated austerity. Spartan minded RAE and Industrial project managers keen to secure state funding, naively tabled bare bones cost plans. Rocket hardware and the related manufacture and testing facilities were planned to be evolved progressively by flight testing in "Staged" configurations until a full specification BA was fired at orbital velocity to certify the design Fit for Purpose, along with a fully established production and test estate.

Without an informed Space Agency to advise HMG, project approval bogged down as various Ministries piggybacked the process on their normal portfolios.

1. The Sir Alec Home Gov: Circa 1964 – Jaded by Blue Streak's massive spending history, this administration cut test firings from 6 to 4 shots before it lost the General election!

2. The Harold Wilson Gov: Circa 1964 – Funded essential Engine, ARU and RAE tasks via quarterly holding contracts while related Industries sponsored their own activities until quarterly contracts were later extended to the entire program. Aimed at keeping a lid on spend rate, the scheme tended to inhibit progress by forcing back program target dates to mask cost overruns.

3. The Edward Heath Gov: Circa 1970 – Revamped the UK space agenda by ending home–grown liquid propelled rocket activities in favour of European and US satellite carriers.

As originally tabled, the BA program entailed six test firings at Woomera until Whitehall officials pressed the RAE to get by on four, a change that forfeited a carefully orchestrated step-by-step production plan for flight hardware that interlocked with a parallel and proportionate expansion plan for the ex BK single file manufacture and testing assents. Furthermore, a four shot plan made it mandatory to launch a fully configured BA with two fully active lower Stages and a passive Stage3 from the maiden flight onwards. This required full capacity production and testing facilities from the word go instead of the progressive introduction as originally envisaged. In the event, actual progress often fell victim whenever quarterly spend limits were threatened, a process that ballooned big time by an engine test bed explosion and total loss of the maiden flight. While such incidents are not unknown in high-energy research, pinchpenny methods can often invite them!

A revamped R1 successfully carried out R0's intended shakedown flight along the WRE westerly centre line, in May'70. As time slipped the X1 Technology Satellite launch date on R3 came under threat, which in turn heaped pressure on the upcoming R2 Fit for Purpose orbital firing with a "Boiler plate" payload. The lack of flight-derived data ahead of the Prospero obligation became a serious concern to the Engineers, Project Managers and Bean Counters alike until Sept'70 when R2, the only remaining BA test vehicle, flew to tick almost every technical box except reaching orbital velocity. The shortfall arose from a 13 sec Stage2 short burn caused by a leaking pressure transducer that depleted the gas bottles early. Ironically the transducer is installed to provide EC5 with kerosene tank pressure readout prior to launch and performs no in flight purpose but shared the external ambient reference datum to the Kerosene tank pressurising system.

Detailed analysis and simulations proved this was not a systematic failure, which allowed the BA design to be declared Fit for Purpose and fit for R3 to carry Prospero. The R2 burn shortfall together with the projects spend rate now became central weapons by those HMG factions who sought program closure in favour of US Scout carriers for later Satellites. While their tenuous arguments required a Crystal Ball to predict BA reliability and launch costs from R2's solitary test flight, powerful political forces ended all HTP rocket activity within UK despite the following facts: –

- HMG imposed test flight limits (R1&R2) thereby curbing flight data acquisition.
- Two BA test firings were not a fair rival to Scout's long launch history.

February 1971 – The Space and Technology Select Committee began taking evidence on UK space activities that led to the Minister for Aerospace, Frederick Cornfield, cancelling the Black Arrow program on 29 July 1971.

The day before R3/Prospero were launched, the Select Committee met and were to make the following observation:

> *The technical concept was sound when the programme was begun, but largely owing to its very modest extent and long drawn out timescale its success was being imperilled. A decision in the early stages of the project to pursue it more realistically and vigorously by increasing the rate of firings might well have achieved successful launchings and eventually a commercial return on its use . . . . . there seems little reason to criticise the Government's decision, but it would be wrong to view it as inevitable from the beginning. As so often in the development of new technology, economy in expenditure has resulted in too little being done to achieve success and the money, time and effort that has been expended has been spent to little purpose. It seems to us to be a classic case of 'penny wise, pound foolish'.*

Despite scant enthusiasm by three consecutive governments and the puny UK annual Space Technology budget, (£4.2M compared with £71.7M, £95.4M and 32.5M for Germany, France and Japan respectively), BA's slender development expenditure demonstrated impressive achievement when R3 took flight and placed Prospero (X1) into the desired earth orbit on 28 Oct' 1971.

The hasty closedown of all BA facilities following R3's success owed more to the US Scout offer and issues playing out across the English Channel, than any thought of a BA legacy with its potential to uphold National credibility in a modern world. Besides disbanding a very specialised workforce, the pursuit of wet rocket technology was abandoned totally in favour of the historic Skylark solid propellant sounding rockets.

Many wise heads saw BA as a low key way to preserve UK's hard won and paid for rocket engine knowhow and to keep a UK foothold on the Space World stage until better times returned.

In later years, a National Space Agency was established and became an agile advocate across numerous space sectors but it never enjoyed defined funding; an impediment that kept many international doors closed.

Except for the occasional exotic propulsion system able to attract subsidy, rocket engine research has remained low key for many years.

<u>One last Pipe Dream:</u>

Had UK plc run the gauntlet and entered the new worldwide Space Market back in those difficult BA days; the nation might now be collaborating with France, Germany and Italy alongside India, Russia and America and participating in their remarkable achievements.

Except for very large satellite tasks such as Hubble and Geostatic Communications, digital techniques have dwarfed satellite sizes to a point where India recently place 104 units into earth orbit from a single rocket.

Readers interested in these times should see the publications by Nicholas Hill and Douglas Millard, referenced in Acknowledgements who offer intellectual exposé of these long ago times.

To appreciate what a modern Rocket Range (Space Port) looks and feels like, look at http://www.arianespace.com/spaceport-facility/practical-information

J'ai terminé – – – I'm off to France

VIVE LA FRANCE – DIAMANT   25

FIG 25–1
(CNES)

<u>General</u> – Towards the end of 1971 the French national space agency, Centre National d'etudes Spatiales (CNES) obtained authority to proceed with a satellite program using three Diamant B–P4 rocket launchers. Updated from the earlier Diamant B, these vehicles enjoyed significant modernisation, including the addition of Black Arrow payload fairings. The fairings were selected for their large satellite volume and aero protection offered to the entire third stage assembly. Along with three vehicle sets, British Hovercraft Corporation (nee Saunders Roe etc, etc) designed and manufactured a suitable adaptor bay to interface the Diamant airframe, supply front line spare parts, handling and hoisting aids together with in field operational procedures. Each fairing set had the following additional features: –

- Internal lining of silver coated Mylar to limit thermal re-radiation.
- External 3mm preformed Norcoat cork skin to limit aero heat input.
- A transfer aerial inlay to access Satellite radio link.
- Self-closing air inlet port for pre launch air conditioning input.

I first became aware of this program when asked to serve as Systems Engineer to cover: -

- Shepherding hardware through the Cowes manufacture phase.
- Devise in field assembly and operation procedures.
- Oversee Integration trials at Saint Medard en Jalles, Gironde.
- Oversee three launch trials at Kourou, French Guiana as follows: -
- Diamant B–P4 1, Satellite Starelette (Geodesic).
- Diamant B–P4 2, Satellites Castor & Pollux.
- Diamant B–P4 3, Satellite Aura (solar UV).)The three vehicles ended the Diamant series to free up resources for the upcoming Arian series. Interestingly, to offset "pay packet" losses to local enterprises, 400 Foreign Legionnaires were drafted to Kourou for intervening years.

Diamant Belonged to a group of rockets that employed high-pressure propellant storage tanks to negate need of complex pump machinery, an attractive simplification that came with its own problems. Because the tanks connect directly to the thrust chamber without intervening machinery, combustion pressure pulsing excited energetic longitudinal resonances (or Pogo vibration) throughout the propellant mass, which was sufficient to damage lightweight upper stage structures and equipments. All BP-4 vehicles were fitted with a very robust structural damping device to tame this sleeping tiger.

Fairings (la Coiffe) – As Shown in Fig 25-2 and Fig B-9 Appendix B, the Fairings replicate those flown on Black Arrow. The aerodynamic form, structure and means of release all remained the same. Because some Diamant payloads were heat sensitive, CNES sought to minimise internal re-radiation by using inner silvered Mylar quilting and external preformed 3 mm thick cork panels, which BHC tailored and cemented to the outer magnesium alloy skins.

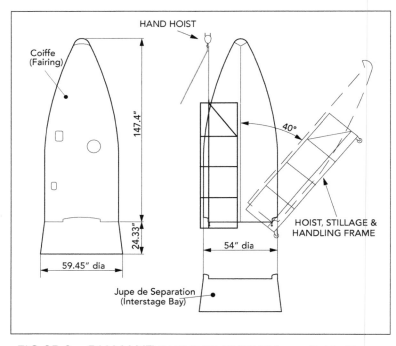

FIG 25-2   DIAMANT PAYLOAD FAIRINGS.   *(D Mack)*

To provide a radio path with the Satellite across the RF imperious fairing structure, a simple parasitic dipole aerial mounted internally was paired with a similar external device. The Diamant application required a Separation Bay to interface Fairing attachment and load paths with the rockets load carrying structure. This structure was also fabricated using Magnesium alloy and was designed as an annular load diffusion beam to disperse fairing hinge loads into the Diamant external skinning.

Vertical Assembly – Late 1974 saw the first Fairing set road freighted to the Vertical Assembly Facility near Gironde where I followed to support the CNES handling crew who would be preparing Diamant for launch at Kourou.

Language – Neither the lead CNES Mechanical Engineer or I were adept linguists, but our combined engineering backgrounds soon laid bare the inner workings of the Fairing design.   The CNES team recognised that fragility of these lightweight structures warranted careful handling to avoid accidental damage and they fully understood the reason for each component and the adjustment features. I returned to Cowes content that the BHC fairings were in good hands, as I prepared to visit Cayenne and Kourou.

Cayenne – Guiana's capital city and international airport lies on the Atlantic coast 30 miles southeast of Kourou. During my time there, Kourou was a compact European style village settlement beside a small native community that totalled about 5000 European and Creole inhabitants that was set to grow larger. The rocket-launching complex extends along a 12mile coastal belt northwest of Kourou village between the Atlantic Ocean and Rainforest. See Fig 25–3. A challenging tropical climate prevails, ranging between 29 and 31°C and with an annual rainfall of 110 inches, conditions that can soon destroy unprotected facilities and machinery.

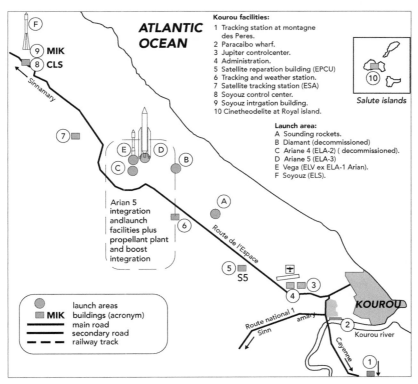

FIG 25-3   KOUROU, FRENCH GUYANA   *(CNES)*

Accordingly, the majority of Centre Spatial Guyanais (CSG) buildings and launch pads are enclosed and air-conditioned.

The CGS Technical and Admin centre stands three miles northwest of Kourou village with the Diamant launch complex six miles further on, a refreshing change from the 30-mile trudge between Woomera village and Area5.

Nowadays, the CSG launch facilities extend seven miles beyond the decommissioned Diamant site to embrace extensive Arian and Soyouz launch areas.

<u>Diamant B–P4 1 Trial</u> – CNES provided open dated Air France tickets via Paris with optional stopovers subject to arrival at Cayenne on due date. This refreshing commonsense standard practice arose because Air France and CNES were both government agencies and CNES staff often broke the outward leg when time allowed. My Project Manager joined me on this first visit and we opted to investigate Guardeloupe for two nights on this outward leg!

Compared to my Black Arrow trials, working as consultant turned out to be a very relaxed affaire. Once a detailed inspection of the Fairing hardware had been done, I merely tagged along as observer during Fairing operations.

<u>Preparation facilities</u> –
The resulting free time allowed me to take stock of the Kourou facilities, rocket preparation and launcher areas.

The Diamant complex was cleverly arranged with a railed link building that joined the service tower and assembly hall as one contiguous hall until launch time.

Thus the Diamant Final Assembly Hall, Admin, Crew-room and all kindred facilities were housed together in this single preparation area beside the launcher, a well-conceived setup.

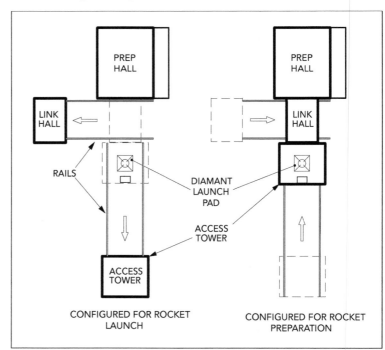

FIG 25-4   DIAMANT LAUNCHER & PREP HALL   *(D Mack)*

Every need was close at hand, (no driving three miles to collect a forgotten item at TS4). Other than the AM & PM Hotel and lunchtime runs plus a few visits to various CSG launch control areas, the personal 2CV was rarely used.

FIG 25-5   DIAMANT BP4-01 ON KOUROU LAUNCHER   *(CNES)*

<u>Recreation</u> – Friendly CNES staff treated us as companions and included us in their many leisure activities, including their pleasant custom of handshaking each other every morning. Many a "French Pidgin English" joke was shared during our enjoyable lunchtime and dinner sessions.

> *A Rain Forest adventure: An expedition up one of many small rain forest rivers was arranged one Saturday. After raiding the local supermarket for bread, tins of pate, cheeses and packs of larger, eight of us ventured forth into the wilderness in two dugout canoes. Murky brown water offered little current but paddling skills in the other boat slowed progress until my "paddle and feather" means to keep moving in a straight line were twigged. Some intrepid long stay CNES guys had gone native by setting up lone semi-permanent weekend sleep-outs by the riverbank. Share our meal with one "wild" man, he added a freshly cut Coeur de Palm. When we suggested the abundant wild life and insects were a dicey way to relax he claimed a good fire kept them at bay and it was an escape from a hectic world. We only managed to spot a few monkeys high in the canopy and one water snake.*

<u>Back to business</u> –

- Oversaw attachment of the Fairing Separation Bay (Jupe de separation 2/3) to the Stage2 upper structure, and the CNES explosives crew fitting, connecting and testing the two pyro-separation units to each half Fairing.
- After the Satellite had been loaded, I observed each half Fairing hoisted secured on the Separation Bay. Handling frame and spring keeper pins were left in place for removal nearer pre fuelling time.

PB4-01 was to place the Starelette satellite into orbit to study Earth geodesy by reflecting fine laser beams from accurately surveyed earth sites.

<u>Launch day</u> – Thursday 6 Feb'1975 saw all personnel except the Launch Pad team evacuated to the GSC admin centre about six miles back and kept abreast of progress via a video display and intercom. As the firing sequence time reached zero we waited and watched for the beast to appear above the nearby treetops and climb away until lost to the naked eye.

Later reports confirmed the flight as successful, our fairings had departed correctly, and Stage3 had put Starelette into orbit.

> *A POST FIRING CELEBRATION: As one might expect of this nation, the standard of their post launch celebrations was without comparison. The entire rocket assembly hall extending from the fixed workshop, through removable link building to the Launch Pad was converted into one continuous buffet area loaded with every kind of European and Guyenne finger food and much wine – a most enjoyable and unequalled event with impromptu sketches and sing-songs all attended by the Maire and many local personalities.*

<u>Diamant B–P4 2 Trial</u>   I travelled alone this time and was met at Charles de Gaulle by a CNES guy toting two, two litre cans of anchovy. It seems the favoured pizza eatery at Kourou was out of stock and I was the only available traveller flying direct to Cayenne.

> *Turtle watching: After taking charge of the anchovy, my CNES couriers sprung a surprise by asking me along on a trip to watch turtles lay their eggs! My fatigue nearly prompted a refusal but all was arranged and I'd regret passing up such a chance later so after a bite to eat we all drove direct from the airport the Mana River on the Surinam border some 125 miles away! I got my head down in the car and awoke to torrential rain hammering down on the unmade track that looked very unsafe but good Rally driving got us through free of mishap. We waited with a few others until these poor creatures laboured to drag their massive bodies up the beach and dig holes with their rear flippers. When about two foot deep, three or four-dozen three-inch diameter pure white rubbery eggs were tumbled in and much time was then spent refilling and disguising the surface before they hauled themselves back to the sea without a further thought for their offspring.*

<u>Back to business</u> – B–P4 2 was to carry aloft a pair of satellites, Pollux (37.5kg) above Castor (77.5kg). The former would space test a hydrazine propulsion device while the latter would collect geodetic data via a super sensitive tri-axis accelerometer.

Telemetry data from the 01 flight revealed that under fairing pressure had lagged behind the ambient fall with altitude. The Fairing was designed to relieve internal pressure by bleeding through the unsealed base line joint. Aero studies concluded the bow shock wave drifting aft as the airframe speed increased, eventually blocked off the design bleed path – the solution was to provide a secondary path.

I was required to pierce six 20mm diameter holes through the Interstage skin at 60° intervals, 400 mm below the Fairing base line. As I'd equipped my self with cutting bits, I sought to borrow a suitable power tool but was thwarted because the storage area was not cleared for power tool use! After a moments thought I decided to introduce modern "Rocket Science" to old world technology by requesting a carpenters hand brace. This did a brilliant job on the Interstage Bays, and the Diamant team enjoyed pulling my leg unmercifully.

As far as I could tell, the trial had progressed without obvious interruption or serious concerns. I often spent several hours sitting in on the Technical Review discussions held each working day, as engineers assessed results from the previous days work – often being confused by my language limitations.

<u>Launch Day, Saturday 17 May</u> – Watched another successful Diamant launch with good flight performance reports.

<u>The Celebration</u> – This equalled the earlier B–P4 1 trial.

<u>Diamant B–P4 3 Trial</u> – On this occasion I was joined by our Chief Systems Engineer, a jolly, talented engineer who enjoyed our stop off at Martinique where we hired a car to tour the coastline before visiting Empress Josephine's family homestead. In those days a fermenting mass of sugar cane waste heaped outside a sugar processing plant close to the airport, was emitting a fantastic heady fermentation of rum fumes.

FIG 25-6   CASTOR & POLLUX SATELLITES ATOP DIAMANT
AT KOUROU – HALF FAIRING REMOVED   *(D Mack)*

A Devils Island adventure: Our CNES friends organised an official trip across to the infamous Ile du Diable that lies about 8 miles off shore directly under the geostationary launch path from Kourou. The Island is administered by CSG who maintains the old prison Administration Building (later to become a tourist hotel) and provides all the utility services along with a rocket tracking station. Together with the close by Ile du Royal and Ile du St Joseph, (collectively termed the Iles du Salut or Salvations's Islands) they formed part of the French penal colony that stretched along the coast to Dutch Surinam from 1852 were until 1946 when it was finally closed. Early missionaries named the Salvations's Islands when they fled there for the constant winds that kept plague carrying Mosquitoes away.

The derelict prison buildings are now overgrown with the vigorous vegetation of many years but evidence of the early inmates artistic skills can be seen in the dilapidated chapel and some cells. Nowadays the Islands have become a popular tourist destination that sports a very modern hotel.

<u>Launch Day</u> – 27th Sept 1975, this last and final Diamant would place the Aura satellite in orbit to study U/V emission from the Sun – Yet another copybook performance.

<u>The Last Celebration</u> – Being the last ever in the Diamant series, outstanding celebrations and feasts persisted for several days, which began with the regular buffet rave up at the launch pad hall. Besides the food and vino, the Team had erected a 2CV, tail end down on the Launch pad and rigged it with cardboard fins and ogive nose and a hoist hook. When proceedings had warmed up the Chef de Mission and Director de Operations were persuaded to don fuelling helmets and climb aboard the mock rocket ship to loud farewells. They were slowly hoisted to about ten feet to roaring cheers before the fire hoses appeared to half fill the car with water before setting it down again. I was fearful for the rigs safety but the guys had done a dummy run at dawn.

Over the next days various outfits threw farewell shindigs to which we were invited. A brilliant one given by the Crew Room concession team provided Campari shots followed by machete beheaded Champaign and endless wine with Anaconda steaks!

Our final party was given by the Mechanical section were whole joints of roasted suckling pi were preceded by Richard shots and a full bottle of claret each. Towards the end singing became compulsory so after much Gallic pressure my Project Manager and I leapt onto the table and ran through a rousing version of "Green Grow the Rushes Grow" with all the actions; by verse five they all had it off by heart.

FIG 25-7   DIAMANT ON KOUROU PAD. BA NOSE FAIRING
CHECKS BEFORE MOUNTING C&P SATELLITES   *(D Mack)*

<u>General Observation</u> – Google or Wikipedia gives good idea of how far France has progressed in the Space business since my Black Arrow days. The modern GSC set up and future plans reflect Frances vision and wisdom in selecting Kourou because: –

1. The site lies only 4° from the equator where low inclination orbital launches can pick up almost all the Earth spin rate.
2. Located on a remote Atlantic coastline with heavy sea cargo docking facilities and unrestricted sea room for spent rocket dumping or recovery operations.
3. A tropical climate enforcing properly sealed air-conditioned installations where sensitive hardware may be serviced in controlled environments.
4. The tropical climate, insects and wild life make landline communication very vulnerable to damage. Consequently most operational areas are microwave linked with local digital computer suites giving efficient on line access to current data and documentation.
5. Remote seclusion yet direct and secure air link and two-week sea link with Europe. Potential to grow a modern mini city with commercially established and operated civilian amenities.
6. A relatively young enterprise, which has profited from lessons learnt at the pioneering rocket ranges.

<u>The Gallic style</u> – My entire time at Kourou was informative and enjoyable. Having admired French engineering ingenuity and their patriotic verve from afar I was eager to join in a typical workday scenario. As demonstrated by their friendly morning handshakes, teamwork, respect for each other's role figured strongly; each day saw progress without trifling strictures or petty supervision that often hampers easygoing progress. My time working alongside several French teams since my Kourou days confirmed these amenable team working ways as normal. Conversely, I've also found that French personnel are often very cautious and reserved when supervised by other nationals; probably an instinctive self-preserving shield we all exercise in unfamiliar circumstances and languages.

<u>An Unexpected Reward!</u> – Some time after the final Diamant trial, CNES invited me to an award ceremony at Evry, their head office outside Paris. Naturally I accepted and took my wife along as a small offset for her many solo times, to meet a few fellow Diamant teammates. The presentation was very formal; along with others I was presented with a CNES diploma for service rendered to the final Diamant rocket program.

Later, we joined a group of CNES pals and their partners who had invited us to dine with them. After a good nights sleep we did a quick tour of central Paris before flying home next morning.

FIG 25–8   WITH ANNE & THREE CNES ASSOCIATES
IN PARIS FOR A DIPLOMA.   *(CNES)*

I.W. man star of space bid

An Isle of Wight engineer has been honoured by the French Government for his work on a space programme.

Mr. Derek Mack (pictured here) of Yarmouth, travelled to Paris with his wife, Anne, and two children to receive a diploma from the President of the French National Centre for Space Studies.

Mr. Mack, systems engineer with the British Hovercraft Corporation, received the award for his contribution to the successful launching of three Diamant rockets which put four scientific research satellites into orbit last year.

The Corporation was awarded a contract to make components for the rockets, and Mr. Mack's work took him to a space centre at Bordeaux and to the launch site in French Guiana.

After serving an aviation apprenticeship, Mr. Mack joined B.H.C. in 1957 and was involved in work on Britain's Black Knight and Black Arrow rockets, both at B.H.C.'s test site at Highdown, Freshwater, and at the launch site at Woomera, Australia.

At the ceremony in Paris, Mr. Mack discovered he was one of only six people in industry to receive diplomas.

FIG 25–9   PRESS CUTTING
(IW County Press)

BLACK KNIGHT DETAILS A

1	INTRO	8	FLIGHT SAFETY
2	PERFORMANCE	9	HAZARDOU SYSTEMS
3	AIRFRAME	10	TELEMETRY
4	TETHER	11	LOADING PROPELLANTS
5	UPPER STAGE	12	SHORESIDE SUPPLIES
6	PROPULSION	13	COUNTDOWN
7	FLIGHTPATH CONTROL	14	PREP & CHECKOUT
		15	THRUST HARVESTING

1 – INTRO: Initially designed as a single stage workhorse to examine high speed re-entry physics for Blue Streak ICBM, Black Knight was later equipped with an upper stage to increase re-entry speeds sought by the Gaslight and Dazzle research programs. The RAE at Farnborough provided various test bodies weighing up to 280lbs and up to 36" diameter, which were released 400 to 500 miles above the Woomera desert to make a free fall re–entry into earth atmosphere (taken as 200,000ft) at speeds up to 11,000ft/sec. The later two-stage Gaslight and Dazzle series fired smaller GW20 cones and 15"dia spheres into the upper atmosphere at 17,000ft/sec.

Fig A–2 outlines a single stage vehicle together with typical Test Body payloads. Fig A–8 and A–9 details the Second Stage configuration.

BK vehicles were propelled by one of two engine types (Gamma 201 and Gamm301), both burnt kerosene and hydrogen peroxide propellants via four trunnion mounted thrust chambers configured to provide three axis thrust vector steering. Armstrong Siddley Motors (ASM) was the primary design and manufacture contractor for both engine types. The 201 engines regulated propellant mixture ratios passively via fix orifices whereas the later 301 engines employed active mixture control via venturi flow metering. To attain the re-entry velocity required, an almost vertical climb took each rocket to an apogee of 400 to 500 miles before freefalling to impact within an instrumented footprint 50 miles down range, a task that required trajectory management during the engine thrust phase. The RAE devised guidance system that employed rear and lateral optical trackers to define a vertical climb up to 19,000ft where a fixed radar beam at a QE of 88° and azimuth of 348° was entered to continue flight path tracking up to All Burnt. The tracking data was used by ground based X and Y pilots to correct drift and apply a 2° down turn by sending radio command pulses to the rockets flight control system. Vehicle attitude was stabilised by on board gyroscopic sensing and servo controlled thrust vector steering.

2 PERFORMANCE:

TABLE A/1

BLACK KNIGHT PERFORMANCE – TABLE A.1

ᵉCuckool ** Cuckoo II   ∧ At 200,000ft

Ident	Num Stage	Eng	Chab'r Press	Dry lbs	HTP ibs	Kero ibs	Mix ratio	AUW lbs	Thrust ibs	IOM G	Burn secs	Apoge miles	Re-entry ∧ft/sec
BK04	1	201	465	1474	10392	1328	7.83	13194	16794	1.27	145.8	499	11740
BK06	1	201	448	1541	10254	1300	7.89	13095	16480	1.26	147	455	11220
BK07	1	201	445	1600	10242	1347	7.60	13371	16340	1.24	148.5	330	11100
BK09	2*	201	452	2022	10375	1342	7.73	13739	16313	1.19	149.5	301	15000
BK13	1	201	463	1555	9939	1319	7.54	12813	16810	1.31	139	427	10870
BK16	2*	301	548	2183	10300	1304	7.90	13787	19190	1.39	128.3	356	14600
BK19	2**	301	634	2228	13763	1756	7.84	17747	21120	1.19	122.8	374	15900
BK21	2**	301	638	2173	13701	1736	7.89	17610	21610	1.23	121.3	404	15000

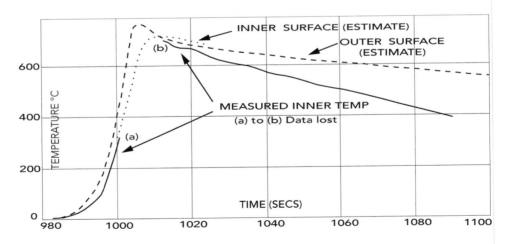

Fig A–1 TYPICAL TEST BODY RE-ENTRY THERMAL TRACE   (Crown copyright)

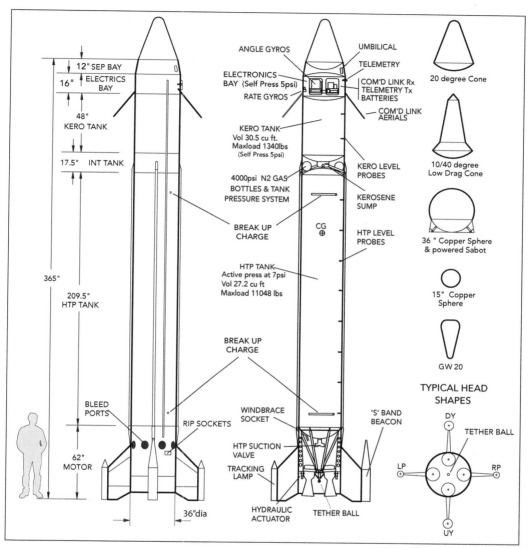

FIG A-2   BK SALIENT DIMENSIONS & ARRANGEMENT   *(Crown copyright)*

3 AIRFRAME ARRANGEMENT:

Interface constraint between Rocket and Launcher together with the release processes are outlined in Fig A–6 below.

3.1 <u>The overall dimensions</u>: Derived from the definitions shown in Fig A–2 as: -

- The 36"dia is the minimum needed to house four Gamma 201 thrust chambers.
- To re-enter 250lb at 11,000ft/sec, a 13000ibs AUW rocket requires 16,000lb thrust for up to 150secs.

- For tanks of 36"dia, 150secs burn time equates to tank wall lengths of 209.5" (HTP) and 48"(Kerosene).
- Motor (62"), Intertank (17.5"), Electronic (16") and Separation (12") bays take the rockets minimum height to 365".
- Each airframe included an adaptor bay individually sized for the Payload experiment; this brought a minimum overall height of 365" (30.4').
- Four rear fins were included to carry electronic and visual tracking aids wide of the engine wake.

3.2 <u>Propellant Storage</u>: To meet the low cost objectives simple engineering techniques and conventional aircraft aluminium fabrication methods were employed throughout. In common with all rocket designs, propellant weight, storage and chemical compatibility invariably present the major structural challenge but HTP eased this task by being aluminium compatible. In pursuit of minimum weight, a prototype was constructed using minimum thickness aluminium alloy skinning, rivet fastened on internal hoop frames with external stiffening stringers, which proved impossible to seal reliably, see Fig A–4 below.

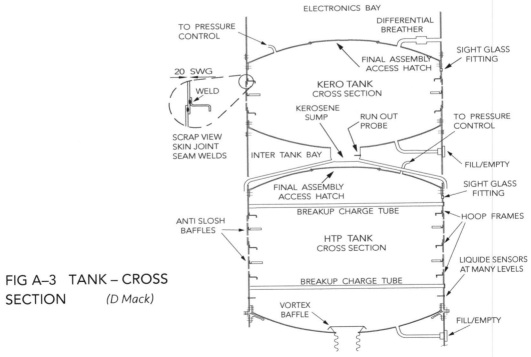

FIG A–3 TANK – CROSS SECTION   (D Mack)

The chosen solution departed from usual aircraft practice by applying a continuous electric seam welding technique that provided reliable leak free jointing on marginally heavier skins, (20swg) without stiffening stringers. A marginal weight penalty resulted continuous QA controlled leak free seams throughout the BK and later BA programs. Chemically milled stretch formed semi hemispherical diaphragms closed out each tank end as shown in Fig A–3 above.

FIG A–4 BK FIRST PROTOTYPE. External stringers & the upper clamp ring is fitted. Lower clamp ring removed to fit the wind brace arms.   *(GKN Aerospace)*

3.3 <u>Engine Bay Detail</u>: – To avoid describing the entire airframe structure, I've chosen to outline the Engine Bay since it offers a mix of line and diffused load paths and deals with the highest loads.

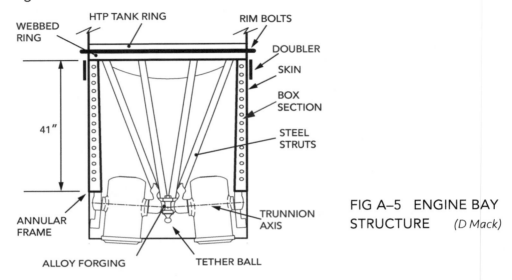

FIG A–5   ENGINE BAY STRUCTURE   (D Mack)

1. At the upper edge, a deep webbed light alloy joint ring is riveted to a stressed skin cylindrical shell, which extends down to a wide annular frame.
2. The webbed joint ring joins the HTP tank base ring via a rim of closely pitched bolts to transfer diffused loads.
3. The cylindrical shell upper zone is heavily skin doubled to form an annular diffusion beam with the webbed ring to focus the diffused HTP tank loads into eight angled steel struts.
4. Each downward sloping strut terminates at a central light alloy forging where the geometry aligns with and extends to the central tethering ball.
5. Thrust Chamber inner trunnion loads are reacted at the central alloy forging.
6. Outer trunnion loads react at the wide annular frame where 4 robust box sections inside the cylindrical shell transfer them up to the deep webbed diffusion beam and onwards via the downward steel struts to the central forging.
7. As the common element, the central forging passes all dead loads to ground via a single ball ended spigot, which offers vertical and lateral constraint with rotational freedom until released at launch.
8. Torsion loads are reacted by two sets of fork and tongue fittings located between launcher structure and motor bay outer skinning at diametrically opposite points.

9. Four tail fins are mount on the outer shell at reinforced fixing points, primarily to carry equipment pods clear of the engine efflux to aid guidance tracking.

3.4 The remaining structure: –

1. Intertank Bay: A reinforced stressed skin structure designed to pass distributed loads between Kero tank and HTP tank. Skin and frame doubling carry flux loads around four large access doors and several service piercings.

2. Electronics Bay: A reinforced stressed skinned structure with four large fully reinforced service hatches that are pressure sealed to sustain 5psi relative, which is vent valve maintained. Four cross rails are arranged to carry several trays of electronic packages and react their loadings.

3. Payload Adapter Bay: Stressed skin unpressurised diffusion structure, terminated with a channel section upper frame and vertical box section longerons at two diametrically opposed explosive bolt housings.

3.5 Safety Factors: Standards were agreed with RAE Structures Dept for unmanned, short-term fatigue applications.

3.6 Airframe Flexure: The high aspect ratio of the slender airframe led to early development problems due to bending and torsion resonance modes, which lay inside the FCS pass band. Lengthy testing led to the introduction lateral rate gyros and electronic notch filtering.

4 – TETHERING:

The basic principle is set out in Fig A–6 and A–7 below. AUW is focused at a central ball-ended spigot projecting below the engine bay and constrained by a gas operated jaw mechanism housed centrally within the launcher structure.

Toppling moments about the release ball are reacted by four diametrically opposed arms that project from the launcher structure to engage with four matching sockets high on the engine bay; counter weights fold these arms outwards as the rocket lifts clear. Two diametrically opposed, registration lugs on the launcher engage with mating slots on the engine bay skirt to resist initial roll motion.

Introduction of the Gamma 301 engine brought the need to reappraise the release jack design because the trunnion axis were repositioned some 8 inches higher than the 201 engine relative to the nozzle exit plain. The structural change needed to align the central alloy forging with the higher trunnion position took the hold down ball and release jack claws with it. To address the unacceptably increase in lift off overlap between engine nozzles and release jack, the jack was redesigned to retract downwards as it opened. Fail-safe release jack circuitry ensured that engine thrust, servo power and zero chamber angles existed before release was initiated.

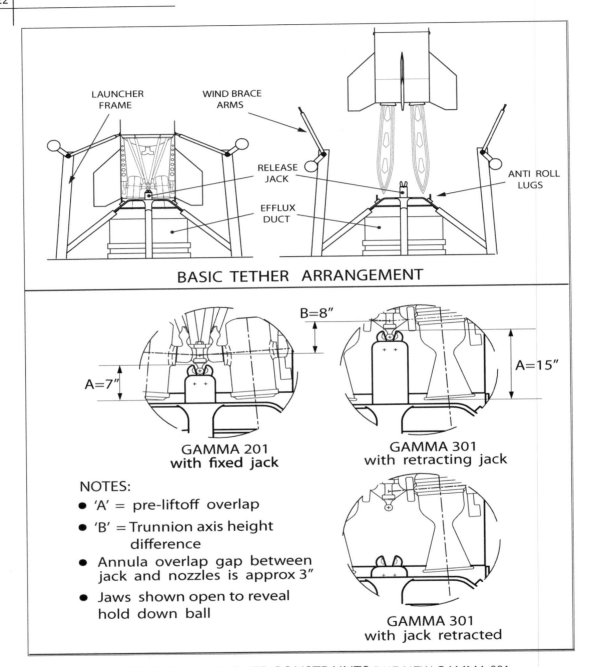

LAUNCHER FRAME

WIND BRACE ARMS

RELEASE JACK

EFFLUX DUCT

ANTI ROLL LUGS

BASIC TETHER ARRANGEMENT

B=8″

A=7″

A=15″

GAMMA 201
with fixed jack

GAMMA 301
with retracting jack

GAMMA 301
with jack retracted

NOTES:

- 'A' = pre-liftoff overlap
- 'B' = Trunnion axis height difference
- Annula overlap gap between jack and nozzles is approx 3″
- Jaws shown open to reveal hold down ball

FIG A–6   ROCKET/ LAUNCHER CONSTRAINTS DUE NEW GAMMA 301
TRUNNION HEIGHT   (D Mack)

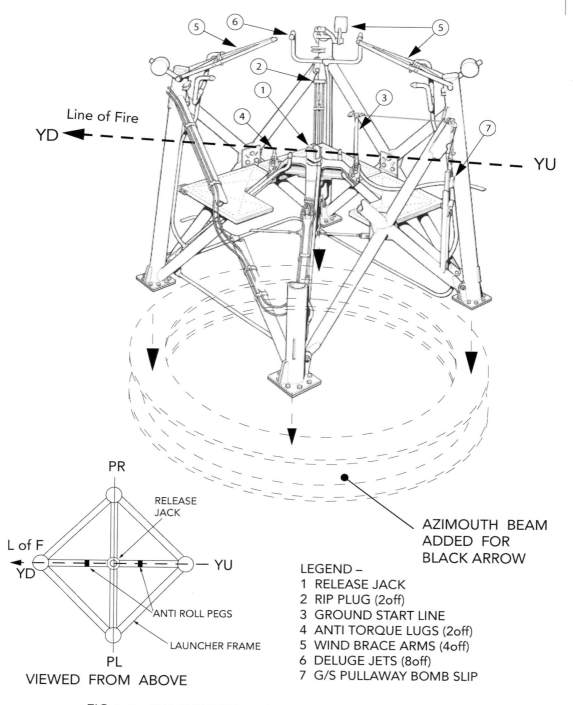

Line of Fire

YD ◄ - YU

PR

RELEASE
JACK

L of F ◄
YD ─── YU

ANTI ROLL PEGS

LAUNCHER FRAME

PL

VIEWED FROM ABOVE

AZIMOUTH BEAM
ADDED FOR
BLACK ARROW

LEGEND –
1 RELEASE JACK
2 RIP PLUG (2off)
3 GROUND START LINE
4 ANTI TORQUE LUGS (2off)
5 WIND BRACE ARMS (4off)
6 DELUGE JETS (8off)
7 G/S PULLAWAY BOMB SLIP

FIG A–7   BK LAUNCHER   (GKN Aerospace + D Mack)

5 – UPPER STAGE DETAIL:

To increase Test Body re-entry speeds for the Gaslight and Dazzle programs, a downward thrusting solid propellant Cuckoo motor was introduced as a second stage. This was secured to an Adapter Bay mounted on Stage1 separation Bay by four double explosive bolts. Nestling within a Sabot unit, the Test Body hung below the Cuckoo motor inside the Adapter Bay, secured by two further explosive bolts.

The Sabot unit sported four small solid fuel boosters aligned to thrust through the Test Body CofG and tethered to the Adaptor Bay by a deploying lanyard.

Located inside a short nosecone fairing and shear pinned to the Cuckoo venturi nozzle, was a compressed gas jet pack designed to lift and spin up the entire upper stage as the Adaptor Bay explosive bolts were fired by thrust sensing inertia switches at Stage1 All burnt.

The spin stabilised Stage2 was designed to coast up to a 360-mile apogee before descending to around 375,000ft where a Phillip's ionisation gauge triggered Cuckoo motor ignition to increase re-entry speed. A delay timer spanning Cuckoo burn time, simultaneously fires the secondary explosive bolts and Sabot boosters to propel the Test Body clear for an uncluttered re-entry at 200,000ft, the Sabot having been lanyard arrested.

Stage2 added 624lbs weight and raised re-entry velocity to 15,000ft/sec, a value that was to reach 17,500ft/sec on later shots using up-rated Cuckoo and Gamma 301 engines.

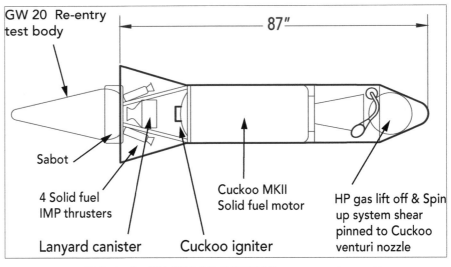

GW 20 Re-entry test body

87"

Sabot

4 Solid fuel IMP thrusters

Lanyard canister

Cuckoo MKII Solid fuel motor

Cuckoo igniter

HP gas lift off & Spin up system shear pinned to Cuckoo venturi nozzle

FIG A–8 BK STAGE 2 DETAIL   *(D Mack)*

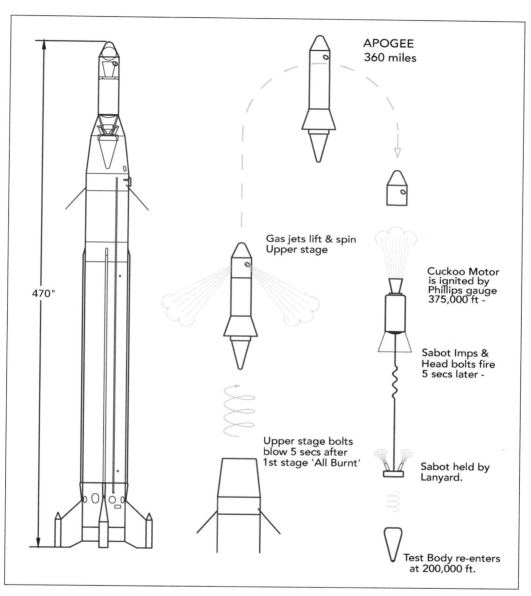

APOGEE
360 miles

Gas jets lift & spin
Upper stage

Cuckoo Motor
is ignited by
Phillips gauge
375,000 ft -

Sabot Imps &
Head bolts fire
5 secs later -

Upper stage bolts
blow 5 secs after
1st stage 'All Burnt'

Sabot held by
Lanyard.

470"

Test Body re-enters
at 200,000 ft.

FIG A–9   BK STAGE 2 SEPARATION SEQUENCE   (D Mack)

6 – PROPULSION:

6.1 <u>High Test Peroxide (HTP):</u> The 3% dilute Peroxide familiar to the domestic world also comes as HTP, an 85% concentrate used with kerosene as a rocket bipropellant. This combination returns a moderate Specific Impulse (SI) of 240 compared to Lox at 280 and Hydrogen at 400 but the following redeeming features reduce airframe complexity:

1. Not cryogenic: Airframe insulation or standby topping up not needed.
2. Hypergolic with Kero: Self ignites in vacuo, low multi chamber ignition spread.
3. Storage: Un-insulated high purity Aluminium tanks at ambient temperature.
4. Water miscible: Wash down and made safe by water dilution.
5. Low volatility: Very mild fuming.
6. Efflux: Exceptionally clean exhaust plume.

Disadvantages:

1. Very catalyst sensitive: All organic, most metallic and plastic materials will induce delayed or immediate violent reactions.
2. Storage surveillance: Daily inspections and good natural ventilation.
3. Obscured activity: Must be alert to slow catalysing.
4. Safe Practice: Continued vigilance of seemingly safe situation.

The peroxide molecule has two hydrogen and two oxygen atoms, which can be split into one free oxygen atom and one water molecule (H_2O) with a suitable catalyst that also releases considerable heat energy. A catalyst pack of heavily silver-plated metallic gauss layers sited at the head of each Gamma combustion chamber, converts high pressure HTP into super heated oxygen rich steam at 500°C.

When this "cold running" is established, hot running is induced by admitting high-pressure kerosene to lift throat temp to 2300°C and the nozzle exit to 1100 °C.

The Gamma engine concept evolved from an original German design taken up by REP Westcott to assist aircraft take off at high elevation airfields and was a single, oxidant cooled thrust chamber producing 4100lbs thrust at sea level

6.2 <u>Gamma 201 Engine:</u> See Figs A–10 & 11 below. Black Knight was formulated around an engine thrust of 16500ib at sea level, which was achieved by enlisting ASM to bundle four separate Wescott units into a cruciform format. Each Thrust Chamber was mounted on a single servo controlled trunnion; aligned with the rocket vehicles pitch, yaw axis to provide full thrust vector steering. Each trunnion axis had a permanent horizontal toe in angle to direct the average thrust vector through the rockets C of G.

With four standard Gamma turbo-pump sets each mounted directly above their respective thrust chamber, propellants were fed via the hollow bore trunnion bearings, an innovation that avoided the use of flexible hoses. HTP entered the cooling jacket of each combustion chamber via a stop valve on the inboard trunnion bearing; Fuel passed through the outer trunnion to a stop valve at the head of each chamber where it was halted by an N2 purge pressure source until chamber steam pressure had attained an acceptable value.

Fixed orifices were sized during calibration firings at Ansty to control propellant flow rates, a method well suited to the engines original application but incapable of maintaining accurate mixture ratio over the BK flight envelope. Typical flight burn times often resulted in over heating and irregular shut down of each thrust chambers.

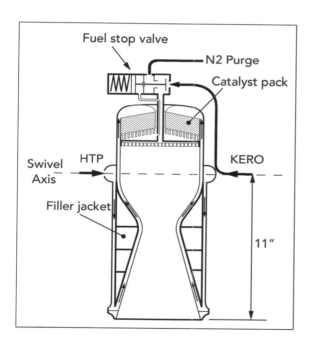

FIG A–10   GAMMA 201
THRUST CHAMBER   *(D Mack)*

6.3 <u>Gamma 301 Engine</u>: Figs A–12 & 13 below detail this upgrade evolved by ASM from the Stentor engine developed for the Blue Steel stand off bomb. The new design benefited from modern lightweight thrust chamber construction, updated turbo-pump technology and fully proportional propellant control that regulated thrust and mixture ratio throughout the BK flight envelope. Two turbo-pump trains, each fed a pair of thrust chambers produced a better thrust decay and propellant usage.

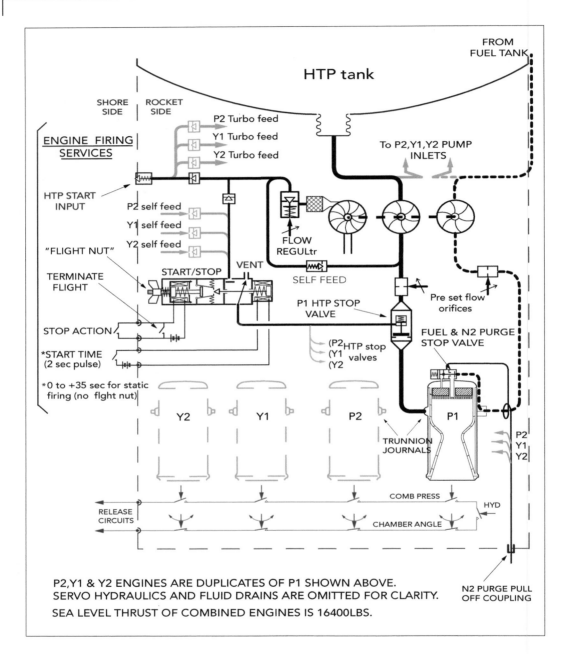

FIG A–11   GAMMA 201 SCHEMATIC   (D Mack)

Thrust chambers were built with stainless steel tubular staves each having a suitably graduated cross section, all seam welded together to form an open-ended barrel. Each stave opened into a common manifold at the nozzle exit and every second stave was sealed at the head end and ported into a common HTP manifold. HTP flowing through each stave loop en route to the catalyst pack, held the running temperature of each "barrel" at the required operating value.

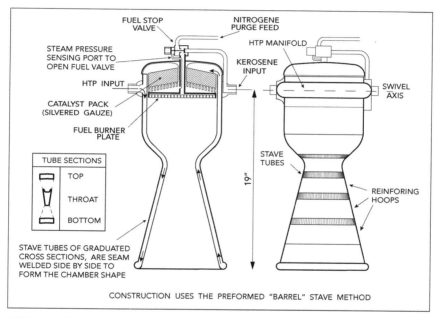

FUEL STOP
VALVE

NITROGENE
PURGE FEED

STEAM PRESSURE
SENSING PORT TO
OPEN FUEL VALVE

HTP MANIFOLD

KEROSENE
INPUT

HTP INPUT

SWIVEL
AXIS

CATALYST PACK
(SILVERED GAUZE)

FUEL BURNER
PLATE

STAVE
TUBES

19"

REINFORING
HOOPS

TUBE SECTIONS

TOP

THROAT

BOTTOM

STAVE TUBES OF GRADUATED
CROSS SECTIONS, ARE SEAM
WELDED SIDE BY SIDE TO
FORM THE CHAMBER SHAPE

CONSTRUCTION USES THE PREFORMED "BARREL" STAVE METHOD

FIG A–12 – GAMMA 301 STAVE TUBE CHAMBER   *(D Mack)*

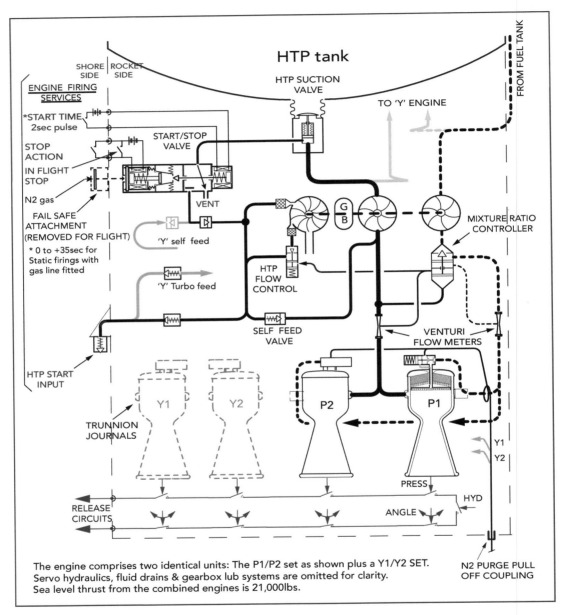

FIG A–13   GAMMA 301 SCHEMATIC   *(D Mack)*

6.4 <u>Gamma 201 Engine Start/Stop Valve</u> – Each combustion chamber is isolated from bulk HTP by hydraulically activated stop-valves located at each HTP trunnion (or in 301 engines, a single suction valve at the HTP tank). A shore-side pressurised HTP source hydraulically opens each stop valve and spins up each turbo pump, the engine becomes self-sustaining when the rising HTP pump delivery pressures exceeds the external source pressure. Executive access to time static firings, take Stop Action or terminate flight is provided via a Start/Stop solenoid valve located in the Engine Bay, which manages hydraulic activation of each HTP stop valve (or 301 suction valve)

The Engine start/stop valve operation must obey the following failsafe rules:

• STATIC FIRINGS: Engine can only be started and kept running while the Start/Stop valve is held open by a shore-side current. Firing must stop when shore side current ceases for any reason.

• LAUNCH FIRINGS: Engine can only be started by shore-side current pulse to the Start/Stop valve and must keep burning at loss of shore side current prior to lift off. Firing must only be stopped by shore-side Stop Action or in Flight Termination.

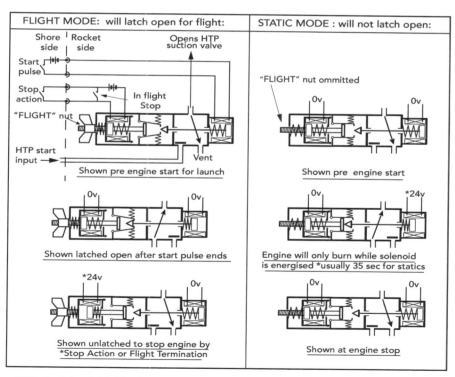

FIG A–14 201 ENGINE START/STOP VALVE SCHEMATIC *(D Mack)*

The "Start/Stop" valve is designed to meet the above opposing rules by using two internal solenoids and a "Flight Nut".

- WITHOUT THE "FLIGHT NUT": This mode meets the Static firing requirement by disabling an internal mechanical latch, which allows the Stop/Start valve to be controlled by the start solenoid alone. Burn time is started or stopped by the duration that electrical power is applied to the first solenoid.

- WITH THE "FLIGHT NUT": This mode meets the Launch firing requirement by allowing the internal mechanical latch to hold the Start/Stop open after a 2sec shore side voltage pulse to the start solenoid. The valve then remains latched open until released by applying a voltage to the stop solenoid that is only accessed by shore-side Stop Action or Flight Termination circuits.

6.5 <u>Gamma 301 Engine Start /Stop Valve</u> – The "Flight Nut" was replaced in favour of an external gas activated attachment for static firings only to inhibit the "Start/Stop" valve latching mechanism. To guard against loss of external gas pressure, the internal engine shutdown battery is always fitted to energise the shore side Stop Action circuit.

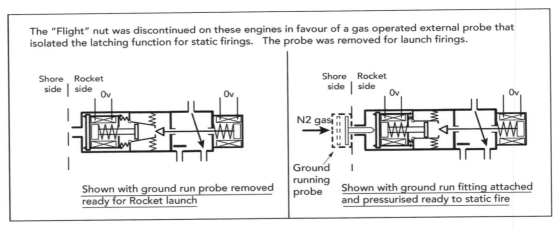

The "Flight" nut was discontinued on these engines in favour of a gas operated external probe that isolated the latching function for static firings. The probe was removed for launch firings.

Shore side | Rocket side — Ov — Ov

Shown with ground run probe removed ready for Rocket launch

N2 gas — Shore side | Rocket side — Ov — Ov

Ground running probe

Shown with ground run fitting attached and pressurised ready to static fire

FIG A–15   301 ENGINE START/STOP VALVE SCHEMATIC   (D Mack)

6.6 <u>Nitrogen Purge System</u>: To prevent damage at engine start up and shutdown, the fuel galleries and burner plates of each thrust chamber must be purged clear of peroxide products by a vigorous flow of nitrogen gas.

A stop valve sited at the head of each chamber admits a shore side nitrogen source, which flows through the fuel galleries and burner plate until catalyst pack steam pressure is high enough to switch it over hot running by admitting kerosene.

The high flow high-pressure nitrogen source for this duty is routed from a bulk store via a Test Post flow control rig to a rocket liftoff connection, as outlined in Fig A–16.

The control rig comprises two dome-loaded controllers, the larger gating and pressure regulating the main gas flow, itself being tightly referenced to the small preset controller to minimises pressure over shoot. A small snubber is included to cushion transients

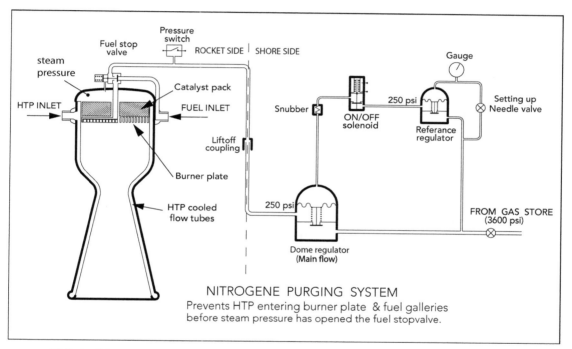

NITROGENE PURGING SYSTEM
Prevents HTP entering burner plate & fuel galleries
before steam pressure has opened the fuel stopvalve.

FIG A–16   NITROGEN PURGING SYSTEM   (D Mack)

6.7 <u>Engine Ground Start System</u>: The engine start sequence needs a shore-side HTP source to spin up its turbo pumps and open its HTP stop valves. The shore-side HTP source was held in a pressurised tank located beside the launcher that was applied to the engine via a pneumatic valve and flexible hosing with self-sealing pull off coupling. Dome controllers as described below for N2 purging system are used to regulate the holding tank pressure. Tank pressurisation and the HTP start valves are time initiated from the central sequence unit in the Equipment Centre.

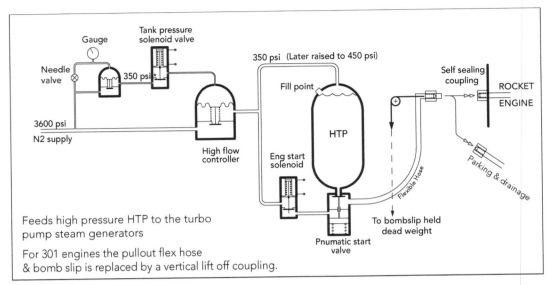

FIG A–17   THE ENGINE HTP GROUND START SYETEM   (D Mack)

7 - FLIGHT PATH CONTROL:

7.1 <u>General</u>: An Autopilot is an elaborate device that controls many aspects of aircraft flight i.e. heading, altitude, rate of climb and descent, airframe attitude, angle of attack and dynamic stability. The needs of BK are far more simple due to it's near vertical flight path that only requires Attitude stabilisation with a 2° down range tilt at 19,000ft and a means of correcting system bias, wind shears and gyro drift until engine thrust ceases at "All Burnt". The equipment to stabilise attitude and receive correction commands is termed the Flight Control System (FCS) and is carried within the rocket itself. The remaining equipment required to track flight path and issue trajectory corrections is termed the Guidance System (GS) and is ground based.

7.2 <u>Flight Control System (FCS)</u>: The system block diagram is shown in Fig A–18.
Is a constant attitude analogue system using Pitch, Yaw and Roll angular data from two fully gimballed displacement gyroscopes located in the Electronics Bay. Lateral gyro and guidance data is electronically combined and control law shaped before being applied to one of four servo amplifiers where Roll demand and thrust chamber angles are added. Each servo amplifier hydraulically adjusts its related thrust chamber angle until the summed inputs reach zero. The collective engine thrust vector that results, realigns the airframe to null the gyro and guidance errors, a process crudely likened to balancing an upright broomstick on the open palm of one hand and moving that hand laterally to keep the stick upright.

To limit costs the FCS hardware was adapted from an earlier thermionic incarnation and repackaged for tray mounting within the Electronics Bay. A clumsy power supply arrangement and total absence of servicing access made the system very difficult to work with. Gain and balance adjustment meant returning the entire tray to the laboratory where an errant subunit could be detached to insert a plug/socket splitter box – an almost unsustainable work cycle.

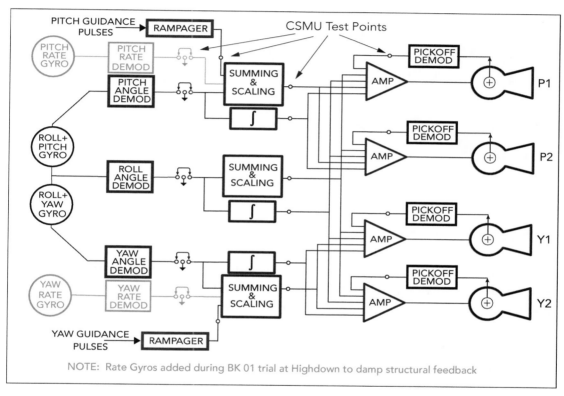

FIG A–18   FLIGHT CONTROL SYSTEM SCHMATIC   (D Mack)

During early trials, serious vibration problems were met when swinging thrust chamber reaction forces easily excited airframe bending and torsion modes, which were felt and by each gyro and fed forward to create three self-sustaining resonance loops. After considerable testing and analysis, the problem was corrected by electronically filtering the high frequency components and introducing lateral rate gyros to damp lateral bending elements that lay inside the FCS pass band.

From BK16 onwards the historic thermionic system was re-engineered using discrete semi conductor elements.

The RAE, EEL and RDD collaborated closely to improve in field servicing and minimise collateral disturbance of adjacent systems. Each subunit was removable at the vehicle; every trim pot was directly accessible at the vehicle and switching mode power supplies streamlined flight system hardware. The revised installation first flew on BK16 and gave a successful trouble free service thereafter.

FIG A-19 Two R&S 2 axis Gyros were flown on each Black Knight   (R&S)

7.3 <u>FCS Sense Testing</u>: The test is aimed at demonstrating the correct FCS control sense with respect to the Range firing line and is achieved by physically tilting/rolling the vehicle airframe through a small angle about the release ball with the FCS and servo hydraulic service active. Because the procedure entails removal of the Wind Brace and Anti Roll lugs, the upper clamp ring is fitted and the Gantry loading rollers are appropriately set to prevent gross airframe displacements.

With the "Flight Plug" fitted, observers are placed to confirm the following as the FCS is run up on with live hydraulics: –

PITCH Chamber exits swing UP RANGE as vehicle head is pitched DOWN RANGE.

YAW Chamber exits swing RIGHT Range as vehicle head is yawed LEFT RANGE.

ROLL Chamber exits move to OPPOSE a CLOCKWISE vehicle rotation, viewed from below.

7.4 <u>Tracking & Guidance System</u>: Flight path perturbations arising from shear winds; gyro drift and system bias were minimised with respect to a combination of optical and radar tracking methods devised by the RAE and manned by DH. A Pitch pilot and Yaw pilot located in EC5, observed rocket flight path error using tracking data pre-selected from the several options by their guidance data supervisor. Each pilot was equipped to send command radio correction pulses to his lateral FCS channel – the Pitch pilot inserted the 2° down range.

0 to 20,000ft tracking – Two ex gunnery optical sighting mounts placed some 3.5 miles Left Flank and Rear of the launch pad provide azimuth and elevation data to the EC5 guidance suite until the radar/telescope beams were entered.

19,000 to 350,000ft tracking – An ex military No3 Mk7, S band radar, with beam axis elevated at 90° x 88° down range, passed lateral displacement and range data to the EC5 guidance suite. To address any loss of radar data, a third pilot steering radar harmonised cross wire telescope aimed at the rocket engine flame, passed lateral data to the EC5 suit.

To aid tracking observations, all BA firings were restricted to dark moonless nights.

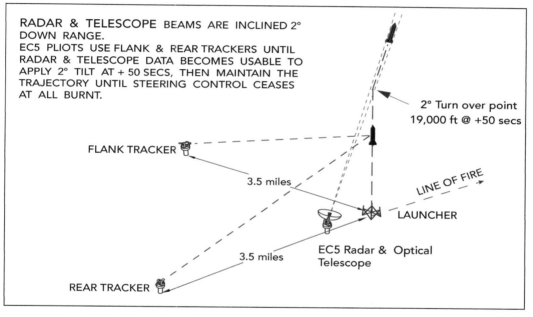

RADAR & TELESCOPE BEAMS ARE INCLINED 2° DOWN RANGE.
EC5 PLIOTS USE FLANK & REAR TRACKERS UNTIL RADAR & TELESCOPE DATA BECOMES USABLE TO APPLY 2° TILT AT + 50 SECS, THEN MAINTAIN THE TRAJECTORY UNTIL STEERING CONTROL CEASES AT ALL BURNT.

2° Turn over point
19,000 ft @ +50 secs

FLANK TRACKER

3.5 miles

LINE OF FIRE

LAUNCHER

EC5 Radar & Optical Telescope

3.5 miles

REAR TRACKER

FIG A–20 – BK GUIDANCE TRACKERS   *(D Mack)*

As engine thrust ends at All Burnt, flight path control ceases and Payload separation is initiated automatically by the rockets thrust sensing inertia switches. The spent rocket continues upwards along a ballistic path to apogee before its descent to impact. The Payload travels a similar path ahead of the rocket as an inbuilt orientation system aligns it for re-entry. To support the tracking and guidance task, an S band transponder beacon carried in one fin pod and two Command Link radios are sited in the Electronics Bay. The latter items also served as the duplicate Flight Termination links.

8 – FLIGHT SAFETY: WRE operate an independent mix of optical and electronic trackers that feed elevation and azimuth data to a central computer suite, to create real time rocket trajectory, velocity and a predicted walking impact plots overlaid on the Range "cut down" boundary map. Together with track perturbation data from the EC5 guidance suite, these displays allow a Flight Safety Officer (FSO) to adjudicate flight path safety. If necessary, he can initiate vehicle destruction via two mutually redundant radio paths to the rocket. The two guidance command link radios provide dual pathways that will shut down the rocket engine and destroy the airframe by diffusing a vigorous catalyst into the HTP tank.

9 - HAZARDOUS ELECTRIC SYSTEMS:

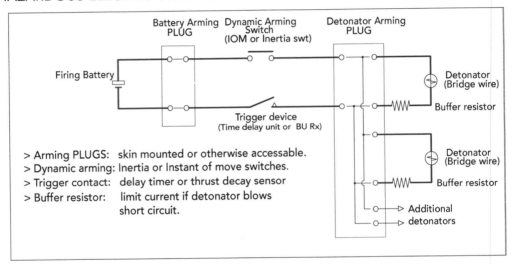

> Arming PLUGS: skin mounted or otherwise accessable.
> Dynamic arming: Inertia or Instant of move switches.
> Trigger contact: delay timer or thrust decay sensor
> Buffer resistor: limit current if detonator blows
          short circuit.

FIG A–21   BASIC ELEMENTS OF EVERY HAZ CIRCUIT   *(D Mack)*

9.1 <u>General</u>: Engine firing, Rocket release and in flight events activated by explosive materials or high pressure gases, are all electrically initiated by circuits rated as "Hazardous" to indicate they must meet specific RAE, WRE and SR design and certification requirements. Two general conventions apply; those circuits residing within the rocket itself are termed "Hazardous Circuits" and those located within a permanent ground installation are termed as "Firing Circuits". Both types must be robust, segregated from general circuitry and embody the same safety checking and intercepts facilities outlined in Fig A–21. While engineering detail will depend on each application, the former "Hazardous Circuits" category must include a dynamic arming element to protect personnel who by definition must be physically close to the hazardous device at arming time.

The "Firing Circuits" where arming facilities are physically remote from the hazardous source, omit the dynamic intercept. Early BK Haz circuits' involved four functions: HTP Tank pressurisation, Engine start and stop, Head separation and Flight Termination. The basic elements in every Haz circuit and their functions are:

- Battery Arming – Isolation/arming + trigger & dynamic arming open tests.
- Detonator Arming – Isolation/arming + no volt & bridge wire loop tests.
- Dynamic Arming – BU arms at I of M, other circuits are armed at > 5g.
- Trigger –Thrust decay sensor, time delay device and flight termination command.

Ground Firing Circuits include Tank pressuring, Engine start/stop Launch release facilities, all of which must embody the same principles applied above but the arming functions are usually replaced by lockable "Safety Bar" switches under Safety Officer jurisdiction. The AOO5 at Area5 also controls a release jack "Safety Bar" to differentiate between Static Firing/Live Firing conditions.

9.2 Inertia Switches: See Fig A–22 below.

BK used these devices to serve two functions: firstly to dynamically arm all non Flight Termination Haz circuits as rocket acceleration exceeded 5g, and secondly to detect engine All Burnt. The switches were developed by the RAE and boast a long established history of arming many research missiles. In basic form, a 20mm diameter thin walled brass cylinder, about 80mm long, is fill with a low viscosity damping oil and closed at each end by an electrically insulted terminal.

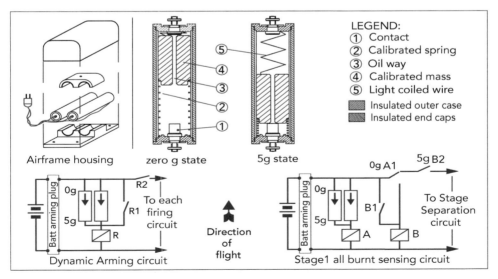

FIG A–22   INERTIA SWITCH & CIRCUIT DETAIL   (D Mack)

A centrally vented piston connects electrically with the top end terminal via a lightly coiled wire and is held against the top terminal by calibrated compression spring.

Under sustained acceleration, the piston compresses the calibrated spring until the bottom terminal is reached to close the circuit and arm the ordnance service. To detect end of engine burn the same type of switch is provided with additional relays to capture the pistons 5g point and its fall back towards 0g.

These "moving part" devices were frequently viewed with suspicion until duplicating each switch and mounting them in a dimensionally stable housing improved reliability.

9.3 <u>Explosive Bolts</u>: See Fig A–23 below. Used to detach airframe structural elements during flight. Each bolt has a weakened head end that is cut free by a single explosive detonator. From BK09 onwards reliability was upgraded by introducing double-ended bolts that housed cutting detonators above and below the structure separation line. The entire Haz circuit, Haz batteries, arming and initiation components were also duplicated above and below the separation line and isolated from each other so that operation of one detonator at each bolt assembly would effect structural separation.

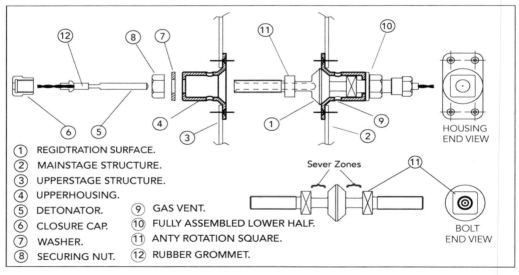

① REGIDTRATION SURFACE.			
② MAINSTAGE STRUCTURE.			
③ UPPERSTAGE STRUCTURE.			
④ UPPERHOUSING.			
⑤ DETONATOR.	⑨ GAS VENT.		
⑥ CLOSURE CAP.	⑩ FULLY ASSEMBLED LOWER HALF.		
⑦ WASHER.	⑪ ANTY ROTATION SQUARE.		
⑧ SECURING NUT.	⑫ RUBBER GROMMET.		

FIG A–23 DOUBLE EXPLOSIVE BOLT   (D Mack)

10 – FLIGHT INSTRUMENTATION:

This system was based on an ancient 465Mhz Telemetry package evolved by the Signals Research and Development Establishment (SRDE) around the late 1950's.

The Sender's 465Mhz transmitter is pulse modulated and multiplexed FM sub-carrier with a frequency range of 130 to 160Khz and frame sync at 180Khz.

The modulator accepts variable voltage or variable inductance inputs, via a motor driven 24-way mechanical multiplexer running at 40rpm with several channels sub-multiplexed by an unsynchronised ¼ frame speed switching unit.

With its long history came reliability but the system required green fingers to maximise RF power output. As I recall, frame sync preceded eight inductive engine pressures at frame speed, 12 FCS voltage signals at frame speed and 2 sub multiplexed housekeeping voltage inputs. Two sub-multiplexed voltage channel sampled propellant tank probes and engine bay temperatures.

1. The BK01 and 02 development firings carried three telemetry installations: -The primary sender sited in the Electronics Bay to deal with engine, FCS and house keeping allocated above.

2. A similar set up in the non-separating Head to monitor dynamics, accelerations, aero pressures and temperatures.

3. A special mini sender to capture engine vibration from several three tri axis accelerometers was located in one Fin Pod.

All later flights routinely carried the electronics bay 24-channel telemetry sender to log rocket system behaviour. The system proved reliable with just the occasional channel lost due to data source failures and one complete sender loss when a Head aerial was damaged at separation.

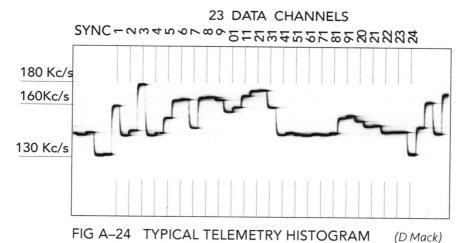

FIG A–24 TYPICAL TELEMETRY HISTOGRAM   (D Mack)

11 – PROPELLANT LOADING:

11.1 Acronyms:

T = Sea level thrust. Declared from test bed calibration firings.

L off G = Lift off acceleration= T divided by AUW (=not less than 1.23g).

AUW = Dry weight (DW) + Propellant weight (PW)

DW = Airframe dead weight including all non-propellant liquids, batteries, ordnance stores and the Payload. The base measurement done at High Down before shipment to Woomera where trials procedures bring it up to lift off value.

PW = AUW – DW.

MR = Mixture ratio = 8.2. Nominal ratio is 8.2 lbs of HTP for every 1 lb of fuel. Catalyst degradation, mixing efficiency, and ambient pressure variation all move actual value towards weaker ratios. Therefore some OISC's sought to adjust for these effects.

KERO LOAD= Equals PW divided by MR+1.

HTP LOAD= Equals Kerosene weight times MR.

*The BK launcher was not instrumented to measure weight; therefore propellant weights were converted to volumetric measure (gallons or litres) using temperature and density data. Tank filling was then done using calibrated sight glasses.

11.2 <u>Tank Filling Accuracy</u>: While accuracy of all above factors was important, experience indicated that in flight MR and tank volumes were the main error sources. Each Gamma 201 was four individual engines with fixed orifice flow regulation all blind to ambient pressure and catalyst variations meant MR during flight was a gamble.

The primary target of reaching maximum velocity occurs when dry weight (DW) is achieved at "All Burnt", meaning the improbability of both propellants depleting together. However, peroxide engines do offer a compromise approach; by marginally under-filling kerosene, the minimum "All Burnt" weight is achieved at the cost of a marginal loss of thrust as the residue HTP cold runs to exhaustion. This ploy became the norm until erratic thrust tail off behaviour caused Payload collisions; so filling bias was reversed to examine hot shutdowns. OISC's continued to struggle with the tail off and MR problems by juggling the filling bias, which remained largely unresolved until the Gamma 301 engine arrived with its active mixture ratio and thrust controls.

11.3 <u>Sight Glass Calibration</u>: Accuracy issues with tank volume calibrations persisted at High Down until swept volume metering pumps with better than 1% accuracy were adopted from the petroleum retail industry.

12 - SHORE-SIDE ELECTRICAL INTERFACES:

To run many system tests, pre-firing checkouts and countdown sequences, 24vdc shore-side supplies and monitor services are routed via an umbilical cable connected to the Electronics Bay near the top of the rocket. Prior to –40secs before launch, all vehicle electronic systems are fed from shore side via the Umbilical route.

At −40secs these systems are switched over to run on rechargeable silver zinc battery packs in the Electronics Bay before the Umbilical cable is ejected at -8secs.

To avoid incidental interruption, the shore-side supplies are derived from float charged lead acid batteries. Critical and executive firing circuits and switching functions that must remain connected until liftoff were routed via rip connectors sited between engine bay and launcher.

13 – FIRING COUNTDOWN:

The Static and Launch firing sequences are almost identical as shown in Table A/2. Two distinct timing phases are involved, an initial period from −20 minutes to -2min embraces manual actions carried out by Equipment Centre team and Range Authority positions, during which moderate time "holds" are allowed.

The second Auto sequence phase from −2min does not allow any "holds", only Stop Actions, which due to one-shot actions that incur recycle actions at the launch pad abort the run. Each Auto sequence event can only execute if its preceding event has succeeded. All events after time zero are engine driven i.e. correct hydraulic pressure; zero chamber angles and acceptable combustion pressures combine to eject the start hose, which opens the release jack.

While using a similar event chain to initiate release, 301 vehicles sit on a retracting release jack that requires engine thrust to be fully established before +4secs when the release jack is armed to open.

TABLE A/2 - BK Static & Launch Firing Countdown

- BK Static & Launch Countdown Timings			
Manually applied Events:	Time ON		Applicability
Switch ON S Band Pre-heat	−20 min	−	√
Switch ON FCS LT	−15 min	−	√
Switch ON Telemetry	−15 min	−	√
Switch ON FCS HT	−12 min	−	√ Pre BK16 standard
Switch on Payload system	-12 min	−	√
Switch ON Extra Services	−10 min	−	√
Close all Readiness switches	−	−	√
Start Auto Sequencer	−2 min	−	√
Automatic applied Events:	Time ON	Time OFF	
Start Recorder sub sequencer	−119 sec	−116 sec	HD only
Pressurise Ground Start tank	−119 sec	+35 sec	√ Reset by Stop Action
Pressurise Rocket HTP tank	−119 sec	− 113 sec	√ Reset by Stop Action
Run internal battery power	−40 sec	−38 sec	HD S&S or Woom S&S&Launch only
Start Duct cooling water	−20 sec	−15 sec	√
Run EC5 recorders	−20 sec	+60 sec	Woomera Static only
Un-cage Gyros	−10 sec	−8 sec	√
Pressurise Gearbox Oil	−8 sec	+10 sec	Gamma 301 only
Start N2 purge	−8 sec	−6 sec	√
Eject Umbilical Plug	−8 sec	−6 sec	HD S&S or Woom S&S&Launch only
Hold open Engine start valve	−4 sec	+35 sec	Statics only (see * below)
Pulse open Engine start valve	−4 sec	−2 sec	Launch only
Apply Ground Start HTP	0	+4 sec	√
Arm release jack	+4 sec	+8 sec	Launch only
Run FCS signal unit(CSSU)	0	+16 sec	Statics only
Auto Stop Action	+10 secs	+12 sec	Launch only
Unlatch Engine start valve	+35 sec	+40 sec	Statics only, Eng battery needed
Stop internal battery power	+45 sec	+50 sec	HD S&S or Woom S&S&Launch only
Stip Duct cooling water	+45 sec	+50 sec	√
Stop N2 purge	+45 sec	+50 sec	√
Consequent Events:	Nominal	Times	
Hydraulic press switch Closes	+1.5 sec	+8 sec	√
Chamber Angle switches Close	+1.5 sec	+8 sec	√
Chamber pressure switches Cld	+1.5 sec	+8 sec	√
Release jack opens (& retracts)	+4 sec	+8 sec	Launch only

* Gamma 201 engines: "Flight Nut" is omitted to prevent latch up
* Gamma 301 engines: External gas line negates latchup. Backup for gas failure uses
  intermal Flight Termination circuit and Haz battery

14 PREPARATION & CHECKOUT:

Each rocket is subjected to two checkout phases: An integration and qualification at High Down, followed by assembly checkout and launch preparation at Woomera.

Both phases followed similar patterns using similar test equipment, procedures and interfaces, the only difference being one of emphasis, test objective and final outcome. Both sites have laboratories dedicated to subassembly testing, calibration and preparation; the UK launch pad and ground system installations replicate those at Woomera in all essential interface detail excepting an active release jack and removable service tower.

TABLE A/3   TRIALS tasks at HIGH DOWN & WOOMERA

INITIAL PREP OF VEHICLE SUB SYSTEMS:		HD	TS2	STATIC FIRING:		HD	Area5
1	Bench test all sub assemblies.	√	√	27	Load Kerosene tank.	Site1/2	√
2	Elect & Mech inspections.	√	√	28	Charge Tank gas bottles.	√	√
3	Haz circuit certification tests.	√	√	29	Flow chk gearbox lub & refill.	√	√
4	Calib't chamber angle sensors.	√	√	30	Prep hydraulics pre engine run.	√	√
5	Pad inductive press rest levels.	√	√	31	Load HTP tanks & wash down.	√	√
6	Calib't Tank & E'Bay vent valves.	√	√	32	Chk Tether & Close check list.	√	√
CHECK OF PROPELLANT SYSTEM:		Site1/2	5A/B	33	Prime exhaust cooling water.	√	√
7	Erect on launcher test stand.	√	√	34	Clear test site.	√	√
8	Cal HTP tank SG & LS volume.	√	—	35	Enter Static Firing Sequence.	√	√
9	Function HTP tank press system.	√	√	36	Drain HTP and examin records.	√	√
10	Cal Kero SG & sump volume.	√	—	37	Dryout Engine.	√	√
CHECKOUT OF ELECTRONIC SYSTEMS:		Site1/2	5A/B	RFI & POST IOM EVENT TESTS:		Site1/2	5A/B
11	Fit & test FCS electronic pack.	√	√	38	Remove Payload & fit int batts.	√	√
12	Test inner loop freq responses.	√	√	39	Refit Payload.	√	√
13	Test FCS stability margin.	√	√	40	Fit & run int system batterys.	√	√
14	Overall FCS sense test.	√	√	41	Install & arm Haz batteries.	√	√
15	Test Tele Txs, C'link & S Band.	√	√	42	Connect & arm det "puffers".	√	√
16	Fit & function chk Payload.	√	√	43	Run & monitor Flight Seq.	√	√
PREP FOR STATIC FIRING:		Site1/2	5A/B	44	Dis shore links ex Rip & Umb'l.	√	√
17	Test Eng start &N2 purge systems.	√	√	45	Run EMC sysyems test.	√	√
18	Cal Engine ground instrument'n.	√	√	46	Test Payload release circuit.	√	√
19	Run FCS demand signals (CSSU).	√	√	PRE SHIPPING TASKS:		P'Area	TS2
20	Check & seal EC Sequence unit.	√	√	47	Acceptance review panel.	√	—
21	Check & seal EC O'ride switches.	√	√	48	Remove Payload & Elect units.	√	—
22	Charge Tank gas bottles.	√	√	49	Return airframe to Prep Area.	√	—
23	Flow chk gearbox lub & refill.	√	√	50	Inventry, bal and weight test.	√	—
24	Fill Eng start tank with demin.	√	√	51	Inhibit Mech systems.	√	—
25	Complete pre S&S check lists.	√	√	52	QA audit and crate up.	√	—
26	Do System & Sequence test.	√	√				

TABLE A/3 (Cont'd)

LIVE FIRING PREPARATION:	AREA5	LIVE FIRING PREP (Cont'd)	AREA5
53 Fit Payload Haz batts & Explosives.	√	64 Spot chk system int batteries	√
54 Refit Payload.	√	65 Complete Rocket Final check lis	√
55 Check & seal EC Sequence unit.	√	66 Close Electronics Bay & Press ch	√
56 Check & seal EC O'ride switches.	√	67 Remove Gantry for RFI tests	√
57 Fit & run int system batterys.	√	68 Run Tele/Mike3 record test.	√
58 Install & arm Haz batteries.	√	69 Conduct Range RFI test	√
59 Fit Payload Sep'tion detonators.	√	70 Replace Gantry	√
60 Chk Eng start and N2 purge systs.	√	71 Do System & Sequence test.	√
61 Load Kerosene.	√	72 Drain start tank & vet S&S result	√
62 Charge Tank gas bottles.	√	73 Load Kerosene tank	√
63 Fill Eng start tank with water.	√		√
LIVE FIRING:	AREA5	LIVE FIRING (Cont'd)	AREA5
74 Charge Tank gas bottles.	√	79 End checklist, pull R'Jack pin.	√
75 Prep flight prep hydraulics.	√	80 Arm Breakup system	√
76 Flow chk gearbox lub & refill	√	81 Remove Gantry	√
77 Load HTP tanks & wash down.	√	82 Clear Pad for Launch sequence	√
78 Fit Breakup charges	√		√

At the UK venue, each rocket undergoes system calibrations, an engine firing, a Flight Sequence test, mutual EMC compatibility survey, RFI assessment and mass balancing. At Woomera, system functional checks precede a further static firing to confirm integrity before installation of the flight Test Body, internal batteries and the ordnance stores.

A full pre launch dress rehearsal with Range authority participation must be successfully concluded before propellants are loaded, flight ordinance circuits are armed and the released jack keeper pin is removed prior to entering the live launch countdown sequence. Each task in Table A/3 above heads a group of subsidiary procedures not shown for clarity.

15 –THRUST HARVESTING:

The original single chamber Gamma rocket engine was designed for low altitude operation and never optimised for the BK sea level to near vacuo envelope. Rocket engines exploit Newton's First and Second Laws by accelerating and expelling gas molecules in a constrained direction to impart motion. However, as gas leaves the combustion chamber it expands until its internal pressure equalises with the local ambient field.

To harvest maximum thrust, the designer fashions a divergent expansion nozzle sized to maintain nozzle contact with the expanding gas envelope for as long as is practical to prolong energy exchange between the departing gas and the rocket airframe.

In doing this, a compromise must be struck between thrust gained versus nozzle size and weight, which means the optimum pressure match will usually occur at an intermediate altitude.

Beyond this point the unconstrained gas leaving the nozzle grows towards an infinite balloon as it seeks balance with the surrounding near zero pressure field.

To address this design problem, large exotic bell shaped and plug nozzles have been created for those projects that can support such sophistication.

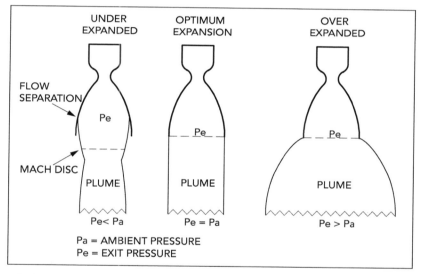

FIG A–25.   NOZZLE EXPANSION REGIMES   (D Mack)

To explore a low cost alternative means of improving better thrust levels, BK07 and BK13 were equipped with installations aimed at testing the effect of partially constraining the ballooning efflux from all four engines as it left the confinement of each combustion chamber exit plane.

The sliding skirt installation on both vehicles was shown to function reliably and did produce a "release" signal via telemetry during engine burn but I've been unable to unearth a report on its in flight behaviour. I'd be surprised if these flimsy structures did survive very long as they descended into the inferno but at least the longitudinal accelerometer should have experienced a tiny blip of the event.

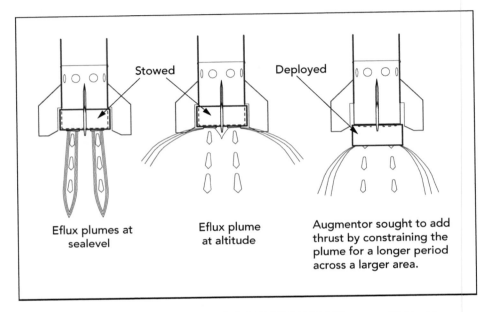

FIG A–26. THRUST AUGMENTOR EXPERIMANT   *(D Mack)*

BLACK ARROW DETAILS | B

1	INTRO	9	PROPULSION
2	PERFORMANCE	10	FLIGHT CONTROL
3	AIRFRAME	11	HAZ SYSTEMS
4	TETHER & EFFLUX	12	FLIGHT SAFETY
5	STAGE3 & SSB	13	PROPELLANT LOADING
6	STAGE SEP SEQUENCES	14	SHORE-SIDE SUPPLIES
7	PAYLOAD FAIRINGS	15	TELEMETRY
8	SPIN TABLE & MAN CLAMP	16	CHECKOUT & COUNT DOWNS

<u>1 – INTRO</u> – Black Arrow was founded on the philosophy, technology and simple engineering methods proven over 22 largely successful Black Knight flights – where simplicity and cost effectiveness ruled. Studies inferred a cost effective solution for a small satellite carrier was a three-stage adaptation of BK with two reconfigured Gamma engines and a bespoke solid propellant third stage motor as outlined below. The vehicle would require a precise autonomous guidance system to overfly sovereign territories also detailed below. Furthermore, the solution would make best use of existing facilities at High Down and Area5 at Woomera.

Treasury constraints cut design proving program from six to four flights and progress fell to a crawl when three monthly holding contracts were imposed. Trickle funding hindered engine development and test site conversion to a point where Saunders Roe and Armstrong Siddley Motors toyed with idea of offering a bridging loan until events took hold due to an engine detonation that wrecked the Ansty test cell and some time later the maiden flight (R0) was terminated soon after lift off. A reworked R1 successfully replace the R0 role but the orbital demo by R2 fell short due loss of Stage 2 HTP tank pressure. Finally despite all ills, R3 expertly placed the Prospero satellite into earth orbit on 28th October 1971 – An event eclipsed by HMG's ill timed scrapping of the BA program along with the UK's entire rocket development industry, possibly to placate ruffled feathers across the channel!

2 – PERFORMANCE –

TABLE B/1

ID	FIRED	OBJECT	PAYLOAD	Stage3	L of Fire	Results
R0	28-Jun-69	Type proving	X0 instrument'd	Inert	West	Terminated early due to a steering servo fault.
R1	04-Mar-70	Type proving	X1 instrument'd	Inert	West	R0 repeat; all stagesworked well, + one fairing hang up.
R2	02-Sep-70	Type proving	X2 instrument'd	Live	5° E of N	Stage2 short burn, tank pressure loss +one fairing hangup.
R3	28-Oct-71	Orbit injection	X3 Prespero satellite	Live	5° E of N	557 x 1598 km at 82° Orbit achieved.

TABLE B/2

Stage1 (lbs)	AUW	Structure	Systems	HTP	Kero	BLACK ARROW WEIGHT BUDGET	
	31090	761	1594	25613	3122		
Stage2 (lbs)						**Interstage	*P'load Fairings
	7935	302	758	5813	709	213	140
Stage3 (lbs)						Propellant	Payload
	975	85.5	26.5	–	–	701	162
Lift off (lbs)	40000						
Thrust (lbs)	50000	** Disgarded at Gamma2 ignition					
Lift off G	0.25	* Disgarded during Gamma2 burn at +180ses					

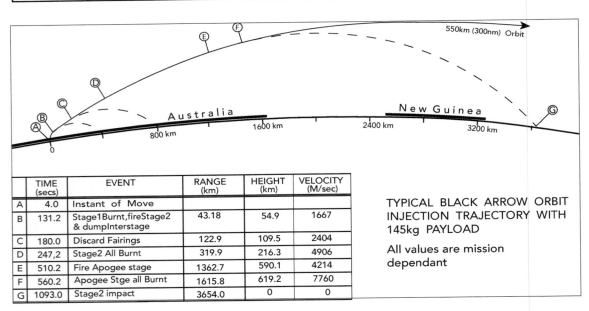

	TIME (secs)	EVENT	RANGE (km)	HEIGHT (km)	VELOCITY (M/sec)
A	4.0	Instant of Move			
B	131.2	Stage1Burnt,fireStage2 & dumpInterstage	43.18	54.9	1667
C	180.0	Discard Fairings	122.9	109.5	2404
D	247,2	Stage2 All Burnt	319.9	216.3	4906
E	510.2	Fire Apogee stage	1362.7	590.1	4214
F	560.2	Apogee Stge all Burnt	1615.8	619.2	7760
G	1093.0	Stage2 impact	3654.0	0	0

TYPICAL BLACK ARROW ORBIT INJECTION TRAJECTORY WITH 145kg PAYLOAD

All values are mission dependant

FIG B–1   BA NORTHERLY TRAJECTORY   *From RAE 69068 (Crown copyright)*

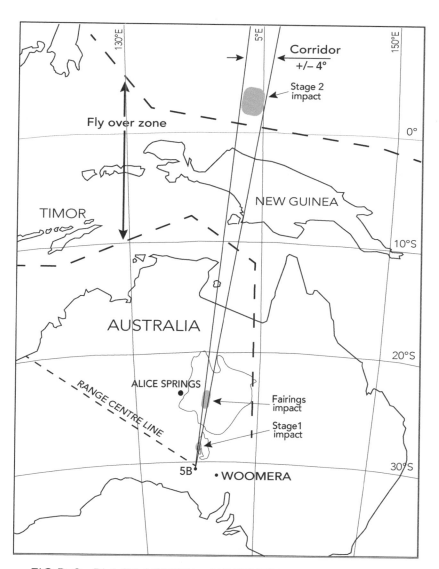

FIG B–2 BLACK ARROW – NORTHERLY CORRIDOR
(Crown copyright)

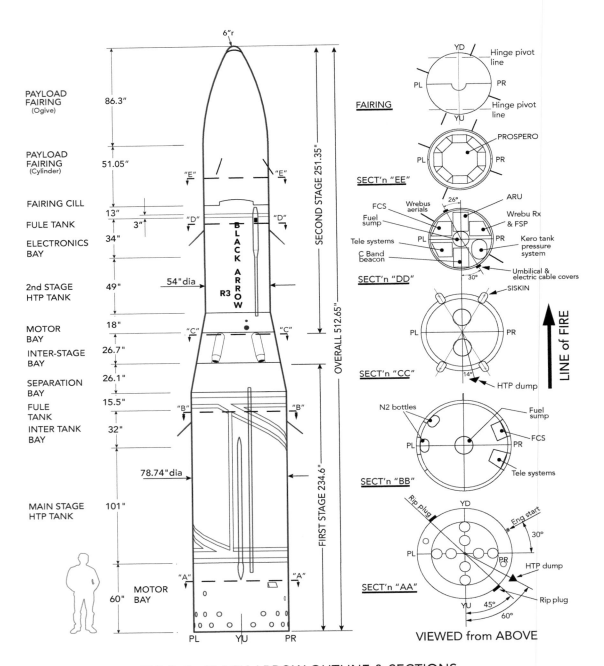

FIG B–3 BLACK ARROW OUTLINE & SECTIONS
From RAE 69068 (Crown copyright)

<u>3 – AIRFRAME STRUCTURE –</u>

The general arrangement and dimensions are as given in Figs B–3 above and B–4 below. Structural principles and detail as pioneered on BK, using traditional aircraft fabrication methods of the time coupled with a specially devised tank electric seam welding technique were applied throughout.

By using existing BK launcher foundations the engine bay diameter was limited to 2M and Stage1 nozzle efflux was squeezed into the Gamma 301 exhaust duct.

Optimised engine performance predictions and staging masses gave burn times of Stage1: 131secs, Stage2: 116 secs, Stage3: 40 secs.

3.1 <u>Stage1: Airframe proportions</u> –

- 131secs burn time required a 101" tall HTP tank and 5.5" tall Kero tank.
- The 60" high Motor Bay and Skirt required to house engine machinery.
- The 32" high Inter Tank Bay enveloped two hemispherical tank ends, a kerosene sump, the HTP tank pressurising gear and all Stage1 electronic systems.
- The 26.7" Separation Bay part of Stage2 conic transition for Gamma2 engine.
- The overall stage height was 234.62".

3.2 <u>Stage2: Airframe proportions</u> –

- A conic transition from Stage1 to 2 is defined by the relative tank diameters and the Gamma2 engine height. It totals 70.8" and divides into Stage1 Separation Bay, Stage2 Interstage Bay and Stage2 Motor Bay.
- Interstage Bay height is 26.12" to embrace the four Siskin separation thrusters.
- The Motor Bay is 18" to provide an annular diffusion beam to the HTP tank.
- The 54" tank diameter derives from an earlier stand alone BK updating study.
- An Engine burn time of 116secs defines propellant tank heights of 49" and 3".
- The 34" Electronics Bay embraces two hemispherical tank ends, tank pressurising gear and all Stage2 electronic units.
- Spin Table & Support structure is set at 39" high to embrace the Waxwing expansion nozzle
- Payload Fairings 149" to fully enclose Stage3 and form a low drag aero profile.

3.3 <u>Stage3: Airframe proportions</u> –

- Stage3 Apogee motor adds **11.86"
- Satellite Separation Bay **12.5"
- Max satellite volume 9.4 cubic feet.

** These dimensions do not add to the vehicles overall height.

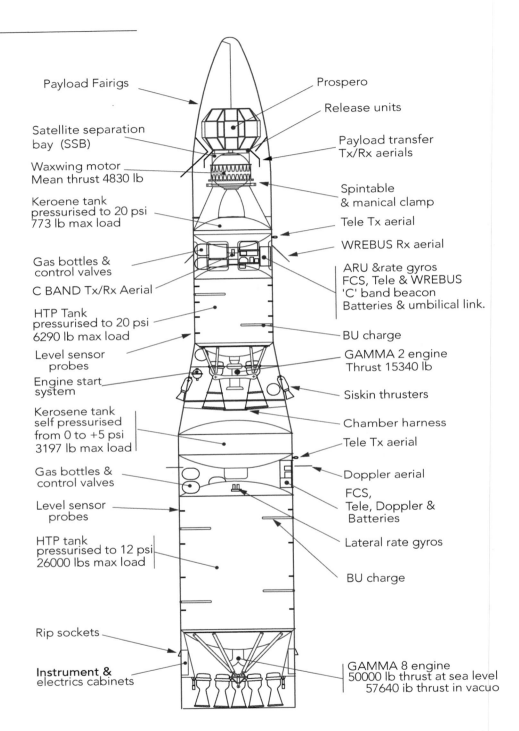

Payload Fairigs

Satellite separation
bay (SSB)

Waxwing motor
Mean thrust 4830 lb

Keroene tank
pressurised to 20 psi
773 lb max load

Gas bottles &
control valves

C BAND Tx/Rx Aerial

HTP Tank
pressurised to 20 psi
6290 lb max load

Level sensor
probes

Engine start
system

Kerosene tank
self pressurised
from 0 to +5 psi
3197 lb max load

Gas bottles &
control valves

Level sensor
probes

HTP tank
pressurised to 12 psi
26000 lbs max load

Rip sockets

Instrument &
electrics cabinets

Prospero

Release units

Payload transfer
Tx/Rx aerials

Spintable
& manical clamp

Tele Tx aerial

WREBUS Rx aerial

ARU &rate gyros
FCS, Tele & WREBUS
'C' band beacon
Batteries & umbilical link.

BU charge

GAMMA 2 engine
Thrust 15340 lb

Siskin thrusters

Chamber harness

Tele Tx aerial

Doppler aerial

FCS,
Tele, Doppler &
Batteries

Lateral rate gyros

BU charge

GAMMA 8 engine
50000 lb thrust at sea level
57640 ib thrust in vacuo

FIG B–4   BLACK ARROW INTERIOR *From RAE 69068 (Crown copyright)*

3.4 <u>Propellant Tanks</u> – All propellant storage tanks were directly scaled up from or styled on the BK tank structure. Propellant bulk loads and imposed loads were carried through 20swg aluminium alloy walls and semi hemispherical ends, terminating at machined joint rings, which formed load diffusion junctions with inter tank bays. Frequent internal hoop frames plus internal pressurisation provided to limit engine pump cavitation provided wall stiffness.

Manufacture tooling and seam welding plant were upgraded to suit the larger geometry and all tanks were fitted with anti slosh and anti vortex baffling as appropriate. A typical tank cross-section schematic is shown in Fig B–5 above.

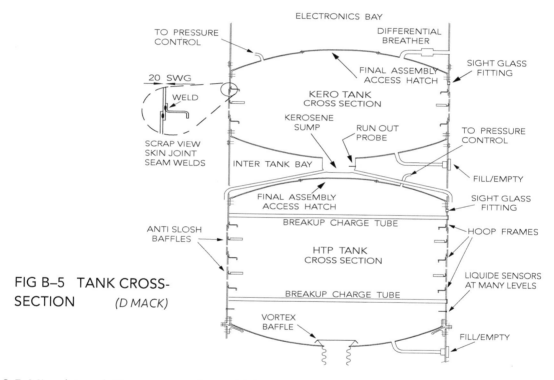

FIG B–5 TANK CROSS-
SECTION   (D MACK)

3.5 <u>Mixed Load Structures</u> – Stage1&2 Motor Bays, Stage1 Separation Bay and the Payload Fairing support structure were all configured to handle mixed line and diffused loads. Each stressed skin assembly was configured as an annular diffusion beam with local skin doubling and stringers to resist localised buckling.

By such means, distributed loads prevailing at propellant tanks were merged with local line load paths at explosive bolts and similar concentration points.

As an example, the two-meter diameter fabricated stressed skin shell enclosing the Gamma8 engine is designed to deal with mixed loads as follows.

1. A deep webbed machined ring is riveted to the top rim where substantial outer skin doubling and the bolted on HTP tank base ring all combine to form an annular load diffusion beam. Beam stiffness maps the HTP tank distributed loads with the line load pathways at eight tubular steel struts sloping down to terminate at a central light alloy forging near the base of the bay structure.
2. Inner trunnion thrust loads react directly with the central light alloy forging.
3. Outer trunnion thrust loads pass to the upper deep webbed joint ring via four reinforced box sections inside the outer shell skinning, and reach the central light alloy forging via the eight steel struts.
4. All dead and live loads developed at the central light alloy forging are grounded via a single ball ended spigot constrained by the Launcher release jack.
5. Two diametrically opposing fork fittings at the base of the outer shell, engage with short vertical lugs on the launcher frame to react torsion forces.
6. Spherical sockets located at fore quadrant points around the top deep webbed machined ring engage with four wind brace arms on the launcher to react topple loads.

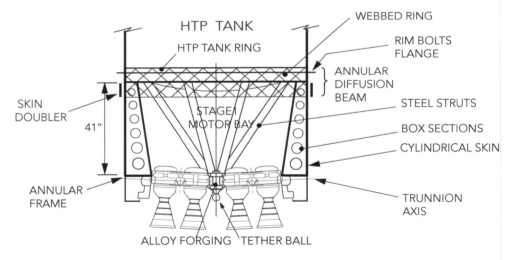

FIG B–6 BA MOTOR BAY– STRUCTURAL OUTLINE   (D MACK)

4 –<u>TETHER & EFFLUX DUCT</u> – The constraining interfaces between vehicle and launcher are similar to that used on BK. (See Figs A–4 through 7 of Appendix A.

By confining each Gamma8 thrust chamber inside a 56″ diameter central zone it proved possible to retain the BK exhaust duct and avoid expensive ground works. The tight chamber grouping and high trunnion axis (introduced with Gamma 301) enforced continued use of a retracting release jack to ensure acceptable liftoff clearances. Figure B–6 below outlines the BA relationship with the launcher structure and the efflux blast duct. The azimuth ring beam frame provides a means of bridging the exhaust duct gully when firing on alternative lines of fire.

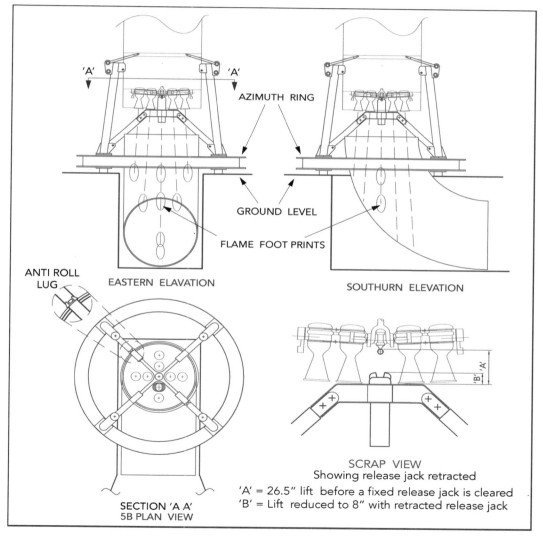

FIG B–7   GAMMA 8 – EXHAUST DUCT & TETHERING   *(D MACK)*

5 – <u>STAGE3 & SSB UMBILICAL ARRANGEMENT</u> – Fig B–8 shows the spring-loaded SSB cable support arms introduced on R3 to avoid the R1/R2 Fairing ejection problems. Each arm was held against its SSB connector by a "cushioned shelf" inside the adjacent fairing. As each Fairing opened to eject at 40°, the arms were released to spring down and lock below the Spin Table rotation plane.

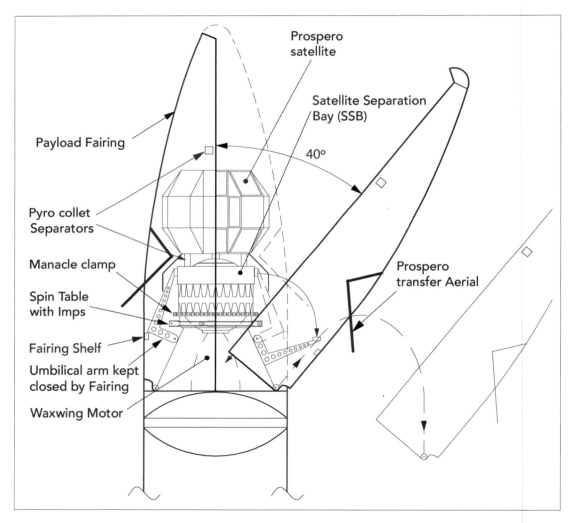

FIG B–8   STAGE3 – FAIRING & SSB UMBILICAL ACTION   (D MACK)

6 – STAGE SEPARATION SEQUENCES

6.1 **AT STAGE1 ALL BURNT**, Loss of Stage1 thrust starts FSP section2 to detach Stage2, initiate Gamma8 start up, begin pitch turn program and jettison the spent Interstage Bay. The FSP then selects WREBUS fail/fire, ejects Payload Fairings and reselects WREBUS fail/safe mode before arming FSP section 3.

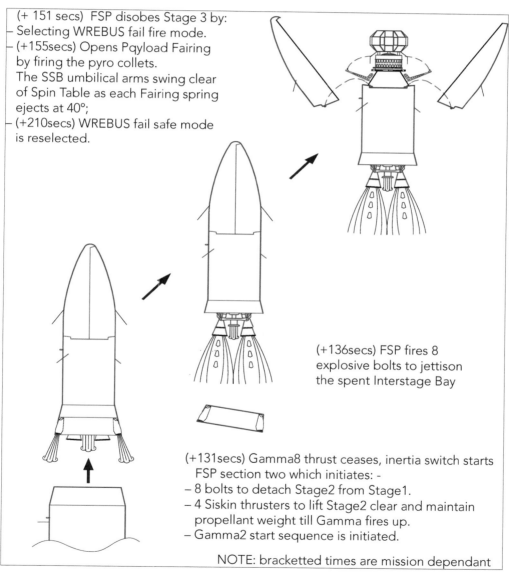

(+ 151 secs) FSP disobes Stage 3 by:
– Selecting WREBUS fail fire mode.
– (+155secs) Opens Payload Fairing by firing the pyro collets.
The SSB umbilical arms swing clear of Spin Table as each Fairing spring ejects at 40°;
– (+210secs) WREBUS fail safe mode is reselected.

(+136secs) FSP fires 8 explosive bolts to jettison the spent Interstage Bay

(+131secs) Gamma8 thrust ceases, inertia switch starts FSP section two which initiates: -
– 8 bolts to detach Stage2 from Stage1.
– 4 Siskin thrusters to lift Stage2 clear and maintain propellant weight till Gamma fires up.
– Gamma2 start sequence is initiated.

NOTE: bracketted times are mission dependant

FIG B–9 STAGE1/2 –SEPARATION SEQUENCES   *(D MACK)*

6.2   <u>AT STAGE2 ALL BURNT</u> – Loss of Stage2 thrust starts FSP section3, which initiates the ACS, continues pitch turn over, starts the SSB and Spin Table time delay relays to unlock and Spin up the Spin Table to 20 radians/sec then firing the Manacle Clamp to release Stage3. SSB delay timers ignite the Waxwing and releases Prospero into orbit.

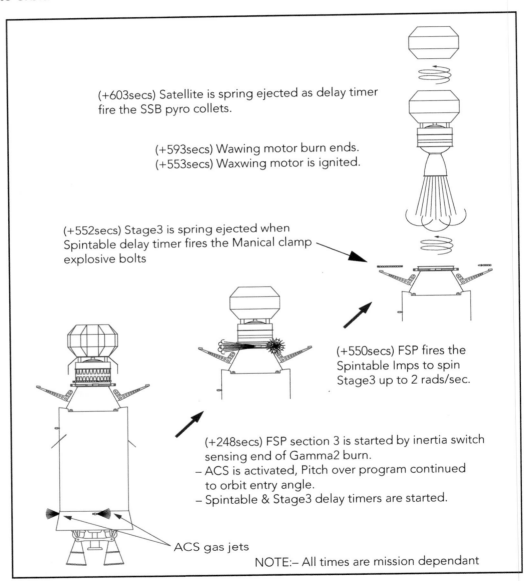

(+603secs) Satellite is spring ejected as delay timer fire the SSB pyro collets.

(+593secs) Wawing motor burn ends.
(+553secs) Waxwing motor is ignited.

(+552secs) Stage3 is spring ejected when Spintable delay timer fires the Manical clamp explosive bolts

(+550secs) FSP fires the Spintable Imps to spin Stage3 up to 2 rads/sec.

(+248secs) FSP section 3 is started by inertia switch sensing end of Gamma2 burn.
– ACS is activated, Pitch over program continued to orbit entry angle.
– Spintable & Stage3 delay timers are started.

ACS gas jets

NOTE:– All times are mission dependant

FIG B–10   STAGE3 – PLACES PROSPERO IN ORBIT   (D MACK)

7 – PAYLOAD FAIRINGS –

7.1 <u>Construction and Operation</u> – See Fig B–11 below. The stressed skinned structure was fabricated from magnesium alloy sheet and press formed framing. The cylindrical ogive form was split longitudinally to provide two identical clamshell halves, each with reinforced channel edge members that housed 5 tongue and fork pairs to maintain skin edge registration and lateral load integrity. One half fairing included a stainless steel nose cap and silicon rubber lip seals restricted air inflow through the vertical and nose cap joints. Each Fairing was secured to Stage2 by two unique hinges that broke apart when opened beyond 40°; an action that enabled powerful compression springs to eject each half Fairing clear. To form an integrated structure, both half Fairings were clamped against the other by debris free, pyro separation collet units sited two thirds up each side of their vertical split line. Each self-contained collet unit was linked to its opposite half partner via an externally inserted pin and tensioning turnbuckle. Each pair of linked pyro units formed a redundant chain to ensure Fairing release if one unit failed. As the pyro units fired, compression springs sited locally and at the foot of each split line, pushed each Fairing half apart towards the ejection 40°-ejection angle. During general handling, all springs were held compressed by keeper pins until removed prior the launch.

7.2 <u>Fairing Handling & Installation</u> – Magnesium alloy is light and strong but brittle and prone to local overload damage. Early handling trials at High Down established that a strong back frame was essential to protect each half fairing during general workshop handling, Gantry hoisting and Stage2 assembly operations.

During rocket vehicle preparation at 5B (and Site1) each fairing was hoisted to level 'F' and stored there until required. Before installation on Stage2, a Waxwing motor and SSB will usually have been set up on the Spin Table. Both umbilical arms must be raised and retained to the SSB by keeper pins red flagged to trail out via the fairing split joint.

To provide a sensitive "operator feel" while manoeuvring and attaching each half Fairing onto its Stage2 interface, a light hand operated two-drop pulley hoist was hung from the main Gantry hoist. This provided gentle hoist control as a technician at each side of the Fairing guided the hinge shanks into the Stage2 housings and secured them.

7.3 <u>Stage3 Final Arming</u> – To give LO5/RUXO access to Spin Table and Stage3 Haz circuits to service batteries and arm ordnance it was necessary to remove the Fairing link pins and partially open the DY fairing. During the re-closure process, both SSB umbilical keeper pins were extracted.

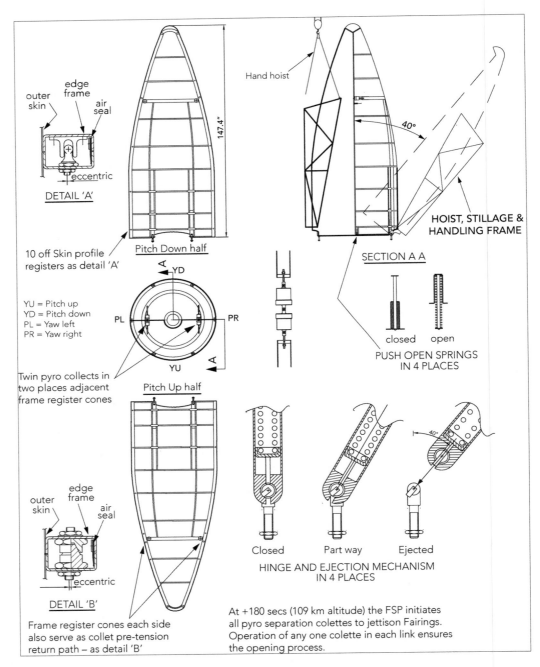

DETAIL 'A'

outer skin / edge frame / air seal / eccentric

10 off Skin profile registers as detail 'A'

YU = Pitch up
YD = Pitch down
PL = Yaw left
PR = Yaw right

Twin pyro collects in two places adjacent frame register cones

Pitch Down half

147.4"

Hand hoist

40°

HOIST, STILLAGE & HANDLING FRAME

SECTION A A

closed   open

PUSH OPEN SPRINGS IN 4 PLACES

A
YD
PL   PR
YU
A

Pitch Up half

DETAIL 'B'

outer skin / edge frame / air seal / eccentric

Frame register cones each side also serve as collet pre-tension return path – as detail 'B'

Closed   Part way   Ejected

40°

HINGE AND EJECTION MECHANISM IN 4 PLACES

At +180 secs (109 km altitude) the FSP initiates all pyro separation colettes to jettison Fairings. Operation of any one colette in each link ensures the opening process.

FIG B–11   BA PAYLOAD FAIRING – GENERL DTAILS   *(GKN Aerospace + D MACK)*

8 – <u>SPIN TABLE & MANACLE CLAMP</u> – The assembly is designed to:
1. Prevent table rotation until Stage3 spin up time.
2. Provide Stage3 with 20 radians per sec gyroscopic stability.
3. Detach and eject Stage3 away from Stage2 by splitting a three-segment Veeband clamp (Manacle Clamp) that activated 30 compression springs.

The fixed and rotating housings were machined from light alloy stock to suit interfaces and incorporate the four-wire ball bearing raceway as shown in Fig B–12

FSP Stage3 timing reaches the Spin Table and SSB delay relays via two spring-back trailing arms, pivoted below and sited at opposite sides of the Table as redundant pathways. Each arm aligned a miniature four-pin socket with a tangentially aligned mating plug slung beneath the Spin Table. When unlocked via a gas operated latch and spun up by the Imp thrusters, Table rotation pulled the connectors apart to let their trailing arms spring down clear of the rotating gizmo above. The FSP signals continued across the Waxwing Vee joint via Clamp split, which allows compression springs to push the Waxwing clear.

8.2 <u>The Manacle Clamp</u> – A Vee-band clamp is divided into three 120° segments and rejoined by single explosive bolts timed to initiate 5 secs after spin Imp ignition.

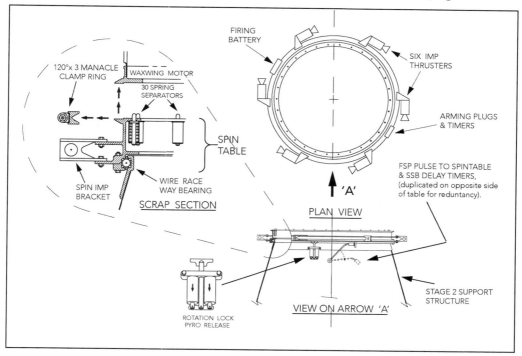

FIG B–12 SPIN TABLE + MANICAL CLAMP DETAIL   *(D MACK)*

9 – PROPULSION –

9.1 <u>Stage1– Gamma 8</u> – Leaving aside various engine and rocket concepts preceding the evolution of Black Arrow, Stage1 engine was derived directly from its BK Gamma 301 predecessor, to meet three basic criteria:

1. To provide a sea level thrust of 50,000lbs.
2. To exploit the flight proven Black Knight engine series.
3. To confine the Nozzle efflux footprint within existing BK exhaust ducts.

These requirements were met by combining two entire BK Gamma 301 style engines, each with two sets of thrust chambers paired on a common trunnion to provide vectored torque steering about the rockets pitch, yaw and roll axis – same, same BK.

Two 301 propellant handling systems were re-piped and re-disposed within the 2 metre diameter motor bay above the thrust chambers. The exit plane of all thrust chambers were kept within the 56" diameter boundary to satisfy the existing launcher efflux ducts, see Fig B–7 above. Each turbo-pump set and mixture ratio controller was arranged to feed four Pitch chambers and four Yaw chambers respectively and power kerosene hydraulic pumps for the steering servos. Start/Stop valve switching between "Static" and "Flight" modes retained the Gamma 301 method where a gas operated attachment is fitted for static firings only.

The new Gamma8 engine provided a lift off thrust of 50,000lb and an SI of 217sec with a minimum burn time of 125sec

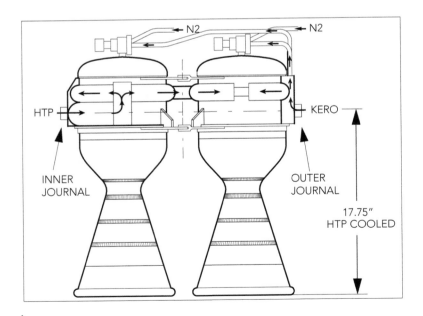

FIG B–13   GAMMA 8
GANGED CHAMBERS
(D MACK + RR)

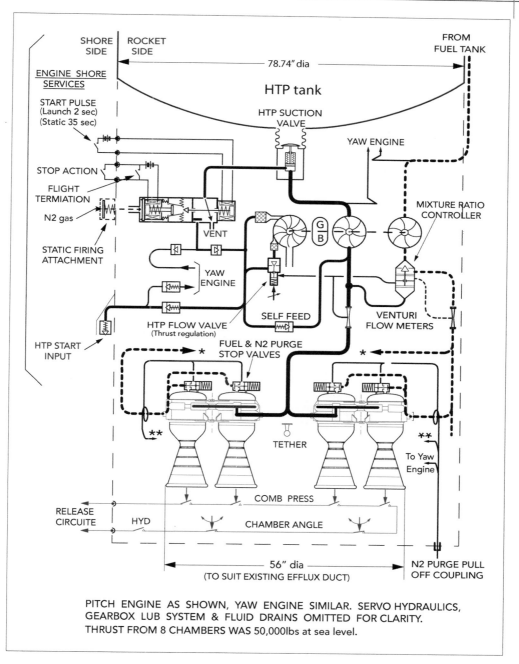

FIG B–14   GAMMA 8 ENGINE SCHEMATIC   (D MACK)

9.2 <u>Gamma 8 Nitrogen Purge & Start Systems</u> – The BK 301 purge system was up rated to twice the flow rate, and the BK 301 start tank system remained unchanged.

9.3 <u>Stage 2 – Gamma 2</u> – Two Gamma 301 thrust chambers were fully gimballed individually to provide roll, pitch and yaw thrust vector control. Kerosene cooled nozzle extensions were added to improve altitude efficiency by raising the expansion ratio to 350:1. The nozzle extensions moved chamber longitudinal CG to the throat area, which created the ideal location for the gimbal assembly. A new turbo pump propellant train was designed to feed both chambers; servo hydraulic power was derived from the kerosene fuel system via a dedicated gear pump and accumulator. The in vacuum thrust is 15350lb with an SI of 267 sec, burn time 110–120sec.

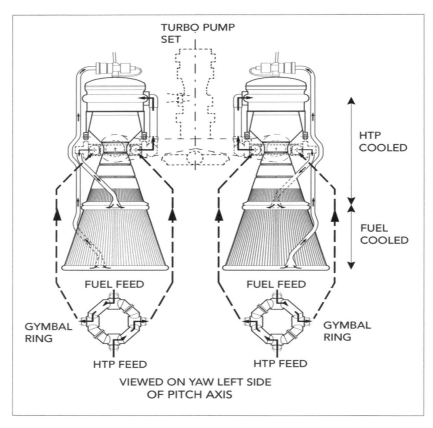

FIG B–15   GAMMA 2 GIMBALED THRUST CHAMBERS   *(D MACK + RR)*

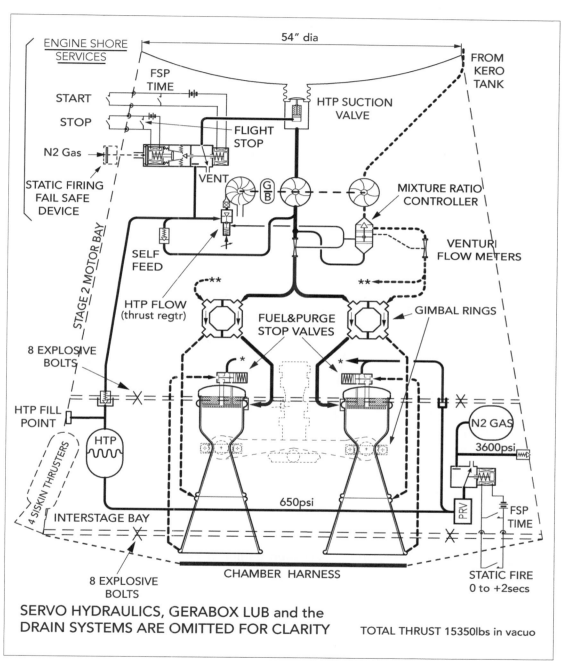

FIG B–16 GAMMA 2 SCHEMATIC (D MACK)

9.4 <u>Stage3 – Waxwing Motor</u> – A bespoke lightweight motor developed at RPE, Westcott and constructed by Bristol Aerojet for BA used a solid propellant formed inside a maraging steel lightweight casing and reinforced resin nozzle. The unit includes a head end cutter to terminate propulsion should it be necessary to terminate flight.

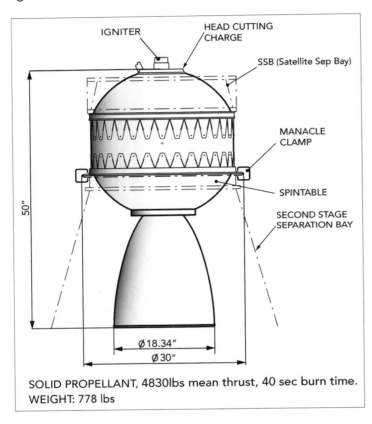

IGNITER

HEAD CUTTING
CHARGE

SSB (Satellite Sep Bay)

MANACLE
CLAMP

SPINTABLE

SECOND STAGE
SEPARATION BAY

50"

Ø18.34"
Ø30"

SOLID PROPELLANT, 4830lbs mean thrust, 40 sec burn time.
WEIGHT: 778 lbs

FIG B–17 STAGE3 –
WAXWING OBITAL KICK
MOTOR
(Crown copyright)

10 - <u>FLIGHT PATH CONTROL:</u> – As seen earlier in Figs B–1 and B–2 the vehicle will travel significant distances overflying sovereign territories, which mandates for an autonomous dead reckoning guidance plan having a pointing accuracy better than 0.2° at Stage3 ignition. Ferranti of Edinburgh came up trumps with a high accuracy Inertial Measurement Unit (IMU) configured as a stable table. Black Knight steering servos were readily adapted and RAE sourced a gas jet ACS system for the long coasting period up to Stage3 separation.

The Flight Control System (FCS) as set out in Fig A–18 below divides into seven packages:

    a. Attitude Reference Unit (ARU)
    b. Stage1 Electronics Pack.
    c. Stage2 Electronics Pack.
    d. Stage1 Thrust Chamber servos.
    e. Stage2 Thrust Chamber servos.
    f. Stage2 Attitude control system (ACS)

10.1a <u>ARU Hardware</u> – Three airborne units located in Stage2 Electronis Bay comprised:

– An Electronics Unit (EU) providing power supplies and servo electronics.
– Atitude Reference Unit (ARU) housing the stable platform.
– Synchro-bias Unit (SU) to convert synchro three phase to FCS two phase.

Ground equipment included:

– Switch On Unit (SOU) and an Alignment Unit (AU) in Equipment Centres and Labs.
– Accurately surveyed rigid test plinth for acceptance testing in each Test Lab.

10.1b <u>The ARU Cluster</u> – Fig B–19 below illustrates the essential features of a four-gimbal stable platform but does little to convey the extreme mechanical complexity. A triad of accelerometer/gyroscope pairs are mounted orthogonally within a hermetically sealed gas filled canister, which also forms the Pitch axis gimbal. Cut away hemispherical shells sized to fit concentrically over each other much like Russian dolls, form each successive gimbal. The inner Roll gimbal is shoe horned in between Pitch and Yaw gimbals has a limited rotation of ±11° that slave drives the outer Roll gimbal via a powerful quick response servo to restore 360° aerobatic freedom and prevent gimbal lock. Platform rotation and direction is sensed by three single degree of freedom gyros and three force feedback accelerometers respectively. Each gyro senses a single axis (around which it can be torque precessed) to which a dedicated gimbal is servo slaved. Each accelerometer is exclusively aligned to one gyro to measure rate changes (and 'g' values) acting along that gyros sensing axis.

Unlike full Inertial Navigators where the accelerometers play the lead role throughout, the ARU only employs them to hold the cluster level while applying Earth de-spin torques to each gyro during ground-based calibration and alignment activities. Forty seconds before liftoff, levelling and alignment is stopped to revert ARU loyalty back to the Star frame where three free gyros and the FSP pitch-over program will dictate rocket attitude and trajectory up to Stage3 ignition.

10.1c <u>Frames of Reference</u> – During the Earth's daily rotation, a spinning gyro appears to rotate 360° bodily, as it stays rigidly fixed to an inertial space reference frame. To be a stable angular reference on Earth this daily gyro rotation has to be halted.

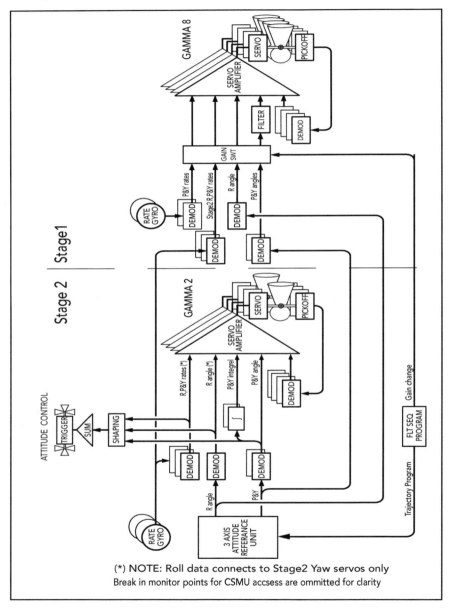

(*) NOTE: Roll data connects to Stage2 Yaw servos only
Break in monitor points for CSMU accsess are ommitted for clarity

FIG B–18 FCS & ACS BLOCK DIAGRAM   (D MACK)

The AU meets this need by levelling the ARU cluster and constantly precessing each gyro with an opposing component of the Earth spin rate prevailing at the test latitude.

10.1d <u>ARU/Airframe Alignment</u> – To avoid a need of gimbal angle resolvers the ARU, FCS and Airframe rotation axis coincide i.e. their Roll, Pitch and Yaw axes are aligned and remain sensibly so throughout flight. ARU performance and accuracy is verified at High Down and Woomera on accurately surveyed rigid plinths.

With the rocket upright on the launcher, the Spin Table upper face and ARU mounting pads are levelled within ±2 arc minutes of the gravity vector by adjustment of the Windbrace Arms. When the ARU is mounted in the rocket it is aligned on the chosen Line of Fire, at the launch point Earth latitude, by the AU using a 12hr precision process. This is followed by physically trimming the airframe Roll (azimuth) angle until the ARU roll synchro reading is zero. A theodolite test follows to confirm an alignment accuracy within 6 arc min with respect to a local survey vertical.

10.1e <u>Initialising the ARU</u> – A notional diagram outlining AU and ARU relationship is given in Fig B–21 below. Cluster alignment involves three phases: Rough levelling, Fine Levelling and Heading alignment.

With the AU appropriately setup, the SOU powers up the ARU to roughly squares-up the gimbals while bringing the system up to operating temperature. The AU then accurately levels the cluster and maintains it so until the close of testing or –40secs pre launch. AU levelling precesses each lateral gyro using Schuler tuned servo loops to bring the lateral accelerometer outputs to a stable zero. When levelled the sensing axes of each gyro is oriented as at launch and the cluster may be slewed to any heading by torquing the azimuth gyro. Since cluster levelling imposes a pendulous couple on the azimuth gyro causing it to act as a North seeking gyrocompass the AU suppresses this effect as it maintains the Line of Fire angle.

When the ARU is just run as support for related system tests where best accuracy is not essential, a simple 2hr ARU power up process is applied that omits gyro drift checking. When best possible accuracy is needed extensive gyro drift calibrations can take up to 12hrs or more.

10.1f <u>Gyro Drift Calibration</u> – Line of Fire and orbital injection accuracy is directly related to gyro stability and the drift component unique to each power up cycle must be assessed and compensated. To make such measurements, each gyro must be isolated from artificial inputs like Earth de-spin torquing and the non-rigid rocket structure. For these conditions cluster slewing aligns the test gyro input axis East/West (in place of the roll or azimuth gyro) and its Earth spin torquing ceases. Cluster levelling duty is swopped to the two gyros not under test and their related accelerometers.

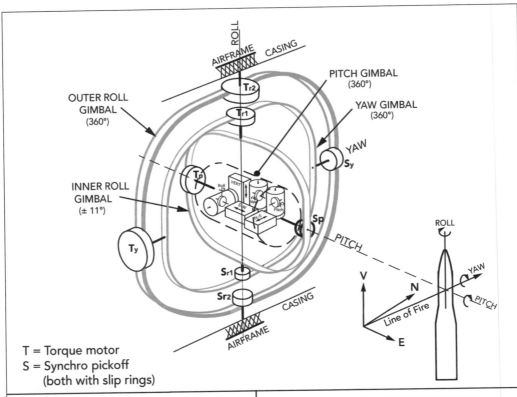

ROLL
AIRFRAME CASING

PITCH GIMBAL
(360°)

OUTER ROLL
GIMBAL
(360°)

YAW GIMBAL
(360°)

Tr2

Tr1

YAW
Sy

INNER ROLL
GIMBAL
(± 11°)

Tp

Roll VERT
E-W
Pitch
N-S

Sp

ROLL

Ty

PITCH

Sr1

Sr2

CASING

AIRFRAME

V

N

Line of Fire

E

ROLL

YAW

PITCH

T = Torque motor
S = Synchro pickoff
(both with slip rings)

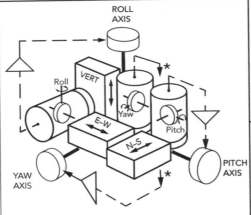

ROLL
AXIS

VERT

Roll

Yaw

E-W

N-S

Pitch

PITCH
AXIS

YAW
AXIS

NOTE: Roll & Yaw gyro spin axis are perminantly
aligned to the cluster pitch axis to isolate them
from the trajectory turn over program.

SINGLE DEGREE of FREEDOM GYRO

Angular motion about
the input axis creates an
output error signal for
slaving the gimbal
drive motor.

A torque motor turns
(precesses) the gyro
around its input axis

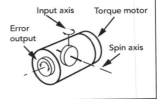

Input axis   Torque motor

Error
output

Spin axis

CLUSTER SENSOR FUNCTIONS

Three rate gyro and accelerometer pairs are mounted
orthogonally in a three axis, four gimbal frame to avoid
gimbal lock. Each gimbal is slaved by its related gyro to
to mirror cluster orientation.

–40secs before launch, the lateral accelerometers torque
the lateral gyros via a Shuler tuned servo loop to keep the
cluster level, thereby aligning all gyros with Earth's frame
of referance. This allows the AU to apply accurate despin
corrections to each gyro.

FIG B–19 ARU CLUSTER & GIMBAL ARRANGEMENT   *(From RAE 69068 + D MACK)*

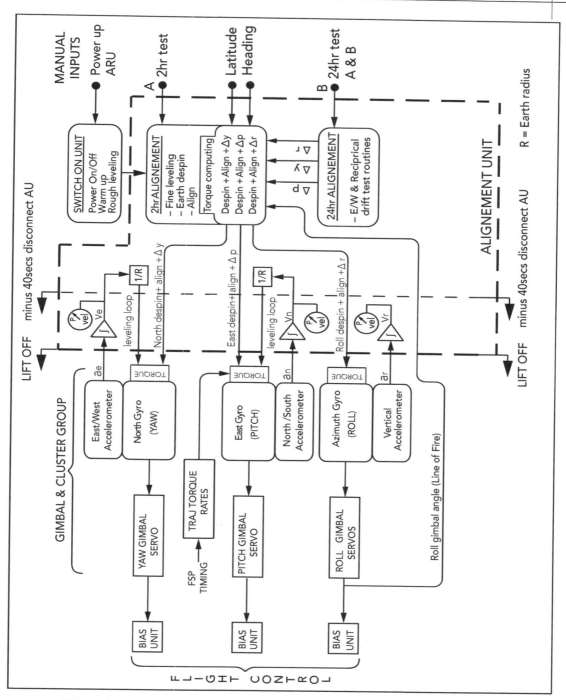

FIG B–20   ARU AND AU NOTIONAL RELATIONSHIP   (D MACK)

Gyro drift polarity is established by a reciprocal measurement with the gyro input axis set to West/East. The AU applies these drift corrections during each accurate alignment, which are done outside normal shift times to limit structural disturbances. Without physical disturbance from wind etc, the procedure may take about 12hr to process three gyros and align the cluster to the required heading. This time period would be intolerable for most applications but it only amounts to a sprinkling of night shifts across a six week BA Trial campaign; a reasonable penalty to secure an angular accuracy of 0.14° at Stage3 ignition, some 10 min after lift off.

10.1g <u>Trajectory input</u> – As seen earlier the ARU roll, pitch and yaw sensing axes coincide with the Rocket steering control axis, which enables the trajectory profile to be inserted by directly torquing the pitch gyro. The resulting ARU gimbal angle is followed up by the FCS, which demands the thrust vector steering angle needed to bring the rocket attitude and restore ARU gimbal angles to zero. A range of pitch (or yaw) trajectory profiles may be created via FSP time selections from four inbuilt torquing currents.

10.1h <u>Platform acceptance tests</u> – Laboratories at High Down and TS4 were equipped with accurately sited rigid plinths where each ARU undergoes searching acceptance testing. In addition to the gyro drift tests mentioned above each test facility is equipped to measure angular scaling using a calibrated ARU tilting rig.

10.1i <u>Launch Sequence</u> – Following a 12hr alignment that corrects gyro drift and aligns on the Line of Fire, the launch countdown is entered and the AU is auto disconnected at minus 40secs. This lets the cluster sensors return to inertial reference frame, free of all Earth constraints for the liftoff. Electrically buffered, extended scale meters in EC5 provided a constant display of three directional velocities integrated from the accelerometers, and three gimbal angles, which all serve as go/no go monitors of ARU integrity until rocket lift off. Experienced engineers observed the velocity patterns as the Platform and Earth launch point converge at time zero.

10. 2 <u>FCS Electronic Packs</u> – These items were engineered and constructed by the EEL department of WHL, Cowes IW, who also produced the BK transistorised control system introduced from BK16 on. To avoid additional redesign costs, the opportunity to upgrade from discrete to integrated semi conductor technology was resisted and BK hardware was directly adapted for BA. See Fig B–17 for block diagram.

10.2a <u>Stage1 Electronics</u> – Comprised the following items that are mounted in the Equipment Bay between the propellant tanks. Items 1 to 5 resided in the crate seen in Fig B–21 below and item 6 was directly mounted on airframe structure:

1. 12 demodulators to recover the DC signal from 12 AC pickoffs.
2. 4 servo amplifiers to sum inputs and drive servo actuators.
3. FSP stepped gain unit with prefixed settings for mass/aero changes.
4. Notch filter to reject structural resonances.
5. Power supplies pack.
6. 2 lateral rate gyros to damp first mode lateral resonances.

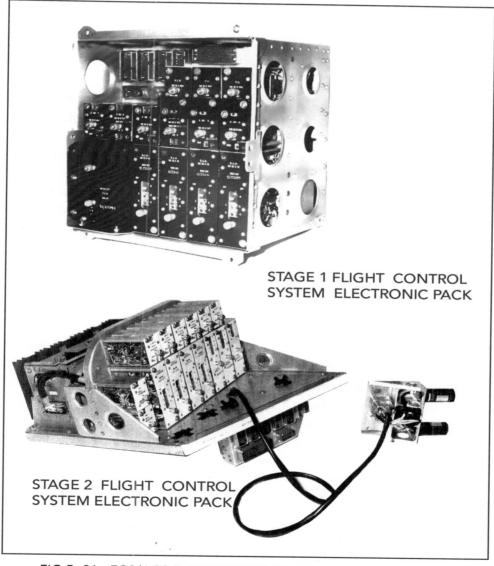

STAGE 1 FLIGHT CONTROL
SYSTEM ELECTRONIC PACK

STAGE 2 FLIGHT CONTROL
SYSTEM ELECTRONIC PACK

FIG B–21   FCS/ACS ELECTRONICS PACKS   *(GKN Aerospace)*

10.2b <u>Stage2 Electronics</u> – Comprised the following items that are mounted in the Electronics Bay between the propellant tanks. Items 1 to 5 residing on the tray shown in Fig B.21 below and item 6 was directly mounted on airframe structure:

1. 12 demodulators to recover the DC signal from 12 AC pickoffs.
2. 4 servo amplifiers to sum inputs and drive servo actuators.
3. 2 Lateral anti-drift Integrators.
4. 6 Attitude Control System (ACS) shaping units.
5. 3 ACS Summing trigger units.
6. 3 rate gyros to damp first mode resonances.
7. 3 ACS Summing trigger units.
8. 3 rate gyros to damp first mode resonances.

10.2c&d <u>Thrust Chamber Servo Loops</u>: The same hydraulic actuators fitted to BK, powered by kerosene were used control Thrust Chamber steering angles in both lower Stages. See FIG B–18 Block diagram.

The relevant outer loop angle and rate error signals are summed at an analogue servo amplifier, which adjusts an actuator spool valve to generate differential hydraulic pressure in opposing piston jacks. Acting via a bell crank, the actuator swings the Thrust Chamber until its angle as metered by an AC pickoff, nulls out the summed servo amplifier error inputs. Hydraulic power is derived via an engine driven gear pump fed from the kerosene delivery pump pressure. Amplitude and phase lag responses of each servo loop is examined across specified frequencies while running on a ground trolley hydraulic supply. With hydraulic power applied, the outer loop ARU and Rate Gyro signals are connected to all inner loops to verify the absence of structural resonance modes.

10.2e <u>Attitude Control System</u> (ACS) – A Bang-Bang gas jet system maintains the Stage2/3 attitude and roll orientation defined by the ARU during the coast phase up to Stage3 release. The system employs eight gas jets; four correcting Roll errors and two in each lateral plane. Attitude angle and rate data are fed by summing amplifiers to jet trigger units that apply gas jet thrusts of 1lb at ±0.25° laterally and ±2.5 ° in roll. This results in a limit cycle of less than ±0.03 °per sec with an error angle of ±0.3°. Trigger units are integral with their respective gas jet assemblies that are arranged around the Stage2 motor bay.

10.2f <u>FCS Overall Sense Testing</u> – The procedure is designed to:

1. Show that each Gamma 2 & 8 thrust chamber and ACS jet operating in any one-control axis would all apply steering torques in the same direction.
2. Show that Stage1 thrust chambers would apply steering torques in opposition to physical error inputs at the ARU.

To show by inference from (1) + (2) that overall FCS sensing was correct.

Prior to the above tests, Stage1 upper handling clamp ring is fitted to constrain he airframe and the ARU must have been 2hr aligned.

<u>1 Above</u> Is met by fitting Stage1 FCS "Flight Plug" in place of Stage1 CSMU monitor cable with live ACS gas and Stage1/Stage2 hydraulic systems. During the test, ARU outputs are isolated at Stage2 CSMU and a Pitch error demand (voltage) is applied to observe that all Pitch thrust chambers and gas jets function in harmony by applying steering torque in the SAME direction, if they were thrusting. This process is repeated for the Yaw and Roll error channels. Stage2 hydraulic power and ACS gas are now powered down.

<u>2 Above</u> Is met by fitting Stage2 FCS "Flight Plug" in place of Stage2 CSMU monitor cable and physically leaning/rotating the rocket structure through a small angle around the release jack ball (An action that entails removal of wind brace arms and anti torque lugs from the rocket, an activity less fearsome than it sounds since rocket is limited laterally from gross movement by the Gantry loading rollers acting against Stage1 upper clamp ring). Observers are placed to confirm the following effects as FCS is powered up and Stage1 hydraulics is applied: –

With the "Flight Plug" fitted, observers are placed to confirm the following as the FCS is run up on with live hydraulics: –

a. PITCH Chamber exits swing UP RANGE as vehicle head is pitched DOWN RANGE.
b. YAW Chamber exits swing RIGHT Range as vehicle head is yawed LEFT RANGE.
c. ROLL Chamber exits move to OPPOSE a CLOCKWISE vehicle rotation, viewed from below.

With all the rocket restraints restored, the ARU is allowed to drift freely in order to log the sign (sense) of the P, Y and R synchro meters on the ARU rack at EC, to avoid test (2) repetition should the need for component replacement ever arise.

BA's moderate size and single ball tethering is probably the only rocket that can entertain this direct sense testing method.

11 <u>HAZARDOUS SYSTEMS</u>:

11.1 <u>Explosive Bolts</u> – The double explosive bolts identical to those developed for BK – (see Fig A–23 in Appendix A), are used and now connect to the Haz circuit using dedicated RF filter units – see Fig 16–4 in Chapter 16.

11.2 <u>Inertia Switches</u> – These items are identical to those used on Black Knight (see Fig A–22, Appendix A) to dynamically arm the ordnance firing circuits during flight. Additionally, Black Arrow uses them to sense Stage1 and Stage 2 engine "All Burnt" to start FSP sections 2 & 3.

11.3 <u>Flight Sequence Programmer</u> (FSP) – A custom Flight Sequence Programmer was developed by the RAE to initiate all in flight events. The electro-mechanical device embodied a synchronous motor activating cam operated micro switches that are segregated into three clutch-selected sections – See Table B/3 below. Section 1 was initiated at minus 10 secs from the Equipment Centre auto sequencer, with sections 2 and 3 being started at stage1 and 2 engine shutdown as shown in FIG B-22 above.

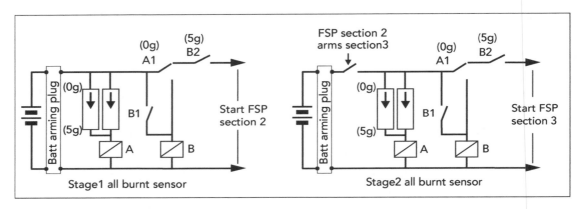

FIG B–22   STAGE1 & STAGE2 ALL BURNT SENSING   *(D MACK)*

Individual solid–state timers residing on the Spin Table and in the Satellite Separation Bay (SSB), spun up Stage3, cut the Manacle Clamp, ignited the Waxwing motor and separated the Satellite, were all pulse initiated by FSP section 2.
The FSP resided in the Stage2 electronics bay.

TABLE B/3: FSP EVENTS

BA nominal FSP sequences (actual times are mission dependant)		FSP FLIGHT TIMES (secs)		*HD TEST TIMES (secs)	
Starting source	FSP Function	Flt Time ON	Flt Time OFF	Time ON	Time OFF
EC Console	Power up systems	−20 min	−	−20 min	−
	Start sync motor	−3 min	−	− 3 min	−
EC Auto Sequence	Start FSP Sect 1	− 10	− 8	− 10	− 8
Instant of move		4	−	−	−
	0.6 turn over	5	10	5	10
	0.6 turn over	34	117	34	117
	FSP gain 1	80	250	80	250
	FSP gain 2	100	270	100	270
Stage1 All Burnt		125			
(inertia switch)	Start FSP Sect 2	126	−	0	−
	Stage1 Ex bolts	131.2	−	5.2	−
	Inter Stage Ex bolts	"	−	"	−
	Sep Rockets	"	−	"	−
	Gamma2 Start	"	−	"	−
	0.116°/sec turn over	"	247	"	121
	Inter Stage Ex Bolts	136	−	10	−
	Stage2 Ex bolts	"	−	"	−
	Arm WREBUS Fail Fire	148	265	22	139
	Init WREBUS Fail Fire	151.2	−	25.2	−
	Release Fairings	155	−	29	−
	End WREBUS Fail Fire	210	−	84	−
	Arm FSP Sec 3	"	298	"	172
Stage2 All Burnt		247			
(inertia switch)	Start FSP Sect 3	248	−	0	−
	Pressurise ACS	251	−	3	−
	0.6°/sec turn over	252	312	4	64
	Gamma2 All Burnt	260	−	12	−
	Uncage Sat gyros	540	−	292	−
	Start Stage3 timers	549	−	301	−
	Fire Unused	599	−	351	−
Stage3 Delay timers	Unlock table	550	−	302	−
	Spin up table	551	−	303	−
	Cut Man clamp	552	−	304	−
	Wax Ignition	553	−	305	346
Waxwing All burnt		593			
	Satellite release	603	−	355	−

* Highdown testing is simplified by running each FSP section separately and consecutively.

12 – FLIGHT SAFETY PROVISIONS –

12.1 <u>Design Qualification Plan</u> – Only three proving firings were permitted. A fully active two stage flight along Range E centre line (55° West) to assess engine behaviour, trajectory control and separation dynamics, while WRE exercised tracking and safety surveillance routines. Firings two and three were to be three active stages fired along the 5° East corridor to prove orbital ability, WRE instrumentation and safety. Firing four being the first formal orbital insertion of a Client satellite.

From + 5 to +312 secs during each firing, the FSP progressively applied a series of pitch turnover rates to the ARU to align Stage3 Apogee motor with the orbital injection angle as shown in Fig B–1 above. The spent Stage1 and Inter-stage would impact 400km from launch, followed by the Payload Fairings at 800km. The spent Stage2 will impact 3650 km into the Indian Ocean for the westerly firings and north of New Guinea on all northerly firings. The safety plan provides early termination dump zones if under performance threaten specified no go areas. See Fig B–2 above.

12.2 <u>WRE Tracking System</u> – Initial lift off observed by three close in Sky Screens, with Stage1 ongoing progress to impact tracked by Optical and Doppler methods. This data also served acquisition data to FPS16 precision radars at Red Lake and Mirikata (25Km and 160 Km from the launcher) as the rocket rises over their local horizon. Radar tracking continued to Stage3 separation. To aid these tasks, Stage1 and Stage2 respectively carried a Doppler transponder and C band beacon. Track data from all sources was managed and digitally processed at the Range 'E' Data Centre for real time distribution to all users and the Flight Safety Officer (FSO).

12.3 <u>WREBUS System</u> – A WRE purpose designed radio system provided mutually redundant radio links to the rockets flight termination circuits. Each radio worked on exclusive frequencies and both were operated in Fail/Safe mode, except during the Fairing ejection window when the FSP time switched them to Fail/Fire mode to guard against any aerial damage. Both radios and the FSP timer were located in the Stage2 Electronics Bay. During flight, two independent WREBUS transmitters at the Range Head constantly radiate a "Prohibit" signal. A "Fire" signal was only transmitted when selected by the FSO.

On detecting a "Fire" signal while in Fail Safe mode, either radio will close its destruct relay and terminate flight. Conversely, operating in Fail Fire mode, both receivers must detect loss of the "Prohibit" signal to close their destruct relays to terminate the flight.

12.4 <u>Rocket Destruction Circuits</u> – From liftoff, closure of WREBUS receiver destruct relays will shut down the running engine and detonate remaining HTP by dispersing manganese dioxide crystals in each tank.

Some 60 secs after lift off, inertia switches will arm each ordnance circuit in all three stages so that WREBUS destruct relays will fire all unfired devices and render the Waxwing motor non propulsive by firing a head cutting charge at motor ignition.

13 – <u>LOADING PROPELLANTS</u> – Load calculations and the loading procedures are identical to those described for Black Knight in Appendix A except loading Stage2 kerosene uses churn weighing.

14 – <u>SHORESIDE INTERFACES</u> – Electrical services between rocket and ground follow one of two routes:

- An umbilical connector feeding shore side electrical power and returning system monitor data, is auto ejected at – 8 secs.
- Rip connectors located at Stage1 Motor Bay are used for executive firing and circuits and time critical functions monitored or controlled until lift off.

The ARU, FCS, 'C' band, Doppler and Telemetry systems all require significant electrical power over extended test periods and are served from shore supply sources until switched to internal batteries at – 40 secs. Batteries are silver zinc cells, boxed in system specific packs that are removed for re-charge and load testing. Where power consumption permits, discrete mercury cells are used in instrumentation systems to avoid cross talk loops. Various Hazardous circuit functions (WREBUS, BU, FSP, Explosive bolts etc) use silver zinc cells housed in localised packs that are not shore supply support as each pack is serviced and load tested prior to final arming.

Mechanical services for mainstage engine starting are routed via 'O' ring sealed pull off couplings that pull apart at lift off. An under Payload Fairing cold air cooling feed via the Umbilical Mast was manually extracted at EC5 prior to the launch countdown.

15 – <u>TELEMETRY</u> – In flight monitoring of system behaviour in each of the lower stages is provided by two 24 x 40 c/sec channel telemetry installations operating at 448MHz and 435 MHz. All system pressures measurements are made using inductive transducers. All other parameters are monitored via direct voltage measurement.

16 – <u>CHECKOUT & COUNTDOWN</u> – These processes mimic those established during the Black Knight program and progress along the follow lines: –

1. <u>Prep Area (TS4)</u> – Physical inspection, Haz Circuit (MAO) tests, FCS and Instrumentation calibrations.
2. <u>Site1 (5A)</u> – Stage2 propellant tank pressure tests, FCS servo frequency tests and the Gamma2 static firing.
3. <u>Site 2 (5B)</u> – Stage1 tested as above plus Stage2 and Gamma8 static firing.
4. <u>Site 2 (5B)</u> – Stage3 load inert Waxwing motor, acceptance testing to confirm all vehicle hardware interfaces and functions correctly as an integrated whole and without any EMC or RFI issues.

5. <u>Transfer</u> to Australia.
6. <u>At Woomera</u> – Live Waxwing motor, Flight Satellite and live ordinance stores fitted. Final RFI tests ahead of full-scale dress rehearsal (S&S test) of the launch countdown. Loading liquid propellants, tipping up gas bottles, sealing off all accesses during final arming and closure of checklists. Begin launch countdown sequence subject to weather conditions!

Full details of above activities have been omitted since they are elaborated in the R0 and R3 trials chapters.

16.8 <u>Procedure Review process</u> – All aspects of trial preparation were regularly visited for relevance and accuracy. Typically, the convoluted Overall Sense Test, commonly called the Rock & Roll test was a candidate for a total overhaul. Carried over from Black Knight where it was relevant to free gyroscope sensors, airframe size and the rotational freedom offered the release jack ball. The Black Arrow airframe size of the two powered stages was barely manageable and very disruptive. The low drift inertial features of the ARU prompted a possible alternate solution to this requirement but the project was cancelled before this was explored.

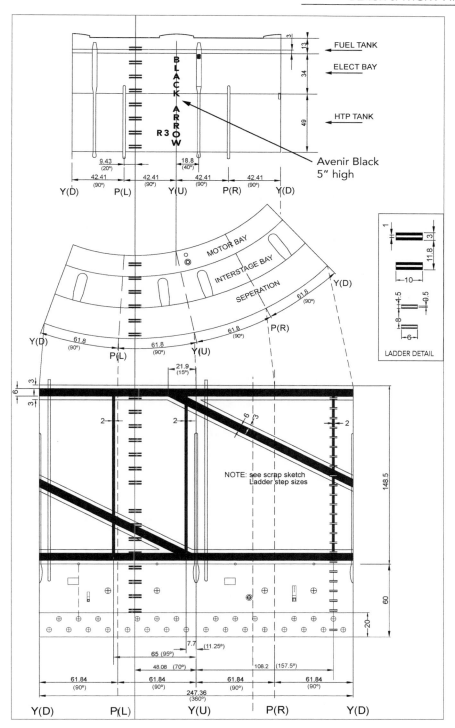

FUEL TANK

ELECT BAY

HTP TANK

BLACK ARROW R3

Avenir Black
5" high

LADDER DETAIL

MOTOR BAY

INTERSTAGE BAY

SEPERATION

NOTE: see scrap sketch
Ladder step sizes

FIG B-23- BA TRACKING GRAPHICS   *(D MACK)*

Days	Site	STAGE 1	STAGE 2	STAGE 3/Fairings	HAZ mat'ls
			TABLE B/4 – BLACK ARROW – Highdown Qualification Trial: Notional Plan of main event		
D-63	Prep	Uncrate Stage1+ inspection	Uncrate Stage2+Interstage	Uncrate SSB	
D-62		Mech chks + non Haz wiring chks	RUXO checks	Uncrate fairings	
D-59		FCS engine cals + service inst tray	Fit/Rem Interstage + RUXO checks		
D-58		Tele padding + cals	Mech chks + Non Haz wiring chks	SSB RUXO chk	
D-57		Fit/Rem Interstage + RUXO chks	FCS engine Cals+Inst tray servicing		
D-56		Continue RUXO chks	Tele padding&cals+Pre 5A chk list	Fair'g RUXO chk	
D-55	Site2		Interstage to Site2 for funct'n chk		
D-52			To Site2+Kero vol cal+press test		
D-51	Site2		HTP tank vol/prob cal+press test.		<> Kero
D-50	Site1	Move Stage1 to Site 1	Load Waxwing+connect ground inst	< Waxwing	
D-49		Kero vol/probe calibration	FCS innerloop chks+ARU pwrup		<> Kero
D-48		HTP vol/probe calibration	Tele syst chkout		<> Kero
D-45			Eng prep+setup sub systs		
D-44			ARU/FCS/ACS bal+CSSU chks		
D-43			S&S for Stage2 static firing		< Kero
D-42			Gamma2 Static firing+post firing		>HTP+Kero
D-41		Fit FCS pack+ set via CSMU	Dry engine +Pess chk E'bay		
D-38		FCS innerloop chks	Strip Stage3+ prep move to Site1	>Waxwing	
D-37		Patch EC/Site1+HTP tank press test			
D-36		Load stage2+interconnect chk	<Interconnect chk+Tank press chk		
D-35			Elec Bay seal test		
D-34		FCS/ stage2 chks	Set up FCS/ARU+Tele chks		
D-33/32			ARU Precision testing		
D-31		FCS Sense test	FCS Sense test		
D-30			Vet Spin Table & gauge tranf aerials		
D-29		Fit Doppler+Full Tele chkout	Fit Wrebus/C-Band+ Full Tele chkout		
D-28		Build Stage3	Fit Inert Waxwi'g+SSB+Payload 'A'	<Waxw+SSB+X?	
D-27		Fit non Haz batts+int test	Fit non Haz batts+int test		
D-24		RFI- Fairings off/on	RFI- Fairings off/on	<Fairings	
D-23		S&S/Firing prep	S&S/Firing prep		
D-22		Static firing S&S test			< Kero
D-21		Gamma8 Static Firing			>HTP+Kero
D-20		Post firing Chks & Engine Dryout			
D-17		Prep FSP runs, fit Haz batts+puffers	Prep FSP runs, fit Haz batts+puffers		< Puffers
D-16		Fit Non Haz batteries+ pwrup ARU	Fit int batteries+ pwrup ARU		
D-15		Fit arming plugs, do FSP test	Fit arming plugs, do FSP test		
D-14		Ditto	Ditto		
D-13		Detonator RFI cks	Detonator RFI cks		
D-10	Prep	Acceptance conference	Strip Payload 'A'/SSB/inert Waxw'g	>X+SSB+Waxw	
D-9		Strip Stages1,2	>> Stage2 to Prep Area		
D-8		To Prep Area+ Prep to Bal & Weigh	Prep for Weigh & balance		
D-7		QA audit + Weigh & Balance	QA audit + Weigh & Balance		
D-6		Prep & Inhibit Stage1	Prep & Inhibit Stage2		
D-3		Loose parts inventory	Loose parts inventory		
D-2		Ditto	Ditto		
D-1		Crate up + close off log books			
D-0		Stage1 sent to shippers	Crate up + close off log books		

Days	Site	STAGE 1	STAGE 2	STAGE 3/Fairings	HAZ
TABLE B/5 – BLACK ARROW – Woomera Launch Trial: Notional plan of main events					
F-50	TS4		Uncrate Stage2+Interstage		
F-49			Physical inspection	Prepare Payload	
F-48		Bench test sub units	Bench test sub units		
F-47		Ditto	Ditto		
F-46		Ditto	Ditto		
Ditto	5A		I'stage to 5A for flow+press chks		
F-43	TS4	Uncrate Stage1+Fit Interstage	Fit Interstage+Inertia swts	Uncrate SSB	
F-42		Physical inspection	MAO Haz wiring chks	Uncrate Fairings	
F-41		Non Haz wiring test+Mech chks	MAO Haz func chk with FSP		
F-40		Cal servo p'offs/swts/servos	Tele inductive+voltage systems		
F-39		Inertia Swts/MAO Haz wiring	Non Haz wiring+v'valves chks	Fairing Haz wiring	
F-36		Tele Inductive+voltage systems	NoneHaz wiring+ servo p'offs'swts		Prep –
F-35		S'down valve chk+Final chklist	Stop valve chk+final chklist		Odnance
F-34			To 5A/Tank pres+Tele chks		items
F-33			Eng servo prep+G'box chks	SSB Haz chks(TS4)	
F-32			Fit FCS+I+loops/Setup ARU gear		
F-29		To 5B/Tele chks/Con&Cal G'inst	ARU fit +12 hr integ test		
F-28		Eng servo prep+FCS servo chks	ARU/FCS bal/ACS bal		<Kero
F-27			SA test +Gas bots+Ld Kero		
F-26	5A		STATIC FIRING S&S test		
F-25			Gamma2 STATIC FIRING		<HTP
F-23/24			Dry engine		
Ditto			Move EC patch across to Pad 5B		
F-22	5B	Load Stage2/Stage1tank test	<<Prep & Move to 5B	Strip Stage3	
F-21		Stage1/2 Elect chks	Stage Elec chks+tank press checks	Spin table chks	
F-20		SetupFCS+Tele channel chks	SetupFCS+Tele channel chks		
F-19		FCS Sense test+Fit Doppler	ARU 12hr chk+FCS sense+Cband		
F-18		Fit non Haz batts+int test	Fit non Haz batts+int test	Fit Wax/SSB/aerials	
F-15		Full Doppler/Tele chkout	Full Wrebus/Cband/Tele chkout	SSB batt+"A"P'Ld	
F-14		RFI Fairings Off+S&S prep	RFI Fairings Off+S&S prep	Run "A" P'load	
F-13		RFI Fairings On+S&S prep	RFI Fairings On+S&S prep	Run "A" P'load	
F-12		STATIC FIRING S&S test			<Kero
F-11		Static firing+post fire chks			<HTP
F-9/10		Dry Engine			
F-8		Eng servo prep	Eng servo prep	Strip dummy Stage3	
F-7		FCS final bal	ARU(G'Comp)/FCS?ACS final bal		
F-6		Load Kero+Prep for FSP runs	Ld Kero+Pres chk E'bay	Ld Flt Waxw+SSB	< Waxw'g
F-5		FSP/ARU/FCS/Haz syst tests	FSP/ARU/FCS/ACS/Haz Syst tests	FSP/Haz syst tests	& Kero
F-4		BU status chk/FSP reset	BU status chk/FSP reset	BU status /FSP reset	
F-3		Fit Haz batts+Ordnance(exBU)	Fit Haz batts+Ordnance(exBU)	Haz batts+Ord'nce	Ord items
F-2		Fit&test int Batts+RFI spot chk	Fit&testInt batts+Payload Fairings	Ld 'F' P'load+	
Ditto		Fill gas bots+BalFCS+	ARU12hr integ+BalFCS+Gas bots		
Ditto		G'box+Hyd+Start+Dump syst	G'box+Hyd+Start+Dump syst		
F-1		LAUNCH S&S test 'A' 'B'& 'C'	Run ARU(24hr)		
F-0		Top Gas+Fill HTP+prime G/B's	Top Gas+Fill HTP+prime G/B's	Service P'load batts	<HTP
Ditto		Arm Haz + BU + Release jack	Arm Haz + BU		
Ditto		LAUNCH SEQUENCE			

TABLE – B/6 STAGE2 STATIC COUNTDOWN HD & WOOMERA

BLACK ARROW – STAGE2 STATIC FIRING COUNTDOWN AT HIGHDOWN & WOOMERA			
Manually activated events	**Time ON**	**Time OFF**	**Applicability**
Switch ON ARU	– 24hrs		√
Switch ON WREBUS	–30 min	–	√
Switch ON C Band	"	–	√
Switch ON FCS power	–20 min	–	√
Switch ON Telemetry	"	–	√
Close all Readiness switches	–3 min	–	√
Start Auto Sequencer	–2 min	–	√
Automatic Timed Events:			
Start Recorder sub sequencer	–119 sec	–116 sec	Highdown only
Pressurise G/S HTP tank	–115 sec	+35 sec	√ Stop Action reset
Pressurise all Vehicle tanks	–115 sec	– 113 sec	√ Stop Action reset
Open duct cooling water valve	–20 sec	–15 sec	√
Start/stop EC5 recorders	–20 sec	+60 sec	Woomera only
Pressurise Gearbox Oil Tank	–8 sec	+10 sec	√
Open N2 purge valve	–8 sec	–6 sec	√
Open/close Engine shutdown valve	–4 sec	+35 sec	√ *See note re external gas line
Open Ground start HTP valve	0	+3 sec	√
Start FCS signal unit (CSSU)	0	+10 sec	√
Close/Unlatch Engine shutdown valve	+35 sec	+40 sec	Eng batt must always be fitted
Close duct cooling water valve	+45 sec	+50 sec	√
Stop N2 purge	+45 sec	+50 sec	√

* Engine shutdown valve must be set in 'Fail Safe' mode by a shore side gas line. This ensures engine will stop when shore side volts are removed. To ensure against loss of shore side gas pressure an engine Flight Termination battery must be installed to activate the external Stop Action circuit.

TABLE – B/7 COMPOSITE STATIC & LAUNCH COUNTDOWN

BLACK ARROW – Composite Static & Launch Countdowns at Highdown & Woomera			
Manually activated Events:	Time ON		Applicability
Power up ARU	–24 hrs	–	
Power up Payload	–30 min	–	
Power up WREBUS	"	–	
Power up Doppler	"	–	
Power up C band	"	–	
Power up Telemetry	"	–	
Power up FCS	–20 min	–	
Switch on FSP sync motor	–3 min	–	
Close all Readiness switches		–	
Start Auto Sequencer	–2 min	–	
Automatic Timed Events:	Time ON	Time OFF	
Start Recorder sub sequencer	–119 sec	–116 sec	Highdown static only
Pressurise G/S HTP tank	–115 sec	+35 sec	Stop Action reset
Pressurise Stage1 & 2 tanks	–115 sec	–113 sec	Stop action reset
Switch Stage1 & 2 to internal power	–40 sec	–38 sec	*Launch & HD test, see note below
Release ARU	-40 sec	+35 sec	
Open duct cooling water valve	–20 sec	–15 sec	
Start/stop EC5 recorders	–20 sec	+60 sec	Woomera Static only
Start FSP Section1	–10 sec	–8 sec	***Launch & HD test, see note below
Pressurise Gearbox Oil Tank	–8 sec	+10 sec	
Open N2 purge valve	–8 sec	–6 sec	
Eject Umbilical Plug	–8 sec	–6 sec	***Launch & HD test, see note below
Open/close Engine Shutdown valve	–4 sec	+35 sec	*** Statics only, see note below
Ditto	-4 sec	-2 sec	**** Launch only, see note below
Open Ground Start HTP valve	0	+3 sec	
Start FCS signal unit (CSSU)	0	+10 sec	Static firing only
Arm Release jack	+5 sec	+10 sec	Launch only, reset by Stop Action
Auto Stop Action	+10 sec	+12 sec	Launch only
Close/Unlatch Engine shutdown valve	+35 sec	+40 sec	Eng valve batt must always be fitted
Revert to external power	+35 sec	+40 sec	*Launch & HD test, see note below
Close duct cooling water valve	+45 sec	+50 sec	
Stop N2 purge	+45 sec	+50 sec	
Consequent Follow on Events:	Nominal Times		
Hydraulic press switch Closes	+2 sec	+8 sec	
Chamber Angle switches Close	+2 sec	+8 sec	
Chamber pressure switches Close	+2 sec	+8 sec	
Release jack opens	+5 sec	+10 sec	Launch only

* For Launch S&S and Launch plus HD S&S and post IoM simulations.

** For Launcg S&S and Launch plus HD post IoM simulations.

***Engine shutdown valve must be set to 'Fail Safe' mode by a shore side gas line. Ensures engine will stop when shore side volts are removed. To ensure against loss of shore side gas pressure an engine flight Termination battery must be installed to activate the extertnal Stop Action circuit.

****Engine shutdown valve must be set to 'Fail Open" mode by removal of shore side gas pressure line to keep valve open for flight when shore side volts are removed at -2 sec.